W9-BYZ-503

WASHINGTON

Scale in Miles

Scale in Kilometers

DOWNTOWN SEATTLE

STREETCAR

MONORAIL

Scale in Miles 0.4

Scale in Kilometers 0.6

MOUNT RAINIER NATIONAL PARK

| Scale in Miles | 0 — 4.8 |
| Scale in Kilometers | 0 — 7.7 |

SPOKANE

| Scale in Miles | 0 — 0.7 |
| Scale in Kilometers | 0 — 1.1 |

HIDDEN ®

Washington

HIDDEN®

Washington

Eric Lucas

THIRD EDITION

Ulysses Press®
BERKELEY, CALIFORNIA

Published by:
ULYSSES PRESS
P.O. Box 3440
Berkeley, CA 94703
www.ulyssespress.com

ISSN 1521-4397
ISBN 1-56975-240-0

Printed in Canada by Transcontinental Printing

10 9 8 7 6 5 4

MANAGING EDITOR: Claire Chun
PROJECT DIRECTOR: Lynette Ubois
COPY EDITORS: Lily Chou, Steven Zah Schwartz
EDITORIAL ASSOCIATES: Marin Van Young, Shola Ogunlana, Melissa Millar, Ryan Gowland
TYPESETTERS: David Wells, Lindsay Mugglestone, Lisa Kester
CARTOGRAPHY: Pease Press
INDEXER: Sayre Van Young
COVER PHOTOGRAPHY:
    FRONT: Larry Ulrich (Red mountain heather, Paradise River, Mt. Rainier National Park)
    CIRCLE & BACK: Craig Blacklock/Larry Ulrich Stock (Mountain goat, Olympic National Park)
ILLUSTRATOR: Glenn Kim

Distributed in the United States by Publishers Group West, in Canada by Raincoast Books, and in Great Britain and Europe by World Leisure Marketing

All color maps copyright © 2000 AAA. All rights reserved. Used with permission. www.aaa.com

Hidden Washington was produced by Ulysses Press in association with VIA Books. VIA Books is a division of the California State Automobile Association (CSAA), 150 Van Ness Avenue, San Francisco, CA 94102. VIA

HIDDEN is a federally registered trademark of BookPack, Inc.

Ulysses Press is a federally registered trademark of BookPack, Inc.

Write to us!

If in your travels you discover a spot that captures the spirit of Washington, or if you live in the region and have a favorite place to share, or if you just feel like expressing your views, write to us and we'll pass your note along to the author.

We can't guarantee that the author will add your personal find to the next edition, but if the writer does use the suggestion, we'll acknowledge you in the credits and send you a free copy of the new edition.

ULYSSES PRESS
3286 Adeline Street, Suite 1
Berkeley, CA 94703
E-mail: readermail@ulyssespress.com

✳

Ulysses Press would like to thank the following readers who took the time to write in with suggestions that were incorporated into this new edition of *Hidden Washington*:

Jennifer Cory; Amy Dennis of Raymond, WA; Lisa Finch of San Francisco, CA; Bill Lewis of Minneapolis, MN; Brian Peterson of Portland, OR; Sarah Primrose of Whidbey, WA; Dorothy Tenhhoff of Olympia, WA.

What's Hidden?

At different points throughout this book, you'll find special listings marked with a hidden symbol:

◀ *HIDDEN*

This means that you have come upon a place off the beaten tourist track, a spot that will carry you a step closer to the local people and natural environment of Washington.

The goal of this guide is to lead you beyond the realm of everyday tourist facilities. While we include traditional sightseeing listings and popular attractions, we also offer alternative sights and adventure activities. Instead of filling this guide with reviews of standard hotels and chain restaurants, we concentrate on one-of-a-kind places and locally owned establishments.

Our authors seek out locales that are popular with residents but usually overlooked by visitors. Some are more hidden than others (and are marked accordingly), but all the listings in this book are intended to help you discover the true nature of Washington and put you on the path of adventure.

Contents

Maps

OUTDOOR ADVENTURE SYMBOLS

The following symbols accompany national, state and regional park listings, as well as beach descriptions throughout the text.

▲	Camping	🏄	Surfing
🚶	Hiking	🎿	Waterskiing
🚲	Biking	⛵	Windsurfing
🐎	Horseback Riding	🛶	Canoeing or Kayaking
⛷	Downhill Skiing	🚤	Boating
🎿	Cross-country Skiing	🚤	Boat Ramps
🏊	Swimming	🐟	Fishing
🤿	Snorkeling or Scuba Diving		

ONE

The Evergreen State

 A place of emerald beauty and scenic grandeur, Washington is the heart of a region that has long fascinated explorers and entrepreneurs, environmentalists and dreamers. This north-westernmost corner of the contiguous United States is nick-named "The Evergreen State"—an appropriate label for a land that boasts eight national forests. Sharing a border with Canada to the north and Idaho on the east, Washington is divided from Oregon on the south by the course of the Columbia River.

Water is a major force, as the Pacific Ocean batters the state's rugged western edge and numerous rivers carve the landscape. Come to Washington and you'll discover wondrous waterfalls, glistening waterways and verdant rainforest. You'll also find mysterious bays, sounds and tributaries, wind-sculpted trees on wave-battered capes and inlets, gossamer mists on towering evergreens, icy summits that cast shadows on pastoral valleys, bustling cityscapes with a cosmopolitan flair, warm breezes through juniper boughs, even a powerful volcano or two.

The heavy rainfall for which Washington is famous helps keep its vegetation lush. The drizzle and clouds that blanket the coastal region during much of the winter and spring nourish the incredibly green landscape that grows thick and fast and softens the sharp edges of alpine peaks and jagged sea cliffs. But there's a flip side: Over half the state (meaning points east of the Cascade Range) is actually warm and dry throughout much of the year.

Much of Washington remains undeveloped and there are vast expanses of wilderness close to all metropolitan centers. In fact, nearly half of the state is covered by forest. Almost without exception, each of its cities is surrounded by countless outdoor recreational opportunities, with mountains, lakes, streams and an ocean within easy reach. It's no surprise that residents and visitors tend to have a hardy, outdoorsy glow. After all, it is the proximity to nature that draws people here.

Hidden Washington will help you explore this diverse area, introduce you to its flora and fauna, tell you of its history. Besides taking you to countless popular spots, it will lead to unusual and unique locales. Each chapter will suggest places to eat, stay, sightsee and shop and to enjoy the outdoors and nightlife. We think you'll find Washington is a place where you can explore for a day, a week or much, much longer.

▼▼▼▼▼▼▼▼▼▼
When to Go

The number of tourists visiting Washington continues to grow as the secrets of its beauty and sunny summer and fall weather get out. Because the landscape is so widely varied, each area with its own appeal, here are brief descriptions of the regions presented in this book to help you decide where you want to go. We begin in the Seattle area, move through southern Puget Sound, the Olympic Peninsula and the Coast, northern Puget Sound and the San Juan Islands, and then to the Cascades and central Washington, finishing with the vast stretch east of the Cascades.

Seattle offers a comfortable mix of cultural sophistication and natural ruggedness. The clustered spires of its expanding skyline hint at the growth in this busy seaport, the shipping and transportation hub of the Northwest. In addition to the downtown/Seattle Center district, this metropolitan community has a number of attractive neighborhoods ideal for strolling, shopping and nightlife. Pastoral Vashon Island is just a quick ferry ride away, while east of the city center is the fashionable Lake Washington district and bedroom/corporate communities such as Bellevue, Renton, Kirkland and Redmond.

Within easy reach of Seattle, **Southern Puget Sound** is a popular day trip and a great way to get acquainted with the Washington State Ferry System. The state capital of Olympia, Tacoma and the charming little community of Gig Harbor all offer easy access to wildlife refuges. Tacoma, Washington's third-largest city, is home to Point Defiance Park, considered the best saltwater park in the state. Bainbridge Island offers art galleries and plenty of scenic beauty. On the Kitsap Peninsula is the Navy town of Bremerton, gateway to the picturesque hamlet of Poulsbo. To the north is the company town of Port Gamble, while south of Bremerton you can discover the rural charms of the Longbranch Peninsula and Harstine Island.

American Indians were probably the first to discover the beauty and bounty of the **Olympic Peninsula and Washington Coast**, with its lush rainforests, stretches of driftwood-cluttered beach, tumbling rivers and snow-capped mountains. Several tribes still live in the area on the outskirts of the massive Olympic National Park alongside fishing villages such as Sequim and Port Angeles and the Victorian-styled logging town of Port Townsend. On the coast, Grays Harbor is a popular maritime area, while the pristine Long Beach–Willapa Bay estuary is famed for oyster farming. This region is ideal for beachcombers, kite flyers and seafood lovers.

Northern Puget Sound and the San Juan Islands, regarded in this book as the coastal area stretched between Seattle and Blaine on the Canadian border, is entirely enchanting, from sea-swept

Washington

island chains to pastoral coastline. Here are rich farming tracts, picturesque forest-covered islands, quaint fishing villages and a shoreline of sloughs and estuaries. Among the cities covered in this section are Everett, La Conner, Mt. Vernon, Bellingham, Ferndale and Snohomish. The arts are strong here, perhaps because of the preponderance of artists drawn by the area's natural beauty. The San Juan Islands are one of the state's authentic treasures and a very popular vacation destination. Island-hopping is perfect for both cyclists and campers. A region lost in time, the San Juans offer everything from plush mansions to romantic bed-and-breakfast hideaways.

A strip of national parks, forests and wilderness areas, including the North Cascades, Snoqualmie and Wenatchee national forests, Mt. Rainier National Park and the Mt. St. Helens National Volcanic Monument, make up the bulk of the spectacular **Cascades and Central Washington**. Leavenworth, a Bavarian-style village, and several small resort towns are also key features here. Some of the best are found in the Lake Chelan area, one of Washington's most desirable summer destinations.

You'll find sagebrush-filled high desert country with shoot-'em up western towns and quiet Indian reservation scattered throughout the **East of the Cascades** zone. Here are the Okanogan Highlands, a scenic northeast Washington region that runs along the Columbia River. Rich in history, this part of the state is popular with backpackers and day hikers, who find it dryer than the Cascades. Spokane, pastoral Yakima Valley wine country, historic Walla Walla, the Palouse Hills, Grand Coulee Dam and the gateway to Hell's Canyon are also popular destinations in this region. Among other highlights are the state's original British settlement, Vancouver, which helped open the door to the Oregon Trail migration west. Other landmarks include Beacon Rock, the remote Maryhill Museum and the Klickitat River, where American Indian dip net fishing remains a way of life.

The Columbia River creates a spectacular natural border between Oregon and Washington known as the **Columbia River Gorge**, a region characterized by towering cliffs, waterfalls and

OBSERVATIONS

Native son William O. Douglas once wrote that visiting his favorite Washington spot, Bird Creek Meadows on the southeast shoulder of Mt. Adams, always made him feel as though he were "standing on the threshold of another world." He also observed "how badly we need high alpine meadows which can only be reached on foot, how badly we need peaks which can only be conquered by daring."

forested bluffs. Here you'll find tremendous opportunities for hiking, salmon fishing, and some of the best windsurfing in the country. The region can be explored by a scenic loop drive over Routes 14 and 84, or by crisscrossing the Gorge and taking time out to explore the spectacular beauty of the Cascade Locks. Watch tugboats ply the waters of the river or marvel at the natural beauty and power of the more than 70 waterfalls in the area.

Seasons

Washington isn't just rain-soaked, snow-covered tundra. In fact, summer and fall days (June–September) are generally warm, dry and sunny. Overall temperatures range from the mid-30s in winter to the upper 80s in summer. There are distinct seasons in each of the primary zones, and the climate varies greatly with local topography.

The enormous mountain ranges play a major role in the weather, protecting most areas from the heavy rains generated over the Pacific and dumped on the coastline. Mountaintops are often covered in snow year-round at higher elevations, while the valleys, home to most of the cities, remain snow-free but wet during the winter months. East of the mountain ranges are temperature extremes and a distinct lack of rain. Travelers can enjoy the rivers, lakes and streams during the hot, dry summers and frolic in the snow during the winter.

The mountainous zones are a bit rainy in spring, but warm and dry during the summer when crowds file in for camping, hiking and other outdoor delights. Fall brings auto traffic and visitors attracted by the changing seasonal colors, while winter means snow at higher elevations that provides the perfect playground for coldweather sports.

The coastal region is generally soggy and overcast during the mild winter and early spring, making this the low season for tourism. However, winter is high season among Washingtonians drawn to the coast to watch the fantastic storms that blow in across the Pacific. Summers are typically warm and dry in the coastal valleys and along the crisp, windy coast, making it the prime season for travelers, who show up in droves, clogging smaller highways with recreational vehicles.

Keep in mind that no matter when you visit Washington, the weather is subject to abrupt change. It is not unusual for surprise snowstorms to hit the Cascades in late spring or early fall. Always bring along warm clothing when traveling in the high country.

CALENDAR OF EVENTS

Festivals and events are a big part of life in Washington, especially when the rains disappear and everyone is ready to spend time outdoors enjoying the sun. Washington's larger cities average at least one major event per weekend during the summer and early fall. Below is a sampling of some of the biggest attractions. Check with local chambers of commerce to see what will be going on when you are in the area.

JANUARY   **Seattle**   The **Lunar New Year Celebration** is a day-long community event, with crafts, music, food and live entertainment.

The Cascades and Central Washington   In addition to catching a dog-sled ride, you'll hear carillon bells and perhaps munch wienerschnitzel at the **Bavarian Ice Fest** in Leavenworth. Winthrop is home of the **Rendezvous Mountain Marathon**, one of the few two-day marathons in the United States.

East of the Cascades   The **Ag Expo/Farm Fest** in Spokane features farm-machinery demonstrations and horseshoe-throwing contests.

Columbia River Gorge   High school bands and vocalists compete for prizes at the **Clark College Jazz Festival** in Vancouver.

FEBRUARY   **Seattle**   **Fat Tuesday** is a week-long Mardi Gras–style festival with a parade, arts and crafts and plenty of jazz and food. Seattle blooms with demonstration gardens and floral displays during the **Northwest Flower and Garden Show**.

Olympic Peninsula and Washington Coast   Aberdeen hosts the annual **Rain or Shine Dixieland Jazz Festival**, which spotlights West Coast musicians.

Northern Puget Sound and the San Juan Islands   Amateur detectives have a field day during Whidbey Island's **Mystery Weekend**, when local merchants offer clues and prizes to solve a whodunit.

The Cascades and Central Washington   Join spring training at the **Winthrop Invitational Snowshoe Softball Tournament**, where participants play ball with a winter twist—in snowshoes. Also popular is Winthrop's **Ski Race of Methow Valley**, featuring classic and freestyle events.

East of the Cascades   In Spokane, the **Northwest Bach Festival** highlights works by the German composer.

MARCH   **Southern Puget Sound**   South of Olympia, you can enjoy the sounds of fiddles, accordions and ragtime piano music at the **Tenino Old Time Music Festival**.

Northern Puget Sound and San Juan Islands   Watch a cooking demonstration, enter a mussel-eating contest or compare your favorite shellfish recipes at the **Penn Cove Mussel Festival** in Coupeville on Whidbey Island. The luck of the Irish will surely be with you at the **Oak Harbor St. Patrick's Day Parade**.

Olympic Peninsula and Washington Coast   Step back in time at Port Townsend's **Victorian Festival**, a celebration of this historic port's heritage, with events portraying Victorian lifestyles.

The Cascades and Central Washington One of the best places to look for art in southern Washington is the **Columbian Artist Spring Show** at Longview. Snow-castle and sculpture competitions are the highlight of the **White Pass Winter Carnival**.

East of the Cascades Indulge in rich candies, ice creams, cakes, drinks and more at **Chocolate Fantasy** in Yakima.

Seattle Bring your umbrellas to watch contestants lure gulls in Port Orchard's **Seagull Calling Contest**. Enjoy some of the first blossoms of spring at the **Daffodil Festival Grand Floral Parade**, which also passes through Tacoma, Puyallup and nearby communities.

Northern Puget Sound and San Juan Islands If you'd rather catch those early-spring colors in all their natural glory, queue up for the drive through the rich farmlands of La Conner and Mt. Vernon during the **Skagit Valley Tulip Festival**.

The Cascades and Central Washington Enjoy over 40 different apple-oriented events during the 11-day **Washington State Apple Blossom Festival** in Wenatchee. Cyclists from all over the evergreen state compete at the **Lake Chelan Mountain Bike Festival**, another major event in this region.

East of the Cascades One of the most colorful events in the area, Clarkston's **Dogwood Festival** celebrates the coming of spring with garden tours, crafts booths, music and road races.

Columbia River Gorge In Woodland, the Hulda Klager Lilac Gardens are open for tours during the **Lilac Days**, which continue into May.

Seattle Storytelling, crafts and a parade are part of the **Norwegian Constitution Day** celebration at the Nordic Heritage Museum. A *biergarten* and a "coffee garden" are featured at the **Pike Place Market Festival**. Considered one of the five best in the nation, the **Seattle International Film Festival** views more than 140 feature films.

Olympic Peninsula and Washington Coast **Sequim Irrigation Festival Parade**, the state's oldest continuous event, features park picnics, an old-fashioned pancake breakfast, dance, parade and a show where loggers demonstrate their skills.

Northern Puget Sound and San Juan Islands A parade, carnival rides, and arts-and-crafts show are held in conjunction with the 85-mile **Ski To Sea Race** between Mt. Baker and Bellingham.

East of the Cascades The ten-day **Spokane Lilac Festival** features a carnival, bed race, torchlight parade, food booths and more. There's also a **Hot Air Balloon Stampede** with nearly 50 balloons in Walla Walla. The Grand Coulee Dam sparkles with a **Laser Light Show** extravaganza every night from Memorial Day through September.

JUNE

Seattle The three-day **Philippine Festival** at Seattle Center celebrates the island chain's Independence Day and cultural heritage with music, dance, food and exhibits.

Southern Puget Sound In Tacoma, thousands flock to **Palmer-Wirf Antique & Collectible Sale**, where you'll find everything from vintage lunchpails to museum-quality pieces. Puyallup's **Meeker Days**, named after one of the town's earliest citizens, celebrates the region's history and its namesake with food stands, crafts booths and music. You'll enjoy hearty servings of strawberry shortcake and performances by Norwegian dancers at the **Strawberry Festival** in Marysville.

Olympic Peninsula and Washington Coast Booths sell sausage, doughnuts, ice cream, baskets, and dolls made of garlic at the **Northwest Garlic Festival** in Ocean Park (Long Beach Peninsula).

Northern Puget Sound and San Juan Islands In addition to a range of nautical events, you'll enjoy a carnival, parade, art show and grand pyrotechnics display during Everett's **Salty Sea Days**. Traditional war-canoe races and ceremonial songs and dances are among the highlights of the **Lummi Stommish** held on the Lummi Indian Reservation northwest of Bellingham. The border town of Blaine is home to the popular **Peace Arch** celebration.

East of the Cascades Spokane takes basketball to the streets during the **Spokane Hoopfest 3-on-3**, when over 2500 teams participate in courts set up all over downtown. Festivities also include a mini food fair, contests and special activities in Riverside Park.

Columbia River Gorge **Sternwheeler Days** marks the return of the Sternwheeler Columbia Gorge to its summer port in Cascade Locks with entertainment and an arts and crafts fair. In Vancouver, the whole city turns out to celebrate **Fort Vancouver Days** with a live jazz show, chili cookoff, beer garden and historic tour.

JULY

Seattle Get ready for alder-smoked salmon and two stages of entertainment at the **Ballard Seafoodfest**. **Millstone Coffee Bite of Seattle**, the city's annual food festival, offers the chance to sample food and wine from dozens of restaurants and wineries.

Southern Puget Sound Behold bagpipe, drum and dance competitions at Enumclaw's **Scottish Highland Games**.

Olympic Peninsula and Washington Coast **Splash Festival!** in Aberdeen features Indian canoe races, a grand parade and a street dance.

Northern Puget Sound and San Juan Islands Festivities at the three-day **Kla Ha Ya Days** in Snohomish include a hot-air balloon show, road race, soccer game and car show. Another winner is the music- and clown-filled **Mount Vernon Children's Art Festival** in Mount Vernon, with hands-on opportunities to make pottery and magic wands. An ideal place to celebrate Independence Day is the **La Conner Fourth of July Fireworks**.

The Cascades and Central Washington The historic river town of Cathlamet hosts the popular **Cathlamet Wooden Boat Festival**.
East of the Cascades The **Sweet Onion Harvest Fest** is a celebration of Walla Walla's famous produce, with food booths, arts and crafts and onion contests. In Lynden is the **Threshing Bee and Antique Equipment Show**, which displays old steam engines and antique farm machinery.
Columbia River Gorge Downtown Vancouver's **International Festival** celebrates Washington's varied heritage with food, music and dance.

AUGUST

Olympic Peninsula and Washington Coast World champions descend on Long Beach to compete in the **Washington State International Kite Festival**.
Northern Puget Sound and San Juan Islands Many of the Northwest's finest artists display their work at top local shows like the **Coupeville Arts and Crafts Festival** on Whidbey Island. Friday Harbor hosts the **San Juan County Fair**, with arts and crafts, agricultural and animal exhibits, a carnival and food booths featuring the bounty of the islands. Also recommended for a selection of Washingtonian art is the **Anacortes Arts Festival**.
The Cascades and Central Washington Located in the shadow of Mt. Adams, the **Trout Lake Community Fair and Junior Dairy Show** is a good place to find local color.
East of the Cascades Classic hot rods, complete with flame-painted hoods, take center stage during Yakima's **Vintiques Street Rod Car Show**.
Columbia River Gorge The **Clark County Fair** has big-name entertainment, horse and art shows, great food and a carnival.

SEPTEMBER

Seattle **Bumbershoot** brings music, plays, art exhibits and crafts to Seattle Center. Learning to live in harmony with the environment is the emphasis of the **Salmon Homecoming Celebration** at the Seattle Aquarium. American Indian dancing, ceremonies, storytelling and crafts are featured. "Do the Puyallup" is the catch phrase of the **Puyallup Fair**, one of the country's largest agricultural fairs.
Southern Puget Sound The state's capital is the port of call for **Olympia Harbor Days**, which celebrates the Sound's maritime heritage with arts and crafts booths, tugboat races and music.
Olympic Peninsula and Washington Coast **Westport Seafood Festival**, held each year around Labor Day, is the ideal place to try fresh salmon, Willapa oysters and dozens of other specialties. **Logger's Play Day** celebrates the life and times of the lumberjack in the coastal town of Hoquiam.
East of the Cascades Broncobusting awaits at the **Ellensburg Rodeo**, held on Labor Day weekend is ranked among the top ten

rodeos in the nation. Enjoy the *biergarten* and German food circus at the **Odessa Deutches Fest**. Wine aficionados can tour the region's wineries and sip estate-bottled vintages at **Catch the Crush** in the tri-cities of Richland, Pasco and Kennewick.

The Cascades and Central Washington   See prize-winning livestock, sample produce and local crafts, nibble cotton candy and enjoy a ride or two at the **Central Washington State Fair** in Yakima.

OCTOBER   **Seattle**   The **Issaquah Salmon Days Festival** in Issaquah features a salmon bake, races, live entertainment, arts and crafts and a parade. South of the city, there's a **Halloween Scavenger Hunt** in Kent.

Olympic Peninsula and Washington Coast   There's plenty of seafood and entertainment along with a shucking contest at the **Oyster Fest** in Shelton.

Northern Puget Sound and San Juan Islands   A great way to get into the Halloween spirit is to attend **Tillinghast's Great Pumpkin/ Scarecrow Contest** in La Conner, or visit the ghosts and ghoulies in **Mt. Vernon's Haunted Forest**.

The Cascades and Central Washington   Leavenworth is ablaze during the **Washington State Autumn Leaf Festival** complete with oompah bands and Bavarian costumes. Airplane buffs will love **Wings over Walla Walla**, which features an air show and displays of antique and military airplanes.

Columbia River Gorge   Candles provide the only light as you step back into 1845 during the **Fort Vancouver Candlelight Tours**.

NOVEMBER   **Seattle**   The Egyptian Theater commemorates women filmmakers during the **Women in Cinema Film Festival**.

Southern Puget Sound   Get into the Christmas spirit at Centralia's **Festival of Trees**, complete with games, storytelling, carolling and, of course, Santa Claus.

Northern Puget Sound   La Conner hosts **Arts Alive**, a three-day celebration of art including demonstrations, live music and displays. There's also the **Annual Whidbey Dance Bonanza**, with workshops, dances and performances.

The Cascades and Central Washington   The **Leavenworth Gala Holiday Food Fair** is a colorful celebration that attracts visitors from all over the state.

East of the Cascades   Spokane's **Winter Knights Snowmobile Show** draws big crowds.

DECEMBER   **Seattle**   To get in the holiday mood, join the hordes of people who gather on Seattle's shoreline to watch the festively decorated **Seattle Christmas Ship**. Seattle Center is all decked out with an ice-skating rink, Christmas train display and arts-and-crafts booths during **Winterfest**, which runs through early January.

Southern Puget Sound   The Point Defiance Zoo & Aquarium hosts **Zoolights**, with half a million lights depicting zoo animals on December evenings. Tacoma's **Holiday Torchlight Parade and Tree Lighting** is one of the region's leading Christmas events. Also popular is the **TideFest Arts and Crafts Show** in Gig Harbor, which features fine arts and crafts for show and sale.

Of the 50 states, Washington is the only one named for a president.

The Cascades and Central Washington   The Bavarian village of Leavenworth looks like a scenic Christmas card during the **Christmas Lighting Festival**.

East of the Cascades   It's holiday time down at the farm during the **Country Christmas Lighted Farm Implement Parade** in Sunnyside.

Columbia River Gorge   Stevenson's **Christmas in the Gorge** offers a tree lighting, crafts bazaar and mystery tour. Boats decorated with Christmas lights sail the Columbia and Willamette Rivers during the **Christmas Parade of Boats**.

Before You Go

For a free copy of the *Washington State Lodging and Travel Guide*, contact **Washington State Tourism**. ~ Department of Trade and Economic Development, 101 General Administration Building, mail stop AX-13, Olympia, WA 98504; 360-586-2088, 800-544-1800; www.experiencewashington.com.

VISITORS CENTERS

Large cities and small towns throughout the state have chambers of commerce or visitor information centers; a number of them are listed in *Hidden Washington* under the appropriate chapter.

For visitors arriving by automobile, Washington provides numerous **Welcome Centers** at key points along the major highways. Visitors can pull off for a stretch, a cup of coffee or juice and plenty of advice on what to see and do in the area. The centers are clearly marked and are usually open during daylight hours throughout the spring, summer and fall.

PACKING

Comfortable and casual are the norm for dress in Washington. You'll want something dressier if you plan to catch a show, indulge in high tea or spend your evenings in posh restaurants and clubs, but for the most part, your topsiders and slacks are acceptable garb everywhere else.

Layers of clothing are your best bet, since the weather changes so drastically depending on which part of the state you are visiting; shorts will be perfectly comfortable during the day in the hot, arid interior, but once you pass over the mountains and head for the coastline, you'll appreciate having packed a jacket to protect you from the nippy ocean breezes, even on the warmest of days.

Wherever you're headed, during the summer bring some long-sleeve shirts, pants and lightweight sweaters and jackets along with your shorts, T-shirts and bathing suit; the evenings can be quite crisp. Bring along those warmer clothes—pants, sweaters, jackets, hats and gloves—in spring and fall, too, since days may be warm but it's rather chilly after sundown. Winter calls for thick sweaters, knitted hats, down jackets and snug ski clothes. It's not a bad idea to call ahead to check on weather conditions.

For an offbeat experience, you might want to try one of Seattle's wheat-grass bars, which serve the ultimate health food drink, clipped fresh and ground into a chloro-phyll-laden treat.

Sturdy, comfortable walking shoes are a must for sight-seeing. If you plan to explore tidal pools or go for long walks on the beach, bring a pair of lightweight canvas shoes that you don't mind getting wet.

Scuba divers will probably want to bring their own gear, although rentals are generally available in all popular dive areas. Many places also rent tubes for river floats and sailboards for wind-surfing. Fishing gear is often available for rent, as well. Campers will need to bring their own basic equipment.

Don't forget your camera for capturing Washington's glorious scenery and a pair of binoculars for watching the abundant wildlife that live here. Also pack an umbrella, just in case. And by all means, don't forget your copy of *Hidden Washington*!

LODGING Lodging in Washington runs the gamut, from rustic cabins in the woods to sprawling resorts on the coastline. Chain motels line most major thoroughfares and mom-and-pop enterprises still vie successfully for lodgers in every region. Large hotels with exceptional service, lavish Sunday buffets and complete business facilities, comfortable pensiones on the European model and waterfront establishments accommodate visitors in all price ranges.

Bed and breakfasts, small inns and cozy lodges where you can have breakfast with the handful of other guests are appearing throughout the region as these more personable forms of lodging continue to grow in popularity. In fact, in areas like the San Juan Islands, they are the norm.

Whatever your preference and budget, you can probably find something to suit your taste with the help of the regional chapters in this book. Remember, rooms are scarce and prices rise in the high season, which is generally summer along the coastline and winter in the mountain ranges. It's a good idea to book ahead in the prime tourists season when conventions can overwhelm the lodging market in cities like Seattle. Off-season rates are often drastically reduced in many places. In general, you can get your best rates in rural areas during the week and in big cities on weekends and holidays.

Lodging in this book is organized by region and classified according to price. Rates referred to are for two people during high season, so if you are looking for low-season bargains, it's good to inquire. *Budget* facilities are generally less than $60 per night and are satisfactory and clean but modest. *Moderate*-priced lodgings run from $60 to $110; what they have to offer in the way of luxury will depend on where they are located, but they often offer larger rooms and more attractive surroundings. At a *deluxe* hotel or resort, you can expect to spend between $110 and $150 for a double; you'll usually find spacious rooms, a fashionable lobby, a restaurant and a few shops. *Ultra-deluxe* properties, priced above $150, are a region's finest, offering all the amenities of a deluxe hotel plus plenty of extras.

Whether you crave a room facing the surf or one looking out on the ski slopes, be sure to specify when making reservations. If you are trying to save money, keep in mind that places a block or so from the waterfront or a mile or so from the ski lift are going to offer lower rates than those right on top of the area's major attractions.

Seafood is a staple in Washington, especially along the coast where salmon is king. Whether it's poached in herbs or grilled on a stake Indian-style, plan to treat yourself to this regional specialty often. While each area has its own favorite dishes, ethnic influences and gourmet spots, Seattle cuisine as a whole tends to be hearty and is often crafted around organically grown local produce. The city's restaurant community is particularly strong on Asian cuisine, including Chinese, Vietnamese and Thai dishes. With numerous open-air eateries and waterfront restaurants, Seattle is also blessed with a generous supply of coffee bars serving first-rate espresso and cappuccino.

DINING

Within a particular chapter, restaurants are categorized geographically, with each entry describing the type of cuisine, general decor and price range. Restaurants listed offer lunch and dinner unless otherwise noted. Dinner entrées at *budget* restaurants usually cost under $8. The ambience is informal, service usually speedy and the crowd a local one. *Moderate*-priced restaurants range between $8 and $16 at dinner; surroundings are casual but pleasant, the menu offers more variety and the pace is usually slower. *Deluxe* establishments tab their entrées from $16 to $25; the cuisine may be simple or sophisticated, depending on the location, but the decor is plusher and the service more personalized. *Ultra-deluxe* dining rooms, where entrées begin at $25, are often gourmet places where the cooking and service have become an art form.

Some restaurants change hands often, while others are closed in low seasons. Efforts have been made to include in this book places with established reputations for good eating. Breakfast and lunch menus vary less in price from restaurant to restaurant than do the evening offerings. If you are dining on a budget and still hope to experience the best of the bunch, visit at lunch when portions and prices are reduced.

TRAVELING WITH CHILDREN

By all means, bring the kids to Washington. Besides the many museums, boutiques and festivals set aside for them, the state also has hundreds of beaches and parks, and many nature sanctuaries sponsor children's activities, especially during the summer months. Here are a few guidelines that can help make travel with children a pleasure.

Many Washington bed and breakfasts do not accept children, so be sure of the policy when you make reservations. If you need a crib or cot, arrange for it ahead of time. A travel agent can be of help here, as well as with most other travel plans.

If you're traveling by air, try to reserve bulkhead seats where there is plenty of room (unless you want to view a movie). Take along extras you may need, such as diapers, a change of clothing for both yourself and your child, snacks and toys or books. When traveling by car, be sure to carry the extras, along with plenty of juice and water. And always allow plenty of time for getting places.

A first-aid kit is a must for any trip. Along with adhesive bandages, antiseptic cream and something to stop itching, include any medicines your pediatrician might recommend to treat allergies, colds, diarrhea or any chronic problems your child may have.

When spending time at the beach or on the snow, take extra care the first few days. Children's skin is especially sensitive to sun, and severe sunburn can happen before you realize it, even on overcast days. Hats for the kids are a good idea, along with liberal applications of sunblock. Be sure to keep a constant eye on children who are near the water or on the slopes.

Even the smallest towns usually have stores that carry diapers, baby food, snacks and other essentials, but these may close early in the evening. Larger urban areas usually have all-night grocery or convenience stores that stock these necessities.

Many towns, parks and attractions offer special activities designed just for children. Consult the calendar listings in this chapter, check local newspapers and/or phone the numbers in this guide to see what's happening where you're going.

WOMEN TRAVELING ALONE

Traveling solo grants an independence and freedom different from that of traveling with a partner, but single travelers are more vulnerable to crime and must take additional precautions.

It's unwise to hitchhike and probably best to avoid inexpensive accommodations on the outskirts of town; the money saved does not outweigh the risk. Bed and breakfasts, youth hostels and YWCAs are generally your safest bet for lodging, and they also foster an environment ideal for bonding with fellow travelers.

Keep all valuables well-hidden and clutch cameras and purses tightly. Avoid late-night treks or strolls through undesirable parts of town, but if you find yourself in this situation, continue walking with a confident air until you reach a safe haven. A fierce scowl never hurts.

These hints should by no means deter you from seeking out adventure. Wherever you go, stay alert, use your common sense and trust your instincts. If you are hassled or threatened in some way, never be afraid to call for assistance. It's also a good idea to carry change for a phone call and to know a number to call in case of emergency, such as the **King County Sexual Resource Center.** ~ P.O. Box 300, Renton, Washington 98057; 24-hour crisis line: 800-825-7273 (call for advice and referrals); www.kcsarc.org.

Many have learned of Washington's charms thanks to poets and writers like Theodore Roethke, Gary Snyder, Annie Dillard, Timothy Egan, and David Guterson.

For more helpful hints, get a copy of *Safety and Security for Women Who Travel* (Travelers' Tales, 1998).

GAY & LESBIAN TRAVELERS

Seattle's Capitol Hill is the hub of urban gay life in Washington, but information hotlines and social and support groups for gay and lesbians also exist in several of the state's other larger cities and towns. Information on gay services and events in the Seattle area can be obtained from the **Gay City Health Project.** ~ 123 Boylston Avenue East, Suite A, Seattle, WA 98102; 206-860-6969; www.gaycity.org. PFLAG **Information Referral Line** offers support and information in Spokane. ~ 509-489-2266. Also in Spokane is the **Rainbow Regional Center**, with gay and lesbian contacts and activities. ~ 509-324-7848. The Seattle–King County Department of Public Health runs an AIDS referral hotline (206-443-1208, CDC National AIDS hotline 800-342-2437).

SENIOR TRAVELERS

Senior citizens will find Washington a hospitable place to visit, especially during the cool, sunny summer months that offer respite from hotter climes elsewhere in the country. Countless museums, historic sights and even restaurants and hotels offer senior discounts that can cut a substantial chunk off vacation costs. The national park system's **Golden Age Passport**, which must be applied for in person, allows free admission for anyone 62 and older to the numerous national parks and monuments in the region. The Passport can be obtained at any national park ranger's office or park office, or in Seattle at the Outdoor Information Recreation Center. ~ REI Building, 222 Yale Avenue North, Seattle.

The **American Association of Retired Persons** (AARP) offers membership to anyone age 50 or over. AARP's benefits include travel discounts with a number of firms and escorted tours with Gray Line buses. ~ 601 E Street Northwest, Washington, DC 20049; 800-424-3410; www.aarp.org, e-mail member@aarp.org.

Elderhostel offers reasonably priced, all-inclusive educational programs in a variety of Pacific Northwest locations throughout the year. ~ 75 Federal Street, Boston, MA 02110; 877-426-8056; www.elderhostel.org.

More apples are grown in Washington than in any other state.

Be extra careful about health matters. In addition to the medications you ordinarily use, it's a good idea to bring along prescriptions for obtaining more. Consider carrying a medical record with you—including your medical history and current medical status, as well as your doctor's name, phone number and address. Make sure your insurance covers you while you're away from home.

DISABLED TRAVELERS

Washington is striving to make more destinations accessible for the disabled traveler.

For more specific advice on traveling in the state, turn to Access Seattle from the **Easter Seal Society**. The Accessible Traveler's Database can be found on their web site. ~ 521 2nd Avenue West, Seattle, WA 98119; 206-281-5700, 800-678-5708; www.seals.org.

There are several places to find more information, including the **Travel Information Center**. ~ 215-456-9603. The **Society for the Advancement of Travelers With Handicaps** is another organization that can provide information. ~ 347 5th Avenue, #610, New York, NY 10016; 212-447-7284, fax 212-725-8253; www.sath.org. **Mobility International USA** is another helpful organization for international exchange travel programs. ~ P.O. Box 10767, Eugene, OR 97440; 541-343-1284; www.miusa.org. Or try **Flying Wheels Travel**. ~ P.O. Box 382, Owatonna, MN 55060; 800-535-6790; e-mail thq@ll.net. **Travelin' Talk**, a networking organization, also provides information. ~ P.O. Box 1796, Wheat Ridge, CO 80034; 303-232-2979; www.travelintalk.net, e-mail info@travelintalk.net. **Access-Able Travel Source** has worldwide information on-line. ~ 303-232-2979; www.access-able.com.

FOREIGN TRAVELERS

Passports and Visas   Most foreign visitors are required to obtain a passport and tourist visa to enter the United States. Contact your nearest U.S. Embassy or Consulate well in advance to obtain a visa and to check on any other entry requirements. Entry into Canada calls for a valid passport, visa or visitor permit for all foreign visitors except those from the United States who should carry some proof of citizenship (voter's registration or birth certificate), including two pieces with photo I.D. Officially, driver's licenses are no longer considered proof of citizenship, although they usually let you pass with one. Bring along a passport, voter registration or birth certificate just in case. The necessary forms may be obtained from your nearest Canadian Embassy, Consulate or High Commissioner.

Customs Requirements   Foreign travelers are allowed to bring in the following: 200 cigarettes (1 carton), 50 cigars or 2 kilograms (4.4 pounds) of smoking tobacco; one liter of alcohol for personal use only (you must be at least 21 years of age to bring in alcohol); and US$100 worth of duty-free gifts that can include an additional quantity of 100 cigars. You may bring in any amount of currency (amounts over US$10,000 require a form). Americans who have been in Canada over 48 hours may take out $400 worth of duty-free items ($25 worth of duty-free for visits under 48 hours). Carry any prescription drugs in clearly marked containers; you may have to provide a written prescription or doctor's statement to clear customs. Meat or meat products, seeds, plants, fruits and narcotics are not allowed to be brought into the United States. The same applies to Canada, with the addition of firearms.

Driving   If you plan to rent a car, an international driver's license should be obtained prior to arrival. United States driver's licenses are valid in Canada and vice versa. Some rental car companies require both a foreign license and an international driver's license along with a major credit card and require that the lessee be at least 25 years of age. Seat belts are mandatory for the driver and all passengers. Children under the age of 5 or 40 pounds should be in the back seat in approved child safety restraints.

Currency   American money is based on the dollar. Bills in the United States come in six denominations: $1, $5, $10, $20, $50 and $100. Every dollar is divided into 100 cents. Coins are the penny (1 cent), nickel (5 cents), dime (10 cents) and quarter (25 cents). You may not use foreign currency to purchase goods and services in the United States. Consider buying traveler's checks in dollar amounts. You may also use credit cards affiliated with an American company such as Interbank, Barclay Card, VISA and American Express.

Electricity and Electronics   Electric outlets use currents of 110 volts, 60 cycles. To operate appliances made for other electrical systems, you need a transformer or other adapter. Travelers who use laptop computers for telecommunication should be aware that modem configurations for U.S. telephone systems may be different from their European counterparts. Similarly, the U.S. format for videotapes is different from that in Europe; National Park Service visitors centers and other stores that sell souvenir videos often have them available in European format on request.

Weights and Measurements   The United States uses the English system of weights and measures. American units and their metric equivalents are as follows: 1 inch = 2.5 centimeters; 1 foot = 0.3 meter; 1 yard = 0.9 meter; 1 mile = 1.6 kilometers; 1 ounce = 28 grams; 1 pound = 0.45 kilogram; 1 quart (liquid) = 0.9 liter.

▼ ▼ ▼ ▼ ▼ ▼ ▼ ▼ ▼ ▼ ▼ ▼ ▼ ▼

Outdoor Adventures

CAMPING

Parks in Washington rank among the top in North America as far as attendance goes, so plan ahead if you hope to do any camping during the busy summer months. Late spring and early fall present fewer crowds to deal with and the weather is still fine.

Though much of Washington's scenic coastline is privately owned, there are a few scattered parks along the shore and even more situated inland in the mountains. It is possible to reserve campsites at several state parks from May 15 through September 16 by calling **Reservations Northwest** at 800-452-5687. You can also contact the **State Parks and Recreation Commission** for more details. ~ P.O. Box 42650, Olympia, WA 98504; 800-233-0321; www.parks.wa.gov.

For information on camping in Washington's national parks and forests, contact the **Outdoor Recreation Information Center**. ~ REI Building, 222 Yale Avenue North, Seattle; 206-470-4060.

PERMITS

Wilderness camping is not permitted in the state parks of Washington, but there are primitive sites available in most parks. Permits (available at trailheads) are required for wilderness camping in parts of the Alpine Lakes wilderness area of the Mt. Baker–Snoqualmie and Wenatchee national forests in Washington. For more information call 800-627-0062. For permits in the Lake Enchantment Area, make reservations in advance (509-548-6977). Campers should check with all other individual parks to see if permits are required. Keep in mind that the popular Mt. Rainier region fills up first in the busy summer months. Consider the Mt. Baker area, the North Cascades or the Okanogan as less-crowded alternatives.

Follow low-impact camping practices in wilderness areas: "Leave only footprints, take only pictures." When backpacking and hiking, stick to marked trails or tread lightly in areas where no trail exists. Be prepared with map and compass since signs are limited to directional information and don't include mileage. For general information on wilderness camping contact **Outdoor Information Recreation Center**. ~ REI Building, 222 Yale Avenue North, Seattle; 206-470-4060.

BOATING

With miles of coastline and island-dotted straits to explore, it's no wonder that boating is one of the most popular activities in Washington. Many of the best attractions in the state, including numerous pristine marine parks, are accessible only by water and have facilities set aside for boaters. Write to or call the **State Parks and Recreation Commission** for a boater's guide to Washington. ~ P.O. Box 42650, Olympia, WA 98504; 800-233-0321; www.parks.wa.gov.

There are several waterways suitable for extended canoeing and kayaking trips. The **American Canoe Association** can provide more information. ~ 7432 Alban Station Boulevard, Suite B232, Springfield, VA 22150; 703-451-0141; www.aca-paddler.org.

Whitewater rafting is particularly popular, especially on the White Salmon where you will find outfitters renting equipment and running tours throughout the summer months.

WATER SAFETY

The watery region of Washington offers an incredible array of watersports to choose from, be it on the ocean, a quiet lake or stream or tumbling rapids. Swimming, scuba diving, walking the shoreline in search of clams or just basking in the sun are options when you get to the shore, lake or river.

Shallow lakes, rivers and bays tend to be the most popular spots since they warm up during the height of summer; otherwise, the waters of Washington are generally chilly. Whenever you swim, never do so alone, and never take your eyes off of children in or near the water.

FISHING

With its multitude of rivers, streams and lakes, and miles of protected coastline, Washington affords some of the best fishing in the world. Salmon is the main draw, but each area features special treats for the fishing enthusiast that are described in the individual chapters of *Hidden Washington*.

Fees and regulations vary, but licenses are required for both salt- and freshwater fishing throughout the state and can be purchased at sporting-goods stores, bait-and-tackle shops and fishing lodges. You can also find leads on guides and charter services in these locations if you are interested in trying a kind of fishing that's new to you. Charter fishing is the most expensive way to go; party boats take a crowd, but are less expensive and usually great fun. On rivers, lakes and streams, guides can show you the best place to throw a hook or skim a fly. Whatever your pleasure, in saltwater or fresh, a good guide will save you time and grief and will increase the likelihood of a full string or a handsome trophy.

For more information on fishing in Washington, contact the **Washington Department of Fish and Wildlife** concerning shellfish, bottomfish, salmon, saltwater sportfish and freshwater game fish. Ask for the Department of Fish Management. ~ 600 Capitol Way North, Olympia, WA 98501; 360-902-2200; www.wa.gov/wdfw, e-mail fishpgm@dfw.wa.gov.

SKIING

As winter blankets the major mountain ranges of Washington, ski season heats up at numerous resorts. Ski enthusiasts head for Mt. Adams, Mt. Rainier and Mt. Baker. For additional information on skiing in Washington, contact the **Pacific Northwest Ski Areas Association**. ~ P.O. Box 2325, Seattle, WA 98111; 206-623-3777; www.skiwashington.com.

TWO

The Washington Landscape

Washington, the northwest placeholder of the contiguous United States, has enough different ecological zones to turn even the most jaded visitor into an amateur geographer. There's a wealth of dramatic scenery found here: rugged coastline, dense forests and two large mountain ranges—one young and aspiring and the other part of a dominant and established volcanic chain.

The young, low-lying Olympic Mountains, home to the only rainforest in the United States outside of Hawaii, reign over the Olympic Peninsula, but are overshadowed by the Cascades to the east, a volcanic chain that starts in western Canada, runs down the middle of Washington and spills out over the state's southern border into Oregon. The Cascades' lower peaks reach over 8000 feet, while Mt. Rainier, the tallest, stretches to a dizzying 14,411 feet and, like some of its neighbors, hosts a family of glaciers. These and other geological wonders fill the state and divide it into its various climate zones. The monumental crests of the mountains trip the clouds, casting a vast "rain shadow" over the eastern part of the state. This rain shadow gives eastern Washington about 12–20 inches of annual rainfall, while the coastal plain to the west of the mountains receives some of the heaviest precipitation in the United States—over 150 inches douses parts of the Olympic Peninsula and sustains the moss-draped rainforest.

The only natural link east to west across the Cascades is the Columbia River, which acts as the Oregon/Washington border. One of the longest rivers in the United States, the Columbia meanders for some 700 miles through Washington alone. The dry, warm flatland climate sucks the cool ocean breezes through the Columbia River Gorge, following the snaking river into the patchwork of rolling plains, irrigated fields and vineyards of eastern Washington.

The greatest concentration of people live in a relatively narrow depression along Washington's western edge that's known as the Puget Trough. Here, you'll find Puget Sound, speckled with the San Juan Islands—more than 170 of them in total.

Wherever you go in the state, there's an abundance of wildlife, from bears to birds, and more types of vegetation than we can do justice to in a few short pages. What follows is a brief overview of some of the highlights of the Washington landscape.

The eruption of Mt. St. Helens in 1980 was only the most recent reminder of the dramatic geological forces that have shaped this state. The Cascade Range began to rise just 20 million years ago, about the time the massive Columbia lava flow, second-largest in the world, formed the Columbia Plateau, which includes Washington and neighboring Oregon. Volcanic eruptions reached a peak about two million years ago with the formation of the Northwest's long chain of "fire mountains," part of the Pacific Rim Ring of Fire. **GEOLOGY**

Volcanoes may have built the mountains, but glaciers carved them into their present form. For the last million years or so they have crept through the valleys and around the mountains, naturally sculpting the land. Within the past 10,000 years, a warmer climate has caused much of the ice mass to melt, adding to the power of already formidable rivers like the Columbia, which has cut its way into the plateau and continental shelf. The withered remains of some glaciers can still be seen on Cascade mountain slopes, still slowly chipping away at their summits. Mt. Baker is dressed with 20 square miles of them.

Some of the state's most intriguing geology is found along the Columbia River basin. A series of volcanic eruptions, giant floods and landslides have combined to create one of Washington's most dramatic landscapes. Traveling through this region, you'll find evidence of numerous lava flows. A geological wonder, the Columbia River basin is littered with pleistocene cinder cones, submerged pinnacles, high benches and eroded scablands.

Washington's forests contain some of the world's biggest trees, holding records in height and circumference, with fir, pine, hemlock and cedar topping 300 feet. While everyone equates coniferous trees with Washington, there is much more to the flora of the region than its abundance of Douglas fir, white pine, red cedar and other evergreens. In fact, the pine-like Western hemlock with its irregular needles is the official state tree, populating the Olympic rainforest, as well as the low slopes of the Cascade mountains, and commonly growing to a height of 200 feet (some reach 300 feet). Each of the distinct geological zones hosts its own particular ecosystem. No matter where you go in Washington, expect to find yourself dazzled by such surprises as the Palouse Hills grasses in spring, the wildflowers of the San Juan Islands or the avalanche fawnlily that grows among patches of snow in Gifford Pinchot **FLORA**

National Forest. Throughout western Washington, you will find bright displays of rhododendron, the state flower. Hundreds of varieties, with their mass of colorful blooms in shades of pink, red and purple, are found growing wild in meadows and parks, making this species a popular icon for photographers. They also have become a cornerstone of Washington backyard gardens.

Thanks to heavy precipitation, this state is one of the greenest in America. Visit the unique rainforests of the Olympic Peninsula, where some 12 feet of rainfall annually support over 1000 species of plant life—trees, flowers and thick carpets of moss and fern. This is the place to look for swordfern, red paintbrush, glacier lily and wood sorrel. Moss-blanketed fir, cedar, maple and spruce create a majestic canopy overhead.

The rainforest is heaven for the spidery, low-lying ferns that enjoy the dank climate. Among the ferns you are likely to find here and elsewhere around Washington are bracken, oak and maidenhair. The maidenhair spleenwort, a short wiry plant with matted roots, grows in the rocky ravines. The high country houses the beautiful mountain holly fern. Up to two feet in length, this scythe-shaped plant is commonly found in cooler shaded areas. The bracken fern thrives in Washington's shaded woodlands and open fields. This triangular plant, ranging up to three feet or more in height, grows fronds all summer long.

In the moist woodlands of the coast, glossy madrones and immense Douglas firs tower over Pacific trilliums and delicate lady's slippers. Bogs full of skunkcabbage thrive alongside fields of fragrant yellow Scotch broom in a riot of color. Look for dune goldenrod, American dunegrass, coastal strawberry and rushes along the shore. Arrowgrass abounds in the salt marshes and you can also expect to find huckleberry, salmonberry and California wax myrtle.

Many different forms of seaweed commonly wash onto the seashore. The hollow tubular plants frequently found along the shoreline at low tide, in tide pools or attached to rocks are known

THE ORIGINAL WOODY WOODPECKER

If you hear a rapid pounding noise, it's probably coming from the pileated woodpecker. Identified by its erect head feathers, it is the largest woodpecker in North America and the model for the cartoon character "Woody Woodpecker." Unlike its cartoon cousin, this bird lives primarily in old-growth forests, drilling for insects under tree bark.

as *enteromorpha intestinalis* (they're the ones used by beachgoing bullies to bludgeon their little brothers). Green hairlike urospora plants are frequently discovered on rocks or driftwood. *Bryopsis corticulans* is a bright green plant with featherlike branches growing from a central tube. You'll find it attached to rocks, shells and driftwood.

In the lowland valleys, alder, oak, maple and other deciduous trees provide brilliant displays of color against an evergreen backdrop each spring and fall. Daffodils and tulips light up the fields, as do azaleas, red clover and other grasses grown by the many nurseries and seed companies prospering in the region. Wild berry bushes run rampant in this clime, offering blackberries, huckleberries, currants and strawberries for the picking. Indian paintbrush, columbine, foxglove, butter cups and numerous other wildflowers line the paths and brush the fields with color.

In the wetlands along the Columbia River and Puget Sound, tall tufts of Douglas fir and hemlock pocketed with maple and alder sprout at the river's edge and creep up the banks. In the spring, scores of violets poke out through the underbrush.

Thick groves of fir and cedar filter the sunlight, providing the perfect environment for mushrooms, lichens, ferns and mosses. As a result, mushrooming has become a favorite pastime of fungusloving locals, as well as a tourist attraction for fine food lovers. Each spring, after a good rainfall, you can spy mushroomers sneaking off alone to their favorite gathering spot, always scanning the ground for the ultimate find: a crop of truffles, part of the mushroom family and an expensive delicacy in French restaurants. **Warning:** New gatherers should bring along an expert to decipher the poisonous mushrooms from the edible. While they will not show you their secret spots, they will steer you away from some serious health problems.

As the snow recedes, alpine wildflowers struggle to live on the rain-soaked meadows, yet a breathtaking array survive. The elegant tiger lily, beargrass, aster, fawnlily and sandwort with its small pin-wheel flowers above a mat of tough leaves, form a rainbow of colors that compliment the gray-green hillsides and decorate the rocky crevasses. Other hardy wildflowers peak through the short wiry grass and dwarf shrubs. Crowberry, red and white mountain heathers and tasty alpine huckleberries blossom and ripen in the early fall.

With the dramatic decrease in rainfall in the plateaus and desert zone comes a paralleling drop in the amount of plant life in eastern Washington, though it is still rich in pine, juniper, cottonwood and sagebrush. Flowers found here include wild iris, foxglove, camas, balsam root and pearly everlasting.

FAUNA

It was the abundance of wildlife that first brought white settlers to Washington, beginning with the trappers who came in droves searching for fur. Beaver and otter pelts, highly valued in China during the 19th century, were heavily hunted. Nearly decimated colonies, now protected by law, are coming back strong. Playful otters are often seen floating tummy up in coastal waters, while the bald eagle can be seen frequently on the Skagit River.

Fish, especially salmon, were also a major factor in the economic development of the region, and remain so to this day, though numbers of spawning salmon are dropping drastically. Nonetheless, fishing fanatics are still drawn here in search of the five varieties of Pacific salmon along with flounder, lingcod, rockfish, trout, bass and many other varieties of sportfish. Angler or not, check out the fish ladders of the Columbia River in the spring where salmon launch themselves out of the water to make it up the huge dams.

Among the more readily recognized creatures that reside in the Pacific Northwest's waters are the orca (killer whales), porpoises and dolphins often spotted cavorting just offshore. When the orca show up, the playful seals and sea lions (the orca's prey) disappear. Constantly one-upping the resident shorelife is the colony of California gray whales that migrate between the Bering and Chukchi seas near Alaska and their warm breeding waters around Baja California. Each year, you can see herds of whales passing the Washington coastline from April through June on their trip north, and again from November through December heading south. Fleets of excursion boats take whalewatchers out to witness these behemoth water mammals that can grow to 42 feet long, weigh over 30 tons and awe spectators with an occasional breach—where 30 tons of whale launches itself completely out of the water. Minke whales are more numerous, as are Dall's porpoises, often mistaken for baby orca because of their similar coloration and markings. Special museums and exhibits throughout the coastal zone attest to the importance of these marine animals to the region. The San Juan archipelago is an excellent place to whalewatch, thanks to three resident pods of killer whales. On

SLUG FEST

The banana slug thrives in Washington's moist climate. Not quite large enough to be mistaken for a speed bump, they leave telltale viscous trails. While it's the bane of gardeners, the slug is still regarded as a sort of mascot for the state. In many souvenir shops, you'll even find plush toy replicas and gag cans of slug soup.

whale watching trips, you're also likely to see Dall's porpoises, splotchy brown harbor seals, bald eagles, great blue herons, cormorants and tufted puffins.

Coastal tidepools offer a closeup look at many fascinating species such as starfish, sea cucumbers, clams, oysters, sea urchins, hermit crabs, anemone, mussels and barnacles. When beachcombing along the coast, you'll find a wide variety of attractive shells. In the Puget Sound area, look for the yellow-gray Japanese littleneck clam. In shallow water you're likely to discover hairy triton, a large yellow white shell. In the same vicinity, keep an eye out for channeled dogwinkle, an inch-long yellow-brown dye shell or the bluish-white barrel bubble. Mudflat areas are a good place to find a shiny tan mollusk called the *cooperella subdiaphana* or a tiny white pear-shaped shell called carp. The brown or black *acmaea limatula* is a limpet found in rocks between tides.

Watch for the Pacific giant salamander in fallen, rotting logs; it is the largest of its kind in the world—growing up to a foot in length and capable of eating small mice.

Among Washington's larger creatures, of the varieties of bear living in the Northwest's remote forests, black bear are most common in southern Washington. Weighing upwards of 300 pounds and reaching six feet tall, they usually feed on berries, nuts and fish and avoid humans unless provoked by offers of food or danger to a cub. Grizzly bears, officially called *horribilis*, are much more aggressive. While extinct in California, these bears, top dog of the bear kingdom, still survive in northern Washington. Even in small numbers, this furry carnivore is a legend. Reportedly, the Lewis and Clark party shot one of these fearsome creatures six times at short range, which apparently only made the animal mad enough to get its half-ton body in motion for a half-hearted chase around the woods. Color does not differentiate a black bear from a grizzly. Some black bears can be light brown, while grizzlies can be almost black. Grizzlies, however, are bigger, have humped shoulders and wield longer claws. They are also known to be meaner and tougher.

Big-game herds of deer, elk, antelope along with moose, cougar and mountain goats range the more remote mountainous areas. Scavengers such as chipmunks, squirrels, raccoons, opossums and skunks are abundant, as well.

The coastal Johns River Habitat Management Area is a good place to look for Roosevelt elk, muskrat, weasel and river otter. An unusual animal, unique to the Olympic Mountains, is the Olympic marmot. These gregarious creatures look like a cross between a ferret and a squirrel, are slightly more curious than lazy and when they are not basking in the sun on top of the pile of rocks they call home, they are exploring and testing, whether its neighboring animals, a sibling, humans or your picnic basket. Visit Olympic National Park and you may run into one of the colonies of marmots who reside there and are said to be the animal world's best people-watchers.

One of the best places in the state to see deer, as well as beaver and mink, is the Columbian White-Tailed Deer National Wildlife Refuge. It's located on the Columbia River near Cathlamet. At Birch Bay State Park on the coast near the Canadian border, beavers, opossums and muskrats can often be seen running along the muddy shoreline. In North Cascades National Park, you're likely to find snowshoe hare, red squirrels, bats, wolverines, mountain goats and, with luck, the elusive bobcat. Eastern Washington's Okanogan National Forest is full of porcupine, black bear and snowshoe hare. The flying squirrel also makes its rounds in the trees of this park, and is actually known more for its gutsy leaping abilities than its aerodynamics. In fact, the flying squirrel cannot "fly," but rather uses the flaps of skin that stretch from its legs to its front paws as a small set of glider wings to extend the range of its leap.

With a proliferation of protected refuges and preserves providing homes for great flocks of snow geese, trumpeter swans, great blue herons, kingfishers, cranes and other species, birdwatchers will be in seventh heaven in Washington, one of the fastest-growing birder destinations on the continent.

Over 300 species of birds live in the Pacific Northwest for at least a portion of the year. Easily accessible mudflats and estuaries throughout Washington provide refuge for egrets, cormorants, loons and migratory waterfowl making their way along the Pacific Flyway. Hundreds of pairs of bald eagles nest and hunt among the islands of Washington along with great blue herons and cormorants. You might see goshawks and spotted owls if you venture quietly into the state's old-growth forest zones.

The spotted owl has been the center of controversy in recent years, the focus of the recurring nature-versus-commerce debate. As logging companies cut deeper into the old-growth forests, which have taken 150 years or more to grow, the habitat for this endangered owl grows smaller. (These nocturnal birds need thousands of acres per pair to support their indulgent eating habits.) The old-growth forests of the Pacific Northwest provide adequate nesting spots in the protected snags and broken branches of tall trees that shelter their flightless young. Recently, old-growth forest has become increasingly hard to come by and the owl's numbers are diminishing—only about 500 pairs survive in Washington today. Some scientists predict their extinction early in the 21st century if logging continues at its present rate. Environmental activists are fighting to keep Washington's forests free and clear of commercial logging roads to preserve their fragile ecosystems.

A Salmon's
Odyssey

The life of a salmon is a long round-trip journey from birth to ocean and back to birthplace. A salmon first enters the world in a small inland stream, where it grows for about a year before departing on its great journey.

Unlike most other fish, salmon live part of their life in saltwater and another part in fresh. Salmon swim downstream to the open sea, changing their camouflage from dots for the river to smooth white for the ocean where they will flow with the currents for about two years. Then they head "home," finding the route back to their original streams by the smell of their home waters and by using the sun as a navigational reference.

These fish are driven to battle ferocious river rapids, swimming upstream against the current to spawn in the same placid pools where they were born. The journey can be as long as 900 miles (to Idaho's Salmon River) and the fish often have to jump up small waterfalls to get to their mates. Ironically, after this long trip and their ritual spawning, the salmon die.

Now with many of the rivers dammed, salmon use manmade fish ladders (that look more like steps) to get back to their streams. Many salmon don't make it upstream past the huge dams, a fact that has prompted government authorities to actually truck some back to their spawning grounds to procreate and then perish.

The Olympic Peninsula area has become a refuge for birders as well as birds. You can see both these groups in full force at Dungeness National Wildlife Refuge near Sequim. Here, you're likely to find a number of binoculars following a wide array of ducks, including greater scaup, bufflehead and green-winged teal. The Nisqually National Wildlife Refuge near Tacoma houses thousands of wintering waterfowl, as well as gulls, sandpipers and passerines. On the Columbia near Vancouver, Ridgefield National Wildlife Refuge has a wide range of birds big and small: widgeons, mallards, red-tailed hawks, goldfinches and red-winged blackbirds are commonly seen darting through the air. At Mt. Baker, far less crowded than popular Mt. Rainier, you'll see red-tailed hawks, bald eagles circling overhead preying on a plentiful supply of grouse, sapsuckers and warblers. In the Spokane area, Turnbull National Wildlife Refuge has a large congregation of forest birds. Bring your binoculars to spot western meadowlark, song sparrows, ducks, killdeer, great horned owls and mountain chickadees.

THREE

History

 There's an intrepid outdoor spirit at the heart of the Washington population. Pacific Northwesterners feel as comfortable lying against a tree as they do sitting behind a desk. This should come as no surprise—anyone raised in a land dotted with lakes, carpeted with forests and cleaved by mountains would grow up familiar with the outdoors. But Washingtonians' love of the outdoors goes well beyond the familiar. They're unfazed by heavy rainfall—true natives leave the umbrellas in the closet—and they revel when the warm sun pokes its head through the usually gray skies. They have an immunity to the harshness of nature, but they also have a strong appreciation for it, which comes from a tradition of explorers and fast growth, retold by living grandparents, remembered by great-grandparents and still present today—it comes from their history.

The story of Washington and the Pacific Northwest is a young one. Romanticized tales of frontier life, from fixing wagon wheels and weathering devastating storms to hunting for food and water in the yet-unsettled territory, dominate our Eurocentric textbooks. But, like other states, Washington's history can be traced back long before the arrival of the Europeans.

THE FIRST TO ARRIVE A popular theory today suggests that 25,000 years ago, at the end of the last ice age, the seas were 300 feet lower and a stretch of land traversed the Bering Strait. The first humans to arrive on the west coast of North America are thought to have used this "land bridge" to walk from Asia to what is now Alaska. From there, they wandered through Canada and down into Washington in search of a warmer climate. Archaeologists have discovered solid evidence of human existence dating back 10,000 years with the find of the "Marmes Man," which are some of the oldest documented skeletal remains in the Western Hemisphere. Along with the partial remains of several individuals, Washington archaeologists, working the dig in the Marmes Rock Shelter (located in eastern Washington), uncovered many of the tools left by this ancient hunter-and-gatherer tribe.

29

Other, more recent evidence of human culture was found at Ozette on the Olympic Coast, the site of one of five major Makah villages. Archaeologists have unearthed well-preserved baskets, harpoons and clothing of the people who lived here an estimated 500 years ago until a mud slide, probably triggered by an earthquake, engulfed and buried the settlement. Because the slide caught the American Indians by surprise, it buried utensils in all stages of use and development. While wooden and textile artifacts have often been destroyed by the region's damp climate, Ozette was beautifully preserved by the great slide. Eleven years of excavation turned up more than 55,000 artifacts, making it possible to paint a complete picture of the early Makah. This find has dwarfed all other projects of its kind and today, 97 percent of all Northwest Coast Indian artifacts are from Ozette.

These ancient people were the ancestors of the numerous tribes that later populated the North American continent. Among them are the Kwakiutl, Haida, Bella Coola, Tlingit, Salish, Yakima, Nez Percé, Paiute, Shoshone, Umpqua and Rogue tribes.

The varying climate of the Pacific Northwest both provided for and dictated the lifestyles of these tribes. Those living inland, east of the mountain ranges, were forced into a nomadic existence, depending primarily on fishing, foraging and hunting game for survival, moving as the climate and animal migrations demanded. They lived in caves during warmer times and constructed large pit houses for winter camp. Many Northwest Coast Indians lived in "longhouses," wooden buildings as much as 100 feet long and 40 feet wide, which could house several families.

The mild climate and abundant resources of the Puget Trough and Pacific coastline led to a fairly sedentary life for the tribes west of the mountain ranges. Here, they constructed permanent villages from the readily available wood, fished the rich waters, foraged in lush forests and had enough free time to develop ritualized arts and ceremonies, as well as an elaborate social structure.

American Indian tribes living on the coast had a wealth of food. Their diets depended on seafood (mostly shellfish, salmon and whale) supplemented by a surplus of potatoes, a common crop for settled tribes. Materialistic and organized, these people had time to create beautiful basketry, hats and wooden whale-fin sculptures inlaid with hundreds of sea otter teeth.

They were also very resourceful people, taking advantage of the malleable consistency of the western red cedar, using its wood for everything from medicinal teas and ointments to houses and canoes. The Makah, one of Washington's most developed coastal Indian cultures, used cedar so proficiently that their woven baskets could be made to hold water and their boxes were used to boil food. Cedar bark was pounded to make soft clothing and woven cedar rain hats helped to keep the people dry in the wet weather of the Olympic Peninsula.

Much of the Makah people's resourcefulness came from their religious beliefs. They took pride in efficiency, using the inedible portions of animals for household utensils so as to please the spirits of the animals who, as they believed, had given themselves up for human benefit. According to their legends, the mountains and the rivers contained great spirits and the salmon were residents of the sea who fed themselves to mankind. For these reasons, the Makah tossed fish bones back into the streams so the salmon people could regenerate to serve the hungry human race once again.

> The American Indians supplied the potato to white settlers and taught them how to grow it successfully in this climate.

To the east, the Yakima and other mid-Columbia Indians developed an elaborate trading culture built around the region's rich fisheries. These tribes were seminomadic, depending on spear-hunted deer, elk, bear, rabbit and squirrel. The tribes that settled by the Columbia River depended on salmon as their main food source.

EXPLORATION AND SETTLEMENT In the 1700s, the heads of several European nations interested in expanding their borders sent explorers to claim chunks of the Northwest coast. The explorers also searched continually for the fabled Northwest Passage, which supposedly connected the Pacific and Atlantic oceans by water. The search for the passage actually had begun much sooner. In the late 1500s, Juan de Fuca, the first recorded explorer to sail along the Washington coastline, thought he had discovered it. However, this Greek traveler, who had adopted his Spanish name as well as flag, was mistaken. What he really found was the mouth of Puget Sound, now called the Strait of Juan de Fuca in his honor.

The Spanish sent out two more parties in 1774 and 1775. Juan Perez, leader of the former, was the first to describe in-depth the region's natural beauty. The other Spanish expedition, led by Bruno de Heceta and Juan Francisco de la Bodega, was much greater in number, as well as purpose. Heceta went ashore along the Washington coastline and claimed the whole Northwest in the name of Spain.

The Russians, not ones to be left out, had sent an expedition in the mid-1700s. They liked what they saw here and sent another group to follow up. Both missions were led by Vitus Bering, who quickly realized the capital potential of the land with its abundance of sea otters and beavers. The Russians moved quickly and erected a number of trading and hunting posts all along the coast, from Alaska as far south as what today is northern California. Bolstered by the prospects of a lucrative fur trade, the Russians were making their first bold move to annex the territory, either ignoring or just ignorant of Spain's outrageous claim.

Arrival of the white explorers brought many changes to the generally peaceful tribes of this relatively well-off region. There is no documentation of the Americans Indians' early interactions with white men, but it is thought that Spanish explorers introduced the horse to the native tribes in the early 18th century, revolutionizing their nomadic lifestyle. The horse allowed hunters to cover much more territory, so tribes were able to remain settled for longer periods of time. By the century's end, traders were beginning to swap guns and ammunition for furs. These weapons helped make the mid-Columbia American Indians proficient bison hunters and fierce warriors. Unfortunately, along with the horses and guns came smallpox. As early as 1775, ships arriving on the Washington coast introduced western diseases that decimated indigenous peoples who had no immunity.

Ironically, the Spanish and Russians were the first foreigners in the region, but they had started a diplomatic territorial battle that they were never to enter. Their sailing expeditions were nothing compared to England's imperialistic machine. The dominating force at the time, England flexed its financial muscle and sent Captain James Cook in 1778 to investigate the maritime fur trade. In 1792, the British commissioned George Vancouver to find the Northwest Passage and map the region, giving him extra leeway with supplies and money. He traveled the inland water routes and named every prominent geological feature after members of his crew.

About the same time, the young and independent United States started looking west. Robert Gray, an American fur trader sent by the Boston Company, explored the Washington coast in 1792 to verify its treasure trove of furry animals. The explorations took him to the mouth of the Columbia River, a discovery that later

A DEADLY MISSION

In 1836, a group of Protestant churches sent out a missionary party led by Dr. Marcus Whitman. The Whitmans settled in Walla Walla at the southeastern corner of Washington and began their mission among the Cayuse tribe. Unfortunately, their good intentions conceived ill results as many of the Cayuse became sick from the laxative remedies and garden poisons used to stave off the insects and animals. When the Cayuse came down with the measles and other western diseases, they turned on the Whitmans. Convinced that the missionaries' goals were to kill them and claim the area for white settlers, the Cayuse murdered the Whitmans and nine others on the mission site.

became the basis for America's claim to the territory. Many American trade companies followed the Boston Company's example and sent hunting parties west. By 1812, the United States dominated the fur trade. The Russians slowly packed up many of their outposts, distracted by the Napoleonic Wars, while the Spanish also lost interest, deterred perhaps by the English presence.

The most famous overland expedition to the west coast was started in 1804 at St. Louis by Meriwether Lewis and William Clark. Their journey, made mostly by canoe and on foot, took the 40-man party two years round-trip. Their goal was a lofty one: to study the geology, plant and animal life of the Louisiana Purchase. And even with that huge task in hand, they did more. They crossed the Rocky Mountains and headed into Washington, paddling down and charting nearly 400 miles of the Columbia River, from the foothills of the Rockies to the Pacific Ocean. In their travels, they encountered many obstacles, from rattlesnakes and grizzly bears to exposure and near starvation, yet only one man died en route. Their success was secured by good relations with the regional American Indians. Lewis and Clark employed French Canadian interpreter Toussaint Charbonneau and, more importantly, his American Indian wife, Sacajawea, who promoted friendship with the Shoshoni and kept the party on good footing with other tribes. The detailed journals and studies kept by Lewis and Clark helped finally dispel the notion of a Northwest Passage.

After Lewis and Clark returned east, a new generation of explorers headed west, convinced they could make a quick fortune in the fur trade. Perhaps the most ambitious of these enterprises was organized by John Jacob Astor, at the time the richest man in America. Eager to monopolize the lucrative fur trade in the uncharted Northwest, he dispatched the ill-fated ship *Tonquin* from New York in the fall of 1810.

In the spring of 1811, just about the time the *Tonquin* was sailing across the Columbia River Bar, a second, overland group sponsored by Astor left St. Louis. They began by following the river route pioneered by Lewis and Clark, but then forged a new trail across the Rockies that would ultimately become part of the Oregon Trail. Among the leaders was Wilson Price Hunt, who was plagued by practically every conceivable misfortune on the journey west. Members of Hunt's party drowned, nearly starved to death, were ambushed by Indians and victimized by strange diseases.

By 1812, when this party limped into the coastal outpost at Astoria, virtually the entire *Tonquin* crew had perished in an Indian raid. A surviving crew member, in a final insane act of revenge, lured the American Indians back on the ship, went below and lit the ship's magazine, killing everyone aboard.

The War of 1812 (in which the United States allied with France against the English) hardly affected the Northwest except for some skullduggery on the part of a British trade company. In September 1812, the remaining Astorians residing on the banks of the Columbia were visited by a party from the English-owned North West Fur Company, a business rival. These newcomers announced that a British warship was en route to seize the new American base Fort Astoria. To make matters worse, they announced that the British had just won the War of 1812. Cut off from the news that would have exposed this lie, the Astorians decided to sell off their pelts for pennies on the dollar and control of the region shifted to the British.

Once the trading companies established permanent outposts in Washington and laid some of the foundation for settlement, the missionaries came to "civilize" the American Indians with their western religion and medicine. However, the intentions of the missionaries often resulted in tension between the American Indians and the new settlers. Eventually, skirmishes escalated into the various Indian Wars of the region, which started in the mid1800s and ended by the turn of the century.

Over time, the territorial struggle came down to the United States and England. After the dust had settled on the War of 1812 (which actually stalemated in 1815), the American and British governments signed a Treaty of Joint Occupation giving both nations the right to trade and settle in the northwest region known as Oregon Country. In 1821, the two reigning British enterprises, Hudson's Bay Company and North West Company, merged and went on to set up a base at Fort Vancouver. This new regional headquarters on the banks of the Columbia exemplified the ability of the British to blend economic and political goals. Unlike Astor's ill-fated pioneers, the region's new landlords showed a deft ability to master this untamed land. Under the aegis of the Hudson's Bay Company, the British turned their Columbia River base into a prosperous trading hub, attracting American Indian tribes from throughout the region.

At the same time, Dr. John McLoughlin, the chief Hudson's Bay factor who befriended American missionaries and settlers, was a superb diplomat. Recognizing the inevitability of American westward expansion, he helped smooth the way for the creation of the new Oregon Territory and the lowering of the British flag in 1848.

Homesteading, fishing, logging, ranching and other opportunities kept the flow of settlers coming. Gold was another early attraction to Washington. A small strike was hit at Walla Walla in the 1850s; however, it was not gold found in Washington that helped this state to prosper. It was the Alaska and Yukon strikes of the late 1890s that attracted droves of prospectors, most of whom passed through Washington buying supplies for their trip up north. Stage routes were established, and river traffic increased steadily. Over the next 40 years, the population expanded from 4000 to over 100,000. As the logging, fishing and shipping industries grew, railroads began pushing into the region, reaching Puget Sound in 1883. Six years later, Washington became our 42nd state and Olympia was named its capital.

THE 20TH CENTURY Rapid industrial development came with the world wars, and Washington emerged as a major player in the shipbuilding and shipping industries. Expansion in lumber, agriculture and fishing continued apace. During World War II, the shipbuilding, aircraft and atomic energy industries all boomed. Modern Washington first found itself in the international spotlight when it hosted two World's Fairs in 12 years: in Seattle in 1962 and Spokane in 1974.

Seattle became the western head of the American airplane industry with the emergence of Boeing as one of the world's largest commercial aircraft companies. Microsoft set up base here in 1975 and within a decade rose to dominate the software industry. Other companies settling in Washington included Sega Corporation, Nike and the Nordstrom corporate headquarters.

The rush of young successful companies combined with the backbone of Boeing attracted a huge influx of people. Until very recently, Seattle was expanding at a phenomenal rate. They could hardly build roads fast enough to handle the traffic. As a result, Seattle is young—from the hoards of yuppie coffee drinkers to the development-speckled suburbs and ultramodern road system.

THE INFAMOUS PIG WAR

Tensions left over from the War of 1812 and the not-yet-forgotten American Revolution caused friction between the Americans and British in the Northwest. The American/British Treaty of 1846 failed to properly define the border of the British territory, instead naming an unspecified "main channel" as the boundary. The Americans and British agreed to use the 49th parallel. However, this latitude divided the San Juan Islands in two, leaving the British and American soldiers staring each other down across the makeshift border. The entente was preserved until a lone British pig wandered into an American settler's garden. The American shot and killed the pig—the only bullet fired during the whole 13-year dispute, a heated diplomatic struggle for control of the islands that came to be called the "Pig War." The "war" was finally resolved in 1872 when the islands were awarded to the United States by a German arbitrator.

The early 1990s were tough for Washington, particularly Seattle. Boeing took some blows, losing big contracts to McDonnell Douglas and Air Bus—and when Boeing hurts, so does Seattle. The regional economy, however, is still very much on its feet, driven by the strong computer and technology companies.

On a cultural level, many American Indian tribes have proudly reclaimed their heritage. A new generation of American Indians has gained prominence in business, education, the environmental movement and the arts. Tribal organizations are also reclaiming lands and fishing rights.

In the early '90s Seattle had its 15 minutes of cultural fame when unlikely members of its lively music scene gained national attention. The "grunge" phenomenon, associated with flannel shirts and a rough rock sound, was shunned by hardcore music fans as pure media hype. Seattle's thriving arts and music scene, however, is anything but hype—it is, after all, Jimi Hendrix's hometown. The large number of students who live there ensure the town's status as a mecca for the young and talented. For alternative sounds, local and otherwise, tune in to KCMU 90.3 FM. Or pick up a copy of *The Rocket*, a free weekly with listings of live music and clubs.

Washington's current challenge is to reconcile its business opportunities with its natural resources, to strike a balance between expansion and preservation that will maintain its rich environmental and economic resources.

FOUR

Seattle and Vicinity

Rain city? Not today. Last night's storm has washed the air clean, swept away yesterday's curtain of clouds to reveal Mt. Rainier in all its astonishing glory. From your hotel room window, you can see the Olympics rising like snow-tipped daggers beyond the blue gulf of Puget Sound. Below, downtown Seattle awakens to sunshine, espresso and the promise of a day brimming with discovery for the fortunate traveler.

The lesson here is twofold: Don't be daunted by Seattle's reputation for nasty weather, and don't limit yourself to anticipating its natural setting and magnificent greenery, awesome as they may be. For this jewel surrounded by water, earning it the nickname "The Emerald City," sparkles in ways too numerous to count after a decade or more of extraordinary growth.

The city, squeezed into a lean, hour-glass shape between Elliott Bay and Lake Washington, covers only 92 square miles, and its population is still under 600,000. But the greater metropolitan area, reaching from Everett to Tacoma and east to the Cascade foothills, now boasts some 3 million.

While most newcomers have settled in the suburbs, Seattle's soaring skyline downtown is the visual focus of a region on the move. No longer the sleepy sovereign of Puget Sound, Seattle today is clearly the most muscular of the Northwest's three largest cities. Its urban energy is admired even by those who bemoan Seattle's freeway congestion, suburban sprawl, crime and worrisome air and water pollution. Growth has been the engine of change, and although the pace has slowed in the '90s, the challenges posed by too rapid an expansion remain persistent topics of discussion.

Seattle offered no hint of its future prominence when pioneers began arriving on Elliott Bay some 140 years ago. Like other settlements around Puget Sound, Seattle survived by farming, fishing, shipbuilding, logging and coal mining. For decades the community hardly grew at all. One whimsical theory has it that because the frontier sawmill town offered a better array of brothels to the region's loggers, miners and fishermen, capital tended to flow into Seattle to fund later investment and expansion.

Whatever the reason, the city quickly rebuilt after the disastrous "Great Fire" of 1889. But it would be another eight years before the discovery of gold in Alaska put Seattle on the map. On July 17, 1897, the ship *Portland* steamed into Elliott Bay from Alaska, bearing its legendary "ton of gold" (actually, nearly two tons), triggering the Klondike Gold Rush. Seattle immediately emerged as chief outfitter to thousands of would-be miners heading north to the gold fields.

Today, Seattle remains tied to its traditions. It's so close to the sea that 20-pound salmon are still hooked in Elliott Bay, at the feet of those gleaming, new skyscrapers. It's so near its waterfront that the boom of ferry horns resonates among its buildings and the cries of gulls still pierce the rumble of traffic. But the city's (and the state's) economy has grown beyond the old resource-based industries. International trade, tourism, agriculture and software giants like Microsoft now lead the way. The spotlight has passed from building ships to building airplanes, from wood chips to microchips, from mining coal to cultivating the fertile fields of tourism.

Seattle has also achieved national—even global—cultural status. Grunge rock swept the music industry in the early '90s, led by local groups such as Pearl Jam, Nirvana, Soundgarden (named after a Seattle park), Alice in Chains and legendary independent record label Sub Pop. All these bands still live and work here (except Nirvana, disassembled by the death of grunge king Kurt Cobain), and music fans can hear the next generation of stars in the city's innumerable clubs and small concert halls.

Starbucks, a home-grown company founded by three University of Washington graduates, fueled the international specialty coffee boom; now Seattle considers itself the coffee capital of the world, and visitors can sample an astonishing array of roasts and blends. With more than two dozen specialty coffee retailers, there's literally a coffee shop on every corner. Nordstrom brought true customer service to the retail industry; Eddie Bauer and REI, two other home-grown institutions, melded flannel and fashion; the city was the test market that proved America would embrace Altoids. In other words, like San Francisco and Los Angeles, Seattle is a good place to see what's coming down the cultural pike.

In the process, one of the nation's most vibrant economies has emerged. You can see that energy in Seattle's highrises, feel it in the buoyant street scene fueled in part by locals' infatuation with espresso. And there is fresh energy beneath your very feet. An " underground" of retail shops (as distinguished from the historic Pioneer Square Underground) has taken shape around the downtown Westlake stations in the Metro Transit Tunnel.

Civic energy has produced a glorious art museum downtown, a small but lively "people place" in Westlake Park, a spacious convention center and additions to Freeway Park. Private enterprise has added hotels, office towers with grand lobbies brimming with public art, shopping arcades, restaurants, nightclubs and bistros.

During the late '80s, as locals struggled with construction chaos, Seattle's downtown briefly suffered the nickname "little Beirut." Again in the late '90s, downtown Seattle is under construction. But this time the atmosphere is one of urban revitalization, as the city gained a new symphony hall, a plethora of condominiums and several upscale shopping and entertainment complexes.

As vibrant as it is, downtown also exhibits the famed Seattle social courtesy and informality. Drivers on many downtown streets still stop to let waiting pedestrians cross, and it's not considered polite to honk your horn. Ask directions of anyone who looks like they know their way around; they'll almost always do their best to help. Only bankers and corporate executives wear suits to work, and not even all of those do. Casual wear is acceptable in almost every social situation; even the symphony and opera draw fans dressed in jeans.

Historically, weather bureau statistics show that mid-July to mid-August brings the driest, sunniest, warmest weather—a sure bet for tourists, or so you'd suppose. But in the last decade or two, that midsummer guarantee all too often has been washed away by clouds or rain. What's the sun-seeking tourist to do?

Consider September. In recent years it has brought modestly reliable weather. Or, simply come prepared—spiritually and practically—for whatever mix of dreary and sublime days that fate delivers. An accepting attitude may be the best defense of all in a region once described in this way: "The mildest winter I ever spent was a summer on Puget Sound."

Have goofy weather, growth, gentrification of downtown neighborhoods and a tide of new immigrants eradicated the old Seattle? Not by a long shot. Pike Place Market's colorful maze is still there to beguile you. Ferry boats still glide like wedding cakes across a night-darkened Elliott Bay. The central waterfront is as clamorous, gritty and irresistible as ever. Pioneer Square and its catacomb-like underground still beckons. The soul of the city somehow endures even as the changes wrought by regional growth accumulate.

But despair not. The legendary Northwest may take a bit more effort to discover, but by almost any standard Seattle and its environs still offer an extraordinary blend of urban and outdoor pleasures close at hand. And growth seems only to have spurred a much richer cultural scene in Seattle—better restaurants serving original cuisines, more swank hotels, superb opera and a vital theater community, more art galleries and livelier shopping in a retail core sprinkled with public plazas that reach out to passersby with summer noon-hour concerts. In this chapter we will point you to familiar landmarks, help you discover some "hidden" treasures and find the best of what's new downtown.

Downtown Seattle

When you fly into Seattle, the central part of this lush region looks irresistible. From the air you'll be captivated by deep bays, harbors, gleaming skyscrapers, parks stretching for miles and hillside neighborhoods where waterskiing begins from the backyard. Central Seattle's neighborhoods offer a seemingly inexhaustible array of possibilities from the International District to Lake Union and the waterfront to Capitol Hill. Eminently walkable, this area can also be explored by monorail, boat and bike. From the lofty heights of the Space Needle to the city's underground tour, this is one of the Northwest's best bets.

SIGHTS Downtown Seattle (Pioneer Square to Seattle Center, the waterfront to Route 5) is compact enough for walkers to tour on foot. Energetic folks can see the highlights on one grand loop tour, or you can sample smaller chunks on successive days. Since downtown is spread along a relatively narrow north–south axis, you can walk from one end to the other, then return by public transit via buses in the Metro Transit Tunnel or aboard the Waterfront Streetcar trolleys, each of which have stations in both Pioneer Square and the International District. The Monorail also runs north–south between Westlake Center and Seattle Center.

A good place to orient yourself is the **Seattle-King County Visitor Information Center**. ~ Level 1, Galleria, 800 Convention Place; 206-461-5840, fax 206-461-8304; www.seeseattle.org.

Pioneer Square and its "old underground" remain one of Seattle's major fascinations. It was at this location that Seattle's first business district began. In 1889, a fire burned the woodframe city to the ground. The story of how the city rebuilt out of the ashes of the Great Fire remains intriguing to visitors and locals alike.

The Pioneer Building, located in historic Pioneer Square, houses Seattle's first electric elevator.

To learn exactly how the underground was created after the new city arose, then was forgotten, then rediscovered, you really need to take the one-and-a-half-hour **Underground Tour**. Several of these subterranean pilgrimages are offered daily to the dark and cobwebby bowels of the underground—actually the street-level floors of buildings that were sealed off and fell into disuse when streets and sidewalks were elevated shortly after Pioneer Square was rebuilt (in fire-resistant brick instead of wood). Admission (reservations recommended). ~ Tour leaves from Doc Maynard's Tavern, 610 1st Avenue; 206-682-4646; 888-608-6337, fax 206-682-1511; www.undergroundtour.com.

Above ground, in sunshine and fresh air, you can stroll through 88 acres of mostly century-old architecture in the historic district (maps and directories to district businesses are available in most shops). Notable architecture includes gems like the **Grand Central Building**, 1st Avenue South and South Main Street, **Merrill Place**, 1st Avenue South and South Jackson Street, the **Maynard Building**, 1st Avenue South and South Washington Street, the cast-iron **Pergola** in Pioneer Square Park and facing buildings such as the **Mutual Life and Pioneer buildings**, 1st Avenue and Yesler Way. More than 30 art galleries are located in the Pioneer Square area. Here you can shop for American Indian art, handicrafts, paintings and pottery.

Yesler Way, located in the heart of the Pioneer Square area, itself originated as the steep "Skid Road" for logs cut on the hillsides above the harbor and bound for Henry Yesler's waterfront mill, and thence to growing cities like San Francisco. Later, as the district declined, Yesler Way attracted a variety of derelicts and became the prototype for every big city's bowery, alias "skid row."

The new city boomed during the Alaska Gold Rush. For a look back at those extraordinary times, stop by the Seattle office of the **Klondike Gold Rush National Historical Park**, where you can see gold-panning demonstrations, a collection of artifacts, films and other memorabilia. ~ 117 South Main Street near Occidental Park; 206-553-7220, fax 206-553-0614; www.nps.gov/klse/home.html.

The main pedestrian artery is **Occidental Mall and Park**, a tree-lined, cobbled promenade running south from Yesler Way to South Jackson Street allowing pleasant ambling between rows of shops and galleries (don't miss the oasis of **Waterfall Park** off Occidental on South Main Street).

Text continued on page 44.

Seattle

DAY 1 • Check in. It makes sense to stay downtown, where most of the key sights are located. Driving from other parts of this long, narrow city can be time consuming. If you *do* stay outside of the downtown area, your best bet is to park at Seattle Center and ride the monorail instead of looking for downtown parking.

• If you haven't done so before starting your trip, make reservations for dinner and the theater tonight and the Underground Tour tomorrow. Seattle runs on reservations, and most locals plan far ahead.

• Stroll **Pike Place Market** and the **waterfront** (see the walking tour on pages 48–49) and visit the **Seattle Aquarium** (page 45).

• Rest your feet on a low-cost, scenic **Washington State Ferry** cruise from the Pier 52 terminal to Bremerton and back.

• On terra firma once more, climb the steep hill to the Westlake Center monorail terminal. Ride the **monorail** to Seattle Center. Take the elevator to the top of the **Space Needle** (page 69).

• Dine in the **Space Needle Restaurant** (page 70) or, more affordably, at the **Seattle Center Food Court**.

• In the evening, enjoy your choice of Seattle Center performing-arts events, which may range from operas and ballets to stage plays and folk-dancing lessons.

DAY 2 • Stroll down to **Pioneer Square** and take the **Underground Tour** (page 41) for a look at the abandoned city that lies hidden beneath downtown Seattle's streets.

• Above ground, ride the elevator to the top of **Smith Tower** (page 44) and imagine the long-ago time when this mini-skyscraper was the city's tallest building.

• Wander through the **International District** (page 44) and take your pick from the many small Asian restaurants along Main and

Jackson streets for lunch. Feast your eyes on the exotic foodstuffs and fine Asian home furnishings at **Uwajimaya**. Complete your exploration of the district with a visit to the **Wing Luke Asian Museum**.

- For dinner this evening, why not enjoy Seattle's favorite food, alder-grilled salmon, at **Ivar's Indian Salmon House** (page 86) on the Lake Union shoreline? Start driving up there early or take a cab; for a popular tourist restaurant, it's a little tricky to find.

- This could be the evening to check out the city's exceptionally lively nightclub scene. (If you don't feel like dyeing your hair green, simply wear your most authentically grungy camping clothes . . . .)

DAY 3
- Is it raining? If not, this could be an ideal morning for urban hiking on the secluded trails of the **Washington Park Arboretum** and **Foster Island** (pages 81–82).

- If it *is* raining, check out the nearby **Museum of History and Industry** (page 82)—the name may sound boring, but the museum is fascinating.

- For lunch, try one of the interesting, affordable restaurants in the University District, such as the **Jitterbug** (page 86).

- Sun still shining? How about a bike ride along **Alki Beach** (page 113) in West Seattle, with its old-time California atmosphere and its great views of the Seattle skyline across the bay?

- Still raining? The city has plenty of other good museums to stay dry in. One good bet is the Boeing's **Museum of Flight** (page 90), tracing the century-long history of the Seattle area's largest employer.

- Consider finishing up your Seattle spree with a big-splurge dinner at **Fullers** (page 62), one of the city's finest restaurants.

For an overview of the whole district, ride the rattling old manually operated elevator to the observation level of the 42-story **Smith Tower**, built in 1914. ~ 2nd Avenue and Yesler Way; 206-682-9393, fax 206-622-9357.

Sharp ethnic diversity has always marked the **International District**, next door to Pioneer Square to the southeast. The polyglot community that emerged on the southern fringes of old Seattle always mixed its Asian cultures and continues doing so today, setting it apart from the homogeneous Chinatowns of San Francisco and Vancouver, across the border in British Columbia. ~ South Main to South Weller streets, 5th to 8th avenues South.

Chinese began settling here in the 1880s, Japanese around 1900, and today the "I.D." as it's commonly known is also home to Koreans, Filipinos, Vietnamese and Cambodians. For all its diversity, the district clearly lacks the economic vitality, bustling street life and polished tourist appeal of other major Chinatowns. Yet some find the International District all the more genuine for its unhurried, even seedy, ambience.

A variety of mom-and-pop enterprises predominates in the I.D. —specialty-food and grocery stores, herbal-medicine shops, dim sum palaces and fortune-cookie factories. You're welcome to poke in for a look at how cookies, noodles, egg rolls and won ton wrappers are made at the **Tsue Chong Company**. Closed Sunday. ~ 801 South King Street; 206-623-0801, fax 206-382-2688.

To see a variety of ethnic foodstuffs, drop by **City Produce**, a wholesale vegetable market with retail sales. Closed Sunday. ~ 710 7th Avenue South at South Lane Street; 206-682-0320, fax 206-682-1876.

The district's single major retail store is **Uwajimaya**; it's not only the largest Japanese department store in the Northwest but also a worthwhile experience of Asian culture even if you're not shopping. ~ 519 6th Avenue South; 206-624-6248, fax 206-624-6915; www.uwajimaya.com.

Wing Luke Asian Museum offers a well-rounded look at the Northwest's Asian Pacific history and culture, representing ten groups of Asian Pacific immigrants. Presentations include historical photography and social commentary on the Asian-American experience. You may also see paintings, ceramics, prints, sculpture and other art. Closed Monday. Admission. ~ 407 7th Avenue South; 206-623-5124, fax 206-623-4559; www.wingluke.com.

The **Nippon Kan Theatre** is the centerpiece of the **Kobe Park Building National Historical Site** and hosts occasional dramas and other cultural presentations. The park and community gardens adjacent to it offer pleasant strolling. ~ 628 South Washington Street; 206-224-0181, fax 206-682-4348.

Hing Hay Park is the scene of frequent festivals—exhibitions of Japanese martial arts, Chinese folk dances, Vietnamese food fairs, Korean music and the like. ~ South King Street and Maynard Avenue South.

The old **waterfront** beginning at the western edge of Pioneer Square remains one of the most colorful quarters of the city and what many consider Seattle's liveliest "people place." On sunny summer days, it is the most popular tourist draw in the city. The waterfront grows more interesting by the year, a beguiling jumble of fish bars and excursion-boat docks, ferries and fireboats, import emporiums and nautical shops, sway-backed old piers and barnacle-encrusted pilings that creak in the wash of wakes.

> Hing Hay Park's colorful pavilion, built in 1975, was donated to the city by Taipei, Taiwan.

The action's concentrated between Piers 48 and 60, and again around Pier 70. Poking around by foot remains the favorite way to explore, but some folks prefer to hopscotch to specific sites aboard the **Waterfront Streetcar**, which runs from Pioneer Square to Pier 70 (you also can climb into a horse-drawn carriage here for a narrated tour). Still another way to do it is via boat (see "Hey! The Water's Fine" at the end of this chapter). Here's a sampler of attractions: As you stroll south to north, you'll encounter a harbor-watch facility, a dozen historical plaques that trace major events, a public boat landing, the state-ferry terminal at Colman Dock and the waterfront fire station whose fireboats occasionally put on impressive, fountainlike displays on summer weekends. Ye Olde Curiosity Shop houses a collection of odd goods from around the world, Ivar's is the city's most famous fish bar, and cavernous shopping arcades include pier-end restaurants, outdoor picnic areas and public fishing. **Central Waterfront Park** is a crescent-shaped retreat from commercialism presenting sweeping views over the harbor.

Dating back to 1899, **Ye Olde Curiosity Shop** is a combination souvenir shop and museum that draws crowds with odd displays such as a Siamese twin calf, rare eskimo walrus-tusk carvings and one of the world's largest collections of shrunken heads. The antique, coin-operated games are an easy way to get rid of pocket change. ~ 1001 Alaskan Way, Pier 54; 206-682-5844.

The **Seattle Aquarium** allows you to descend to an underwater viewing dome for up-close looks at scores of Puget Sound fish. Other exhibits include a sea otter pool, a coral reef tank teeming with sharks, and a giant Pacific octopus on an all-he-can-eat crab diet in an attempt to beat the size record set by the aquarium's last giant octopus, which reached 78 pounds before being released into the ocean in January 2000 so he could mate. Salmon are born at the aquarium and allowed to migrate to the open sea, returning later to spawn. Admission. ~ Pier 59 at Pike Street; 206-386-4320, fax 206-386-4328; www.seattleaquarium.org.

Next to the aquarium is the **IMAX Dome** (formally the Omnidome), the only IMAX dome theater in Seattle. This highly recommended program features 70mm films such as the 1980 Academy Award–nominated *Eruption of Mt. St. Helens*. Admission. ~ Pier 59; 206-622-1868; www.seattleimaxdome.com.

The Pike Hillclimb across Alaskan Way leads up—almost straight up, 155 step's worth—past several decent restaurants and shops to the famed **Pike Place Market**. (There's an elevator for the walk-weary. You can also reach the north end of the Market from a stairway/elevator complex opposite the Pier 62/63 public wharf.) You'll also pass some piers whose sheds have been leveled to provide public access, the last vestiges of working waterfront on the central harbor—fish-company docks and such—as well as the Port of Seattle headquarters.

The venerable market, born in 1907, has proved itself one of the city's renewable treasures. Saved from the wrecking ball by citizen action in the early '70s, the market was later revitalized through long-term renovation. Today, the nine-acre **Pike Place Market National Historic District** and the surrounding neighborhood are in many respects better than ever. The main historic market now offers hundreds of different products in hundreds of categories, from clothing to different types of zucchini. Some 250 businesses, about 120 farmers, 160 craftspeople and a good 40 restaurants and eateries. In all, a market experience unparalleled in the nation! To learn more, call for more information or stop at the Info Booth at 1st Avenue and Pike Street. ~ Virginia Street to just south of Pike Street, 1st to Western avenues; 206-682-7453, fax 206-625-0646; www.pikeplacemarket.org.

There are so many ways to enjoy the market that we can scarcely begin to list them. Come early for breakfast and wake up with the market (at least a dozen cafés open early). Come at noon for the ultimate experience of marketplace clamor amid legions of jostling shoppers, vendors hawking salmon and truck-farm produce, and street musicians vying for your contributions. Come to explore the market's lower level, often missed by tourists, a warrenlike collection of secondhand treasures, old books, magazines, posters and vintage clothing. Come to shop for the largest collection of handmade merchandise in the Northwest on handcraft tables at the market's north end. Come to browse all the "nonproduce" merchandise surrounding the main market—wines, exotic imported foods, French kitchenware, jewelry and avant-garde fashions.

Among the market's many virtues, perhaps the best is that it is a real-life urban amenity popular with Seattleites every bit as much as visitors. What downtown workers do lends itself to travel itineraries equally well: Walk to the market late morning and enjoy the atmosphere a few minutes. You could buy a coffee drink at Starbucks and listen to the street musicians invariably set up out front —perhaps the King Jesus Disciples, four excellent gospel singers who once prowled downtown streets as transients. Yes, this is the original **Starbucks** store, the very first of 3300 around the world; it opened in 1971. ~ 1912 Pike Place; 206-448-8762.

After you've loaded up on coffee and tasty treats from the food vendors, wander down to **Victor Steinbrueck Park**, a small plaza ◄HIDDEN at the north end of Pike Place, overlooking Elliott Bay and the

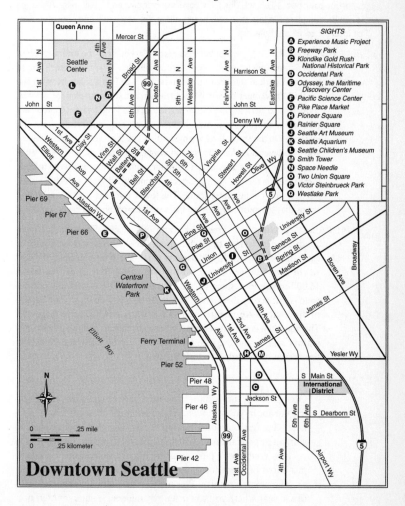

SIGHTS

- A Experience Music Project
- B Freeway Park
- C Klondike Gold Rush National Historical Park
- D Occidental Park
- E Odyssey, the Maritime Discovery Center
- F Pacific Science Center
- G Pike Place Market
- H Pioneer Square
- I Rainier Square
- J Seattle Art Museum
- K Seattle Aquarium
- L Seattle Children's Museum
- M Smith Tower
- N Space Needle
- O Two Union Square
- P Victor Steinbrueck Park
- Q Westlake Park

Downtown Seattle

WALKING TOUR
Seattle's Waterfront

Nowhere is the distinctive character of Seattle more visible than along the water-front between Piers 52 and 70 and the adjacent Pike Place Market. (Of course, the waterfront contains many more piers south of this area, but they are used for industrial shipping and are inaccessible on foot. The best way to get a look is from a harbor tour boat.) This walking tour covers about two and a half miles. Although it can be completed in less than two hours, along the way you'll find enough points of interest to fill a whole day.

PIKE PLACE MARKET   Start at Pike Place Market, near the intersection of Pike Street and 1st Avenue on a steep hillside above the waterfront. (If you must park in this area, you're most likely to find a space beneath the Alaska Way Viaduct downhill from the market. A better plan for drivers, though, is to park at one of the big lots around the Seattle Center and ride the monorail downtown. It lets you off just four blocks from the market.) On the street level are more than 100 food vendors' stalls where you'll find plenty of fresh fruits and veggies to snack on while you wander, free samples of tasty edible souvenirs, and fishmongers hawking fresh local seafood such as giant geoduck (pronounced "gooey duck") clams, along with arts-and-crafts stands. The lower level has small eateries and shops that sell exotica imported from such far-off lands as Egypt and India.

HARBOR STEPS PARK   From the south end of Pike Place Market, head south a short distance to Harbor Steps Park. (Here you're practically in front of the **Seattle Art Museum** (page 50); if time permits, it's well worth a visit either now or on the way back.) Walk down the broad 16,000-square-foot steps to Western Avenue. The waterfront prome-nade is just across the avenue. The steps take you down to Pier 59, site of the **Seattle Aquarium** (page 45) and the **IMAX Dome** (page 46). The aquarium is a must-see stop, where attractions include jellyfish, mi-gratory salmon and the largest octopus in captivity. The aquarium is in the middle of the public waterfront area.

Olympics. On sunny days the crowd here ranges from backpack-ing European youths to bankers to religious proselytizers to Japa-nese schoolgirls on tour, holding hands. There's no better place to gain an appreciation of Seattle's cultural diversity. On your way back to your hotel, pick up some gifts to take home, or maybe just a loaf of bread for dinner. ~ Pike Place and Western Avenue.

The next pier north, Pier 62/63, is a public park ten months of the year where you can often see anglers for squid at high tide.

PIERS 62–70   If you walk north, you'll pass **Piers 62–63**, a bare-wood park serving as a 4000-seat municipal concert venue that has hosted such performers as Lyle Lovett, Jonny Lang, Judy Collins and Los Lobos. Between Anthony's Pier 66 Restaurant and the Edgewater Inn on Pier 67 is **Odyssey, the Maritime Discovery Center** (page 50). Beyond the Edgewater Inn are departure piers for the **Victoria Clipper** (summer-only ferry service to Victoria, B.C.; Pier 69) and *Spirit of Puget Sound* (lunch and dinner cruises; Pier 70).

PIERS 55–57   If you walk south from the aquarium, you'll pass a large dining and shopping complex at **Pier 57**, where the central attraction for kids is a vintage carousel. **Gray Line Water Tours** (206-623-4252) boats also depart from this pier, while **Pier 56** is the departure point for tour boats to **Tillicum Village** (206-443-1244, 800-426-1205), a replica Salish Indian village on a small island where trips include a traditional grilled salmon buffet. **Pier 55** is home to **Argosy Cruises** (206-623-1445), offering daily boat tours of Seattle Harbor.

PIER 54   Pier 54 is the site of two venerable Seattle landmarks. **Ivar's Fish Bar** (206-467-8063), the original home of the clams and fish-and-chips restaurant that now has locations all over the Northwest, was started in 1938 by the late Ivar Haglund while he was director of Seattle's first aquarium next door. **Ye Olde Curiosity Shop** (page 45) is a combination souvenir shop and free museum.

PIER 52   Pier 52 is the terminal for the **Washington State Ferries** that run frequently to Bremerton, Winslow and Vashon Island. Taking any of these ferries as a foot passenger makes for a relaxing, low-cost scenic cruise and an introduction to the ferry system that will serve you well as you travel to other parts of the Puget Sound area.

PIONEER SQUARE   From the ferry terminal, you can either return the way you came, climbing back up the Harbor Steps, or go a few more blocks south to Pioneer Square, returning to central downtown along 2nd Avenue with its towering skyscrapers.

During July and August, the pier becomes a world-class outdoor theater, with evening concerts by pop, rock and blues music acts such as Chris Isaak and Robert Cray. The setting is unparalleled, with the Olympic Mountains across the sound lit pink by the summer sunset. Admission. ~ Summer Nights at the Pier, 206-281-8111; www.onereel.org.

Just a bit north is the Port of Seattle's **Pier 66**, the Bell Street Pier. With a small-craft marina, three restaurants, a museum, a conference center and a skybridge leading up to the booming Belltown shopping/restaurant district along 1st Avenue, this recent development has become a popular stop for travelers.

At Pier 66 on the waterfront, **Odyssey, the Maritime Discovery Center** contains three galleries of high-tech interactive exhibits for kids and adults that reveal how the industrial waterfront works, focusing on fishing, trade and boating. Children can try loading a 20-ton cargo container onto a ship, experience a simulation of a fishing vessel on a stormy sea and explore a scaled-down fishing boat. Other displays explain fishery management, the global economy, marine safety and environmental preservation. Admission. ~ 2205 Alaskan Way; 206-374-4000, fax 206-374-4002; www.ody.org, e-mail education@ody.org.

It costs less than a dollar to ride the Monorail, which zips between Seattle Center and Westlake Center in two minutes.

If you continue north on the waterfront, past the handsome port headquarters building, you reach **Myrtle Edwards Park**, at the end of Alaskan Way, a greenbelt that offers downtown Seattle's best jogging route.

South of Pike Place Market is the **Seattle Art Museum**, designed by the husband/wife architectural team of Robert Venturi and Denise Scott. The five-story, limestone-faced building highlighted with terra-cotta and marble has quickly become a regional, postmodern landmark. You'll enter the museum via a grand staircase, but to see the collections, you'll have to ascend by elevator to the galleries. Known for its Northwest Coast American Indian, Asian and African art, the museum also features Meso-American, modern and contemporary art, photography and European masters. Do not miss the superb collection of African masks. Admission. ~ 100 University Street; 206-654-3100, fax 206-654-3135; www.seattleartmuseum.org.

Located across the street from the Seattle Art Museum, the Seattle Symphony's massive **Benaroya Hall** gives the symphony its own dedicated concert facility after years of sharing space at Seattle Center with the opera and ballet. The grounds include a memorial garden dedicated to Washington residents who died in military conflicts from World War II to the present. ~ 200 University Street; 206-215-4700, fax 206-215-4701; www.seattle symphony.org.

City center, or **Downtown**, has undergone a remarkable rejuvenation. It's a delightful place to stroll whether you're intent on shopping or not. Major downtown hotels are clustered in the retail core, allowing easy walks in any direction. Here's one way to sightsee:

Start at the south end of **Freeway Park**—also called Ellis Park —which offers five-plus acres of lawns, gardens and fountains, and is the nation's first major park to be built over a freeway. The park's many waterfalls and pools create a splashy, burbling sound barrier to city noise. Beds of summer-blooming flowers, tall evergreens and leafy deciduous trees create a genuine park feeling, inspiring picnics by office workers on their noon-hour break. Amble north through the park, and take a short detour beneath a street overpass toward University Street (steps next to more waterfalls zigzag up to Capitol Hill and dramatic views of city architecture). ~ 6th Avenue and Seneca Street.

Continue north as the park merges with similarly landscaped grounds of the **Washington State Convention and Trade Center**, which offers occasional exhibits. Maps and information are on hand at the Tourist Information Center (206-461-5840, fax 206-461-8304), located on the first level of the Convention Center. ~ 800 Convention Place; 206-447-5000, fax 206-694-5399; www.wsctc.com.

Head west through linking landscaping that leads you past yet more waterfalls and flowers in the main plaza of **Two Union Square**. Cross 6th Avenue and enter **Pacific First Center** located on the corner of Union Street. This handsome building's lower levels are lined with upscale shops and a theater complex, bold sculptures and stunning exhibits of colorful art glass. Wander and admire for a bit, stop for a meal or an espresso, then continue by leaving the building at the 5th Avenue and Pike Street exit. Cross 5th Avenue past what used to be the striking Coliseum Theater, now renovated and occupied by Banana Republic. Head west on Pike Street to 4th Avenue and turn right to enter triangular **Westlake Park** at 4th Avenue and Pine Street, which offers a "water wall" against street noise, a leafy copse of trees and an intriguing pattern of bricks that replicate a Salish Indian basket-weave design best observed from the terraces on the adjoining Westlake Center.

Westlake Center is an enormously popular, multilevel shopping arcade, a people place offering cafés and espresso bars, a brew pub, flower vendors, handicrafts and access to what's been heralded as downtown's "new underground." The marbled, well-lighted, below-street-level arcades were created as part of the city's new downtown transit tunnel. Metro buses (propelled electrically while underground) rumble by on the lowest level. Just above it are mezzanines full of public art, with vendors and shops, and underground access to a string of department stores.

Walk south on 4th Avenue a few blocks to **Rainier Square**, between 4th and 5th avenues and University and Union streets, and discover another burgeoning underground of upscale enterprises. Follow its passageways eastward past a bakery, restaurants and access to the venerable **Fifth Avenue Theatre**. Continue east, up an escalator back to Two Union Square and Freeway Park.

To the south and west of downtown, surrounded by saltwater on three sides, **West Seattle** offers the finest aggregation of seaside parks and paths in town with stupendous views of the city shining across the waters of Elliott Bay. Some seven miles of roads follow the water's edge, including Harbor Avenue Southwest, Alki Avenue Southwest and Beach Drive Southwest. At low tide, there are miles of sandy strands, tide flats and a sprinkling of tidepools.

Offshore on Blake Island is **Tillicum Village**, a huge cedar longhouse styled after the dwellings of the Northwest Coast American Indians, situated on the edge of a 475-acre marine state park. The village presents traditional salmon bakes and performances by the Tillicum Village Dancers. Tillicum Village charters Argosy vessels from Pier 55/56 on Seattle's central waterfront year-round. ~ 206-623-1445, fax 206-623-5474; www.tillicumvillage.com. **Kitsap Harbor Tours** depart for Blake Island from the Bremerton waterfront in summer ~ 360-377-8924.

LODGING

Lodgings vary widely in style and price throughout the Seattle area. Downtown, there's a thick cluster of expensive luxury hotels interspersed with a few at moderate and even budget rates.

HIDDEN ►

The **Pioneer Square Hotel** combines a prime location with Four-Diamond historic charm. The essence of comfort is captured here by turn-of-the-20th-century decor and remarkably quiet rooms. Rates are quite reasonable by downtown standards. The Pioneer Square Historic District surrounding the hotel is a haven for fascinating restaurants, taverns, art galleries, shops and more. The ferry terminal and Seattle Art Museum are also within a few blocks. ~ 77 Yesler Way; 206-340-1234, fax 206-467-0707; www.pioneersquare.com. ULTRA-DELUXE.

The **Alexis Hotel** is an elegant little haven two blocks from the waterfront and close to downtown stores and business centers. The 109 rooms have soft colors and contemporary furnishings mixed with a few antiques, all done in good taste. Some of the roomy suites have fireplaces. The service is unmatched in this renovated historic hotel. ~ 1007 1st Avenue; 206-624-4844, 800-426-7033, fax 206-621-9009; www.alexishotel.com. ULTRA-DELUXE.

Pensione Nichols offers European-style lodging within a block of Pike Place Market. Ten rooms on the third floor of a historic building share four baths and a large common space with a stunning view of the bay, while two rooms share one bath on the second floor. The rooms are painted a cheerful yellow; some have windows, while others only have skylights. They are simply furnished with antiques. There are also two ultra-deluxe suites that sleep five and have fully equipped kitchens and private baths. A continental breakfast is served. ~ 1923 1st Avenue; 206-441-7125,

800-440-7125, fax 206-448-8906; www.seattle-bed-breakfast. com. DELUXE TO ULTRA-DELUXE.

The downtown location for **Green Tortoise Backpackers Guest-** ◀ HIDDEN
house is convenient to most central-Seattle attractions—among them Pike Place Market, just a block away. With functional private and dorm rooms, 24-hour check-in, a common room and a fully equipped kitchen, it's much like a hostel, with one extra advantage: a free breakfast. Many guest services, such as tours and discounts at local clubs, pubs and restaurants, add value as well. ~ 1525 2nd Avenue; 206-340-1222, fax 206-623-3207; www. greentortoise.com. BUDGET.

Hotel Monaco offers stylish, upscale accommodations in 189 funky, plush rooms and suites. The grand high-ceilinged lobby has columns and pilasters and a white stucco fireplace spotlighted by azure hues. Make sure to take advantage of their in-room pet goldfish adoption program. ~ 1101 4th Avenue; 206-621-1770, 800-945-2240, fax 206-624-0060; www.monaco-seattle.com. ULTRA-DELUXE.

This is a city of readers: the Seattle Public Library has the fourth-highest circulation of any municipal library in the United States.

One of Seattle's historic landmarks, the **Four Seasons Olympic Hotel** is the epitome of elegance and style, worth a peek whether you stay here or not. When the hotel opened in 1924, it was the ultimate in fine lodgings of the day. The modified Italian Renaissance brick building, on a prime downtown site owned by the University of Washington, was filled with antique mirrors, marble, Italian and Spanish oil jars and bronze statuary. Terrazzo floors were laid by Italian workers brought to Seattle for the project. The proud Washington State Hotel Association labeled its metropolitan member "a bit of New York transplanted to the Pacific Northwest." For years, the Olympic is the preferred site for social events, banquets, weddings and debutante balls. With time its elegance faded, but today the Four Seasons Olympic is again operating as the queen of hotels in the Pacific Northwest. ~ 411 University Street; 206-621-1700, 800-223-8772, fax 206-682-9633; www.fourseasons.com. ULTRA-DELUXE.

Seattle has only one place to stay that is directly on the waterfront: the **Hotel Edgewater**. It began as a top-flight hotel on Pier 67, built in the 1960s for the World's Fair. It later slid into decay and was renovated in "mountain lodge" style—meaning plaid comforters and natural-log furniture in the rooms and an antler chandelier in the lobby. Half of the 238 rooms and suites have stunning views of Elliott Bay, West Seattle and the Olympic Peninsula. Guest rooms are comfortable, and the staff is accommodating. The restaurant has a fine water view. ~ 2411 Alaskan Way; 206-728-7000, 800-624-0670, fax 206-441-4119; www.noble househotels.com. ULTRA-DELUXE.

Between downtown and Seattle Center is **Sixth Avenue Inn**, a five-story motor inn with 166 rooms. The rooms, done in crisp blue and cream, are a cut above those in most motels. They contain blond furniture and assorted plants and books. Those on the north and in back are the quietest. No pets. Parking limited but complimentary. There's a restaurant overlooking a small garden. ~ 2000 6th Avenue; 206-441-8300, 800-648-6440, fax 206-441-9903. DELUXE.

The **West Coast Camlin Hotel**, on the edge of downtown and a block from the convention center, was built in 1926 and has been renovated in recent years. The 130-room hotel has a lovely lobby of marble with oriental carpets, a restaurant and lounge on the 11th floor and a conference room on the lobby level. Most of the oversized, classically furnished rooms have work areas, a popular feature for business travelers. ~ 1619 9th Avenue; 206-682-0100, 800-426-0670, fax 206-682-7415; e-mail camlinhotel@sprint mail.com. DELUXE.

Hostelling International—Seattle is a low-priced establishment on the edge of Pike Place Market. In addition to 197 sleeping units, the bright, clean hostel has a kitchen, dining room, lounge, TV room and small library. Also available are bike storage and laundry facilities. ~ 84 Union Street; 206-622-5443, 888-622-5443, fax 206-682-2179; www.hiseattle.org. BUDGET.

A retreat from the throngs in Pike Place Market is **Inn at the Market**. The hotel, several shops and a restaurant are centered by a brick courtyard with a 50-year-old cherry tree. Small 69-room, light and airy and furnished in French country style, the inn is one of Seattle's best. Rooms have views of the city, courtyard or water. ~ 86 Pine Street; 206-443-3600, 800-446-4484, fax 206-448-0631; www.innatthemarket.com. ULTRA-DELUXE.

The **Renaissance Madison Hotel** offers luxury accommodations with views of Puget Sound, Lake Union and downtown. The 553 rooms are furnished in casual and contemporary earth-toned decor and guests enjoy access to the health club, pool and spa on the top floor. ~ 515 Madison Street; 206-583-0300, 800-278-4159, fax 206-447-0092. ULTRA-DELUXE.

The **Sorrento Hotel** is known for its personal service and attention to detail. A historic building that has been remodeled, Sorrento is on a hilltop a few blocks above the downtown area. Beyond the quiet, plush lobby are a notable restaurant and an inviting lounge. The Sorrento has been called one of the most romantic hotels in Seattle. All 76 rooms and suites have a warm, traditional, European atmosphere. ~ 900 Madison Street; 206-622-6400, 800-426-1265, fax 206-343-6155; www.hotelsorrento.com. ULTRA-DELUXE.

Considered a luxury hotel in the 1930s, the **Pacific Plaza Hotel** is now a dignified, quiet downtown classic with 160 rooms.

Author Picks

CHAPTER FAVORITES

Pike Place Market is lots of fun, but I find it even more fascinating to wander up and down the food aisles of **Uwajimaya**, trying to identify the exotic ingredients sold there—many of them bright pink and most of them labeled only in Japanese. *page 64*

When money's no object, my favorite Seattle lodging choice is the **Hotel Edgewater**. It has changed completely since the days when the Beatles used to fish for sand sharks from the windows, but the location is still hard to beat. *page 53*

Touristy though it may be, the great view, alder-grilled fish, interesting decor and historic photos of native Salish people in old-time Seattle combine to make **Ivar's Indian Salmon House** my favorite Seattle restaurant. *page 86*

I highly recommend a visit to the **Château Ste. Michelle** winery, even for teetotallers, because the spacious, parklike grounds surrounding the château are among the most beautiful places in the Seattle area for a relaxing stroll or a picnic. *page 97*

Though updated, it hasn't lost its old-fashioned flavor, with windows that open, ceiling fans and traditional furniture in rather small rooms. A continental breakfast and morning newspaper are provided in a lounge off the multitiered lobby. The concierge is very helpful. ~ 400 Spring Street; 206-623-3900, 800-426-1165, fax 206-623-2059; www.pacificplazahotel.com. MODERATE TO DELUXE.

The **Inn at Virginia Mason** is an attractive, nine-story brick building owned by the medical center next door. On the eastern edge of downtown, it caters to hospital visitors and others looking for a convenient location and pleasant accommodations at reasonable prices. The 79 rooms have dark-wood furnishings and teal and gray decor. Two suites have a fireplace and whirlpool tub. There's a small restaurant by a brick terrace. ~ 1006 Spring Street; 206-583-6453, 800-283-6453, fax 206-223-7545. MODERATE TO DELUXE.

The **Sheraton Seattle Hotel & Towers** manages to deftly combine the facilities of a large urban hotel with a personal touch. It has 840 rooms and suites, a highly acclaimed restaurant and a sprawling lobby with stunning displays of art, mostly glass. The pool and exercise room on the 35th floor have a grand view of the city with the Olympic Mountains as a backdrop. Stay in the Club Level (floors 31–33) and you'll have private champagne check-in and breakfast, tea and evening hors d'oeuvres in the Club Lounge.

The Towers (top floor) offer the same perks as the Club Level, but with even more luxuries and amenities including butler service. ~ 1400 6th Avenue; 206-621-9000, 800-325-3535, fax 206-621-8441. ULTRA-DELUXE.

Two smaller boutique hotels offer elegant lodging in more intimate settings in the heart of the shopping district. The **Mayflower Park Hotel** is right next to Westlake Center and Nordstrom; in fact, it's connected to Westlake and offers covered access to Nordstrom and the Bon Marche. A handsome, renovated 1927 stone building whose thick walls ensure quiet, the Mayflower's 172 rooms are furnished with brass and Asian antiques. As was common in the '20s, the rooms are somewhat small, but its location is hard to beat. ~ 405 Olive Way; 206-623-8700, 800-426-5100, fax 206-382-6997. ULTRA-DELUXE.

Just three blocks away, the **Hotel Vintage Park** is a refurbished classic, with 126 upscale rooms and an excellent Italian restaurant. It offers luxury hotel amenities such as terry-cloth robes, fully stocked honor bars and soundproofed double-pane windows. The hotel provides a nightly hosted wine hour by the wood-burning fireplace in its lobby. ~ 1100 5th Avenue; 206-624-8000, 800-624-4433, fax 206-623-0568. ULTRA-DELUXE.

The Warwick, on 4th Avenue a few blocks north of Westlake, is a '60s-style highrise with some great views of Queen Anne Hill and downtown from the upper floors. Rooms are in the Sheraton class, with queen-size beds, cream and floral furnishings and balconies. It has a swimming pool and exercise facilities, and an in-house dining room. The Seattle Center is within easy walking distance. ~ 401 Lenora Street; 206-443-4300, 800-426-9280, fax 206-448-1662. MODERATE.

Located in a former 1920s apartment building, the **Claremont Hotel** provides spacious guest rooms converted from studio apartments. Decorated in soft tones of peach, green and blue, the rooms retain some art deco architectural details and include sitting areas with love seats and large rooms with pedestal sinks and large bathtubs. ~ 2004 4th Avenue; 206-448-8600, 800-448-8601, fax 206-441-7140; e-mail salesdpt@claremonthotel.com. DELUXE TO ULTRA-DELUXE.

Villa Heidelberg is a bed and breakfast in a Craftsman-style home on a corner hillside. The inn has a wide wraparound porch that overlooks gardens of roses and rhododendrons. Inside, the atmosphere is comfortable and relaxed. The house features leaded glass windows, beamed ceilings and the original 1909 gaslight fixtures and embossed wall coverings. The six guest rooms are decorated in pastel florals and feature brass or oak beds and oak dressers. A full breakfast is served. ~ 4845 45th Avenue Southwest, West Seattle; 206-938-3658, 800-671-2942, fax 206-935-7077; www.villaheidelberg.com. MODERATE TO DELUXE.

Seattle's
Street System

Newcomers to Seattle often find street signs bewildering; the city is divided into several sections, each with different area designations. Here's how the system works: All avenues run north–south and are followed by a geographical indicator (1st Avenue Northwest, 23rd Avenue South); all streets run east–west and are preceded by the direction (East Ward Street, Northwest 65th Street). Exceptions are noted below.

The city's sections are:

Northwest, bounded by Puget Sound on the west, Lake Washington Canal on the south, and 1st Avenue Northwest on the east.

North, bounded by 1st Avenue Northwest, Denny Way and 1st Avenue Northeast. South of Lake Washington Canal, the streets have no geographical indicators.

Northeast, bounded by 1st Avenue Northeast, the Canal and Lake Washington.

West, bounded by Puget Sound, Lake Washington Canal, Denny Way and Queen Anne Avenue.

East, bounded by the Canal, Eastlake Avenue, Broadway, Yesler Way and Lake Washington. South of Denny Way, the avenues have no geographical indicators.

Downtown, bounded by Elliott Bay, Denny Way, Broadway and Melrose avenues and Yesler Way. There are no geographical indicators.

South, bounded by Yesler Way, Lake Washington and Elliott Bay and 1st Avenue South.

Southwest, bounded by Puget Sound, Elliott Bay and 1st Avenue South.

Adding to the confusion is a maze of freeways, bridges and angled streets. But with a map and some experience, the system isn't as difficult as it first appears.

DINING

The fine **al Boccalino** serves some of the city's best Italian dinners. Located in a brick building near Pioneer Square, the restaurant's atmosphere is unpretentious and intimate, the antipasto imaginative, and the entrées cooked and sauced to perfection. Saddle of lamb with brandy, tarragon and mustard is a favorite. There are daily specials for every course. ~ 1 Yesler Way; 206-622-7688, fax 206-622-6918. MODERATE TO DELUXE.

Artwork is the main dish at **The Painted Table**, where each place setting features a colorful handpainted charger plate signed by a local artist and the terra-cotta walls are adorned with changing art exhibitions. The menu is artful as well, with entrées crafted with fresh ingredients provided by small local farms. Among the seasonal specialties are ahi tuna salad with caviar, shredded green papaya, pea shoot sprouts and chilled coconut water; and pan-roasted Oregon squab with pumpkin ravioli, asparagus and dates. ~ 92 Madison Street; 206-624-3646, fax 206-340-8861. DELUXE.

Ten times more specialty coffees are sold in Seattle than in other U.S. cities, and you'll find espresso stands on almost every corner.

For a romantic dinner, try **Il Terrazzo Carmine** in the Merrill Place Building. For patio diners, a cascading reflecting pool drowns out some of the freeway noise. Entrées include *zuppa di pesce napoletana* (spicy shellfish soup) or veal piccata with capers and lemon. The restaurant also features an extensive Italian wine list. ~ Pioneer Square, 411 1st Avenue South; 206-467-7797, fax 206-447-5716. MODERATE.

White-linen tablecloths, black-rattan furnishings and loads of plants await you at **La Seafood Restaurant,** an upscale Cantonese restaurant in the International District. In the foyer, the specials such as hot and smokey crab in a spicy sauce, red-pepper beef, fresh fish with vegetables or clams in black-bean sauce are posted on the blackboard. ~ 424 7th Avenue South; 206-622-8181, fax 206-622-8186. MODERATE TO DELUXE.

For great Vietnamese food at low prices, try **Saigon Gourmet**. After the green oilcloths and the white-lace curtains, there's no decor to speak of—just hungry patrons eager for a dish of shrimp, Cambodian noodle soup or papaya with beef jerky. Shrimp rolls here are some of the best in town. Closed Sunday. ~ 502 South King Street; phone/fax 206-624-2611. BUDGET.

On the outskirts of the International District you'll find **Chau's Chinese Restaurant,** a small, unpretentious restaurant that offers great seafood such as Dungeness crab with ginger and onion, clams in hot garlic sauce, bird's-nest scallops and rock-cod fillets with corn sauce. Choose the fresh seafood entrées over the standard Cantonese dishes. ~ 310 4th Avenue South; 206-621-0006. BUDGET TO DELUXE.

HIDDEN ▶

It's impossible not to get thoroughly filled at **Zaina**, a friendly, low-key Greek eatery in the midst of the lower downtown business district. The place is packed with office workers at lunch, but the crowd thins out after 1 p.m. The food is filling and flavorful. ~ 108 Cherry Street; phone/fax 206-624-5687. BUDGET TO MODERATE.

Inside Hotel Monaco is the upscale **Sazerac**, named for a New Orleans cocktail of bourbon and peychaud bitters. The seasonal Southern-inspired menu may feature spicy gumbo, fried catfish with cole slaw or braised shortribs in red gravy. Mahogany booths and windows, velvet curtains and cushions, whimsical artwork and jazz playing in the background complete this trendy scene. ~ 1101 4th Avenue; 206-624-7755, fax 206-624-0050. DELUXE.

Hidden away in the Pike Place Market is **Place Pigalle**. Wind your way past a seafood vendor and Rachel, the brass pig (a popular market mascot), to this restaurant with spectacular views of Elliott Bay. The dark-wood trim, handsome bar and other touches make for a European-bistro atmosphere. The restaurant makes the most of fresh ingredients from the market's produce tables. Dine on fresh Penn Cove mussels with bacon, celery and shallots in balsamic vinaigrette, calamari in a dijon-ginger cream sauce, or one of the daily fresh salmon specials. The dishes are artfully presented. Patio dining available. Closed Sunday. ~ Pike Place Market, 81 Pike Street; 206-624-1756. DELUXE.

Tucked into a hillside in Pike Place Market, **Il Bistro** is a cozy cellar spot with wide archways and oriental rugs on wooden floors. Light jazz, candlelight and well-prepared Italian food make it an inviting spot on a rainy evening. Several pastas are served; the entrées include rack of lamb, veal scallopine, fresh salmon and roasted half-chicken served with garlic mashed potatoes. ~ 93-A Pike Street; 206-682-3049, fax 206-682-7880. DELUXE TO ULTRA-DELUXE.

Across the cobbled street, you can observe the eclectic mix of shoppers and artists in the Pike Place Market at **Three Girls Bakery**, a popular hangout. This tiny lunch counter and bakery with just a few seats serves good sandwiches—the meatloaf sandwich is popular—and hearty soups, including chili and clam chowder. You have more than 50 kinds of bread to choose from. The sourdough and rye breads are recommended. If you don't have room for pastries, buy some to take home. You won't regret it. ~ 1514 Pike Place; 206-622-1045, fax 206-622-0245. BUDGET.

◄ HIDDEN

The food at **Oriental Mart** is a combination of Filipino and Asian—and it's very good and very inexpensive. Try the pork *adobo* if they have it that day; otherwise, any of the chicken preparations are excellent. There's no better place for lunch at the Market. The lunch counter is in back of the food-and-novelties store. ~ 1506 Pike Place Market; 206-622-8488. BUDGET.

In Post Alley, behind some of the market shops, you will find more than just a wee bit of Ireland at **Kells**. This traditional Irish restaurant and pub will lure you to the Emerald Isle with pictures and posters of splendid countryside. A limited menu includes salmon with an Irish dill sauce, leg of lamb, Irish stew and meat pies. From the heavy, dark bar comes a host of domestic and imported beers. Irish musicians play live music seven days a week. ~ 1916 Post Alley; 206-728-1916. MODERATE TO DELUXE.

HIDDEN ▶

Talk about hidden—this place doesn't even have a sign. You enter through the pink door off of Post Alley. **The Pink Door**, with its Italian kitsch decor, is lively and robust at lunchtime. Especially good are the *lasagna della porta rosa* and a delicious cioppino. In the evening, the pace slows, the light dims and it's a perfect setting for a romantic dinner. In the summer, rooftop dining offers views of the Sound. Closed Sunday and Monday. ~ 1919 Post Alley; 206-443-3241, fax 206-443-3341. MODERATE TO DELUXE.

Off a brick courtyard above Pike Place Market, **Campagne** is one of the city's top restaurants. Diners enjoy French country cooking in an atmosphere both warm and elegant. The menu changes six times a year. Entrées may include rack of lamb brushed with puréed anchovy and garlic sauce or roasted sea bass with tarragon, lemon and tiny herb dumplings. The simply prepared dishes are usually the best: young chicken stuffed with ricotta, spinach and roasted herbs and served with sage-infused jus and rosemary roasted potatoes, for example. ~ 86 Pine Street; 206-728-2800. DELUXE TO ULTRA-DELUXE.

HIDDEN ▶

Right below Campagne, off Pine Street, is **Cafe Campagne**, the larger restaurant's hugely popular, less expensive bistro. The café's food is even heartier than that upstairs, typified by sausages, roast meats, extravagant breakfasts and country-style desserts. The atmosphere is definitely more homey; since it doesn't take reservations for lunch (like a true country café), the wait at midday can be lengthy. ~ 1600 Post Alley; 206-728-2233. MODERATE TO DELUXE.

HIDDEN ▶

Overlooking the market itself, **Copacabana** is Seattle's only Bolivian restaurant, but that isn't its greatest virtue. Tucked into the second floor of a lengthy, triangular historic brick building, its outdoor balcony tables offer mind-boggling views on sunny days. In the distance, the Olympic Mountains loom above the shimmering waters of Puget Sound. In the foreground below is the market's colorful bustle. Copacabana's food, typified by shrimp soup and *huminta*, a spicy corn pie, is decent; it's the view that causes local office workers to line up at the entrance, a curved wrought-iron stairway at the foot of Post Alley, before it opens at 11:30 for lunch. All the outside tables are gone by noon on clear days, so get there early. ~ 1520½ Pike Place; 206-622-6359. MODERATE.

A stone's throw away is **Chez Shea**, also occupying the upper floor of a historic brick building. This intimate cubbyhole dining room offers great views (all indoors, alas) and superb Northwest regional cuisine with French influences, and enhancements such as excellent seafood. The prix-fixe menus include rich, inventive soups, salads and main dishes based on hearty ingredients such as roast chicken and lamb. Timing your dinner to coincide with sunset will produce an incomparably romantic experience. Closed Monday. ~ 94 Pike Street; phone/fax 206-467-9990. ULTRA-DELUXE.

Every meal served at **El Puerco Lloron** includes wonderfully fresh tortillas, made by hand while hungry diners watch from the cafeteria line. The *chile rellenos* compare with the best and the tamales and taquitos are all authentic and of good quality. There's a Mexican fiesta atmosphere in the warm, steamy room. ~ Pike Place Market Hillclimb, 1501 Western Avenue; 206-624-0541. BUDGET.

Artists and others without a lot of money for eats hang out at **The Two Bells Tavern** in Belltown. Local artwork on the walls changes every two months. This funky bar with 25 kinds of beer and a host of inexpensive good food is a busy place. You can always find good soups, sandwiches, burgers, salads and cold plates. Some favorites are an Italian-sausage soup and the hot beer-sausage sandwich. ~ 2313 4th Avenue; 206-441-3050, fax 206-448-9626. BUDGET.

Also on 4th Avenue, anchoring the less glitzy side of Belltown, is a restaurant/laundromat that's quintessentially Seattle but little known to visitors. Is **Sit & Spin** a '50s diner, with its chrome-edged formica tables, jukebox and retro-cafeteria menu? Is it just a utilitarian hangout where patrons scarf bargain meals while they wash their clothes? Is it a New Age shrine where herbal teas and vegetarian sandwiches tread lightly on the metabolism? Is it a hot spot of Seattle's arts and music culture, where the sharp-eyed visitor might spy a rock star in town to record at a famed nearby studio? It's all of these, a memorably unique establishment with live bands on weekends that's also a great place for lunch. ~ 2219 4th Avenue; 206-441-9484, fax 206-448-7210. BUDGET.

◄ HIDDEN

TAKE ME OUT TO THE BALL GAME

Seattleites are solid fans of their teams. The **Mariners** play baseball April through September at SAFECO Field. ~ 206-346-4001. At Husky Stadium on the University of Washington campus, the **Seahawks** football team kicks off August through December. ~ 206-827-9766, 206-628-0888, 888-635-4295. The **Supersonics** basketball team shoots hoops from October through April at the Key Arena. ~ 305 Harrison Street; 206-283-3865, 206-628-0888. In the minor leagues, the **Thunderbirds** hockey team plays from September to March at Key Arena. ~ 206-448-7825.
College football takes place in Husky Stadium on the University of Washington campus. ~ Montlake Boulevard; 206-543-2200.

A favorite among downtowners is the **Botticelli Café**. The small café is known for its *panini*—little sandwiches made of toasted focaccia bread and topped with olive oil, herbs, cheeses, meats and vegetables. The espresso and ices are good, too. Closed Sunday. ~ 101 Stewart Street; 206-441-9235. BUDGET.

Contemporary, international cuisine prepared with imagination is served at the **Dahlia Lounge** near the shops of Westlake Center. Bright red walls and ceiling, a neon sign and paper-fish lampshades create a celebratory atmosphere. The chef draws upon numerous ethnic styles and uses Northwest products to develop such dishes as potstickers filled with lobster, shrimp and shiitake mushrooms served with sake sauce. ~ 1904 4th Avenue; 206-682-4142, fax 206-467-0568. DELUXE.

Padded white tablecloths, carpeting and an amber glow from the light fixtures give **Tulio** appealing warmth. Usually packed and festive, it's a place for great food and lively conversation rather than a quiet rendezvous. Go for the specials, such as pan-fried swordfish with fennel, and the desserts, which range from a rich tiramisu to delicate pistachio gelato. ~ 1100 5th Avenue, 206-624-5500, fax 206-623-0568. MODERATE TO DELUXE.

Original Northwest art hangs above the booths in **Fullers**, an internationally acclaimed restaurant in the Sheraton Seattle Hotel & Towers. The decor is plush and sophisticated and the cuisine always top quality. Chef Monique Barbeau calls her food "globally influenced, regionally inspired." Though the menu changes seasonally, examples may include sea scallops with ginger and risotto, or beef tenderloin served with an herbed bread pudding and truffled asparagus. Validated valet parking. Closed Sunday. ~ 1400 6th Avenue; 206-447-5544, fax 206-621-8441. DELUXE TO ULTRA-DELUXE.

In the Westin Hotel is **Nikko**, where there's a sushi and *teppan yaki* bar and private rooms for groups of six or more. Tempura, sukiyaki, sushi and sashimi are among the Japanese delicacies served. No lunch on Saturday. Closed Sunday. ~ 1900 5th Avenue; 206-322-4905, fax 206-441-2946. MODERATE TO DELUXE.

The decor is spare and clean in **Wild Ginger**, and the menu is Chinese and Southeast Asian. Dark-wood booths fill the big, open room; at one end is a satay bar where skewered chicken, beef, fish and vegetables are grilled, then served with peanut and other sauces. The wondrous Seven Elements Soup, an exotic blend of flavors, is a meal in itself. No lunch on Sunday. ~ 1400 Western Avenue; 206-623-4450, fax 206-623-8265. MODERATE TO DELUXE.

Spend a perfect summer day at Alki Beach in West Seattle, then take in dinner at the **Alki Café**, where a well-rounded menu that changes four times a year includes great salads, seafood, meat, chicken and pasta dishes. Specials of the evening are listed in the

Parking
Solutions

The best solution to parking in central Seattle is to leave your car behind. That's not always possible; a few strategies will help ease the struggle.

The basic principle is that, the farther from main points of interest you are, the easier and cheaper parking becomes. Especially troublesome spots are the Westlake Center area; Pioneer Square; the waterfront; Pike Place Market; Capitol Hill. If you have to park in central downtown, expect to pay $4 to $6 an hour in a parking garage; many garages fill up just before lunch time.

One reasonably priced garage that usually has space is the **IBM Building** (the garage entrance is actually on University between 5th and 6th avenues). ~ 1200 5th Avenue; 206-623-2675. Another similarly priced garage is at the **Washington Athletic Club**. ~ 1325 6th Avenue; 206-622-7900.

Metered parking is available under the **Alaskan Way Viaduct** along the waterfront; most spaces are taken by 10 a.m. **Public Market Parking** often has space, and offers a free hour to those on quick errands. ~ 1531 Western Avenue; 206-621-0469.

Once you reach downtown's edges, price goes down and availability goes up. On 7th Avenue north of the major hotels, **Key Park NW** offers full-day parking for $10. ~ 2301 7th Avenue; 206-443-8400. **Bruce Caplan Parking** a half block farther charges $5 a day. ~ 2111 7th Avenue. And by the time you go three blocks farther, another **Key Park** at 7th Avenue and Denny Way offers a full day for $4. All these lots are within a ten-minute walk of Seattle Center, Westlake Center and the Washington State Convention & Trade Center.

two dining areas. Be sure to leave room for dessert—a lovely fruit torte, gingerbread grillcakes or delicious cheesecake made in the bakery. The bakery offers up hearty omelettes, French toast, muffins and cinnamon rolls. Coffee, espressos, lattes, beer and wine are good, too. If you've overindulged, you can always take another stroll on the beach. ~ 2726 Alki Avenue Southwest, West Seattle; 206-935-0616. BUDGET TO MODERATE.

"Alki," the state motto, is an Indian word that means "bye and bye."

Also in West Seattle, the **Cat's Eye Cafe** has great coffee, excellent muffins and super sandwiches . . . not to mention plenty of feline pictures and paraphernalia. Soup and sandwich for lunch is an excellent choice. Breakfast and lunch only. ~ 7301 Bainbridge Place Southwest; 206-935-2229. BUDGET.

The **Santa Fe Cafe** is more upscale, offering a fussier version of Southwestern cuisine, more avocados and cilantro than beans and tortillas. Chile-flavored beer, anyone? Wags might call it Northwest/Southwest Contemporary cuisine; it's worth a visit after a trip to the Woodland Park Zoo. ~ 5910 Phinney Avenue North; 206-783-9755. MODERATE.

SHOPPING The oldest and loveliest structure in Pioneer Square is the Pioneer Building. Here is the **Pioneer Square Antique Mall** in the basement has more than 6000 square feet of space devoted to antiques and collectibles and maintained by some 80 dealers. ~ 602 1st Avenue; 206-624-1164.

Grand Central Arcade Building houses 17 shops. Visitors can also enjoy drinks and baked goods at lobby tables adjacent to a brick fireplace. ~ 214 1st Avenue South; 206-623-7417. **Millstream NW** sells Northwest sculpture, prints, pottery and jewelry by local artisans. ~ 120 1st Avenue South; 206-233-9719.

Mary Vitold Gallery & Framing has been dealing in paintings, fine-art prints and sculptured works produced by up-and-coming Northwest artists. The gallery has monthly rotating shows. ~ 112 South Washington Street; 206-624-9336.

In the heart of the Pioneer Square district is the **Elliott Bay Book Company** featuring over 150,000 titles, including an outstanding stock of Northwest books. You're bound to enjoy browsing, snacking in the on-premises café or listening in on frequently scheduled readings by renowned authors. ~ 101 South Main Street; 206-624-6600.

Seattle's connection with the Pacific Rim is legendary, and **Uwajimaya** demonstrates the tie with shoji screens and lamps, kanji clocks and watches, lacquerware music boxes, goldimari ceramic pieces and Japanese, Chinese, Thai, Vietnamese, Filipino and American canned and frozen foods. ~ 519 6th Avenue South; 206-624-6248.

Known as an "Oriental Woolworth's," **Higo Variety Store** has all kinds of small toys, bowls and sundries in the five-and-dime category. Also on hand are some more expensive articles such as hapi coats, kimonos and obi sashes. Closed Sunday. ~ 604 South Jackson Street; 206-622-7572.

Along the waterfront, Piers 54 through 70 are shoppers' delights. You'll love **Ye Olde Curiosity Shop**, a Seattle landmark where the mummies "Sylvia" and "Sylvester" preside over souvenirs, American Indian totem poles and masks, Russian stacking dolls, lacquerware and Ukrainian eggs. ~ 1001 Alaskan Way, Pier 54; 206-682-5844.

Called the "Soul of Seattle," the **Pike Place Market** has been in business since 1907. Saved from the wrecking ball by citizen action in the early '70s, Pike Place is now a bustling bazaar with 250 businesses, 120 farmers (selling produce and flowers at tables and stalls), 100 local artists and crafts people and 40 eateries. ~ 85 Pike Street; 206-682-7453; www.pikeplacemarket.org.

A notable establishment within the market is the **Pure Food Fish Market**, which ships fresh or smoked salmon worldwide. ~ 1511 Pike Place Market; 206-622-5765. Also here is **Hands of the World**, where the specialty is ethnic jewelry, masks and home accessories such as carved picture frames and folkloric art from Asia and Africa. ~ 1501 Pike Place Market; 206-622-1696.

Just south of Pure Food Fish is **DeLaurenti Specialty Food Markets**, a wondrously well-stocked specialty food store with hundreds of cheeses, pâtés, canned goods, spices, breads, meats and, in season, fresh black truffles at $395 a pound. Closed Sunday. ~ 1435 1st Avenue; 206-622-0141. Behind DeLaurenti, **Marketspice** offers, among dozens of teas and spices, its own distinctive clove-tinged spiced tea blend; it makes a great Christmas gift. ~ 85-A Pike Place; 206-622-6340. ◄ *HIDDEN*

Across Pike Place from the main arcade is **Jack's Fish Spot**, where the fish is as good as that at the more famous fish stands, the prices are at least 50 cents a pound better—in some cases as much as $3 cheaper per pound—and the Dungeness crab, cooked on the spot, is the freshest in the market. They'll ship fresh salmon anywhere, and Jack's smoked salmon, which comes from the only smokehouse in the market, is also the best. ~ 1514 Pike Place; 206-467-0514. ◄ *HIDDEN*

A few feet away, at the foot of Post Alley, **El Mercado Latino** carries Caribbean and Central American delights ranging from red bananas to pasilla chiles to habañero sauces. ~ 1514 Pike Place; 206-623-3240.

Sub Pop Mega Mart holds grunge culture artifacts found almost nowhere else. Sub Pop is the independent record label whose creative support and imaginative promotion of local bands ◄ *HIDDEN* brought them world fame. Here are the original LPs of seminal groups such as Mudhoney and Green River, made before Nirvana's success catapulted the Seattle sound to prominence. The poster rack includes photos by legendary black-and-white grunge-scene photographer Charles Peterson. ~ 1514 Pike Place #14; 206-652-4356.

Yes, it is true that a Nordstrom worker once accepted a pair of tires returned by a customer—even though Nordstrom stores do not sell tires! That's service.

On 1st Avenue just above the market, two stores across the street from each other offer uniquely Seattle wares. At **Dilettante Chocolates**, the family recipes, rich and dark, derive from the delights ancestor Julius Rudolph Franzen made as chocolatier for the last Romanov czar, Nicholas II. ~ 1603 1st Avenue; 206-728-9144. Literally across the street, **Simply Seattle** is the best place downtown to get a gift or memento reflecting the city. It could be a Seattle Mariners T-shirt; it could be a carved wooden slug. ~ 1600 1st Avenue; 206-448-2207.

Close by is **Opus 204**, a small shop filled with a wondrous display of unusual and fine clothing, handicrafts, imports and gifts. ~ 2004 1st Avenue; 206-728-7707.

HIDDEN ▶

In the downtown area, 5th Avenue, Seattle's fashion street, is lined with shops displaying elegant finery and accessories. **Nancy Meyer** specializes in very fine European lingerie. ~ 1318 5th Avenue; 206-625-9200. **Rainier Square** at 1333 5th Avenue houses several prestigious retail establishments. **Turgeon Raine** is an exceptionally good, locally owned jewelry store. ~ 1407 5th Avenue; 206-447-9488. **Totally Michael's** has contemporary, upscale clothing. ~ 521 Union Street; 206-622-4920. **Biagio** specializes in handsome leather goods—handbags, luggage, business and attaché cases. ~ 1405 4th Avenue; 206-623-3842.

At the **Westlake Center**, located at 4th Avenue and Pine Street, pushcarts loaded with jewelry, scarves and other small trappings lend a European flavor to the 80 retail establishments here. **Fireworks Galleries** takes its name from unusually fired sculptures. Also offered are a variety of intriguing home accessories, gifts and jewelry. ~ 400 Pine Street, Suite 118; 206-682-6462. Fast foods, available on the third floor, include teriyaki, baklava, enchiladas, yogurt and quiche.

Alhambra offers high-end women's clothing, Indonesian furniture and a variety of jewelry. ~ 101 Pine Street; 206-621-9571.

Adjoining Westlake Center is the flagship store for **Nordstrom**, the department store chain that achieved prominence with its no-holds-barred customer service and chic goods. Located in the old Frederick & Nelson building, Nordstrom's has saltwater and freshwater aquariums in the children's department as well as a four-story atrium with a grand piano played by a rotating roster of musicians. ~ 500 Pine Street; 206-628-2111. A few blocks away, **Nordstrom Rack** is a favorite haunt of Seattleites seeking elegant bargains. ~ 1601 2nd Avenue; 206-448-8522.

Seattle's nightlife, music and club scene is astounding for a city its size. More than 50 clubs, lounges, restaurants and taverns feature live or deejay-spun music, and dozens more have occasional performances. The offerings run the gamut from folk to punk/metal; dance venues range from midnight raves in port district warehouses to salsa nights at Latin bars.

NIGHTLIFE

The best guide to the city's entertainment scene is *The Stranger*, an alternative weekly newspaper that carries a complete calendar of shows, dances, plays, cinema, performances, readings, art galleries and other goings-on. *The Stranger* also offers the most entertaining classified section in town, as well as down and dirty love-life columnist Dan Savage, a Seattle celebrity. It's available free every Thursday at coffee shops, cafés, taverns, bookstores and newsstands throughout the Seattle area.

The *Seattle Times* also publishes a club guide in its Thursday entertainment section. And Microsoft's Sidewalk online city-guide service is encyclopedic in its scope: www.seattle.sidewalk.com.

Half-price same-day tickets to many Seattle musical events, as well as most theater stagings, are available at **Ticket/Ticket**, which maintains booths at Pike Place Market and on Capitol Hill. Call for directions, but they won't say over the phone what tickets they have that day. ~ 402 Broadway East (Broadway Market, Second Level); Pike Place Market, 1st Avenue and Pike Place; 206-324-2744.

◄ HIDDEN

Unexpected Productions offers comedy performances and workshops in improvisational theater techniques. ~ The Market Theater, 1428 Post Alley, Pike Place Market; 206-781-9273.

There are many fine nightclubs in Pioneer Square, and on "joint-cover" nights, one charge admits you to nine places within a four-block radius. Among them is **Doc Maynard's**, heavy on rock-and-roll with live music on weekends. Cover. ~ 610 1st Avenue; 206-682-4646. The **New Orleans Creole Restaurant** offers live jazz and blues nightly along with Cajun Creole food in an eclectic, laidback atmosphere. Cover. ~ 114 1st Avenue South; 206-622-2563. Over at the **Bohemian Café/Lounge & Backstage** a mixed crowd enjoys live blues, reggae and ska Monday through Saturday. Cover. ~ 111 Yesler Way; 206-447-1514. And at **Swannies Comedy Underground**, comics entertain nightly. Cover. ~ 222 South Main Street; 206-628-0303.

The Showbox nightclub features local, national and international live bands and all types of music, complete with restaurant and full bar. Cover. ~ 1426 1st Avenue; 206-628-3151.

Belltown, near the Pike Place Market, has lots of activity after dark. **Crocodile Café**, one of Seattle's legendary spawning grounds for grunge, punk, rock and alternative bands, attracts a young crowd for live music. Closed Monday. Cover. ~ 2200 2nd Avenue; 206-441-5611.

The **Seattle Symphony**'s large performance space, **Benaroya Hall**, has enabled it to vastly expand its schedule and repertoire. Noted especially for its attention to American composers, the symphony, under the direction of Gerard Schwarz, is one of the top recording orchestras in the United States. ~ 200 University Street; 206-215-4700, tickets 206-215-4747; www.seattlesymphony.org.

At the north side of the Pioneer Square district, **Fenix Pool Hall & Fenix Underground** is a two-stage mainstay of the Seattle music scene, specializing in national alternative rock acts and reggae. Enjoy a game of pool before a show. ~ 315 2nd Avenue; 206-467-1111; www.fenixunderground.com.

Folk and jazz dominate at the **O.K. Hotel** down near the waterfront. ~ 212 Alaskan Way South; 206-621-7903.

An after-dark stop made-to-order for travelers, **Sit & Spin** is a combination bar, nightclub and laundromat where you can catch live music, poetry readings or live theater while your clothes whirl. ~ 2219 4th Avenue; 206-441-9484.

Dimitriou's Jazz Alley is a downtown dinner theater and premier jazz club with international acts. Cover. ~ 6th Avenue and Lenora Street; 206-441-9729.

For satirical/comical revues try the **Cabaret de Paris** dinner theater. Closed Sunday. Cover. ~ Rainier Square, 1333 5th Avenue; 206-623-4111.

The **Paramount Theatre**, the elaborate movie palace of the 1920s, now offers Broadway shows and musicals. ~ 9th Avenue and Pine Street; 206-682-1414.

FESTIVALS OF SUMMER

The Seattle Center grounds are the home of three popular and worthwhile annual events. The **Folklife Festival** on Memorial Day weekend attracts hundreds of thousands of fans for music of every possible description, especially ethnic. Folklife also features art and crafts, food, dance, mime, improv theater, juggling and acrobatics—all free, though a donation is suggested. ~ 206-684-7300. **Bumbershoot** occupies the other end of summer, Labor Day weekend, charging a modest admission but offering an equally kaleidoscopic lineup of music, food and arts, including national acts like B. B. King, Pearl Jam, Bonnie Raitt and George Thorogood. ~ 206-281-7788. The midsummer **Bite of Seattle** attracts dozens of the city's restaurants to the grounds, where patrons can try modestly priced samples of everything from ostrich to sautéed geoduck. ~ 206-684-7200.

Video games, beer and pub food—sounds like a classic video arcade. But **Gameworks** is much more than that. With the latest in electronic games, virtual-reality games and adventures, this has become the highly successful (and highly publicized) prototype for what is now a national chain. ~ 1511 7th Avenue; 206-521-0952.

LINCOLN PARK 🏃 🚲 🏊 This major multipurpose park for southwest Seattle is situated on a nose-shaped bluff just south of the Fauntleroy Ferry Terminal. There are rocky beaches strewn with tidepools and a network of quiet paths winding through groves of madrona, Douglas fir, cedar and redwoods. The park also offers play and picnic areas, an outdoor heated saltwater pool, tennis courts, football field and several miles of bike paths. ~ Located south of West Seattle, off Fauntleroy Avenue Southwest; 206-684-8021, fax 206-233-7023.

PARKS

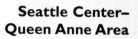

Seattle Center– Queen Anne Area

Northwest of downtown a familiar landmark rises skyward—the Space Needle. This symbol of the city nestles comfortably among museums, cultural centers and a sports arena at the Seattle Center. Just north of the arts and entertainment complex sits the stunning Queen Anne area, a hilly neighborhood of fanciful homes and great views. This is the part of Seattle where the downtown bustle starts to give way to the more peaceful charms of the outlying neighborhoods.

Seattle Center, once the site of the 1962 World's Fair, is now a 74-acre campus with 10 buildings that house a variety of offices, convention rooms and theaters. Locals and visitors continue to flock to the **Space Needle** (206-443-2111, fax 206-905-2211; www.spaceneedle.com; admission) for the view or a meal, to summer carnival rides at the **Fun Forest**, to the **Food Fair**'s short-order ethnic eateries, to see opera and live theater and to check out wide-ranging exhibits and demonstrations at the **Pacific Science Center** (206-443-2001, fax 206-443-3631; www.pacsci.org; admission). The Charlotte Martin Theater is the site of the **Seattle Children's Theater** (206-443-0807, fax 206-443-0442), which has jovial performances geared to a young audience. The **Pacific Northwest Ballet** (tickets, 206-292-2787, fax 206-441-2440; information, 206-441-9411; www.pnb.com) has its offices and rehearsal space at the Phelps Center (where the public can watch the corps rehearse through a glass wall). There is also a large skateboard park, which is open most of the year just in case you get the urge to hop on a slab of plywood with four wheels and "get radical." And you can play ball at the **Nate McMillan Basketball Park** near the 5th Avenue parking lot. ~ Seattle Center: Two miles north of the

SIGHTS

downtown core between Denny Way and Mercer Street; 206-684-7200, fax 206-684-7366; www.seattlecenter.com.

Kids will also enjoy visiting the center's **Seattle Children's Museum** on the ground floor of Center House. The collection features a kid's-size neighborhood and multicultural global village, a two-story walk-through re-creation of a mountain forest and mechanically oriented displays. There are also a giant Lego room, a small lagoon for children and a drop-in art studio. ~ Seattle Center; 206-441-1768, fax 206-448-0910; www.thechildrensmuseum.org.

For an interactive history lesson on American rock-and-roll, stop by **Experience Music Project** (EMP). Among the many highlights at this 140,000-square-foot space-age facility are a vintage guitar collection, a rock fashion exhibit and the Jimi Hendrix Gallery. Those with rock-star fantasies will get a kick out of the Sound Lab, where you can perform on stage to your adoring fans. Admission. ~ 325 5th Avenue North; 206-367-5483 877-367-5483, fax 206-770-2727; www.emplive.com, e-mail experience@emplive.com

For a breathtaking view of Seattle's skyline and Elliot Bay, go to Queen Anne district's **Kerry Park** at West Highland Drive and 2nd Avenue West.

LODGING Conveniently located a block from Seattle Center, half of the **Best Western Executive Inn**'s rooms offer views of the Space Needle. In the lobby guests enjoy a fitness center with jacuzzi, a full-service restaurant and lounge. ~ 200 Taylor Avenue North; 206-448-9444, 800-351-9444, fax 206-441-7929. DELUXE.

On Lower Queen Anne Hill is the **Hampton Inn & Suites**. Standard rooms have either a king-size or two double beds, while studio, one- and two-room suites are also available. Full breakfast buffet included. ~ 700 5th Avenue North; 206-282-7700, fax 206-282-0899. MODERATE TO ULTRA-DELUXE.

DINING At the **Space Needle Restaurant,** the entertainment—from 500 feet up—in either the restaurant or the observation deck is seeing metropolitan Seattle, its environs, Puget Sound, the Olympic Mountains and Mt. Rainier, the Queen of the Cascade Range, as you rotate in a 360° orbit. The restaurant serves various seafood, beef, pasta, poultry and lamb dishes, such as vegetarian pasta and chicken with salsa fresca. Breakfast, lunch, dinner and Sunday brunch. ~ 219 4th Avenue North; 206-443-2100, fax 206-905-2262. DELUXE TO ULTRA-DELUXE.

HIDDEN ▶ On the plaza at Five Point Square, next to the Chief Seattle statue, the **Five Point Cafe Chief's Lounge** is a distinctive Seattle landmark. With a sign on the door warning nonsmokers that smokers are welcome, and "Pinball Wizard" inevitably playing on the jukebox, it's a real joint. Why go? The food is good, no-

nonsense and quite economical, and no one leaves hungry. Try
the fish and chips or the meatloaf sandwich (yes, it's that kind of
restaurant). ~ 415 Cedar Street; 206-448-9993. BUDGET.

For sublime breakfast pastries and delicious Mediterranean-
inspired lunch items, head for **Macrina Bakery**, a cozy European-
style bakery and café where the moss green walls are adorned
with scrolls, ironwork, paintings and other work by local artists.
Breakfast items include house-made coffee cakes, cereals and fruit
pastries, while a changing lunch menu may offer such dishes as
tartlet of roast chicken and goat cheese or cheese polenta with red
chard. Brunch on weekends only. ~ 2408 1st Avenue; 206-448-
4032, phone/fax 206-448-4089. MODERATE.

When Kaspar Donier moved his acclaimed restaurant to the
Seattle Center area, he lost the old location's view atop an office
building, but gained a nicer home and a different dinner crowd.
Now, symphony, opera and ballet patrons flock to **Kaspar's** to feast
on his intriguing blend of contemporary Northwest cuisine with
hearty Swiss cookery. Kaspar's braised lamb shanks, for instance,
may be the Northwest's best; his scallops are sumptuous and plentiful. Dinner only. Closed Sunday and Monday. ~ 19 West Harrison Street; 206-298-0123, fax 206-298-0146. DELUXE.

Near the Seattle Center and the Queen Anne district, **Asiana**
serves authentic Thai cuisine in a friendly, comfortable setting.
There are oriental art objects and artwork from Thailand to look
at while you wait for your order of Bathing Rama (beef or pork
in a peanut-chili sauce over spinach) or *tom yum potek* (spicy and
sour soup) or another of the menu's 60-plus items. They vary in
hotness and are rich with the flavors of coconut, curry, garlic, pea-
nuts and peppers. ~ 101 John Street; 206-285-9000, fax 206-
286-3126. BUDGET TO MODERATE.

Chutney's occupies a tidy, elegant space just a block from the
Seattle Center. Its Indian menu is rich and varied, leaning heavily on hearty lentil and vegetable concoctions. The lunch buffet is
unbelievably filling. Ask for the excellent garlic/chile chutney. No
lunch on Sunday. ~ 519 1st Avenue North; 206-284-6799, 206-
284-6801. MODERATE.

DREAMWORKS

For a rewarding, spur-of-the-moment visit, drop by Seattle Center
on a summer evening for a contemplative quarter-hour of gazing at
the **International Fountain**. The combination of changing lights and
waterworks synchronized to music the first 15 minutes of every hour
against a rose-tinted summer sunset, can lull you into a dreamy state.

HIDDEN ►

Three blocks away, but still within easy walking distance of Seattle Center, **Tup Tim Thai** is the Thai restaurant locals favor over its better-known cousins north of the center. Tup Tim's soups and curries are the best in Seattle; it's advisable to arrive early for lunch, or for dinner on nights there are events at the center. Closed Sunday. ~ 118 West Mercer Street; 206-281-8833. BUDGET TO MODERATE.

NIGHTLIFE
Home of the 1962 World's Fair, the **Seattle Center** still offers innumerable nighttime diversions. ~ 305 Harrison Street; 206-684-8582.

Sharing facilities at the Seattle Center Opera House, a World's Fair–era concert hall, are the city's opera and ballet, each with its own claim to fame. Founded in 1964, **Seattle Opera** is dedicated to producing theatrically compelling, musically accomplished opera. The leading Wagner company in America, Seattle Opera will stage a new production of Richard Wagner's *Ring* in 2001. ~ 206-389-7676, 800-426-1619.

Pacific Northwest Ballet's annual production of Tchaikovsky's *Nutcracker*, with fanciful sets designed by famed children's illustrator Maurice Sendak, is a perennial favorite. ~ 301 Mercer Street; 206-441-2424.

Music director Gerard Schwarz has led the **Seattle Symphony** to prominence by focusing on baroque and romantic classics and formerly little-known American composers such as Alan Hovhaness (a longtime Seattle resident), David Diamond and Howard Hanson. Masterpiece symphony concerts are Thursday and Saturday evenings. The fact that symphony concerts rarely sell out offers visitors the chance to see one of the top orchestral ensembles in the United States. ~ 206-215-4748; www.seattlesymphony.org, e-mail info@seattlesymphony.org.

The **Seattle Repertory Theatre** plays an eclectic mix from musicals to classic dramas at the **Bagley Wright Theatre** and the **Leo K. Theatre**. ~ 155 Mercer Street between Warren Avenue and 2nd Avenue North; 206-443-2222. The nearby **Intiman Theatre** presents plays by the great dramatists, as well as new works. ~ 201 Mercer Street at 2nd Avenue North; 206-269-1900.

A Contemporary Theater at 7th and Union streets in the old Eagles Auditorium next to the Convention Center (206-292-7676) and **The Empty Space Theater** at 3509 Fremont Avenue North (206-547-7500) specialize in works by new playwrights.

▼▼▼▼▼▼▼▼▼▼
Capitol Hill

Seattle's sizable gay population and diverse array of gay inns, clubs and meeting places is one of the many reasons travelers are increasingly flocking to the city. While gay activities and nightlife are found throughout the city, the highest concentration is in Capitol Hill, one of Seattle's most cosmopolitan neighborhoods. Take a walk down Broadway in Capitol Hill, and you'll see one of the most vibrant gay communities in the country.

Capitol Hill is a mixed neighborhood that is a fun place to browse. Within a block or two you can toss back an exotic wheatgrass drink at a vegetarian bar, slowly sip a double espresso at a sidewalk café, shop for radical literature at a leftist bookstore or hit a straight or gay nightclub. If you can't find it on Capitol Hill, Seattle probably doesn't have it. Broadway Avenue is the heart of this region known for its boutiques, yuppie appliance stores and bead shops.

Home of some of the city's finest Victorians, this neighborhood also includes **Volunteer Park**. Be sure to head up to the top of the water tower for a great view of the region. ~ East Ward Street from 11th to 17th avenues.

The building that used to house the Seattle Art Museum is now the home of the **Seattle Asian Art Museum**. This Arte-Moderne building was a gift to the city in the 1930s by Dr. Richard Fuller, who was the museum's director for the next 40 years. The Japanese, Chinese and Korean collections are the largest, but the museum also has south and southeast Asian collections. Japanese folk textiles, Thai ceramics and Korean screen paintings are some of the highlights. One admission fee will get you into here and the Seattle Art Museum downtown. Admission. ~ Volunteer Park, 1400 East Prospect Street; 206-654-3100, fax 206-654-3135; www.seattleartmuseum.org.

On Broadway, the public art will give you a free dance lesson—just follow the bronze "Dancing Feet" imbedded in the sidewalk.

Not far away, **St. Mark's Episcopal Cathedral** is an imposing Romanesque edifice from the outside; an austere, cavernous space inside whose unusual shape (more a square than a long rectangle) was dictated by its location on a bluff overlooking downtown. The cathedral's superb acoustics and massive Flentrop organ mean it is often the site of recitals. ~ 1245 10th Avenue East; 206-323-0300, fax 206-323-4018.

Nostalgia reigns in Capitol Hill's **Harvard Exit Theater**. Once the elegant home of a women's club, it still has the parlor with a fireplace and piano. This is the place to see award-winning foreign and art films. Auditoriums are wheelchair accessible. ~ 807 East Roy Street; 206-323-8986.

A mother-daughter team runs the **Salisbury House**, a quiet, dignified, gracious Capitol Hill home two blocks from Volunteer Park. Cathryn and Mary Wiese offer five crisp, clean rooms (all have private baths) furnished with antiques and wicker. Fresh flowers, duvets on the beds, a full (meatless) breakfast and thoughtful innkeepers make this a well-done bed and breakfast. There are fireplaces in the living room and library and a refrigerator guests may use. ~ 750 16th Avenue East; 206-328-8682, fax 206-720-1019; www.salisburyhouse.com. MODERATE TO DELUXE.

Also in the popular, busy Capitol Hill area, **Gaslight Inn** is a bed and breakfast brimming with urban flair. The 1906 house is furnished with oak, maple and glass antiques. Various period styles have been effectively combined with modern amenities in the 16 guest rooms. Most have private baths, and six boast fireplaces. Gaslight has a heated, outdoor swimming pool (closed in winter) and an outdoor deck that overlooks the city. They serve a continental buffet breakfast. ~ 1727 15th Avenue East; 206-325-3654, fax 206-328-4803; www.gaslight-inn.com. MODERATE TO ULTRA-DELUXE.

Expect a friendly welcome and lots of conversation at **Roberta's Bed & Breakfast**. The comfortable, traditional home located on Capitol Hill hosts a mixed clientele in four rooms on the second floor and a fifth under the eaves on the third floor. There are cozy window seats, gleaming woodwork, skylights, shelves full of books, a piano and a full, meatless breakfast. ~ 1147 16th Avenue East; 206-329-3326, fax 206-324-2149; www.robertasbb.com. DELUXE.

Located on Millionaire's Row on Capitol Hill, the **Shafer-Baillie Mansion** is a turreted and gabled reminder of an earlier era with its wide porches, library, formal dining room and ballroom with a copper fireplace. Built in 1914 the grand 15,000-square-foot mansion is the largest on Capitol Hill. This bed-and-breakfast inn has 11 suites, all with refrigerators and televisions and most with private baths. ~ 907 14th Avenue East; 206-322-4654, 800-922-4654, fax 206-329-4654. MODERATE TO DELUXE.

On Capitol Hill near Volunteer Park in the Harvard-Belmont Historic District is the **Bacon Landmark Mansion,** a historic 1909 Tudor stucco home. In addition to the two-story carriage house, which has a living room, dining room and two guest rooms with a private bath in each, there are ten guest rooms in the main house, six with private bath. The Capitol suite has a sun room with wet bar, fireplace, queen-size four-poster bed, view of the Space Needle and a big bathtub. ~ 959 Broadway East; 206-329-1864, 800-240-1864, fax 206-860-9025; www.site-works.com/bacon. MODERATE TO DELUXE.

DINING

Hearty Northwest fare with a German accent is on the menu at **Szmania's,** a popular spot with an exhibition kitchen in the residential area of Magnolia. The specialties include sea bass over Mediterranean couscous with a ginger-soy vinaigrette; roast duckling served with sweet cherries and red cabbage; and Alaskan halibut in a pinot noir sauce with lobster mashed potatoes. Dinner only. Closed Monday. ~ 3321 West McGraw Street; 206-284-7305, fax 206-283-8303. MODERATE TO DELUXE.

Seattle's
Coffee Wars

It doesn't take long for visitors to notice that Seattle's primary energy source is coffee. Coffee bars, the preferred business and social meeting spots, do a booming business, and it seems as if there's a drive-up espresso kiosk on every block. Some folks think it's the weather that makes the steamy, mood-lifting beverage more popular than Prozac, but the real reason for Seattle's identification with coffee is that the concept of selling fresh-roasted whole beans in bulk originated here.

In 1971, "fresh coffee" still meant a new five-pound can of Folger's from the supermarket. Then Jim Stewart, with backing from his brother Alan, started Stewart Brothers Coffee, a small stand selling coffee beans in Pike Place Market. Jim first used a peanut roaster he'd bought from a vendor on a southern California beach but soon traveled to Italy to learn the art from master espresso roasters and purchased a real coffee-bean roaster. The unfamiliar smell of fresh roasted coffee wafted through the market and made his stand an instant hit. Later that same year, a second coffee-bean stand opened in Pike Place Market under the name Starbucks.

Soon the two rivals began buying coffee beans from different parts of the world, developing assorted distinctive blends and adding flavorings. In 1984 Starbucks started its first coffee bar at 4th and Spring streets in downtown Seattle under the name Il Giornale. Meanwhile, Stewart Brothers began selling whole-bean coffee in bulk through supermarkets. Learning that there was another coffee wholesaler named Stewart, the brothers abbreviated the company's name to SBC Inc., which in turn inspired its trade name, Seattle's Best Coffee.

Today, SBC is the world's leading seller of specialty coffee beans, while Starbucks has expanded to more than 3300 coffee bars, including locations in Tokyo, Beijing, Manila and Kuwait. Both companies have their headquarters in Seattle, and the city now boasts 26 other retail and wholesale coffee-roasting companies as well as five green brokers (importers of unroasted coffee beans).

HIDDEN ▶ . Not far from 1st Avenue, you'll find the thriving Belltown shopping, dining and nightlife scene. **Marco's Supperclub** is a little-known purveyor of fine, eclectic multiregional dishes; the deep-fried sage leaves, an appetizer, are a true original. Quite filling meals are reasonable by Belltown standards. Dinner only. ~ 2510 1st Avenue; 206-441-7801, fax 206-441-4258. MODERATE TO DELUXE.

Ayutthaya is a corner restaurant in Capitol Hill renowned for its Thai cookery. Small, clean-lined and pleasant in blue and lavender, Ayutthaya features plenty of chicken and seafood dishes along with soups and noodles. Flavors blend deliciously in the curried shrimp with green beans, coconut milk and basil. Or try the chicken sautéed in peanut-chili sauce. No lunch on weekends. ~ 727 East Pike Street; 206-324-8833, fax 206-324-3135. BUDGET TO MODERATE.

Near the University of Washington, **Kokeb** is a pleasant restaurant offering the hotly spiced dishes of Ethiopia. The finger food is eaten with chunks of a large, flat bread. The atmosphere is rustic, with an open-beamed ceiling. Dinner only. ~ 926 12th Avenue; 206-322-0485, fax 206-324-3618. BUDGET TO MODERATE.

Café Septième is Kurt Timmermeister's re-creation of small Parisian cafés that cater to the literati and students. This full-service restaurant carries plenty of reading material and turns out cups of good coffee, lattes and light fare. A favorite luncheon sandwich is eggplant with roasted peppers. Desserts include shortbread, carrot cake, a variety of cookies and other mouthwatering treats. Breakfast, lunch and dinner. ~ 214 Broadway Avenue East; 206-860-8858, fax 206-860-0760. BUDGET TO MODERATE.

The **Broadway New American Grill** is a famed mainstay of the Capitol Hill scene. Its food is mainstream-grill breakfast and burger fare, moderately priced and dependable if unimaginative. But it's better known as a place to hang out and watch the passing parade on Broadway. ~ 314 Broadway East; 206-328-7000, fax 206-325-4734. BUDGET TO MODERATE.

More health-conscious nibblers head for the **Gravity Bar**, a full-service vegetarian restaurant with white woodwork and modern cone-shaped glass-topped tables. The extensive menu includes tofu avocado rollups, a tempeh burger, ambrosia rice salad and a selection of vegetable and fruit juices. ~ 415 Broadway East; 206-325-7186. BUDGET.

HIDDEN ▶ Since Capitol Hill never truly closes, its two dessert emporia are integral to the area's atmosphere. You can buy a box of chocolate truffles at **Café Dilettante**, but you'd be missing a divine late evening experience—a midnight table in a crowded, mirrored room. Try the Coupe Dilettante, the restaurant's exceptional ice cream sundae swimming in Dilettante's dark Ephemere sauce, or any of dozens of other desserts. This is among the best chocolate in the country. ~ Dilettante Chocolates, 416 Broadway East; 206-329-6463, fax 206-329-0782. BUDGET.

At **Famous Pacific Dessert**, the emphasis is less on chocolate, ◄ *HIDDEN*
the atmosphere is a bit more cozy than glitzy and the late-night crowds are large. Diners can choose from 25 to 30 different pies, cakes and European-style tortes. ~ 127 Mercer Street, 206-284-8100, fax 206-935-2535. BUDGET.

The trendy boutiques of Capitol Hill draw shoppers looking for **SHOPPING**
the unusual, though there are many standard stores, too. You'll see dozens of shops with new and vintage clothing, pop culture items, and ethnic wear and artifacts, all interspersed with myriad cafés and coffeehouses.

If you're in the market for a potato gun, would like to snack on Pez candy, crave a glow-in-the-dark slug or are searching for a popping Martian, head on over to **Archie McPhee's** near Lake Union, west of the university. This novelty-and-toy store offers more than 10,000 exotic items from all over the world. ~ 2428 Northwest Market Street; 206-297-0240.

Seattle-based **Recreational Equipment, Inc.,** is better known as REI, the largest cooperative in the United States. Its flagship store offers an astonishing array of outdoor clothing and equipment—as well as a huge climbing wall, the largest indoor freestanding climbing structure in the world. ~ 222 Yale Avenue North; 206-223-1944, 888-873-1938.

> Gay clubs and stores are concentrated on Broadway, as well as nearby streets like 15th Avenue East and East Olive Way.

Capitol Hill's **Broadway Market** is filled with popular shops like **Urban Outfitters**. Featuring casual urban ware, this shop offers new and vintage clothing, jewelry, housewares and shoes for the hip crowd. ~ 401 Broadway Avenue East; 206-322-1800.

Bailey/Coy Books is well-stocked with reading material, including gay and lesbian literature. ~ 414 Broadway East; 206-323-8842.

Chocoholics can get their fix in the Capitol Hill district at **Dilettante Chocolates**, a combination chocolatier and café. ~ 416 Broadway East; 206-329-6463.

Capitol Hill offers a number of popular gay and lesbian clubs **NIGHTLIFE**
and bars, including the following:

Fox's Tavern features Sunday-night karaoke and female impersonators on most evenings. ~ 1501 East Olive Way; 206-720-9963.

Not your ordinary Seattle café, **Coffee Messiah** beckons you with a large pink neon cross perched on the rooftop. The interior is painted a deep purple, with red velvet curtains and religious images. A pilgrimage to this coffee shrine would not be complete without a trip to its coin-operated discotheque bathroom, decorated to simulate Hell. Pictures of the devil surround a black sink and red toilet equipped with its own heat lamp. Nightly entertainment includes movie night on Tuesday. Open mike Wednesday, Thursday and Saturday. ~ 1554 East Olive Way; 206-860-7377.

One of the biggest clubs in the area is **R-Place Seattle Pub**. Depending on your mood, you can plunk down at the sports bar, throw darts, enjoy a music video, shoot pool, enjoy tunes from the jukebox or play a low-stakes gambling game called pull tabs. ~ 619 East Pine Street; 206-322-8828.

In the Capitol Hill neighborhood, the **Elite Tavern** has a busy pub atmosphere. ~ 622 Broadway East; 206-324-4470.

Also popular is **Neighbours Disco** offering deejay dance music seven nights a week. Cover. ~ 1509 Broadway; 206-324-5358.

Founded in 1984, **Wildrose** claims to be the oldest women's bar on the West Coast, offering food and drink as well as camaraderie. Occasional live music. ~ 1021 Pike Street East; 206-324-9210.

The leather crowd favors **The Cuff** and **Seattle Eagle**, two more Capitol Hill taverns. ~ The Cuff, 1533 13th Avenue, 206-323-1525; Seattle Eagle, 314 Pike Street East, 206-621-7591.

There's a piano bar and dinner service at **Thumper's**, which is also a lunch and brunch place. Cabaret on Sunday. Cover. ~ 1500 Madison Avenue East; 206-328-3800.

With the largest dancefloor in Seattle, the **Timberline** historic lodge draws enthusiastic mixed crowds for country line dance sessions, deejayed '70s music and other down-home events. It's located between Capitol Hill and the Space Needle. Cover. ~ 2015 Boren Avenue; 206-622-6220.

Vogue is the mecca of the leather/lace/latex enthusiasts in downtown Seattle. Partly gay and partly not, it features industrial and new-wave deejay music most nights. Themes vary—for instance, Wednesday is gothic night while Sunday is fetish night. There's

---

STARGAZING

Why did celebrity-watchers flock to Capitol Hill in May 1995 to catch a glimpse of Mel Gibson? The Hollywood star was in town for the world premiere of his eventual Oscar winner *Braveheart*—so far, the headiest moment in the entire history of the **Seattle International Film Festival**. Each spring, SIFF draws hundreds of thousands of cinema lovers for its 25-day run in Capitol Hill theaters, and each year one of the SIFF favorites goes on to national acclaim. Screenings, lectures and receptions abound at this large, well-attended film festival. Admission. ~ 206-464-5830.

live music on Tuesday and a vamp variety show on Thursday. Cover. ~ 1516 11th Avenue; 206-324-5778.

BOREN/INTERLAKEN PARKS   A secret greenway close to downtown is preserved by these neighboring parks on Capitol Hill; it's just right for an afternoon or evening stroll. ~ Located from East Roanoke Avenue to Lake Washington Boulevard East and Washington Park.

PARKS

◄ *HIDDEN*

While downtown is the city's magnet, some of Seattle's best parks, sightseeing and nightlife can be found in its nearby neighborhoods. Arboretums and science museums, lakeside dining and shopping worth a special trip are all in this region.

▼▼▼▼▼▼▼▼▼▼▼▼▼▼▼▼▼▼
Outlying Neighborhoods

Few guidebooks look at the **Lake Washington Ship Canal** as a single unit. Yet it ties together a wondrous diversity of working waterfront and recreational shoreline along eight miles of bay, lake and canal between Puget Sound and Lake Washington. Construction of the locks and canal began in 1911 and created a shipping channel from Lake Washington to Lake Union to Puget Sound. Along its banks today you can see perhaps the liveliest continuous boat parade in the West: tugs gingerly inching four-story-tall, Alaska-bound barges through narrow locks; rowboats, kayaks, sailboards and luxury yachts; gill-netters and trawlers in dry dock; government-research vessels; aging houseboats listing at their moorings; and seaplanes roaring overhead.

SIGHTS

All in all, the ship canal presents a splendid overview of Seattle's rich maritime traditions. But you'll also discover plenty that's new—rejuvenated neighborhoods like Fremont and south Lake Union's upscale shoreline, a renovated Fisherman's Terminal and a handful of trendy, waterside restaurants. Amid the hubbub of boat traffic and ship chandlers, you'll also encounter quiet, street-end parks for birdwatching, foot and bike paths, the best historical museum in the city and one of the West's renowned arboretums. Here's a summary, west to east.

Ballard is one of Seattle's most distinctive neighborhoods, exemplified by the wry slogan, "Ya, sure, y'betcha," a nod to its Nordic heritage. Ever tried lutefisk? If you want to (few do), this is the place. Ballard shut down to greet Norway's royal family on one of their state visits to the United States. The royals even checked out the **Nordic Heritage Museum,** the only facility of its kind in the country. Here artifacts such as antique boats demonstrate why timber and fisheries are what drew Scandinavians here more than a century ago; the museum also maintains an extensive research library. Closed Monday. Admission. ~ 3014 67th Street Northwest; 206-789-5707, fax 206-789-3271.

Hiram M. Chittenden Locks in Ballard is where all boats heading east or west in the ship canal must pass and thus presents the quintessential floating boat show; it's one of the most-visited attractions in the city. Visitors crowd railings and jam footbridges to watch as harried lock-keepers scurry to get boats tied up properly before locks are either raised or lowered, depending on the boat's direction of passage. Terraced parks flanking the canal provide splendid picnic overlooks. An underwater fish-viewing window gives you astonishing looks at several species of salmon, steelhead and sea-going cutthroat trout on their spawning migrations (June to November). Lovely botanical gardens in a parklike setting offer yet more diversion. ~ 206-783-7059, fax 206-782-3192.

Fisherman's Terminal is home port to one of the world's biggest fishing fleets, some 700 vessels, most of which chug north into Alaskan waters for summer salmon fishing. But you'll always be able to see boats here—gill-netters, purse-seiners, trollers, factory ships—and working fishermen repairing nets, painting boats and the like. Here, too, are net-drying sheds, nautical stores and shops selling marine hardware and commercial fishing tackle. One café opens at 6 a.m. for working fishermen; there's a fish-and-chips window and one good seafood restaurant (Chinook's) overlooking the waterway. ~ On the south side of Salmon Bay about a mile east of the locks. ~ 206-728-3395, fax 206-728-3393.

The **Fremont** neighborhood is locally famous for the sculpture *Waiting for the Interurban*, whose collection of lifelike commuters is frequently seen adorned in funny hats, scarves and other cast-off clothing. Centered around Fremont Avenue North and North 34th Street at the northwest corner of Lake Union, the district is top-heavy with shops proffering the offbeat (handmade dulcimers, antiques and junk).

Perhaps most offbeat of all is the **Fremont Troll**, another famous sculpture found beneath the north footings of the Aurora Bridge. When the nearby Magnolia Bridge was damaged by mudslides, Fremont residents archly averred that their bridge escaped harm because it was under a troll's guardianship. ~ 35th Street North, under the Aurora Bridge.

Gas Works Park occupies property that dangles like a giant green tonsil from Lake Union's north shore. Until 1956, the park's namesake "gas works" produced synthetic natural gas from coal and crude oil. Some of the rusting congeries of pipes, airy catwalks, spiraling ladders, tall towers and stubby tanks were torn down during park construction, but enough remains (repainted in snappy colors) to fascinate youngsters and old-timers alike. ~ Foot of Wallingford Avenue North off North 34th Street.

On the south side of Union Bay, 175-acre **Washington Park** at Lake Washington Boulevard East and East Madison Street presents enough diversions indoors and out to fill a rich day of exploring in all sorts of weather. Most famous is the **Washington Park Arboretum** (which occupies most of the park with 14,000 plants), at its best in the spring when thousands of rhododendrons and azaleas—some 10 to 15 feet tall—and groves of spreading chestnuts, dogwoods, magnolias and other flowering trees leap into bloom. Short footpaths beckon from the Visitors Center. But two in particular deserve mention—Azalea Way and Loderi Valley—which wend their way down avenues of pink, cream, yellow, crimson and white blooms. The arboretum's renowned Japanese Garden (admission) is especially rewarding in the spring months, and both arboretum and garden present splendid fall colors in October and early November. In the Winter Garden, everything is fragrant, and the Woodland Garden highlights the arboretum's acclaimed collection of Japanese maples. ~ Visitors Center: Arboretum Drive East; 206-543-8800, fax 206-325-8893; www.depts. washington.edu.wpa.

Miles of duff-covered footpaths lace the park. For naturalists, the premier experience will be found along the one-and-a-half-mile (each way) **Foster Island Trail** at the north end of the park on Foster Island behind the Museum of History and Industry (see later in this section). This footpath takes you on an intriguing bog-walk over low bridges and along boardwalks through marshy wet-

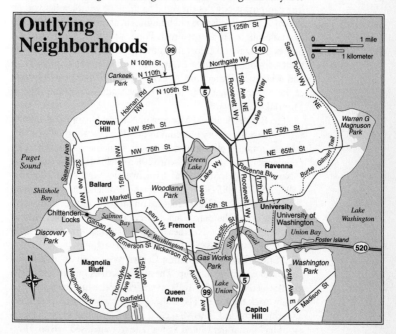

Outlying Neighborhoods

lands teeming with ducks and wildfowl, fish and frogs and aquatic flora growing rank at the edge of Lake Washington.

In summer, you can join the canoeists paddling the labyrinth of waterways around **Foster Island**, sunbathers and picnickers sprawling on lawns, anglers casting for catfish and trout and the swimmers cooling off on hot August afternoons. Canoes are for rent through the University of Washington.

On rainy days the **Museum of History and Industry** is a fitting retreat. It's the city's best early-day collection and pays special tribute to Puget Sound's rich maritime history, as befits any museum located next door to this vital waterway. Closed Monday. Admission. ~ 2700 24th Avenue East; 206-324-1125, fax 206-324-1346; www.seattlehistory.org.

The Washington Park Arboretum boasts the largest holly collection in the country.

Exceptional architecture, a garden setting and easy access make a campus tour of the **University of Washington** (or U-dub, as locals call it) a highlight of a Seattle visit. The university began downtown in 1861; in 1895, it was moved to its present site. The Alaska–Yukon–Pacific Exposition of 1909 was held on the campus, and several of its fine buildings date from that event. The campus borders the canal north of Montlake Cut (part of the waterway) and is a haven for anyone who enjoys the simple pleasure of strolling across a college campus. It boggles the mind to think of what awaits you on its 694 acres—handsome old buildings in architectural styles from Romanesque to modern; Frosh Pond; red-brick quads and expanses of lawn and colorful summer gardens; canal-side trails on both sides of the Montlake Cut; access to the Burke-Gilman Trail; and a lakeside **Waterfront Activity Center** (206-543-9433) with canoe and rowboat rentals. ~ Husky Stadium parking lot, off Montlake Boulevard.

The **Burke Memorial Museum of Natural History and Culture** is the oldest university museum in the West. Established in 1885, it has a notable collection of American Indian artifacts. There's a popular coffeehouse, the **Boiserie** (206-543-9854), in the basement. ~ Northeast 45th Street and 17th Avenue Northeast; 206-543-5590, fax 206-685-3039; www.washington.edu/burkemuseum.

The **Henry Art Gallery** focuses on modern and contemporary art. Don't miss the marvelous collection of textiles here. Admission. ~ 15th Avenue Northeast and Northeast 41st Street; 206-543-2281, fax 206-685-3123; www.henryart.org.

At the **Visitors Information Center**, you can pick up a useful (and free) walking tour map. The map describes quirky bits of UW history as the hour-plus walk meanders under tall trees and past stately brick buildings. The College of Forest Resources resembles a Gothic cathedral. The Medicinal Herb Garden may be the largest of its kind in the United States. The tree-enclosed Sylvan Theater is the site of numerous trysts, plays and weddings. Fountains, ponds, a rose garden and views of Lake Washington add texture to the lovely campus. ~ 4014 University Way Northeast; 206-543-9198, fax 206-616-6294.

A mile or so north of the ship canal, Woodland Park and Green Lake Park straddle Aurora Avenue North (Route 99) and together offer 530 acres of park, lake and zoo attractions.

The star of the parks is **Woodland Park Zoo**, which since 1979 has won praise for its program of converting static exhibits into more natural, often outdoor environments. Most notable are the African Savannah, Gorilla Exhibit, the Marsh and Swamp and the Elephant Forest where you can see Thai elephants working at traditional tasks. There's also a Tropical Rain Forest, heralded as a "journey through different levels of forest," and a seasonal contact yard and family farm. The Trail of Vines, an Asian rain-forest where Indian pythons, lion-tailed macaques, orangutans, Malayan tapirs and siamangs live. Admission. Fremont Avenue North and North 50th Street; 206-684-4800, fax 206-615-1070; www.zoo.org.

Green Lake Park, enormously popular with all ages and classes of Seattleites, is simply the best outdoor people-watching place in the city. Two loop trails circle the shore (the inner trail is 2.8 miles long, the outer 3.2 miles) and welcome all comers. On summer days, both paths are filled with strollers and race-walkers, joggers and skaters, bikers and nannies pushing prams. On the lake you will see anglers, canoeists, sailboarders, swimmers, birdwatchers and folks floating in inner tubes.

LODGING

Seattle's neighborhoods offer several hotels and numerous bed-and-breakfast accommodations. A bed and breakfast can be a great value, offering a casual atmosphere, home-cooked food included in the room rate and personal contact with an innkeeper who usually knows the city well. Contact **A Pacific Reservation Service**. ~ 206-784-0539, fax 206-431-0932; www.seattlebedandbreakfasts. com.

The MV **Challenger** is a "bunk and breakfast" on Lake Union. The opulent interior of the renovated, 96-foot tugboat is done in mahogany and oak. It has a salon with a fireplace and eight cabins with nautical furnishings. They all overlook the lake and city sky-line. Captain's Cabin, the largest, includes the former pilothouse. The Challenger also offers cabin quarters on two yachts beside the main tugboat. ~ 1001 Fairview Avenue North; 206-340-1201, fax 206-621-9208; www.pathfinder.com/offers/roadtrip. MODERATE TO ULTRA-DELUXE.

A favorite of visitors to the University of Washington, both gay and straight, the **Chambered Nautilus Bed & Breakfast Inn** is only a block from the campus. Breezily casual, the spacious home

has a family atmosphere. Games and books, soft chairs by the fireplace and all-day tea and cookies add to the homeyness. Six guest
rooms on the second and third floors have antique furnishings. All
have private baths and four feature private porches. A full gourmet breakfast is served, sometimes on the sun porch. ~ 5005 22nd
Avenue Northeast; 206-522-2536, 800-545-8459, fax 206-528-
0898; www.chambernautilus.com. MODERATE TO DELUXE.

Also in the University District is **Edmond Meany Hotel**, a 15-
story tower with 155 corner rooms. All units have views of the
mountains or the lake and cityscape. Standard hotel furnishings
adorn the spacious rooms, decorated in art deco style. A handsome
restaurant and lounge are on the floor below the lobby. ~ 4507
Brooklyn Avenue Northeast; 206-634-2000, 800-899-0251, fax
206-547-6029. ULTRA-DELUXE.

The **University Plaza Hotel** is a three-story motor hotel adjacent to Route 5, west of the University of Washington. There are
135 comfortably furnished rooms centered around a pool courtyard. Rooms on the freeway side can be noisy. On the ground floor,
behind a mock-medieval England facade, are a restaurant, lounge
and beauty salon. ~ 400 Northeast 45th Street; 206-634-0100, 800-
343-7040, fax 206-633-2743; MODERATE.

DINING

After visitors watch the ships go through the locks in the Ballard
area, they stop at **Pescatore's** for Italian seafood and views of the
channel. For your comfort the terrace has fireplaces and a retrac-
table awning. Choices include an antipasto platter, pizzas from a
woodburning stove, penne gorgonzola, shellfish stew and house-
made desserts. ~ 5300 34th Avenue Northwest; 206-784-1733,
fax 206-783-4574. DELUXE.

When you're nostalgic for an old coffeehouse with an upbeat,
neighborhood flavor, head for **Still Life in Fremont Coffeehouse**.
Set in the unpretentious Fremont District, it has high windows, a
friendly atmosphere, music, great soups and generous sandwiches.
~ 709 North 35th Street; 206-547-9850. BUDGET.

Ponti Seafood Grill is near the Fremont Bridge on the Lake
Washington ship canal. The Mediterranean-style restaurant offers spectacular views of the canal from flower filled patios. The
menu has mostly seafood, though there are good pasta and
chicken dishes as well. No lunch on Saturday. ~ 3014 3rd Avenue
North; 206-284-3000, fax 206-284-4768. DELUXE TO ULTRA-
DELUXE.

On the south shore of Lake Union is **Chandler's Crabhouse
and Fresh Fish Market**. The whiskey crab soup is good for starters
before digging into a steamed crab, grilled salmon or other fresh
seafood plate. During Oyster Hour (3 to 6 p.m.) the first oyster's
free and the rest are only $1.25. Grab a table with a view of the

water and enjoy. ~ 901 Fairview Avenue North; 206-223-2722, fax 206-223-9380. DELUXE TO ULTRA-DELUXE.

Bicycles hang from the rafters. T-shirts are on sale in the lobby. **Cucina! Cucina!** is an open, spacious, noisy Italian restaurant with a large deck overlooking Lake Union where you can watch float planes land and take off or see kayakers gently paddling by. Diners can see into the open kitchen to watch the staff making pizzas large and small for baking in the woodburning ovens. One of the most interesting toppings is the barbecue chicken. You will find a variety of pasta dishes, such as linguine with roasted chicken and goat cheese, vegetarian or meat-filled calzones and good spinach and caesar salads. ~ 901 Fairview Avenue; 206-447-2782, fax 206-223-9372. MODERATE.

The hillside overlooking Lake Union is a long way from Trinidad, but **Bandoleone** succeeds smashingly at its mix of Caribbean and Central American cuisine. Chile-seared fresh fish and roast lamb marinated in plum-pepper sauce typify the highly imaginative and seasonally changing offerings. The bar becomes a cigar smokers' haven late in the evening. ~ 2241 Eastlake Avenue East; 206-329-7559. MODERATE TO DELUXE.

Also on Lake Union's east shore is a sushi restaurant much loved by north downtown workers. **I Love Sushi** overlooks Lake Union and a small marina; a lunch repast is so reasonable—a large plate of expertly prepared sushi under $10—that you can dream of bidding on the boats for sale in the water next to the deck. ~ 1001 Fairview Avenue North; 206-625-9604. MODERATE.

A colorful and lively Spanish-eclectic restaurant in the Madison Park area, **Cactus** serves a cuisine representative of many different cultures, but mostly influenced by Southwestern food. Start with one of the most unusual items on the menu—a salad of baby field greens topped with beer-battered goat cheese, candied hazelnuts and a roasted-jalapeño-and-green-apple vinaigrette. One of the more unusual entrées is ancho-cinnamon chicken—marinated in ancho chile, cinnamon and Mexican chocolate and glazed with honey. ~ 4220 East Madison Avenue; 206-324-4140. MODERATE.

LAKE UNION—SPEND THE DAY EXPLORING

The six miles or so of shoreline circling **Lake Union** present a varied mix of boat works and nautical specialty shops, street-end pocket parks, boat-in restaurants, seaplane docks, rental-boat concessions, ocean-research vessels, houseboats and flashy condos. You could spend a day exploring funky old warehouses and oddball enterprises. The lake's south end offers extensive public access to the shore behind a cluster of restaurants, a wooden-boat center and new park.

Not too far away, in a small house surrounded by gardens, is **Rover's**, which specializes in five-course meals of Northwest cuisine with a French accent and is just the place for those romantic occasions. Chef Thierry Rautureau creates the ever-changing menu based on locally available, fresh produce. In addition to sea-food in imaginative sauces, entrées might include rabbit, venison, pheasant and quail. A good selection of Northwest and French wines is available. Service is friendly and helpful, and there is patio seating in summer. Closed Sunday and Monday. ~ 2808 East Madison Street; 206-325-7442, fax 206-325-1092. ULTRA-DELUXE.

HIDDEN ►

Seattle is a poor place to sample Mexican food. One happy exception is the **Chile Pepper**, an unpretentious Wallingford café where they know what pasillas, moles and poblanos are. The chiles rellenos are quite good. Closed Sunday. ~ 1427 45th Street North; 206-545-1790. BUDGET TO MODERATE.

A favorite seafood place for tourists is **Ivar's Indian Salmon House** with its dugout canoe hung overhead and Northwest American Indian longhouse-style architecture and decor. The restaurant also features views of the kayak, canoe, tugboat, windsurfer and yacht activity on Lake Union. The menu includes alder-smoked salmon and black cod, Northwest American Indian–style, and prime rib. ~ 401 Northeast Northlake Way; 206-632-0767, fax 206-623-0715. MODERATE TO DELUXE.

Near the University of Washington, make a beeline for **Jitterbug**. Upbeat and lively, this is the place to go for generous portions of well-prepared Northwest regional food with Southwestern and Asian influences. The ever-changing menu may include *huevos rancheros* or grilled fresh fish. ~ 2114 North 45th Street; 206-547-6313, fax 206-548-1069. MODERATE.

Union Bay Café serves Northwest regional foods with an Asian and Italian influence. The seasonal entrées might include grilled sturgeon with roasted garlic, tomato and dill and hazelnut chicken on sautéed spinach with lemon butter. More unusual is the filet of ostrich grilled and served with Walla Walla sweet onions and a sauce of port wine, green peppercorn and sage. Lighter entrées are available in the simple, classic café. The appe-

NORTHWEST CUISINE, SEATTLE STYLE

In the Northwest, regional cooking at its best emphasizes the bounty of fresh produce and seafood available; in Seattle, innovative chefs have turned it into a distinctive cuisine showcasing the dazzling variety of ingredients that pour in from farms and boats. Combined with fine wines from Washington's 75-plus wineries, it makes for meals that critics rave about.

tizer list is almost as long as the regular menu. Closed Monday.
~ 3515 Northeast 45th Street; 206-527-8364, fax 206-527-0436.
MODERATE TO DELUXE.

On a busy commercial street between the University and Ravenna districts is **Ciao Bella Ristorante**. The authentic Italian cuisine has been drawing raves since the little, L-shaped ristorante
opened. On the menu are several classic pizzas, veal and chicken
entrées and delectable pasta dishes. Chicken breast sautéed with
gorgonzola cheese and fish soup with clams, mussels, calamari
and prawns are flavored with artistry. Dinner only. ~ 5133 Northeast 25th Avenue; 206-524-6989. MODERATE TO DELUXE.

Guido's Pizza is a funky, unpretentious place in Ravenna, the
aromas from which send people walking by into Pavlovian sali-
vation. You can buy pizza by the whole or slice, delicious salads
and good cappuccinos. The artichoke pizza is wonderful. ~ 2108
Northeast 65th Avenue; 206-525-3042, fax 206-374-0818.
BUDGET TO MODERATE.

At the **Washington Park Arboretum Visitor's Center Gift Shop**   **SHOPPING**
are gardening books, cards, china, earrings, necklaces, serving trays
and sweatshirts. You can also buy plants from the arboretum
greenhouse. ~ 2300 Arboretum Drive East; 206-543-8800.

Dominated by the UW campus is the University District, a com-
mercial neighborhood overflowing with a vast array of retail shops.
One that attracts many tourists is the **Folk Art Gallery La Tienda**.
Here you'll find handpicked craft items from all over the world
including those made by 200 selected American artisans. ~ 4138
University Way Northeast, 206-632-1796; and 2050 Northwest
Market Street.

The largest bookseller in Washington is **University Book Store**,
where addicted readers can browse happily for hours. There's a
huge selection of literature, technical books and college texts, as
well as music and camera sections, some clothing and stationery.
~ 4326 University Way Northeast; 206-634-3400.

Seattle's most active small **cinema district** is near the University   **NIGHTLIFE**
of Washington in a cultural mecca along and near 45th Street.
These theaters are all operated by the same company and all spe-   ◀ *HIDDEN*
cialize in foreign, art and independent films. ~ **The Guild 45th
Street Theater**, 2115 45th Street North, 206-633-3353; **Metro Cin-
emas**, 4500 9th Avenue Northeast, 206-633-0055; **Neptune Theater**, 1301 45th Street Northeast, 206-633-5545, **Seven Gables
Theater**, 911 Northeast 50th Street, 206-632-8820; and **Varsity**,
4329 University Way Northeast, 206-632-3131. This neighborhood is also the home of a profusion of small cafés and restaurants catering to the evening before-and after-show crowd.

Conor Byrne's has live Irish music on the weekends and dancing every Tuesday and Thursday evening in the summer. The old-world building has exposed bricks, high ceilings and low light. Weekend cover. ~ 5140 Ballard Avenue; 206-784-3640.

Club crawlers frequent the **Ballard Firehouse** for rock, reggae and salsa. Cover. ~ 5429 Russell Avenue Northwest; 206-784-3516. **Tractor Tavern** offers a mix of live rock, country, Celtic and alternative music. Cover. ~ 5213 Ballard Avenue Northwest; 206-789-3599.

Near the University of Washington, you will find an array of clubs and places to park yourself at night.

There are cocktail service, full dinner and comedy shows Thursday through Saturday at **Giggles Comedy Niteclub**. Cover. ~ 5220 Roosevelt Way Northeast; 206-526-5347.

Located just barely off campus, the happening student hang-out in the University District is the **Big Time Microbrewery & Alehouse,** which offers beer, pizza and a rowdy young crowd. Seattle's oldest brewpub (c. 1988), it has an antique bar, shuffleboard in the back room and a museum-like collection of beer bottles, cans, signs and memorabilia. ~ 4133 University Way; 206-545-4509.

Nearby, **Tommy's Nightclub & Grill** features deejay dance music and live reggae and rock on alternating nights and some of the cheapest beer in town. ~ 4552 University Way Northeast; 206-634-3144.

In Fremont, the popular, cheery **Trolleyman Pub** serves Red-hook ales and a variety of pub fare. It also houses a tasting room. ~ 3400 Phinney Avenue North; 206-548-8000.

BEACHES & PARKS

DISCOVERY PARK 🏃 🚲 With two miles of beach trail and nine miles of footpaths winding through mixed forest and across open meadows, this bluff-top preserve (Seattle's largest at 535 acres) protects a remarkable "urban wilderness." Here are sweeping vistas, chances to watch birds (including nesting bald eagles) and study nature, the **Daybreak Star Indian Cultural Center** (206-285-4425, fax 206-282-3640) featuring art and cultural exhibits from various tribes, an interpretive center with environmental displays and educational programs, four miles of road for bicycling and an 1881 lighthouse (oldest in the area). Fort Lawton Historic District includes Officers' Row and military buildings surviving from the park's days as an Army fort. There are areas suitable for picnics; restrooms and a visitors center are at the park's east gate. ~ Located a quarter-hour drive north of downtown in the Magnolia district. The main entrance is at 3801 West Government Way and 36th Avenue West; 206-386-4236, fax 206-684-0195.

CARKEEK PARK 🚶 🚲 Tucked into a woodsy canyon reaching toward Puget Sound, this 224-acre wildland protects Piper's Creek and its resurrected runs of salmon and sea-going trout. Signs explain how citizens helped clean up the stream and bring the salmon back. Trails lead past spawning waters, to the top of the canyon and through a native-plant garden. You will find picnic areas, restrooms, play areas and beachcombing (as long as you take nothing home with you) and a pioneer orchard. ~ Take 3rd Avenue Northwest to 110th Street Northwest, turn and follow the signs; 206-684-0877, fax 206-364-4685.

GOLDEN GARDENS 🚶 🏊 🛶 🚤 ⚓ North of Ballard on Shilshole Bay, this 88-acre park has waterfront, woods, a creek and a sandy beach that swarms with young picnickers and sunbathers in summer. You can watch glorious sunsets from here. There are fire pits, a boat ramp, basketball hoops, wheelchair accessible soccer and football fields and trails, and a public fishing pier. On the slope east of the beach, the park has numerous walking paths under the trees. ~ 206-684-4075, fax 206-684-4853.

> Adjacent to the Warren G. Magnuson Park is the National Oceanic Atmospheric Administration's Sound Garden. The park that gave the Seattle rock band its name is full of sculptures that move and chime when the wind blows.

WARREN G. MAGNUSON PARK 🏊 🛶 🚤 This 194-acre site carved from the Sand Point Naval Air Station presents generous access to Lake Washington and wide views across the lake. It's a favorite place to launch a boat, swim or toss a frisbee. You'll find picnic areas, restrooms, softball fields, tennis courts, swimming beaches with summer lifeguards and a wheelchair-accessible wading pool. ~ Located on Lake Washington, northeast of downtown Seattle, at Sand Point Way Northeast and 65th Avenue Northeast; 206-684-4075, fax 206-684-4853.

SEWARD PARK 🚶 🚲 🏊 🛶 🚤 ⚓ On Bailey Peninsula, this 278-acre park jutting into Lake Washington encompasses Seattle's largest virgin forest. Walking through it on one of several footpaths is the prime attraction, but many come to swim and sunbathe, launch a small boat, fish or visit a fish hatchery. Seward Park offers a rare opportunity to see nesting bald eagles in an urban setting. The best introductory walk is the two-and-one-half-mile shoreline loop stroll; to see the large Douglas firs, add another mile along the center of the peninsula. The swimming beaches' gentle surf is ideal for children, and there are lifeguards in summer. You can fish from the pier for crappie and trout. There are picnic areas, restrooms and play areas. ~ Located on the west shore of Lake Washington, southeast of downtown, at Lake Washington Boulevard South and South Orcas Street; 206-684-4075, fax 206-684-4853.

▼▼▼▼▼▼▼▼▼▼
Seattle South

Meander from the heart of the city and you'll find one of the world's great aviation museums. Inviting saltwater beaches provide a convenient retreat from urban living. Seattle South serves as the city's back door to the wilderness.

SIGHTS

About ten miles to the south of downtown Seattle, off Route 5 at Boeing Field, you'll encounter the **Museum of Flight**. Centered in a traffic-stopping piece of architecture called the Great Gallery, the museum is a must. In the glass-and-steel gallery, 22 aircraft hang suspended from the ceiling, almost as if in flight. In all, some 50 aircraft (many rare) trace the history of more than 70 years of aviation. You'll see a 1916 B&W float plane, 1917 Curtis Jenny biplane, 1929 Boeing 80-A biplane, 1932 Yakima Clipper sail plane, 1935 DC-3, 1962 A-12 Blackbird, 1944 B-29 Superfortress and many homebuilts.

The 1909 **Red Barn** houses one wing of the museum. The so-called barn was originally a boat-building factory on the banks of the nearby Duwamish River. Later Bill Boeing bought it and turned it into the original headquarters for the Boeing Corporation. Relocated several times, the Red Barn now houses exhibits on Boeing's early days in the airplane business, a far cry from today's mammoth factories. Visitors can also tour the operating air traffic control tower. Admission. ~ 9404 East Marginal Way South; 206-764-5720, fax 206-764-5707; www.museumofflight.org.

LODGING

A stone's throw from Sea-Tac Airport, the **Seattle Marriott** is a wonderfully luxurious hotel featuring a 20,000-square-foot tropical atrium five stories high. Around it are 459 guest rooms. A restaurant, lounge, whirlpool, health club with massage therapy (by appointment) and gameroom round out the amenities. Airport shuttle is provided. ~ 3201 South 176th Street; 206-241-

AERONAUTIC ACROBATICS

In 1954, when Boeing's first commercial jet prototype was about to be unveiled, public skepticism about its ability to fly was widespread. So Chief Pilot Tex Johnston took the plane up for an unauthorized flight on Seattle's Seafair Sunday, when hundreds of thousands of fans would be lining the shores of Lake Washington to watch the hydroplane races. Johnston not only did a fly-by, he barrel-rolled the plane barely 2000 feet overhead—a performance captured by news cameras to forever dispel rumors the plane couldn't fly.

2000, 800-643-5479, fax 206-248-0789; www.marriott.com. ULTRA-DELUXE.

DINING

An excellent Thai restaurant convenient to Sea-Tac Airport is **Bai Tong**. Located in a former A&W drive-in, this eatery is known for its steamed curry salmon, grilled beef with Thai sauce and marinated chicken. The carpeted dining room is lush with potted plants, and the walls are adorned with photos of mouthwatering dishes. ~ 15859 Pacific Highway South, Sea-Tac; phone/fax 206-431-0893. BUDGET.

For an unusual experience in low-priced dining, head west of the airport to the increasingly Latino suburb of Burien, where you'll find **El Trapiche Pupusería & Restaurant**. This homespun, unpretentious little restaurant serves authentic Salvadoran specialties such as *pollo asado* (a skinless, boneless chicken breast chargrilled in annatto-seed marinade), *pescado frito* (whole deep-fried tilapia), *pupusa de chicharrón* (cornmeal rounds stuffed with shredded pork and served with spicy slaw) and beef hoof soup (an acquired taste, to be sure). Practically the only Central American eatery in the greater Seattle area, El Trapiche's novelty draws a growing clientele from all parts of the city. ~ 127 Southwest 153rd Street, Burien; 206-244-5564, fax 206-242-2120. BUDGET TO MODERATE.

PARKS

ED MUNRO SEAHURST COUNTY PARK A well-designed, 140-acre site where landscaping divides 4000 feet of saltwater shoreline into individual chunks just right for private picnics and sunbathing. A nature trail and some three miles of primitive footpath explore woodsy uplands and the headwaters of two creeks. An artificial reef just offshore is popular with divers and anglers with boats. Other facilities include picnic areas, restrooms, showers, playground and marine laboratory with fish ladder and outdoor viewing slots. ~ Located at 16th Avenue Southwest and Southwest 140th Street, via Exit 154B from Route 5, Burien; 206-296-4281.

SALTWATER STATE PARK You'll share this busy park with lots of locals, nearly 800,000 visitors a year, so don't expect solitude. But among the 88 acres, do revel in the fine views, some 1500 feet of shoreline and quiet woods with two miles of hiking trails. A sunken barge about 150 yards offshore from a prominent sandspit attracts a variety of perch and seasonal fish and divers. There are picnic areas, restrooms, showers, play areas and a concession stand. ~ Located on Marine View Drive (Route 509) about halfway between Seattle and Tacoma, west of Route 5 via Exit 149; 800-233-0321, fax 360-664-8112.

▲ There are 47 sites for tents, two primitive hiker/biker sites and two sites with full hookups; $10 per night.

▼▼▼▼▼▼▼▼▼▼
Vashon Island

No shopping malls, no fast-food restaurants—just natural beauty and a hometown feel. That's the draw to Seattle's neighboring Vashon Island. A mecca for artists, this 14-mile island is fast becoming known as the bed-and-breakfast island. Since you can reach pastoral Vashon Island by state ferry from the Fauntleroy dock in West Seattle (a 15-minute crossing), we include it in this section of the book. However, Vashon Island stretches south for 13 miles toward Tacoma (accessible by another 15-minute ferry from Tahlequah), creating a lovely Seattle-to-Tacoma country-road alternative to Route 5. The ferry to Tacoma lands next to one of the city's highlights, splendid Point Defiance Park.

SIGHTS

Since Vashon is also served by a passenger-only ferry that leaves from downtown Seattle's main ferry dock, it's a popular destination for bicyclists and backpackers heading for the island's youth hostel, or one of its many B&Bs. The island's little-traveled back roads offer long, leisurely rides through deep second-growth forests and pastoral farmland, with a smattering of U-pick berry and fruit farms. Time seems to stand still, partly because the landscape is so bucolic, partly because Vashon society operates on "island time." You can't get a shirt starched on the island, but you can pick cherries and raspberries at local farms.

Vashon is home to a thriving community of artists, potters, weavers and other craftspeople—many of whose studios are periodically open to passersby, especially during holiday weekends —as well as writers and musicians. It's also home to a growing gay and lesbian community.

Vashon Highway runs the length of the island, passing through the town, with its smattering of small shops and restaurants, and on south past **Seattle's Best Coffee.** Housed in a turn-of-the-20th-century freighthouse, this roastery is a great place to stop and fill your cup with fresh-brewed Guatemala or Costa Rican estate coffee, a great bargain at 50 cents. You can also buy gift packages to take home. ~ 19529 Vashon Highway; 206-463-3932, fax 206-463-5051.

Burton, a small community halfway down the island, has several small galleries and gift stores, a restaurant and two inns. It's also the turnoff for a secluded, lovely beach park, **Burton Acres County Park,** an excellent place to go for a picnic or a beach stroll, to launch canoes or kayaks, or even to swim in the cool salt water of Quartermaster Harbor. On July Fourth, a local anonymous benefactor pays for a fireworks show on a barge in the middle of the harbor; it's one of the best displays on the West Coast. ~ Burton Acres Park, Bayview Drive Southwest, outer loop.

HIDDEN ►

Side roads beckon from the highway to a handful of poorly marked state beaches and county parks. **Point Robinson County Park** on Maury Island (linked to Vashon via an isthmus at the hamlet of Portage) is easier to find and particularly interesting since it's next door to the Coast Guard's picturesque Point Robinson Lighthouse (not open to the public).

LODGING

Vashon Island, befitting its pastoral, low-key nature, has no hotels or motels, and attempts to build anyway would provoke local outcry. It does, however, have more than two dozen fine small inns and B&Bs. Most of Vashon's inns and B&Bs are secluded, idyllic places where quiet prevails and the island's beauty is at the visitor's doorstep.

Vashon Island abounds with bed-and-breakfast inns, some of them in quaint old farmhouses surrounded by meadows and orchards. One is the **Betty MacDonald Farm,** the former home of Betty MacDonald who authored *The Egg and I, Onions in the Stew,* and all the Mrs. Piggle Wiggle children's books. The first two books wryly chronicle life on the Olympic Peninsula and

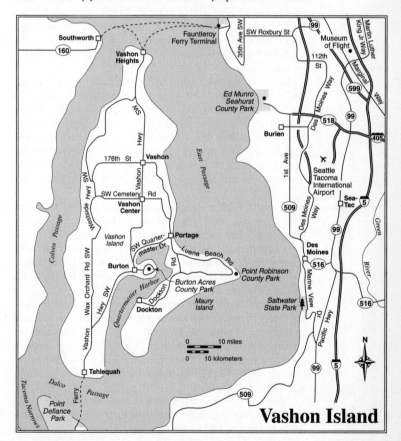

Vashon Island. The six-acre farm overlooks Puget Sound and Mt. Rainier and offers two guest accommodations, a cedar-paneled loft and a private cottage both furnished with oriental carpets, Northwest Indian print fabrics, antiques, full kitchens and wood-burning stoves. Guests also enjoy a full breakfast, beach access, trail bikes, private decks and gardens. For nighttime reading, there are books by MacDonald. ~ 12000 99th Avenue Southwest; 206-567-4227, 888-328-6753, fax 206-567-4555; www.bettymacdonaldfarm. com. DELUXE.

Vashon's annual Strawberry Festival, the weekend after July Fourth, is highlighted by a Saturday parade that features the Antique Tractor Society, the Vashon Island Marching Kazoo Band and the local grocery store's precision grocery cart drill team.

Located in an 1890s farmhouse painted blue with white trim, the **Old Tjomsland House** is surrounded by apple and pear trees and deer fields. The inn features a two-bedroom suite and a one-bedroom cottage, both furnished with family antiques and offering kitchenettes and living space. Includes a huge breakfast of fresh fruit, turnovers, oatmeal, eggs and, occasionally, roasted salmon. ~ 17011 Vashon Highway Southwest; phone/fax 206-463-5275, 888-255-2706; www.old tjomslandhouse.com. MODERATE TO DELUXE.

Situated in the tiny town of Burton, the **Back Bay Inn** is a New England–style lodging with an airy, open dining room downstairs and four spare, elegant bedrooms up. The inn's hardwood and fir floors warm its stucco walls; a brick entryway is edged with bright flowers six months of the year. Breakfasts, especially weekend brunch, are excellent. It's also open for dinner Tuesday through Saturday, serving Northwest cuisine. ~ 24007 Vashon Highway Southwest, Burton; 206-463-5355, fax 206-463-6663. MODERATE TO DELUXE.

HIDDEN ►

Peabody's B&B is about as hidden as you can get—an elegant 1910 Craftsman-style farmhouse set on beautifully landscaped grounds way out on Maury Island. It offers a stunning view of Puget Sound and the lights of Seattle at night. Peabody's two units, one upstairs, one down, have side rooms for toddlers and children. Full breakfast. ~ 23007 64th Avenue Southwest (Luana Beach Road); phone/fax 206-463-3506. MODERATE.

The AYH **Ranch/Hostel**, about a mile outside the town of Vashon, caters to bicycle and foot travelers; free pickup is provided from the bus stop in town. Hostel lodgings range from campsites and tepees to one private room and bath. Extensive grounds allow room for roaming. Free pancakes for all. Closed November through April. ~ 12119 Cove Road Southwest; 206-463-2592, fax 206-463-6157. BUDGET.

Also in a pastoral setting with resident deer, **Artist's Studio Loft** offers a carriage house cottage with a beamed ceiling, skylights, ceiling fan, kitchenette and outdoor hot tub. Other accommodations include a suite with a private entrance, French doors, cathedral ceilings, and potted palms, a smaller room decorated with Mexican tiles and wicker furnishings, and a cottage. The rate includes a continental breakfast. ~ 16529 91st Avenue Southwest; 206-463-2583, fax 206-463-3881; www.asl-bnb.com. MODERATE TO DELUXE.

DINING

Vashon Island is one of the least likely places to find decent Mexican food, but there it is at **Casa Bonita**, a small family-run enclave in the town of Vashon. Here are such unusual (for the Northwest) delights as chicken en mole and *molcajete*, a hearty stew. Meals are filling and economical. ~ 17623 100th Avenue Southwest; 206-463-6452. MODERATE.

◄ HIDDEN

If you want to act like a real islander on Vashon, breakfast consists of a visit to **Bob's Bakery**, a tiny storefront on the main highway in town. Each morning Bob bakes up more than a dozen different delights, ranging from poppyseed pound cake to cranberry/orange scones. Grab a goodie, a cup of coffee and the newspaper, have a seat on the bench out front and watch the world go by for a half hour or so. Closed Sunday and Monday. ~ 17506 Vashon Highway; 206-463-5666. BUDGET.

The old island hangout is **Sound Food Restaurant**. The restaurant is known for its casual atmosphere—windows overlooking the gardens and lots of wood inside. Saturday and Sunday brunches result in long waits, but the food—whole-wheat waffles, blintzes with fresh fruit, potato pancakes, omelettes with wonderful sauces and breads and pastries from the bakery—is usually worth it. A variety of soups, salads and sandwiches of baked bread is available for lunch. Dinner entrées include pasta primavera, seafood dishes and a number of large salads. Desserts—sigh—come fresh from the bakery. ~ 20312 Vashon Highway Southwest; 206-463-3565. BUDGET.

SHOPPING

◄ HIDDEN

Two miles down the highway, near Seattle's Best Coffee, **Owen's Antiques** has 11 rooms of 19th-century antique furniture and accessories, a quilt room, an Asian room and a country room. Closed Sunday through Tuesday. ~ Vashon Highway and Cemetery Road; 206-463-5193.

A mile farther down the highway is the **Country Store**, an eclectic collection of clothing, garden supplies, food products, gifts and nursery plants. Spring is a great time to stroll the grounds and experience the vast array of flowers. ~ 20211 Vashon Highway Southwest; 206-463-3655.

Across the street, **Minglement** has a wide selection of island crafts, especially pottery, plus other oddments including holistic foods and dietary supplements. ~ Vashon Highway and Ellisport Road Southwest; 206-463-9672.

▼▼▼▼▼▼▼▼▼▼▼
Seattle North

Heading north from Seattle, you'll cross the county line (into Snohomish County) toward the less urban and more maritime cities and villages lining Northern Puget Sound. You don't have to travel far to catch a glimpse of the region's past, before Seattlemania lured businesses and families to relocate here. North of Seattle you'll find a slower pace and strong reminders of Washington's history.

SIGHTS

Northeast of Seattle, the long-time mill town of **Edmonds** has a lively charm and provides a link to the Olympic Peninsula. Ferries leave hourly from the Edmonds ferry landing, on a waterfront that has a recently redone beach park, a long fishing pier and an underwater park that is popular with divers. The park teems with marine life that swims around sunken structures: boats, a dock, a bridge model and others. On shore, the **Edmonds Beach Rangers** host summer beach walks. ~ 425-775-2525, fax 425-771-0253.

The Edmonds Art Walk map points out the public art-works on display: bronze and copper sculptures, tile murals, stained glass and others.

The **Edmonds Chamber of Commerce** wins the prize for quaintness. It's housed in a pioneer log cabin that looks like a storybook house. ~ 121 5th Avenue North, Edmonds; 425-670-1496, fax 425-712-1808; www.edmondswa.com.

A visit to the **Edmonds Historical Museum** with its working shingle-mill model, maritime heritage exhibits and collections of logging tools and household furnishings gives a better understanding of the pioneer heritage and industrial history of Edmonds. A walking tour takes you past the old shingle mills, Brackett's Landing (where the earliest pioneers settled), and numerous buildings constructed in the late 1800s and early 1900s. Closed Monday. ~ 118 5th Avenue, Edmonds; 425-774-0900.

LODGING

The **Maple Tree**, a renovated 1923 vintage home, offers charming accommodations complete with private bath and balcony. A light breakfast is included. ~ 18313 Olympic View Drive, Edmonds; 425-774-8420, fax 425-775-9039; www.visit.to/themaple tree. BUDGET TO MODERATE.

Hidden away in a little business complex full of shops and restaurants, the **Edmonds Harbor Inn** provides basic motel-style accommodations with updated pastel decor and light wood furnishings, a breakfast area and a meeting space. Sadly, none of the rooms has a view of the harbor. ~ 130 West Dayton, Edmonds; 425-771-5021, 800-441-8033, fax 425-672-2880. MODERATE.

Rooms in the three-story **Travelodge** are comfortably decorated and clean, with dark blue carpets, curtains and bedspreads and cable television. There are even a few kitchenette and jacuzzi units. Other amenities include hot tubs and continental breakfast. ~ 23825 Route 99, Edmonds; 425-771-8008, 800-771-8009, fax 425-771-0080; www.travelodge.com. MODERATE.

If you venture up to Edmonds, try **Ciao Italia**. This small restaurant on the main drag doesn't look like much from the outside— thankfully the lace curtains block out most of the traffic view. Best choices include spaghetti *mirechiaro* (a garlicky seafood pasta in white-wine sauce) and veal piccata. Dinner daily, and lunch Wednesday through Friday. ~ 546 5th Avenue South, Edmonds; 425-771-7950. MODERATE.

A café and bakery, **Brusseau's** features country-style breakfasts, homemade meatloaf sandwiches, homemade soups and a wide variety of desserts. The restaurant has a pleasant courtyard with planters and picnic tables. Try their quiche Lorraine or omelette special. Breakfast and lunch only. ~ 117 5th Avenue South, Edmonds; 425-774-4166, fax 425-650-2516. BUDGET TO MODERATE.

Every table at **Arnies at the Landing** has a dandy second-floor view of Puget Sound and the Edmonds harbor. Chicken, steak and pasta are on the regular menu, but your best bet is to order from the fresh daily seafood list. There's a variety of fresh broiled fish, and the clam chowder has won awards. The four-course early dinner (until 6 p.m.), available Sunday through Friday, is a bargain. Sunday brunch. ~ 300 Admiral Way, Edmonds; 425-771-5688, fax 425-771-7624. MODERATE TO DELUXE.

Located a block from the ferry landing, **Café de Paris** is known for its French cuisine, served in a small dining room or on the glass-enclosed sunporch. No lunch on weekends. ~ 109 Main Street, Edmonds; 425-771-2350. MODERATE TO DELUXE.

Chanterelle Specialty Foods has a rustic atmosphere, with wooden floors and American cuisine. It's bright, cheerful and busy at mealtimes with patrons ordering salads and sandwiches. Open daily for breakfast, lunch and dinner. ~ 316 Main Street, Edmonds; 425-774-0650, fax 425-771-5783. MODERATE.

There are a number of good shops in the renovated **Old Mill Town**. Within it, check out the **Edmonds Antique Mall** where you can find dolls, glasses and antique furniture. ~ 201 5th Avenue South, Edmonds; 425-771-9466.

Over 200 dealers sell their wares at the **Aurora Antique Pavilion**. ~ 24111 Route 99, Edmonds; 425-744-0566.

DINING

SHOPPING

Seattle East, extending from the eastern shore of Lake Washington to the Cascade foothills, blends the urban and rural assets of this metropolitan region. Here you'll find wineries and archaeological sites, prime birdwatching areas and homey bed and breakfasts.

Seattle East

Located just south of Woodinville, **Château Ste. Michelle** is the state's largest winery with daily tasting and tours. Situated on a turn-of-the-20th-century estate, it also has duck and trout ponds,

SIGHTS

experimental vineyards and outdoor concerts on summer weekends. ~ Route 202; 425-415-3300; www.ste-michelle.com.

Bellevue is the fourth-largest city in Washington, its suburban sprawl broken by ten high-rise complexes of office buildings, shops and department stores. **Bellevue Square**, with some 200 stores, is one of the largest malls in the state. ~ Northeast 8th Street and Bellevue Way; 425-454-2431.

Like Boeing, Seattle's other economic giant, Microsoft, also has its own museum, but it only exists in cyberspace. Look it up at www.microsoft.com/mscorp/museum.

The **Bellevue Art Museum** displays a variety of exhibits, especially Northwest contemporary artworks. Admission. ~ Bellevue Way at Northeast 6th Street; 425-519-0770.

Bellevue boasts a surprisingly diverse network of parks embedded within its neighborhoods. **Mercer Slough Nature Park**, stretching north from Route 90 off Bellevue Way with the entrance at 2102 Bellevue Way Southeast, is the biggest and may be the best with some 300 acres of natural wetland habitat and ten miles of trails. **Wilburton Hill Park**, between 128th Southeast and 118th Avenue on Main Street, is centered around the Bellevue Botanical Gardens, filled with native and ornamental Northwest plants. The park covers over 100 acres and has more than three miles of hiking trails as well as softball and soccer fields. ~ 12001 Main Street off 116th Avenue Northeast; 425-452-2750; www.ci.bellevue.wa.us.

To see what Bellevue used to be like before freeways, commuters and office towers, stroll the short stretch of shops along Main Street westward from 104th Avenue Southeast in **Old Bellevue**.

Adults and children alike are enchanted with the **Rosalie Whyel Museum of Doll Art**. Hundreds of antique and modern dolls are on display in a building that is patterned after a brick Victorian mansion. Admission. ~ 1116 108th Avenue Northeast, Bellevue; 425-455-1116, fax 425-455-4793.

North of Bellevue, hugging the Lake Washington shore, is **Kirkland**, with remnants of small-town charm. Pedestrian traffic is encouraged, with easy access to the lake and a one-and-a-half-mile walking/biking path. At Moss Bay, there's a public boat ramp and marina, shops, cafés and a brewery. The **Arthur Foss**, a 112-foot tugboat built in 1889, is open for tours in the summer. Originally steam-powered, the tug was given a diesel engine in 1935.

Seattle's rock legend Jimi Hendrix is buried south of Bellevue. A caretaker can show you the guitarist's grave at **Greenwood Memorial Park**. ~ 350 Monroe Avenue Northeast, Renton; 425-255-1511, 425-271-6045.

LODGING   The **Bear Creek Inn** is a Cape Cod house set among trees on an acre of land. There's a large rock fireplace in the sitting room, a patio and a deck with a hot tub. The three rooms feature wood furniture with oak and pine trim painted with flowered designs. ~ 19520 Northeast 144th Place, Woodinville; 425-881-2978. MODERATE.

Set on three-plus acres, **A Cottage Creek Inn** has its own creek, pond and gazebo on the grounds. The English Tudor house features four guest rooms, one with a brass bed, one with an antique bed, all with their own bathrooms. There's full jacuzzis in the two larger rooms. There's a pleasant sitting room with a piano,

Seattle East

which guests are encouraged to play. Full breakfast included. ~ 12525 Avondale Road Northeast, Redmond; phone/fax 425-881-5606; www.cottagecreekinn.com. MODERATE TO DELUXE.

Big, pink and broad-shouldered, the **Hyatt Regency Bellevue** is the classiest place to stay in Bellevue. The mood is corporate, quality's high and access is convenient. The 382 rooms are painted in earth tones, and have soft lighting, contemporary furnishings and all the amenities, including room service. For a fee, guests may use the adjoining health club. ~ 900 Bellevue Way Northeast, Bellevue; 425-462-1234, 800-233-1234, fax 425-646-7567. ULTRA-DELUXE.

The **Woodmark Hotel at Carillon Point** is a handsome, four-story brick structure on Lake Washington's shore. Its small scale, residential-style lobby, and comfortable bar with a fireplace and shelves of books create the ambience of a welcoming, stylish home. The 100 rooms, in subdued pastels, have all the amenities: mini-bars, two televisions, robes and hair dryers. Rooms on the lake side have panoramic views. ~ 1200 Carillon Point, Kirkland; 425-822-3700, 800-822-3700, fax 425-822-3699. ULTRA-DELUXE.

Evergreen Point Floating Bridge, crossing Lake Washington between Seattle and Bellevue, is the world's longest floating bridge (1.4 miles).

The **Shumway Mansion** is a historic mansion with a New England flavor. To save it from demolition, the present owners had it moved to a knoll in north Kirkland, where it now stands as a bed-and-breakfast inn and accommodates guests, weddings and social functions. When a group takes over, overnight visitors can retreat to a tiny reading alcove on a second floor. The formal inn contains European furnishings, rugs out of the Orient, lace curtains and silk floral arrangements. Each of the eight rooms has a queen-size bed and antiques and easy chairs. The innkeepers serve a full breakfast on crystal and china. ~ 11410 99th Place Northeast, Kirkland; 425-823-2303, fax 425-822-0421; www.shumwaymansion.com. MODERATE.

HIDDEN ▶

In a quiet wooded area southeast of Seattle is the **Maple Valley Bed and Breakfast**. The two-story contemporary home has open-beamed ceilings, peeled-pole railings, cedar walls and detailed-wood trim. Guests like to relax on the antique furniture on the front porch. The two guest rooms are individually decorated and color coordinated with French doors that open onto a large deck. Both have log beds. On cool nights, heated, sand-filled pads ("hot babies") are used to warm the beds. A full breakfast is served on country-stencil pottery in a dining area that overlooks trees, wandering birds and ponds with ducks. ~ 20020 Southeast 228th Street, Maple Valley; 425-432-1409, 888-432-1409, fax 425-413-1459; www.nwlink.com/~holihedge/ssba.html. MODERATE.

Sophistication is definitely not the attraction at the **Armadillo**, Woodinville's outpost of Texas-style barbecue. Service is accompanied by wisecracks; the menu is one big collection of bad puns; the decor has been described as "road kill." But the food—hearty ribs, brisket and chicken—is as close to decent barbecue as you will get in the land of salmon. And the hot sauce is actually hot. ~ 13109 175th Street Northeast, Woodinville; 425-481-1417, fax 425-485-8525. MODERATE.

The open kitchen at **Andre's Eurasian Bistro** is as entertaining as the food. This restaurant offers a menu with Vietnamese specialties like spring rolls or chicken with lemongrass, as well as Continental selections, such as lamb with garlic. Vietnamese chef Andre Nguyen comes with experience from some of Seattle's best restaurants. Closed Sunday. ~ 14125 Northeast 20th Street, Bellevue; 425-747-6551, fax 425-747-4304. MODERATE.

You wouldn't expect to find a good restaurant in this little shopping strip, but here it is. At **Pogacha**, a Croatian version of pizza is the mainstay. The pizzas, crisp on the outside but moist inside, are baked in a brick oven. Because the saucing is nonexistent or very light, the flavor of the toppings—pesto and various cheeses, alone or over vegetables or meat—is more apparent. Other entrées include Adriatic-inspired grilled meats and seafood, salads and pastas. ~ 119 106th Avenue Northeast, Bellevue; 425-455-5670, fax 425-455-0108. MODERATE.

The one, lone reason to visit **Sushi-Ten Hama** is more than sufficient. Plunk down $20 and you'll get all the fresh-made sushi you can eat—and when they say "all," that's exactly what they mean. Sit at the sushi bar and order 'til you drop; the yellowtail, ahi and salmon are especially good, but don't overlook more exotic delights such as octopus and roe. ~ 2217 140th Avenue Northeast, Bellevue; phone/fax 425-643-6637. MODERATE.   ◄ HIDDEN

Bis Restaurant features a blend of American and European cuisine, offering specialties such as the *vol au vent*, a puff-pastry ring filled with either shrimp and artichokes or mushrooms. Reservations encouraged. ~ 10213 Main Street, Bellevue; 425-455-2033, fax 425-455-2720. MODERATE.

The best spot for a view of Lake Washington while you dine is **Yarrow Bay Grill and Beach Café**. In the upper-level Yarrow Bay Grill, booths and tables are set against windows that extend in a wide semi-circle overlooking the lake. The Northwest cuisine emphasizes fresh seafood; salmon and chicken are smoked in-house, and the flavorful clam chowder is excellent. Downstairs, the more casual Yarrow Beach Café offers an interesting menu with specials that travel to different ports-of-call every eight weeks, and a bar with Northwest wines and microbrewed beers. The bargain here at the café is happy hour on weeknights when, with a drink purchase, you can choose from generous portions of appetizers such as Cajun popcorn shrimp, steamed mussels and smoked salmon for half-price. ~ 1270 Carillon Point, Kirkland; 425-889-0303 or 425-889-9052, fax 425-803-2982. MODERATE TO DELUXE.

HIDDEN ▶

One of the best Japanese restaurants in all of Puget Sound is hidden in the Totem Lake West shopping center in suburbia. **Izumi** features an excellent sushi bar. Entrées are fairly standard—beef, chicken sukiyaki and teriyaki and tempura—but the ingredients are especially fresh and carefully prepared. Service is friendly. Closed Monday. ~ 12539 116th Avenue Northeast, Kirkland; 425-821-1959. MODERATE TO DELUXE.

HIDDEN ▶

Overlooking Juanita Creek north of Kirkland, **Cafe Juanita** is a pricey but dependably excellent restaurant. Intimate and quiet, the creekside atmosphere is romantic. The Northern Italian food centers on game, poultry and pasta; the wine list is superlative. Dinner only. ~ 9702 120th Place Northeast, Kirkland; 425-823-1505, fax 425-823-8500. MODERATE TO DELUXE.

A couple of local residents who grew up in Pakistan and Bangladesh have opened **Shamiana**. The food is cooled to an American palate but can be spiced to a full-blown, multistar *hot*. A buffet of four curries, salad, *nan* and *dal* is offered at lunch. Dinners are à la carte, and include entrées such as lamb curry with rice *pulao* or chicken *tikka*. ~ 10724 Northeast 68th Street, Kirkland; 425-827-4902, fax 425-828-2765. MODERATE.

SHOPPING

In Bellevue, **Bellevue Square** has 200 of the nation's finest shops, department stores and restaurants. ~ Northeast 8th Street and Bellevue Way.

One of the most elegant shops in Bellevue is **Alvin Goldfarb Jewelers**. Specializing in 18-carat gold pieces crafted by an in-house goldsmith who also works with precious and semiprecious gems,

ALL ABOARD FOR DINNER

Dining cars built in the 1930s and 1950s, refurbished in style, offer unusual views of the Seattle area to passengers who book a ride on the **Spirit of Washington**. The train travels from Renton north for 22 miles along the east shore of Lake Washington to Woodinville. Top-quality meals at ultra-deluxe prices are served during the journey—dinners daily, and lunch and brunch on weekends. In Woodinville, passengers disembark for a tour of the beautifully landscaped Columbia winery. On the return journey, they enjoy dessert and coffee and watch the scenery go by. The train crosses Wilburton Trestle, the longest (102 feet) wooden trestle in the Northwest. ~ P.O. Box 835, Renton, WA 98057; 800-876-7245.

this is a mecca for discriminating people who desire a one-of-a-kind item. Closed Sunday. ~ 305 Bellevue Way Northeast, Bellevue; 425-454-9393.

If you're looking for the unusual, browse through **Ming's Asian Gallery**, two stories full of Asian antiques and art from China, Korea and Japan. ~ 10217 Main Street, Bellevue; 425-462-4008.

Collectors of marine antiques can pick up old brass lights, wooden wheels, telescopes or diving equipment of days gone by on two floors at **Cuttysark**. They also have a large collection of old U.S. and foreign flags. Closed Sunday. ~ 10235 Main Street, Bellevue; 425-453-1265.

Five miles north of Bellevue is the downtown **Kirkland Square**, a minimall easily identified by its handsome, ten-foot-high clock. ~ 215 Main Street, Kirkland. Hunters of antiques appreciate the **Kirkland Antique Gallery**. The mall has nearly 100 dealers selling antiques and collectibles. ~ 151 3rd Street, Kirkland; 425-828-4993. If you're tired of shopping 'til you drop, kids (and some adults) rave about **Quarters**, where you can play video games. ~ 206 Main Street, Kirkland; 425-889-2555.

Excellent Northwest pottery, ceramics, jewelry and blown glass make **Lakeshore Gallery** a fine place to stop even if you have no intention of buying. The carved woodwork is especially well done. ~ 15 Lake Street, Kirkland; 425-827-0606. Around the corner, **The Tobacco Patch** has the East Side's best selection of cigars and pipe tobaccos, plus many tobacco-related gifts. ~ 125 Central Avenue, Kirkland; 425-739-4782.

Refurbished farmhouses, a barn and a feed store are stocked with handicrafts and artful, designer clothing at Issaquah's **Gilman Village**. Among the 40-plus shops clustered in these historic structures is **Northwest Gallery of Fine Woodworking** (425-462-5382), owned by 30 woodworkers and stocked with fine handcrafted furniture, custom cabinetry, boxes and screens. ~ 601 108th Avenue, Plaza 100, Bellevue; 206-625-0542. **Made in Washington** (425-392-4819) handles pottery, specialty foods and wine, dinnerware and wood carvings. ~ 317 Northwest Gilman Boulevard, Issaquah.

Satisfy your sweet tooth at **Boehm's Candies**, where hundreds of chocolates are hand-dipped every day. You can tour the factory (reservations are required; this is a popular spot) and watch the skilled workmanship that goes into making candies of this quality. ~ 255 Northeast Gilman Boulevard, Issaquah; 425-392-6652.

Daniel's Broiler has a jazz guitarist on Sunday and Monday, piano Tuesday through Saturday and a Sunday jazz showcase; music nightly. ~ Bellevue Place, 10500 Northeast 8th Avenue, 21st Floor, Bellevue; 425-462-4662.

NIGHTLIFE

Live sports events via satellite plus an extensive bar menu are on tap at **Chadfield's Sports Pub** located in the Hyatt Regency Bellevue. ~ 900 Bellevue Way Northeast, Bellevue; 425-462-1234.

New Jake O'Shaughnessey's is a grill and bar with four televisions in the lounge. ~ 401 Bellevue Square, Bellevue; 425-455-5559.

With a welcoming fireplace, the **West Coast Bellevue Hotel** invites you into their lounge. ~ 625 116th Avenue Northeast, Bellevue; 425-455-9444.

Good things come in small packages, and the **Village Theater** proves it. The local casts here will tackle anything, be it Broadway musicals, dramas or comedy. ~ 303 Front Street North, Issaquah; 425-392-2202.

Enjoy live jazz and blues on Friday and Saturday at **Forecasters Redhook Ale Brewery**. ~ 14300 Northeast 145th Avenue, Woodinville; 425-483-3232

BEACHES & PARKS

MARYMOOR COUNTY PARK 🚶 🚴 🐎 This roomy, 520-acre preserve at the north end of Lake Sammamish in Redmond is a delightful mix of archaeology and history, river and lake, meadows and marshes, plus an assortment of athletic fields. A one-mile footpath leads to a lakeside observation deck, and there's access to the eight-mile Sammamish River Trail. The circa-1904 Marymoor Mansion houses a historical museum, with a pioneer windmill nearby. Facilities include picnic areas, restrooms, play areas, baseball and soccer fields, tennis courts, a model-airplane airport, a bicycle velodrome with frequent races, a climbing wall and archaeological site. ~ Located on Westlake-Sammamish Parkway (Route 901) off Route 520 just south of Redmond city center; 206-296-2964, fax 206-296-2968.

KELSEY CREEK PARK 🚶 This unique park is a 130-acre farm with an old homestead and farm animals in the barnyard. There are hiking trails, jogging paths, wooded glens, a creek and an 1888 log cabin. ~ 13204 Southeast 8th Place, Bellevue; 425-452-6881, fax 425-452-2804.

SAINT EDWARDS STATE PARK 🚶 🚴 ⛵ 🎣 This former Catholic seminary still exudes the peace and quiet of a theological retreat across its 316 heavily wooded acres and 3000 feet of Lake Washington shoreline. Except for a handful of former seminary buildings, the park is mostly natural, laced by miles of informal trails. To reach the beach, take the wide path just west of the main seminary building. It winds a half mile down to the shore, where you can wander left or right. Side trails climb up the bluff for the return loop. There's also a beach (no lifeguard) and year-round indoor pool (fee). You'll also find picnic areas, restrooms, a tennis court, a horseshoe pit, soccer and baseball fields, basketball,

Where Are They Now?

Nearly 30,000 visitors each year make pilgrimages to Seattle to visit the gravesites of deceased superstars. The headstone of martial arts film hero **Bruce Lee** (1940–1973), engraved in English and Chinese, is found in Lake View Cemetery on Capitol Hill, just north of Volunteer Park. Alongside, another headstone marks the final resting place of his son, **Brandon Lee** (1965–1993), who died in a freak gunshot accident while filming *The Crow*. ~ 1554 15th Avenue Northeast, Seattle; 206-322-1582.

Lake View Cemetery is also the final resting place of several Seattle historical figures—among them founding fathers Henry L. Yesler (1830–1892) and David "Doc" Maynard (d.o.b. unknown–1873), and Chief Seattle's daughter Princess Angeline (1811–1896).

Legendary guitarist **Jimi Hendrix** (1942–1970), who reigned as Seattle's most famous rock musician until his fatal drug overdose a year after his landmark appearance at Woodstock, is interred at Greenwood Memorial Park in suburban Renton. Because of the large number of fans who still visit the grave, plans have been announced for a larger gazebo-style memorial to be erected on the site. ~ 350 Monroe Avenue Northeast, Renton; 425-255-1511.

Incidentally, Jimi Hendrix attended central Seattle's Garfield High School (class of '61), where Bruce Lee met his future wife Linda Emery (class of '63) while he was giving a guest lecture on Chinese philosophy at Garfield High. Jimi and Bruce also shared the same birthday, November 27.

Don't look for the grave of Seattle's other deceased rock superstar, **Kurt Cobain** (1967–1994), lead singer and guitarist of the grunge group Nirvana. His remains were cremated and the ashes scattered in the Wishleah River near the south boundary of Olympic National Park. The river provides the water supply for the city of Aberdeen, Washington.

volleyball, badminton and a gymnasium (fee). ~ Located on Lake Washington's eastern shore, between Kenmore and Kirkland on Juanita Drive Northeast; 425-823-2992.

JUANITA BEACH COUNTY PARK Juanita Beach County Park draws big crowds of area residents from late June through September, with good reason. Its sandy beach is one of the best on Lake Washington; the roped-off swimming area is vast; and the water warms up fairly early in the shallow bay. There's a concession building and adequate changing facilities, a picnic area and plenty of room for anglers to ply their craft without interfering with swimmers. ~ Access from Juanita Drive Northeast, five minutes north of downtown Kirkland. Across the bay, **Juanita Bay Park** is basically undeveloped, offering wildlife watchers a huge wetland area that attracts waterfowl, blackbirds and the occasional eagle or osprey. ~ Access is from Market Street North, five minutes north of downtown Kirkland. General information on King County Parks; 206-296-2966, fax 206-296-1437.

HIDDEN ▶

HIDDEN ▶

O.O. DENNY COUNTY PARK Also located on Lake Washington, just north of Kirkland, O.O. Denny offers miles of heavily wooded hiking trails and a sheltered picnic area on the lake. While there are no lifeguards, people do swim and fish. Restrooms are available. ~ From Route 405 take Northeast 116th Street Exit, head west on Juanita Drive Northeast, and turn left on Holmes Point Drive Northeast; 206-296-4129, fax 206-296-1437.

LUTHER BURBANK COUNTY PARK At the northeast corner of Mercer Island in Lake Washington, this little jewel presents some 3000 feet of shoreline to explore along with marshes, meadows and woods. The entire 77-acre site is encircled by a loop walk. You can fish from the pier for salmon, steelhead, trout and bass, and in summer swim at the beach. Among the facilities are picnic areas, restrooms, a play area, tennis courts and an amphitheater with summer concerts. ~ Entrance is at 84th Avenue Southeast and Southeast 24th Street, via the Island Crest Way exit from Route 90 on Mercer Island, east of Seattle; 206-296-4232, fax 206-296-4341.

GENE COULON BEACH PARK At the south tip of Lake Washington in Renton, this handsomely landscaped site is most notable for the loads of attractions within its 55 acres: one-and-a-half miles of lakeside path, the wildfowl-rich estuary of John's Creek and a "nature islet," a lagoon enclosed by the thousand-foot floating boardwalk of "Picnic Gallery," a seafood restaurant, a fast-food restaurant, and interesting architecture reminiscent of old-time amusement parks. A logboom-protected shoreline includes a fishing pier. There's a boat harbor with an eight-lane boat launch, and good fishing from the pier for trout and salmon. The bathing beach is protected by a concrete walk-about with summer lifeguard. There are picnic grounds and floats, restrooms, play areas, and volleyball and tennis courts; there's a restaurant on park grounds and others nearby. ~ Bordered by Lake Washington Boulevard North in Renton, north of Route 405 via Exit 5 and Park Avenue North; 425-235-2568, fax 425-430-7665.

Students at the Center for Wooden Boats can build a boat in a week.

LAKE SAMMAMISH STATE PARK 🏃 ⛵ 🚣 🚤 A popular, 431-acre park at the southern tip of Lake Sammamish near Issaquah, it offers plenty to do, including swimming (no lifeguard), boating, picnicking, hiking and birdwatching along 6858 feet of lake shore and around the mouth of Issaquah Creek. Look for eagles, hawks, great-blue heron, red-wing blackbirds, northern flickers, grebes, kingfishers, killdeer, buffleheads, widgeon and Canada geese. Picnic areas, restrooms, showers, soccer fields and a jogging trail are the facilities here. ~ Located at East Lake Sammamish Parkway Southeast and Southeast 56th Street, two miles north of Route 90 in Issaquah (15 miles east of Seattle) via Exit 17; 425-455-7010, fax 503-872-5289.

Salmon is the Sound's most famous fish, but scores of other species make sportfishing a signature attraction here. A combination of migratory and "resident" stocks offer angling for Chinook and Coho almost year-round. And when salmon fishing slows, you can try your luck for some 200 types of bottom-fish that also populate these waters—colorful fellows like the Red Irish Lord and copper rock fish, as well as greenling, halibut and many varieties of cod.

Outdoor Adventures

SPORT-FISHING

SEATTLE AREA Ballard Salmon Charters offers full-day salmon-fishing trips. Bait and tackle are included. ~ Shilshole Marina, Seattle; 206-789-6202.

Pier 54 Adventures offers year-round, half-day sportsfishing in Puget Sound for salmon and flounder. They also provide half-hour speedboat trips across Elliott Bay into the Sound. ~ Pier 54; 206-623-6364.

SEATTLE NORTH All Seasons Charter Service operates five boats for salmon or bottomfish. ~ Port of Edmonds; 425-743-9590.

KAYAKING & BOATING

If your nautical knowhow extends no further than a good row across a lake, then head for Lake Union, on the northern edge of Seattle's downtown center. On a bright summer day, the waters of Lake Union are dotted with kayaks, small wooden rowboats and sailboats.

SEATTLE AREA To rent a single, double or triple kayak, call **Northwest Outdoor Center** to reserve ahead. Kayaking on Lake

Union is very popular, and it's not unusual for all the center's 120 kayaks to be rented on a nice day. Classes and guided trips from one day to five days are available. ~ 2100 Westlake Avenue North; 206-281-9694; www.nwoc.com. At the **Center for Wooden Boats**, not only can you rent one of several different kinds of classic wooden rowboats, you can also learn a bit about their history. There are also several small sailboats for rent, but only experienced boaters can rent one. The center is a nonprofit, hands-on museum that also offers sailing instruction and other heritage maritime skills such as knot-tying, navigation and boat building. ~ 1010 Valley Street; 206-382-2628; cwb.org. To rent a "kicker boat" for do-it-yourself sportfishing, you'll have to leave the lake.

VASHON ISLAND The owners of **Vashon Kayak Guide Company** have both kayaks and canoes to rent, and will meet you at your desired starting point. They offer instruction as well, and in summer months lead kayak tours around the island's shores, a day-long odyssey that almost always includes heron, eagle, sea lion and seal sightings. The island's inner harbor is safe for novices; tricky tidal currents can make a foray out into the main channels more risky. ~ P.O. Box 908, Vashon, WA 98070; 206-463-9257; pugetsoundkayak.com.

WIND-SURFING

Serious windsurfers head south to Columbia Gorge—when they have the time for a four-hour drive. When they don't, **Lake Washington**, **Elliott Bay** and **Quartermaster Harbor** on Vashon Island are prime spots for windsurfing—there's almost always a breeze, often fairly stiff, and the air temperature is usually above 40°.

The water is another story: Puget Sound boarding requires a dry suit, and it's a good idea on Lake Washington as well in spring and fall. Prime put-ins are beach parks on the east side of Lake Washington, especially Houghton Beach Park in Kirkland, Luther Burbank Park on Mercer Island and Gene Coulon Beach Park in Renton. On Lake Sammamish, Lake Sammamish State Park at the south end of the lake, in Issaquah, is popular. On Elliott Bay, Alki Beach in West Seattle is best, although some boarders put in at Myrtle Edwards park in downtown Seattle.

The top rental and general information place in the Seattle area is **Urban Surf**, near the University of Washington on the shores of the Lake Washington Ship Canal. ~ 2100 North North Lake Way; 206-545-9463.

SWIMMING

Do people swim in Puget Sound? Sure—most of the time on a dare. The area's salt waters don't warm much past 50°, even in August. But a few sheltered bays get considerably warmer than that, and on a sunny summer day a dip can be stimulating. Any other place, any other time, requires caution, not to mention foolhardiness—hypothermia can arrive in less than two minutes if

Hey! The Water's Fine

Even if you're a diehard landlubber, do not fail to go sightseeing here by boat at least once. Simply put, if you leave Seattle without plying its surrounding waters your trip will be incomplete. So don't hesitate, dear traveler: Head to the downtown central waterfront and make some waves.

On a clear day you can see forever, or so it would seem aboard one of the **Washington State Ferries**. Headquartered at Colman Dock, the ferries make frequent departures to Bremerton and to Bainbridge Island, both across Puget Sound to the west. But getting there is much of the fun because from your watery perch you'll be treated to grand views of Mt. Rainier, Mt. Baker and the Olympics (the Mountains, not the Games, silly). Up closer you'll see pleasure boats and other craft, and you may even catch a glimpse of an orca (killer) whale. To Bremerton, you can ride the car-and-passenger ferry, the passenger-only boat or the fast-ferry for pedestrians. At Pier 50 next door, you can board a passenger-only ferry to Vashon Island. ~ Pier 52; 206-464-6400.

This is your captain speaking. That's just part of the show on **Argosy Cruises**, which offer at least three tours every day year-round. On the harbor spin you'll get grand mountain views and see boat traffic like you won't believe: freighters, tugboats, sailboats, ferries, you name it. The narrator spices up the trip. ~ Pier 55; 206-623-4252, 800-642-7816.

Argosy and **Gray Line Water Sightseeing** join forces for their "locks tour." The tour goes north to Shilshole Bay, eastward through the Hiram M. Chittenden Locks into the Lake Washington Ship Canal and then on to the south tip of Lake Union. You return to the waterfront by bus. Going through the locks is an experience in itself, plus you'll get to see zillions of other boats doing the same. And along the way you might even see salmon jumping. ~ Pier 57; 800-426-7505.

For something different, **Spirit of Puget Sound** presents half-hour "mini-cabaret" performances as the highlight of its cruises, all of which serve meals. Lunch, dinner, and moonlight cruises go throughout the week. Longer tours feature live music and dancing. ~ Pier 70; 206-443-1442.

A narrated harbor tour is included in the **Tillicum Tours-Blake Island** four-hour excursion to 55-acre Blake Island Marine State Park, which has tons of things to see and do. ~ Piers 55 and 56; 206-443-1244.

S.S. Virginia V is the last authentic operating steamboat of the legendary "Mosquito Fleet," the motley flotilla of steamboats that once carried foot passengers and cargo around Puget Sound before the coming of highways and autos. Today, the *Virginia V* is under renovation, but with the right funding she should sail soon. ~ 206-624-9119.

you're unprepared. Puget Sound's many freshwater lakes are another story; by midsummer they've usually warmed near 70° and attract hordes of bathers on sunny days.

Nude beaches? Try Hawaii.

FRESHWATER   The best swimming beaches on Lake Washington are at Juanita Beach County Park; Houghton Beach Park in Kirkland; Gene Coulon Park in Renton; and Seattle's Seward Park, Colman Park, Madrona Park, Madison Park and Matthews Beach Park. Lake Sammamish State Park is the place to go on Lake Sammamish in Issaquah; many smaller outlying lakes offer public beaches.

SALTWATER   There aren't any truly warm bays in the immediate Seattle area; hardy souls hit the saltchuck at Alki Beach in West Seattle when the sun burns bright in August.

Better swimming is found west and south, at Ostrich Bay in Bremerton; Quartermaster Harbor on Vashon; and Penrose Point State Park on the Key Peninsula west of Tacoma. It's not for wimps; even Puget Sound natives are prone to ask if you really did go in that water. But if you truly want to immerse yourself in a visit to Puget Sound, immerse yourself.

SCUBA DIVING   Puget Sound's hundreds of miles of shoreline, scores of public beaches, extraordinary marine life and numerous underwater parks offer considerable opportunities for diving. But the Sound's average temperature of around 55° means wetsuits are *de rigeur*, and full scuba gear is the frequent choice of divers. Of the many exciting dive spots in the area, one standout is **Brackett's Landing Underwater Park** in Edmonds. Numerous dive shops with equipment rentals and lessons are located around major population centers. With 12 locations between them, **Underwater Sports Inc.** (800-252-7177) and **Lighthouse Diving Centers** (800-777-3483)

A SIDE TRIP TO VICTORIA

The picturesque Canadian town of **Victoria** in British Columbia combines a rich British heritage with a relaxed lifestyle. Winsome, gracious and colorful, Victoria is full of history and natural beauty, offering museums and gardens, grand old hotels and quaint shops. Located west of the San Juan Islands and just across the Strait of Juan de Fuca from Washington's Olympic Peninsula, Victoria is just a pleasant ferry ride away from the Seattle area and makes for a scenic day trip or overnight excursion. Whichever you choose, consider capping off your visit with high tea at the landmark Empress Hotel. (For information on getting to Victoria, see the "Ferry" section at the end of the chapter.)

are convenient to most Seattle-area locations. They offer lessons and trips, and they rent and repair equipment.

SEATTLE SOUTH A full-service scuba shop, **Northwest Sports Divers Inc.** rents any equipment you might need. They also offer scuba certification classes. Closed Sunday. ~ 8030 Northeast Bothell Way, Kenmore; 425-487-0624.

SEATTLE NORTH **Underwater Sports Inc.** has shops in Seattle, Edmonds and Everett. ~ Seattle: 10545 Aurora Avenue North, Seattle; 206-362-3310, 800-252-7177. Edmonds: 264 Railroad Avenue; 425-771-6322. Everett: 205 East Casino Road; 425-355-3338.

Lighthouse Diving Centers offers outposts in Seattle and Lynnwood. ~ Seattle: 8215 Lake City Way Northeast; 206-524-1633. Lynnwood: 5421 196th Street Southwest; 425-771-2679.

SEATTLE EAST You'll find local branches of **Underwater Sports** in Bellevue and Kirkland. ~ Bellevue: 12003 Northeast 12th Street; 425-454-5168. Kirkland: 11743 124th Avenue Northeast; 425-821-7200.

In Bellevue, **Silent World** has classes, gear and rentals. There are night dives and beach dives on Sunday, as well as some one-day and two-day trips to the San Juans, Canada and tropical destinations. ~ 13600 Northeast 20th Street; 425-747-8842.

INLINE SKATING

It takes about an hour to skate around Seattle's **Green Lake** on the paved multi-use trail. You can rent inline skates at **Gregg's Greenlake Cycle.** ~ 7007 Woodlawn Avenue Northeast; 206-523-1822.

JOGGING

In a generally cool climate, with pastoral back roads on the outskirts of much of Seattle and Tacoma, and an extensive network of public trails and greenbelts, runners will find innumerable routes. Some of the better-known trails, such as Seattle's Burke-Gilman and Green Lake, are often quite crowded, especially on weekends and after work in the summer.

Seattle's Washington Park Arboretum is an exceptionally beautiful mid-city forest enclave, landscaped with hundreds of native and exotic shrubs and trees. Trails are numerous; a typical loop would comprise a 5K.

GOLF

Except when the occasional snowstorm closes them down, golf courses in the area are open year-round.

SEATTLE NORTH **Jackson Golf Club** is a public 18-hole course with a par 3. Though the course has a few hills, it isn't very challenging. ~ 1000 Northeast 135th Street, Seattle; 206-363-4747. Golf pro Freddy Couples grew up at the **Jefferson Park Golf Club**, which has 18 holes with an executive par 3. You can rent carts and clubs, and you can see the lake and the city at some points. ~ 4101 Beacon Avenue South, Seattle; 206-762-4513. **Kayak Point Golf Course**, about 30 miles north of Seattle, is hilly and overlooks the Olympic Mountains and Puget Sound. This public championship course with a double fairway is worth the drive. Amenities include an 18-hole putting course; shoes, clubs and carts for rent; and a restaurant in the same building. ~ 156th Street, Stanwood; 360-652-9676.

SEATTLE EAST **Bellevue Municipal Golf Course** is one of the most active courses in the state, probably because it's a good walking course with moderate hills. This public course has 18 holes and cart rentals. ~ 5500 140th Avenue Northeast; 425-452-7350.

TENNIS

Northwest precipitation practically turns tennis into an indoor sport. You'll have to call a few days in advance to reserve an indoor court at one of these public facilities.

SEATTLE SOUTH It helps to mention that you're an out-of-town visitor when you call—at least six days in advance—to reserve one of the ten hardtop indoor courts at **Seattle Tennis Center**. The center also has four public outdoor courts. Tennis pros are available for lessons by appointment. ~ 2000 Martin Luther King Jr. Way South; 206-684-4764.

SEATTLE EAST The City of Bellevue operates the public courts at **Robinswood Tennis Center**. There are four indoor and four lighted outdoor courts; call six days in advance (start dialing at 8:30 a.m.). Pros are available for lessons. Fee. ~ 2400 151st Place Southeast at Southeast 22nd Street; 425-452-7690.

RIDING STABLES

Take off on a guided ride to the top of a mountain east of Seattle.

SEATTLE EAST One of the best places for a ride is Bridle Trails State Park in Bellevue. Crisscrossed with 20 miles of riding trails the park is thickly forested with evergreens, firs and cedar. Used mainly by local riders, the park has no rental mounts. On a clear day, you can see more than 100 miles atop Tiger Mountain near Issaquah. **Tiger Mountain Outfitters** will get you there in a three-hour trail ride that will let you see Mt. Rainier 65 miles away in the distance and possibly black bear, deer and cougar within several yards. Call for reservations. ~ 24508 Southeast 133rd Street, Issaquah; 425-392-5090.

BIKING

It's no surprise to learn that Seattle has earned a nod from *Bicycling* magazine as one of the top bicycling cities in the country. Bicycle programs are administered by state, city and county transportation agencies, which has resulted in a network of bicycle lanes and trails throughout the region, many of them convenient for visitor recreational use.

Helpful information, including bicycle route maps, is available from several agencies. The Washington Department of Transportation operates the **Bicycle Hotline** to request a route map and informative brochure. ~ P.O. Box 47393, Olympia, WA 98504; 360-705-7277. **The Seattle Bicycling Guide Map** is available from the Seattle Transportation Department and can usually be found in bike stores and public libraries. ~ 600 4th Avenue, Room 708, Seattle, WA 98104; 206-684-7583. **King County** publishes a bicycling guide map; it's distributed free at bike shops countywide and at Metro Transit centers. Or call the King County Bike Hotline at 800-542-7876. The **Cascade Bicycle Club** serves as an all-purpose club, for riders of all skill levels. The club operates a hotline, which provides general information about bicycling in the area and club-sponsored weekend rides. ~ 206-522-2453.

> Seattle was built on seven hills, though only six remain: the seventh hill, Denny, was scraped off and dumped into Puget Sound.

DOWNTOWN SEATTLE In West Seattle, the **Alki Bike Route** (6 miles) offers miles of shoreline pedaling—half on separated bike paths—from Seacrest Park to Lincoln Park. Besides changing views of the city and Puget Sound, you should have great views of the Olympic Peninsula mountains.

OUTLYING AREAS The three-mile loop around **Green Lake** is the most leisurely and rich in recreational detours. Although the central city is fairly hilly, especially if you're biking in an east–west direction, there are trails within Seattle that run near the water and on lower and flatter terrain that are ideal for recreational bicyclists. The most famous, of course, is the multi-use **Burke-Gilman Trail**, popular with bikers, walkers and joggers. It's flat, paved and, following an old railroad right of way, it extends from Gas Works Park on Lake Union, through the university campus, past lovely neighborhoods next to Lake Washington and on to Kenmore. In Kenmore, it links up with the **Sammamish River Trail**, which winds through Woodinville (and its wineries) and on to suburban Redmond. It's a lovely city-to-farmlands tour.

SEATTLE NORTH Pedal past Puget Sound parks, beaches and the bustling Edmonds port, home of the largest charter fleet on the West Coast, on the three-mile **Edmonds Waterfront Trail** running between Edmonds Underwater Park and Deer Park Reserve. **Bike Rentals** For bike rentals, repairs, new bikes and accessories in Seattle, try **Gregg's Greenlake Cycle.** ~ 7007 Woodlawn Avenue Northeast; 206-523-1822; www.greggscycles.com. The **Bicycle Center of Seattle,** near the Burke-Gilman Trail, has mountain bikes, hybrids and tandems. ~ 4529 Sand Point Way Northeast; 206-523-8300. The place to buy and repair a bike on Alki

Beach is the **Alki Bike & Board Company**. ~ 2611 California Avenue Southwest, Seattle; 206-938-3322.

HIKING   Nearly every park mentioned in the "Beaches & Parks" sections of this chapter offers at least a few miles of hiking trail through forest or along a stream or beach. One great park is Discovery Park in Seattle. All distances listed are one way unless otherwise noted.

DOWNTOWN SEATTLE   For short strolls in downtown Seattle, try **Freeway Park** and the grounds of the adjoining Washington State Convention Center (.5 mile) and **Myrtle Edwards** and **Elliott Bay parks** (1.25 miles) at the north end of the downtown waterfront. Just across Elliott Bay, West Seattle offers about four miles of public shoreline to walk around Duwamish Head and Alki Point.

SEATTLE SOUTH   The trail along **Big Soos Creek** (4.5 miles), now protected in two parks, is an inviting ramble on a blacktop path next to one of the few wetland streams still in public ownership hereabouts. The trail winds from Kent-Kangley Road to Gary Grant Park. In Kent, south of Seattle, follow signs off Route 516 (Kent-Kangley Road) at 150th Avenue Southeast.

SEATTLE NORTH   For a longer walk, the **Burke-Gilman Trail** (12 miles) extends from Gas Works Park in Seattle to Logboom Park in Kenmore and on to Redmond.

The **Shell Creek Nature Trail** (.5 mile) in Edmonds' Yost Park at 96th Avenue West and Bowdoin Way, is an easy walk along a stream. Contact Edmonds Parks and Recreation for a guide to the area. ~ Edmonds Parks Department: 700 Main Street; 425-771-0227.

SEATTLE EAST   Three foothills peaks nicknamed the "Issaquah Alps" (King County's Cougar Mountain Regional Wildland Park, Squak Mountain State Park and Tiger Mountain State Forest) south of Issaquah (about 15 miles east of Seattle) include miles and miles of trail and road open to hikers year-round. **Cougar Mountain Regional Wildland Park** (206-296-4145) is the best bet for visitors with resident deer, porcupines, bobcats, coyotes, black bears and four square miles of untouched land with trails. Call for trail maps. Another good resource is the **Issaquah Alps Trails Club** (206-328-0480), which publishes several hiking guidebooks and offers excursions, group hikes and general hiking information. One representative hike is the **West Tiger 3, 2, 1 Trail** (8–10 miles), which meanders to an elevation of 3000 feet at the summit of West Tiger 3 for stunning aerial views. Leave Route 90 at the High Point exit (the first exit east of Issaquah) and you will see the small parking lot where the trailhead is located.

Seattle lies along Puget Sound east of the Olympic Peninsula in the state of Washington. **Route 5** enters Seattle
from Olympia and Tacoma to the south and from Ev-
erett from the north. **Route 90** from Eastern Washington goes near
Snoqualmie and through Bellevue on its way into Seattle. **Route
405** serves the Eastside suburban communities of Bellevue, Kirkland and Redmond. **Route 169** leads from Route 405 southeast
of Renton to Maple Valley, Black Diamond and Enumclaw.

Transportation

AIR

About 20 miles south of downtown Seattle is **Seattle-Tacoma International Airport**, also called Sea-Tac, which is served by Aeroflot Russia, Air B.C. and Canada Airlines, Alaska Airlines, Alaska
Commuter Service, America West Airlines, American Airlines, Asiana Airlines, British Airways, Canadian Regional Airlines, Continental Airlines, Delta Air Lines, EVA (Evergreen), Frontier Airlines,
Harbor Alaska Commuter Airlines, Hawaiian Airlines, Horizon
Air, Northwest Airlines, Reno Air, SAS, Southwest Airlines, Trans
World Airlines, United Airlines, USAir and several smaller charter airlines. For general information, call 206-431-4444. There's
a visitors information center on the baggage level of Sea-Tac
International Airport (206-433-5218).

FERRY

The **Washington State Ferry System** serves Seattle, Port Townsend, Tacoma, Southworth, Vashon Island, Bainbridge Island,
Bremerton, Kingston, Edmonds, Mukilteo, Clinton, the San Juan
Islands and Sidney, B.C. Most are car ferries. ~ 206-464-6400;
www.wsdot.wa.gov/ferries.
  The **Victoria Clipper** passenger catamaran service operates
daily trips (a two-and-a-half-hour trip) between Seattle and Victoria, B.C. ~ 206-448-5000.

BUS

Greyhound Bus Lines serves Seattle. The terminal is at 811 Stewart Street. ~ 800-231-2222. **Gray Line Airport Express** provides
inexpensive bus service from the airport to hotels and the downtown area. ~ 206-626-6088.

TRAIN

Rail service in and out of Seattle is provided by **Amtrak** on the
"Empire Builder," "Coast Starlight" and "Cascadia." Call for
more information on connections from around the country. ~
800-872-7245.

CAR RENTALS

Most major car-rental businesses have offices at Seattle-Tacoma
International Airport. Rental agencies include **Avis Rent A Car**
(800-331-1212), **Budget Rent A Car** (800-527-0700), **Dollar Rent
A Car** (800-800-4000), **Hertz Rent A Car** (800-654-3131) and
Thrifty Car Rental (800-367-2277). **XtraCar Discount Rentals**
(800-227-5397) offers low rates and shuttle service to the airport.

PUBLIC TRANSIT

Bus transportation provided by **Metro Transit** is free in downtown Seattle. Metro Transit provides service throughout the Seattle-King County area. ~ 206-553-3000.

Deemed transportation for the future, the **Monorail** was built for the 1962 World's Fair. It runs between downtown and the Seattle Center every ten minutes. ~ 206-441-6038.

Waterfront Streetcar trolleys run along the waterfront from Seattle's historic Pioneer Square to Pier 70. ~ 206-553-3000.

In the Kitsap Peninsula area, the **Poulsbo-Kitsap Transit** provides routed service in all of Kitsap County. ~ 360-373-2877.

The downtown hub for both the monorail and the bus system is at Westlake Center, on Pine Street between 4th and 5th avenues. The monorail arrives on an elevated platform above the street-level mall, while buses load in an underground terminal. The buses are uniquely designed so they can switch from diesel to electric power when they enter the subterranean transit tunnels.

TAXIS

In the greater Seattle area are **Checker Cab** (206-622-1234), **Farwest Taxi** (206-622-1717), **North End Taxi** (206-363-3333) and **Yellow Cab** (206-622-6500).

FIVE

Southern Puget Sound

First-time visitors to southern Puget Sound may find that it's the constantly changing geography that's the region's most memorable and striking feature. On a map, Southern Puget Sound looks like a fistful of bony fingers clawing at the earth. This maze of inlets, peninsulas and islands presents plentiful saltwater access and invites days of poking around.

What nature created here, partly by the grinding and gouging of massive lowland glaciers, is a complex mosaic. From the air, arriving visitors see a green-blue tapestry of meandering river valleys weaving between forested ridges, the rolling uplands dotted by lakes giving way to Cascade foothills and distant volcanoes, the intricate maze-way of Southern Puget Sound's island-studded inland sea.

From on high it seems almost pristine, but a closer look reveals a sobering overlay of manmade changes. Even as Seattle's downtown becomes "Manhattanized," the region is being "Los Angelesized" with the birth of a freeway commuter culture stretching from Olympia on the south to Everett on the north and beyond Issaquah on the east. Some commuters arrive by ferry from Bainbridge Island to the west. Farmlands and wetlands, forests and meadows, are giving way to often poorly planned, hastily built housing tracts, roads and shopping centers.

For the traveler, such rapid growth means more traffic and longer lines for the ferry; more-crowded campgrounds, parks and public beaches; busier bikeways and foot trails; more folks fishing and boating and clam-digging. Downtown parking can be hard to find and expensive. But don't despair. South of the heart of Seattle you'll still find a wealth of parks and wilderness, waterways and beaches. With an ample array of outdoor activities, southern Puget Sound serves as Seattle's back door to the wilderness.

To the southwest of Seattle, the Tacoma/Olympia region is rich in history, parks, waterfalls and cultural landmarks. Tacoma features numerous architectural gems; nearby villages like Gig Harbor are ideal for daytrippers. One of the nation's prettier capital cities (and here you may have thought Seattle was the capital of Washington!), Olympia is convenient to the wildlife refuges of southern Puget Sound, as well as to American Indian monuments and petroglyphs.

Venture west of Seattle across Puget Sound and you'll find some rare treasures such as a company town operating in the time-honored manner, a fascinating Indian cultural show, a marine-science center and inns that look like they were created for a James Herriott book. From the islands of Puget Sound west to Hood Canal, this is also a region rich in parks and natural areas. You'll also want to tour the Kitsap Peninsula, Bremerton's Naval Heritage and the parks of Southern Puget Sound.

▼▼▼▼▼▼▼▼▼▼▼▼▼▼▼

Tacoma and Olympia

Despite a lingering mill-town reputation, Tacoma, the city on Commencement Bay, has experienced a lively rejuvenation in recent years and offers visitors some first-rate attractions. Charles Wright, president of the Great Northern Railroad, chose it as the western terminus of his railroad, and he wanted more than a mill town at the end of his line. Some of the best architects of the day were commissioned to build hotels, theaters, schools and office buildings.

SIGHTS

Today, **Tacoma** is the state's "second city" with a population of 179,000. The city jealously protects its treasure trove of turn-of-the-20th-century architecture in a pair of historic districts overlooking the bay on both sides of Division Avenue. The 1893 **Old City Hall** at South 7th and Commerce streets was modeled after Renaissance Italian hill castles. The 1889 **Bostwick Hotel** at South 9th Street and Broadway is a classic triangular Victorian "flatiron."

The **Pantages Theater**, an exquisitely restored 1918 masterpiece of the vaudeville circuit designed by Marcus Priteca, is the centerpiece of Tacoma's thriving theater district, and one of the finest of its kind in the nation. The 1615-seat Pantages is home to symphony, opera, ballet and major national touring acts. (And it outstrips in sheer opulence, Tacomans like to point out, anything Seattle has to offer.) The Pantages is worth visiting simply to gawk at its glittering grandeur. It's joined in the Broadway Center for the Performing Arts by the **Rialto Theater**, another restored 1918 belle, and the **Theatre on the Square**, devoted to its resident drama company, Tacoma Actors Guild. ~ Broadway Center, 901 Broadway, Tacoma; tickets, 253-591-5894; tours and general information, 253-591-5890, fax 253-591-2013.

A mile away, history adds more depth to Tacoma's appeal at the **Union Station/Washington State History Museum** complex. The side-by-side buildings not only are aesthetically appealing—the restored copper-domed Union Station is now the federal courthouse, the history museum is a sweeping, arched modern counterpart—they also offer cultural wealth inside.

Union Station's 70-foot diameter rotunda dome rises 60 feet above ground level; the Beaux-Arts neoclassical–style building dates from 1911. The rotunda holds one of the world's finest exhibits of glass art made entirely by Tacoma native Dale Chihuly, the renowned founder of the Pilchuck School of blown-glass art. ~ 1717 Pacific Avenue, Tacoma; 253-572-9310.

The **Washington State History Museum** next door offers a comprehensive view of the state's human cultures, from the original inhabitants dependent on salmon to the logging, fishing and farming that first brought settlers to the Northwest. Interactive exhibits allow visitors to sit in the driver's seat of a covered wagon, take a stab at separating wheat from chaff and experience a coal

Southern Puget Sound

mine cave-in. Closed Monday. Admission. ~ 1911 Pacific Avenue, Tacoma; 253-272-3500, fax 253-272-9518; www.wshs.org.

Down the street a few blocks, the small but vigorous **Tacoma Art Museum** hosts international-class shows, such as an exhibit featuring Picasso's ceramics and works on paper. The permanent collection focuses on Northwest artists, with a special emphasis on glass art. Admission. ~ 1123 Pacific Avenue, Tacoma; 253-272-4258, fax 253-627-1898.

Without a doubt, Tacoma's prettiest garden spot is the **W. W. Seymour Botanical Conservatory**, a graceful Victorian domed conservatory constructed at the turn of the 20th century with over 12,000 panes of glass. Inside are exotic tropical plants, including birds of paradise, ornamental figs, cacti and bromeliads; seasonal displays of flowers; a collection of orchids; and a fish pond with waterfall. ~ 316 South G Street, Tacoma; phone/fax 253-591-5330; www.tacomaparks.com.

A treat for both kids and adults is **Point Defiance Park**, set on a sloping peninsula above the south Puget Sound shore. This 700-acre urban park has an outstanding zoo and aquarium with a Pacific Rim theme. You can watch the fish from above or through underwater viewing windows. The **zoo** (253-591-5337, fax 253-591-5448) has penguins, beluga whales, polar bears, an elephant barn and a farm where city children can pet goats and sheep. In Point Defiance, you can also see Camp 6 Logging Museum; Fort Nisqually, a reconstruction of the original 1850 Hudson's Bay Company post (closed Monday and Tuesday except in summer); a children's fantasy land (Never Never Land, open in the summer); rhododendron, rose, Japanese and native Northwest gardens; and numerous scenic overlooks. A good beach walk is at the base of the bluff edging the park, heading west from Owen Beach. Since the water is swift here, it's best to walk at low tide. The **Boathouse Marina** offers boat rentals and fishing (253-591-5325, fax 253-305-1085). ~ North 54th and Pearl streets, Tacoma; 253-305-1000; www.tacomaparks.com.

Halfway between Point Defiance and downtown, just off the Ruston Way waterfront, **Puget Gardens** is a little-known oasis in the city. Not only is this idyllic three-acre enclave rarely crowded, it is exceptionally well landscaped, with a walking path, footbridge and meandering creek. ~ On Alder Street, just off Ruston Way, Tacoma; 253-305-1000, fax 253-305-1098.

HIDDEN ►

A half hour east of Tacoma, in the **Puyallup Valley**, a series of river-bottom flower farms blaze with daffodil and tulip blooms. One of the largest growers is **Van Lierop Bulb Farm**, a family-operated farm since 1934. Van Lierop welcomes visitors to its shop and gardens during the height of the bloom season in March. ~ 13407 80th Street East, off Pioneer Avenue East, from Route 512, Puyallup; 253-848-7272, fax 253-848-9142.

Tacoma and Olympia

HIDDEN ▶

Steilacoom about five miles south of Tacoma is a quiet counterpoint to Gig Harbor's bustle. Founded by Yankee sea captains in the 1850s, it exudes a museum-like peacefulness and preserves a New England look among its fine collection of clapboard houses. Get a self-guiding brochure at **Steilacoom Historical Museum**. Closed Monday and the month of January. ~ 112 Main Street, Steilacoom; 253-584-4133.

At the 1895 **Bair Drugstore** you can order an old-fashioned float from the 1906 soda fountain. ~ On Lafayette Street near Wilkes Street, Steilacoom; 253-588-9668, fax 253-474-9823.

Fort Lewis, astride Route 5 south of Tacoma, is one of the most important army posts in the United States, having gained strength during the Pentagon consolidation. Nearby **McChord Air Force Base** has grown in stature as well. Both posts offer museums open to the public. The **McChord Air Museum** has historic aircraft, a flight simulator for visitor use, and other artifacts covering the base's history from World War II on. Closed Monday. ~ On the base near the main entrance, Route 5, Exit 125; 253-984-2485. The **Fort Lewis Military Museum** covers the history of the post from 1917 to the present. Open Wednesday through Sunday afternoons. ~ Building 4320, on post, right off Route 5, Exit 120; 253-967-7206.

At the southern tip of Puget Sound, **Olympia**'s state capitol dome rises boldly as you approach on Route 5, a tempting landmark for travelers and an easy detour from the busy freeway. But this community of some 39,000 offers visitors more to peruse than government buildings and monuments. Nevertheless, the capitol campus may be the best place to begin your explorations.

You can take a daily guided tour seven days a week through the marbled halls of the Romanesque **Legislative Building** and see other buildings on the grounds—**Temple of Justice, Executive Mansion** and **State Library**.

The nearby **State Capitol Museum** includes a fine collection of Northwest Coast Indian artifacts. Closed Monday. Admission. ~ 211 West 21st Avenue, Olympia; 360-753-2580, fax 360-586-8322; www.wshs.wa.gov.

Downtown, the handsomely restored **Old Capitol**, at 7th Avenue and Washington Street across from stately Sylvester Park, will catch your eye with its fanciful architecture. But most of downtown is a potpourri of disparate attractions—the **Washington Center for the Performing Arts** at 512 Washington Street Southeast, galleries, the **Capitol Theater** at 5th Avenue and Washington Street with its old films and local theater, and a bit of Bohemia along 4th Avenue West.

HIDDEN ▶

Percival Landing is an inviting, harborside park with observation tower, kiosks with historical displays, picnic tables, cafés and boardwalks next to acres of pleasure craft. ~ At the foot of State Avenue at Water Street, Olympia.

For a longer walk, head south on Water Street, cross 4th and 5th avenues, then turn west and follow the sidewalk next to the Deschutes Parkway (or get in your car and drive) around the park-dotted shores of manmade **Capitol Lake**, which is two and a half miles from the town of Tumwater.

Tumwater marks the true end of Puget Sound. Before Capitol Lake was created, the sound was navigable all the way to the Deschutes River. **Tumwater Historical Park**, at the meeting of river and lake, is rich in both history and recreation. One of two pioneer houses here was built in 1860 by Nathaniel Crosby III (Bing Crosby's grandfather). Down by the river you can fish, have a picnic, explore fitness and hiking trails, watch birds in reedy marshes and see more historical exhibits. Across the river, a handsome, six-story, brick brew house built in 1906 marks an early enterprise that lives on in a 1933 brewery a few hundred yards south. ~ 777 Simmons Avenue, Tumwater; 360-754-4160, fax 360-754-4166.

Follow Deschutes Parkway south to **Tumwater Falls Park** (not to be confused with Tumwater Historical Park), a small park that's a nice spot for a picnic lunch and whose main attraction is the namesake "falls," twisting and churning through a rocky defile. Feel the throb of water reverberating through streamside footpaths. Listen to its sound, which the Indians called "Tumtum." You'll find plenty of history in the headquarters exhibit, including an American Indian petroglyph and a monument recounting the travails of the first permanent settlement north of the Columbia River here in 1845. ~ Deschutes Way and C Street, Tumwater; phone/fax 360-943-2550.

Ten miles south of Olympia are **Mima Mounds**, an unusual group of several hundred hillocks spread across 450 acres. Scien-

BLACK DIAMOND—COAL AND BREAD

Black Diamond (about 35 miles southeast of Seattle on Route 169) is an old coal-mining town with the odds and ends of its mining, logging and railroading history on display at the **Black Diamond Historical Society Museum**. This intriguing museum is housed in an 1884 railroad depot. Open Thursday and weekends or by appointment. ~ Baker Street and Railroad Avenue; 360-886-1168. But the real reason most folks stop here—on their way to Mt. Rainier, the Green River Gorge or winter ski slopes—is the famous **Black Diamond Bakery**. At last count, the bakery and its wood-fired ovens produced some 30 varieties of bread. ~ 32805 Railroad Avenue.

tists think they could have been created by glacial deposits or, believe it or not, giant gophers. There is a self-guided interpretive trail offering a close look at this geologic oddity, as well as several miles of hiking trails. ~ Wadell Creek Road, Littlerock; 360-748-2383, fax 360-748-2387.

Howl with the wolves at **Wolf Haven International** southeast of Olympia. The 80-acre refuge shelters about 30 gray wolves. Guides give tours daily in summer and on weekends in other months. On summer weekends, visitors gather for singing, storytelling and joining in the wolves' howls. Closed Tuesday. Admission. ~ 3111 Offut Lake Road, Tenino; 360-264-4695, fax 360-264-4639.

LODGING

Many of Tacoma's historic residences have been transformed into small inns and B&Bs. The **Greater Tacoma Bed & Breakfast Reservations Service** can help arrange lodging. ~ 253-759-4088, 800-406-4088, fax 253-759-4025.

The Villa is a 1925 Italianate mansion also on the National Historic Register. Six sizable guest rooms have jacuzzis or soaking tubs, fireplaces and views. The verandas, patio with fountain, and landscaped gardens add to the Mediterranean allure. Guests will also enjoy a hot tub, exercise room and carriage house. ~ 705 North 5th Street, Tacoma; 253-572-1157, 888-572-1157, fax 253-572-1805. DELUXE TO ULTRA-DELUXE.

The **Sheraton Tacoma Hotel** is an elegant hotel next to the Tacoma Convention Center. The 319 rooms have a contemporary decor and most have views of Mt. Rainier or Commencement Bay. The concierge levels (24th and 25th floors) serve complimentary continental breakfast and late-afternoon hors d'oeuvres. ~ 1320 Broadway Plaza, Tacoma; 253-572-3200, 800-845-9466, fax 253-591-4105. DELUXE.

Chinaberry Hill, an 1889 Victorian bed and breakfast, offers three spacious romance suites with bay windows, double jacuz-

---

THE BEST BOAT WATCHING GIG—HARBOR, THAT IS

Gig Harbor across the Tacoma Narrows off Route 16 is a classic Puget Sound small town. The community that arose around the harbor was founded as a fishing village by Croatians and Austrians. Today you're more likely to see every sort of pleasure craft here; it's one of the best boat-watching locales on Puget Sound. The tight harbor entrance funnels boats single-file past dockside taverns and cafés where you can watch the nautical parade. Or, rent a boat from Rent-A-Boat & Charters and join the flotilla. ~ 8829 North Harborview Drive; 253-858-7341; www.ptinet.net/~rntaboat.

zis, private baths with showers and harbor views or a fireplace. The adjacent two-story carriage house, with its cabin atmosphere, is ideal for families featuring a queen-sized curved iron canopy bed, a double bed loft and a jacuzzi alcove. Appointed with period antiques and surrounded by gardens, the inn is an inviting retreat. ~ 302 Tacoma Avenue North, Tacoma; 253-272-1282, fax 253-272-1335; www.chinaberryhill.com. DELUXE TO ULTRA-DELUXE.

No Cabbages Bed and Breakfast is a comfortable, old-fashioned beach house built against a wooded hillside. It has two guest rooms, which have their own entrance and share a bath. They feature knotty-pine walls and great views of the deck terrace and harbor. A third, moderately priced room is open in the summer. The house is filled with eclectic art and interesting conversation. The innkeeper serves an outstanding breakfast. ~ 7712 Goodman Drive Northwest, Gig Harbor; 253-858-7797; e-mail trout@harbor. net. MODERATE.

The Harbinger Inn is a restored, 1910 mansion with period antiques and a manicured lawn and garden. The living room, a first-floor porch with wicker furniture and a second-floor veranda overlook the marina, capitol building and the Olympic Mountains. Four of the five well-furnished rooms also have views. All units have private baths. The owners lend bicycles, as this is a choice area for bicycling, and serve a continental breakfast. ~ 1136 East Bay Drive, Olympia; 360-754-0389, fax 360-754-7499. MODERATE.

High above Capitol Lake, on a grassy bluff with a view of the manmade lake and capitol dome, is the West Coast Olympia. Popular with business and government travelers, it has 177 commodious rooms with practical furnishings, a lounge, a restaurant overlooking the lawns and water, and an outdoor swimming pool. Waterside rooms have the best views and are the quietest. ~ 2300 Evergreen Park Drive, Olympia; 360-943-4000, fax 360-357-6604. MODERATE.

Eight blocks from the Capitol, the Ramada Governor House is the latest version of a vintage downtown hotel. Its 122 rooms —some with views of the lake, harbor and Capitol building—are spread over eight floors. The hotel has above-standard furnishings, though most rooms are small, and a seasonal pool, exercise room and sauna. A number of packages and discounts are available. ~ 621 South Capitol Way, Olympia; 360-352-7700, 800-228-2828, fax 360-943-9349. MODERATE TO ULTRA-DELUXE.

The Tyee Hotel, three miles south of Olympia, is just off Route 5, but traffic noise is muted by walls. The 145-room, two-story Tyee has some resort amenities: 17 acres of grounds, a pool, a spacious lobby with a fireplace. The restaurant serves three meals a day, and the pastel rooms are well-furnished and comfortable. ~ 500 Tyee Drive, Tumwater; 360-352-0511, 800-386-8933, fax 360-943-6448. MODERATE.

DINING

Do you enjoy good tempura? Then don't walk, run to **Fujiya** in downtown Tacoma. Masahiro Endo, owner and chef, is a great entertainer with his knife at the sushi bar. Chicken sukiyaki is delicious. Closed Sunday. ~ 1125 Court C, Tacoma; phone/fax 253-627-5319. MODERATE.

Sophistication and elegance describe the ambience at **Altezzo** in the Sheraton Tacoma Hotel. There are superb views of Commencement Bay and Mt. Rainier from this gourmet Italian restaurant, located several stories above the city. The menu changes daily; entrées include grilled pork loin chop stuffed with fontina cheese and artichoke hearts and cioppino, a hearty tomato-based stew of Dungeness crab, prawns, calamari, clams and other fresh seafood. Reservations recommended. Dinner only. Closed during summer holidays. ~ 1320 Broadway Plaza, Tacoma; 253-572-3200, fax 253-591-4105. MODERATE TO DELUXE.

Mandarin and Szechuan fare is the specialty at **Charlie Chan's**, a family-run establishment where pictures of the owner with such celebrities as Jeff Smith (TV's Frugal Gourmet and a fellow Tacoman) are proudly displayed. Especially good are the Mongolian beef, vegetable dishes and sizzling rice soup. ~ 1009 Bridgeway Southwest, Tacoma; 253-588-5555, fax 253-581-9591. BUDGET TO MODERATE.

One of those time-warp kind of restaurants that has had the same waitresses and clientele for decades, **Harbor Lights** is where locals go for certified Angus beef and chops, huge buckets of steamed clams, Dungeness crab, grilled salmon and other unpretentious seafood dishes. ~ 2761 Ruston Way, Tacoma; 253-752-8600, fax 253-752-4679. MODERATE TO DELUXE.

If you've a hankering for barbecued ribs, fried chicken or catfish, try **Southern Kitchen**. This is no antebellum mansion, just a plain, well-lighted café with good food. Just as good as the entrées are the greens, grits, yams, fried okra, biscuits, homemade strawberry lemonade and melt-in-your-mouth corncakes served up alongside. The cooks are Southern stock themselves, so you can count on this fare being authentic. Breakfast is served all day. ~ 1716 6th Avenue, Tacoma; 253-627-4282. BUDGET.

HIDDEN ► The storefront setting is equally unprepossessing, but ethnic food of an entirely different sort is the fare at **May's Vietnamese Restaurant**, where curries and sautés reflect the slightly European spin Vietnamese cuisine applies to Southeast Asian food. May's chicken curry, dark and rich, is divine. ~ 2514 Proctor Street North, Tacoma; 253-756-5092, fax 253-761-8547.

HIDDEN ► At the **Spar Tavern**, in Old Town (Tacoma's original settlement site, two miles north of downtown), pub food reaches unaccustomed heights. The Spar is famous for "chicken & jos," deep-fried chicken and potato pieces not recommended for health enhancement. You can also get a remarkably good Caesar salad, along with crab sandwiches in season. Breakfast served on weekends. ~ 2121 30th Street North, Tacoma; 253-627-8215, fax 253-627-0895. BUDGET.

One of the best views in Olympia is from **Falls Terrace**, through huge windows overlooking Tumwater Falls on the Deschutes River. A good way to start your meal is with some Olympia oysters. The menu features pasta dishes, an excellent bouillabaisse and an array of chicken and beef entrées. Desserts are more ice-cream theatrics than tasty morsels. Reservations recommended. ~ 106 South Deschutes Way, Olympia; 360-943-7830, fax 360-943-6899. MODERATE TO DELUXE.

Hidden across from the Farmers' Market is **Gardner's Seafood and Pasta**. It is no secret to locals, who flock to this small restaurant. While seafood is the specialty here, there are several pastas that are very good, too. Try the pasta primavera. The Dungeness crab casserole is rich with cream, chablis and several cheeses. Homemade ice cream and other desserts fill out the meal. Dinner only. Closed Sunday and Monday. ~ 111 West Thurston Street, Olympia; 360-786-8466. MODERATE TO DELUXE.

◄ HIDDEN

Before the Alaska Gold Rush thrust Seattle into prominence at the turn of the 20th century, Tacoma was Puget Sound's leading city.

Patrons don't usually go to a restaurant for the water, but at **The Spar** it truly is exceptional because it comes from the eatery's own artesian well. Once a blue-collar café, the restaurant features large photographs of loggers felling giant Douglas firs. On the menu are thick milkshakes, giant sandwiches, prime rib and Willapa Bay oysters. ~ 114 East 4th Avenue, Olympia; 360-3576444, fax 360-352-2969. BUDGET TO MODERATE.

Boaters, legislators, lobbyists, tourists and waterfront strollers congregate at the **Budd Bay Cafe** at Percival Landing. You can sit outside on the big deck and watch the boats come and go while you enjoy some of the specialties: fresh pasta and seafood, homemade soups, micro beers (including their own Budd Bay Ale), Northwest wines and desserts from the in-house bakery. An elaborate champagne brunch is served Sunday. ~ 525 North Columbia Street, Olympia; 360-357-6963, fax 360-786-8474. MODERATE.

The **Whale's Tail Dockside Deli and Espresso Bar** is a bright little café on the boardwalk at Olympia's Percival Landing. Fast and friendly service, tasty homemade soups and sandwiches, deep-dish quiche and a fine view of Budd Bay have made this spot a favorite. Try the chunky muffins, hand-dipped ice creams and espresso. ~ 501 North Columbia Street, Olympia; 360-956-1928, fax 360-956-0110. BUDGET.

In a neighborhood less frequented by tourists, **Portafino Restaurante** is a charming little restaurant in a turn-of the-20th-century home. Seven tables fill the former living and dining rooms, with more tables on the enclosed porch. Classical music plays softly in a subdued atmosphere. Fresh Northwest foods are served, often under mild sauces. Dinner only. Closed Monday. ~ 101 Division Street, Olympia; 360-352-2803, fax 360-943-8812. MODERATE.

In downtown Olympia, the **Urban Onion** serves sizable breakfasts, good sandwiches and hamburgers and a hearty lentil soup. Dinners include chicken, seafood and *gado gado*—a spicy Indonesian dish of sautéed vegetables in tahini and peanut sauce, along with Mexican entrées. They also offer several vegetarian specials. The restaurant is part of a complex of shops in the former Olympian Hotel. ~ 116 Legion Way, Olympia; 360-943-9242, fax 360-754-2378. MODERATE.

The Olympia area isn't the place you'd expect gourmet French-Northwest cuisine, but chef Jean-Pierre Simon exceeds expectations at **Jean-Pierre's Garden Room**. Located in a historic old home near the Olympia Brewery, Simon serves up luscious crêpes, pastas and fish entrées that meld French Provincial influences with local ingredients—such as Dungeness crab. Closed Sunday. ~ 316 Schmidt Place, Tumwater; 360-754-3702, fax 360-754-1352. MODERATE TO DELUXE.

SHOPPING   In the Proctor District in north Tacoma you can find Northwest foods, gifts and clothing at the **Pacific Northwest Shop**. ~ 2702 North Proctor Street, Tacoma; 253-752-2242. Fine Irish imports are in stock at **The Harp & Shamrock**. ~ 2704 North Proctor Street, Tacoma; 253-752-5012. The **Old House Mercantile** offers gifts for the kitchen and garden as well as a selection of teapots and jewelry. ~ 2717-A North Proctor Street, Tacoma; 253-759-8850. Educational toys are found at **Teaching Toys**. ~ 2624 North Proctor Street, Tacoma; 253-759-9853. The **Museum Store** at the Washington State History Museum features gifts, jewelry, games and books. ~ 1911 Pacific Avenue, Tacoma; 253-798-5880.

Near the Tacoma Dome downtown, **Freighthouse Square** is a thriving collection of shops and eateries in an old railroad warehouse. A dozen restaurants comprise an often-crowded food court; dozens of shops offer local crafts, jewelry, ethnic gifts, flowers and food items. ~ 25th and East D streets, Tacoma; 253-305-0678.

O'Leary's Bookstore carries used titles. ~ 3828 100th Street Southwest, Tacoma; 253-588-2503.

For sportswear and outdoor gear in Tacoma, try **Sportco**. Shop warehouse-style for hunting, fishing, camping gear and guns. ~ 4602 East 20th Street, Tacoma; 253-922-2222. Or visit **Duffle Bag Army Navy Inc.** for camping, hunting and workwear. ~ 8207 South Tacoma Way, Tacoma; 253-588-4433.

In Gig Harbor, **The Beach Basket** features, of course, baskets and other gifts. ~ 4102 Harborview Drive, Gig Harbor; 253-858-3008. Scandinavian utensils, books and gifts can be found at **Strictly Scandinavian**. ~ 7803 Pioneer Way, Gig Harbor; 253-851-

Author Picks

CHAPTER FAVORITES

I can't think of a better way to spend a clear, brisk morning than by window-shopping along the quaint streets of **Poulsbo**, a slice of Scandinavia in the Pacific Northwest. *page 136*

Chocolate left on my pillow is but one of the reasons I have sweet dreams when I stay at **Chinaberry Hill**, a luxurious bed and breakfast with lovely gardens and bay vistas. *page 124*

A great view always seems to enhance my meals, which is why I choose to savor **Madrona Waterfront Cafe**'s Northwest seafood stew on the deck overlooking the water. *page 134*

I like to unwind by clamming the shores of **Kitsap Memorial State Park**, which is also an ideal choice for hiking, fishing and family camping. *page 140*

5959. **Kelly's Toys & Gifts** features stuffed animals and games. ~ 7806 Pioneer Way, Gig Harbor; 253-851-8697. **Mostly Books** stocks books (you're kidding), bookmarks and postcards. ~ 3126 Harborview Drive, Gig Harbor; 253-851-3219.

Downtown Puyallup has several fine antique stores within walking distance of each other on Stuart Street and Meridien Way. Check out **Antique City**'s collection of '50s cowboy toys, dolls, furniture, books and cookie jars. ~ 105 South Meridien Way, Puyallup; 253-840-4324.

In Olympia, contemporary women's clothing and accessories are found at **Juicy Fruits**. ~ 113 West 5th Avenue; 360-943-0572. **Olympic Outfitters** is housed in a restored, brick-and-metal building and is stocked with everything from backpacking to cross-country ski gear. ~ 407 East 4th Avenue; 360-943-1114.

NIGHTLIFE

Pete's BBQ Rib and Steak House, or "Barbecue Pete's" as locals know it, has darts, pull-tabs, pool and a dancefloor. ~ 1314 East 72nd Street, Tacoma; 253-535-1000.

In the Lakewood area try **Happy Days Diner and Time Tunnel Lounge**, where deejays spin Top-40. Cover. ~ 11521 Bridgeport Way Southwest, Tacoma; 253-582-1531.

Drake's Downtown Café & Cabaret offers karaoke, happy-hour specials and deejay dancing on weekends. Cover. ~ 734 Pacific Avenue, Tacoma; 253-572-4144. **Katie Downs Tavern** is an adults-only pub overlooking Commencement Bay with a menu featuring local microbrews, seafood and pizza. ~ 3211 Ruston Way, Tacoma; 253-756-0771. Boasting one of the largest selections of draught beer in the state is the **Ale House Pub**. ~ 2122 Mildred Street West, Tacoma; 253-565-9367.

The **Tacoma Little Theatre** is a community theater producing five plays a year. ~ 210 North I Street, Tacoma; 253-272-2281.

Christie's Lounge features live bands playing Top-40 music Thursday through Saturday. Cover on weekends. ~ Best Western Executive Inn, 5700 Pacific Highway East, Fife; 253-922-0080.

The Tides Tavern in Gig Harbor features live bands Friday and Saturday night playing '50s and '60s rock and some rhythm-and-blues. Cover for live shows. ~ 2925 Harborview Drive, Gig Harbor; 253-858-3982.

BEACHES & PARKS

Green River Gorge is less than an hour from downtown Seattle but is worlds away from the big city. The heart of the gorge covers only some six miles on the map but is so twisted into oxbows that it takes kayakers 14 river miles to paddle through it. Just 300 feet deep, the steep-walled gorge nevertheless slices through solid rock (shale and sandstone) to reveal coal seams and fossil imprints and inspire a fine sense of remoteness. State and county parks flank the gorge.

The **Green River Gorge Conservation Area** includes three state parks. Here we pick the two developed parks at the entrance and exit of the gorge and one nearby state park on a lake. ~ 253-931-3930, fax 253-931-6379.

FLAMING GEYSER STATE PARK 🏃 🚲 🛶 ⚓ Once a resort, this 667-acre park downstream from the exit of Green River Gorge offers four miles of hiking trails and nearly five miles of riverbank. Originally, the flaming geyser area was a test site for coal samples, but miners found natural gas instead, which, when lit, produced a 20-foot flame. The "flaming geyser" is only eight inches high now, and can be seen off one of the trails. Pick up a trail map and brochure at the main office. Fish for rainbow trout and steelhead in season (check the posted regulations). There are picnic areas, restrooms, play areas, volleyball courts, a horseback riding area (but no stables) and horseshoe pits. ~ Located on Green Valley Road three miles west of Route 169, south of Black Diamond; 253-931-3930, fax 253-931-6379.

KANASKAT-PALMER STATE PARK 🏃 🚲 🛶 ⚓ Lovely walking on riverside paths, especially in summer, is the hallmark of this 320-acre park upstream from the entrance to Green River Gorge. During fishing season, try for steelhead and trout (check posted regulations). Picnic areas, restrooms, showers, volleyball courts and horseshoe pits are the facilities here. ~ Located on Cumberland-Kanaskat Road off Southeast 308th Street, 11 miles north of Enumclaw and Route 410; 360-886-0148, fax 360-886-1715.

▲ There are 31 developed sites and 19 with partial hookups; $10 to $16 per night.

NOLTE STATE PARK 🚶 🚴 🏊 ⛵ 🎣 ⛴ Surrounding Deep Lake, 117-acre Nolte Park is famous for its huge Douglas firs, cedars and cottonwoods. A one-and-a-quarter-mile path circles the lake taking you around nearly 7200 feet of shoreline and past the big trees; a separate nature trail interprets the forest. You can swim at the lake (no lifeguards); motorboats are prohibited. The lake is open for fishing year round, offering trout, bass, crappie, catfish and silvers. There's a minimal picnic area. Closed October to mid-April. ~ Located on Veazie-Cumberland Road just south of Southeast 352nd Street, six miles north of Enumclaw and Route 410; 360-825-4646, fax 360-802-9960.

WEST HYLEBOS WETLANDS STATE PARK 🚶 A rare chunk of   ◄ HIDDEN
urban wetland tucked between industrialization and subdivisions, the 68-acre park offers examples of all sorts of wetland formations along a one-mile boardwalk trail—springs, streams, marshes, lakes, floating bogs and sinks. You'll also see remnants of ancient forest, plentiful waterfowl, more than a hundred species of birds and many mammals. Facilities are limited to portable toilets. ~ Located on South 348th Street at 4th Avenue South, just west of Route 99 and Exit 142.

DASH POINT STATE PARK 🚶 🚴 🏊 🎣 🚣 ⛴ Nearly 500 acres of forested wildland with 3300 feet of saltwater shoreline preserve a bit of solitude just barely outside the Tacoma city limits. Seven-and-a-half miles of trail ramble through mixed forest of second-growth fir, maple and alder. The park's beach is one of the few places on Puget Sound where you'll find enjoyable saltwater swimming—shallow waters in tide flats are warmed by the summer sun. Tides retreat to expose a beachfront nearly a half-mile deep. There's fishing from the pier at Brown's Point Park south of Dash Point State Park, and swimming in tide flat shallows (no lifeguard). Facilities include picnic areas, restrooms and showers. ~ Located just northeast of Tacoma on Southwest Dash Point (Route 509); 253-661-4955, fax 253-661-4995.

◆◆◆

LET'S MAKE A DEAL

Midwestern timber baron George Weyerhaeuser arrived in Tacoma in September 1900 ready to do a deal. He wound up buying 900,000 acres of wilderness timberland for $1 million. Not only was that the start of the Northwest's giant timber companies, it was the largest single check ever written to that point.

▲ There are 100 developed sites ($10 per night) and 38 sites with hookups ($15 per night); 800-452-5687.

POINT DEFIANCE PARK 🚶 🚴 🏕 ⚓ ⛵ 🛥 🚣 Jutting dramatically into Puget Sound, this 700-acre treasure is hailed by some as the finest saltwater park in the state, by others as the best city park in the Northwest. Here are primeval forests, some 50 miles of hiking trails, over three miles of public shoreline and enough other attractions to match almost any visitor's interests. Five Mile Drive loops around the park perimeter with access to trails, forest, beach, views, attractions and grand overlooks of Puget Sound. The park is also known for its zoo and aquarium, particularly the shark tank (fee). Popular with boaters, there's a fully equipped marina with boat rentals, a boathouse (253-591-5325) and a restaurant. You can fish from the pier or in a rented boat. You'll find picnic areas, restrooms, play areas, tennis courts and a snack bar at the boathouse. ~ The entrance is on North 54th and Pearl streets; 253-305-1000, fax 253-305-1098 (Attn. Susan).

The Nisqually National Wildlife Refuge is an important stop for migratory shorebirds and waterbirds on the Pacific Flyway.

KOPACHUCK STATE PARK 🚶 🚴 🚤 🎣 🎿 ⚓ ⛵ 🛥 🚣 Spectacular views across Carr Inlet toward the Olympic Mountains from a half-mile of shoreline gives Kopachuck much to boast about. Many car-top boaters launch from the beach near the park to fish for bottomfish and salmon or paddle out to Cutts Island Marine State Park a half-mile away. No lifeguard is on duty. There are picnic areas, restrooms and showers. ~ Located on Kopachuck Drive Northwest at Northwest 56th Street about seven miles west of Gig Harbor and Route 16; 253-265-3606, fax 360-644-8112.

▲ There are 41 sites for tents and RVs ($11 per night); no hookups are available. Closed October through April.

NISQUALLY NATIONAL WILDLIFE REFUGE 🚶 ⚓ 🚣 This 3000-acre refuge's ecosystem is a diverse mix of conifer forest, deciduous woodlands, marshlands, grasslands and mud flats and the meandering Nisqually River (born in Mt. Rainier National Park). Here, the river mixes its fresh waters with the salt chuck of Puget Sound. The refuge is home to mink, otter, coyote and some 50 other species of mammals, over 200 kinds of birds and 125 species of fish. Trails thread the refuge; longest is the five-and-a-half-mile dike-top loop that circles a pioneer homestead long since abandoned. Fishing yields salmon, steelhead and cutthroat. Facilities include an education center and restrooms. Fee, $3 per family. ~ Located about 25 miles south of downtown Tacoma via Exit 114 from Route 5; 360-753-9467, fax 360-534-9302.

TOLMIE STATE PARK 🚶 🚤 🎣 🎿 ⚓ ⛵ 🚣 A salt marsh with interpretive signs separates 1800 feet of tide flats from forested uplands overlooking Nisqually Reach. The sandy beach is fine for wading or swimming; at low tide you may find clams. A two-and-a-half-mile wheelchair-accessible perimeter hiking trail loops through the park's 106 acres. An artificial reef and three sunken barges 500 yards offshore and almost-nonexistent current make the underwater park here popular for divers. Fishing yields salmon and cod. You'll find picnic areas, restrooms and showers. ~ Located on Hill Road Northeast, northeast of Olympia via Exit 111 from Route 5; phone/fax 360-456-6464.

MILLERSYLVANIA STATE PARK
Some 840 acres of primeval conifer forest and miles of foot trail are this park's big appeals. But visitors also come to enjoy its 3300 feet of shoreline along Deep Lake, where you can swim, launch a small boat (no wake) or fish for trout, bass, perch and crappie. Facilities include picnic areas and restrooms. ~ The park is located at Exit 95 just east of Route 5, ten miles south of Olympia; 360-753-1519, fax 360-664-2180.

▲ There are 125 developed sites ($11 per night) and 40 sites with hookups ($16 per night). No reservations necessary October through May (800-452-5687).

Bainbridge Island

To the north, Bainbridge Island offers a much more attractive destination for most travelers, and you can see it on foot. The picturesque town is located on an island of the same name, just a 35-minute ferry ride from Colman Dock (pick up a self-guiding brochure with map, *A Downtown Guide to Bainbridge Island*, before boarding).

SIGHTS

To see more than obvious attractions on **Bainbridge Island,** head for the mile-long waterfront footpath called **Walkabout** to the left of the ferry landing. Follow it along the shoreline, past shipyards and hauled-out sailboats under repair, to **Eagle Harbor Waterfront Park** and its fishing pier and low-tide beach. Carry on to a ship chandler and pair of marinas. Return as you came or make it a loop trip by walking up to **Winslow Way,** where you can stop for espresso or shop. If you tire of boutiques, step into **Winslow Hardware,** where the local folk come to chat and buy essential tools.

Bainbridge Island Vineyards and Winery is the only winery in the Seattle area that grows its grapes on-site. There is a tasting room, gardens, a wine museum of antiques and a picnic area on this family farm estate winery. The Ferryboat White label is popular with visitors. Open afternoons Wednesday through Sunday; open only on weekends in January. ~ 682 Route 305, Bainbridge Island; 206-842-9463.

If you enjoy gardens, don't miss a tour of the famous **Bloedel Reserve.** Once a private estate, the reserve has 150 acres of forest, meadows, ponds and a series of beautifully landscaped gardens. Reservations are required for a tour. Closed Monday and Tuesday. Admission. ~ 7571 Northeast Dolphin Drive, Bainbridge Island; 206-842-7631, fax 206-842-8970; www.bloedelreserve.org.

LODGING

On Bainbridge Island, **The Beach Cottage Hideaway** is built over the water and has a kitchen (with breakfast ingredients in the refrigerator), a private deck, a fireplace and views of Eagle Harbor and the Olympic Mountains. It accommodates up to four people. Continental breakfast included. ~ 5831 Ward Avenue Northeast, Bainbridge Island; 206-842-6081. DELUXE.

Serenity and comfort in the countryside characterize **Bombay House**, a 1907 Victorian set on a hilltop. The five-room bed and breakfast has a bright, cheery atmosphere. The rooms, which vary in size and decor, view the sea or the lavish flower and herb gardens. ~ 8490 Northeast Beck Road, Bainbridge Island; 206-842-3926, 800-598-3926. MODERATE TO DELUXE.

DINING

Specializing in mesquite-grilled steaks and seafood, the **Island Grill** provides casual fine dining amid a dark green and burgundy color scheme with hardwood floors. Dishes include fresh Northwest seafood, prime steaks, pastas and salads. Weekend brunch. ~ 321 High School Road Northeast, Bainbridge Island; 206-842-9037. MODERATE TO DELUXE.

In a large Tudor house nestled in the trees is the **Bistro Pleasant Beach**. The white-linen tablecloths and low lighting bespeak a comfortable island elegance. The chef specializes in Northwest seafood but includes a couple of succulent chicken dishes, pastas and aged beef entrées. The leg of lamb, served with roasted garlic, fresh herbs and shallot–rose cabernet sauce, comes recommended. Made-to-order pizzas are baked in the wood-fired oven. ~ 241 Winslow Way, Bainbridge Island; 206-842-4347, fax 206-842-6997. MODERATE.

The town that used to be called Winslow is now known just as Bainbridge Island.

Exotic flavors and innovative sauces are what you'll find at the **Four Swallows**, an upscale Italian restaurant located in a spacious 1880s farmhouse. The kitchen staff, utilizing fresh Northwest ingredients, whips up gourmet, thin-crust pizzas and zesty pastas. The entrées show the chef's creativity, and include grilled veal chops with porcini-mushroom sauce and *brodetto*, a fresh fish-and-shellfish stew in a rustic saffron-tomato-fennel broth. Dinner only. Closed Sunday and Monday. ~ 481 Madison Avenue, Bainbridge Island; 206-842-3397; e-mail gkf424@aol.com. MODERATE TO DELUXE.

A pleasant spot to relax with a beer and a sandwich or fish and chips is the deck at the **Madrona Waterfront Cafe**. The view from the deck above the water is always a delight, and it's only about five blocks from the ferry dock. The food, which includes salmon sandwiches, Northwest seafood stew and gorgonzola chicken fet-tuccine, is reasonably priced, but high for what you get—stick with something simple and enjoy the view. ~ 403 Madison Avenue South, Bainbridge Island; 206-842-8339. MODERATE.

The cozy **Pegasus** is a traditional coffeehouse with lots of reading material, conversation, freshly baked pastries and assorted coffees. No dinner. ~ 131 Parfitt Way, Bainbridge Island; 206-842-6725. BUDGET.

Walk into the **Streamliner Diner** and it's like stepping back into a midwestern diner. There are eight tables, a small bar and an open kitchen that serves up breakfast burritos, fried egg sandwiches, scrumptious omelettes and buttermilk waffles. Lunches include soups, salads and quiches. Breakfast and lunch only. ~ 397 Winslow Way, Bainbridge Island; 206-842-8595. budget.

FAY BAINBRIDGE STATE PARK A small park (17 acres), it nevertheless curls itself around a long sandspit to present some 1400 feet of shoreline. The only campground on Bainbridge Island is here. Facilities include picnic areas, restrooms, showers, a play area, horseshoe pits and volleyball courts. ~ At Sunrise Drive Northeast and Lafayette Road about six miles north of the town of Bainbridge Island at the island's northeast tip; 206-842-3931, fax 360-753-1594.

▲ There are 25 developed sites with partial hookups ($11 per night) and ten walk-in sites ($8 per night). Closed mid-October to mid-April.

FORT WARD STATE PARK Located at the south end of Bainbridge Island, this park offers 137 acres of paths, forest and picnic sites, as well as a mile-long beach, complete with salmon and lingcod fishing for day-use visitors. Locked service road is accessible by walking. ~ 206-842-4041, fax 360-385-7248.

BEACHES & PARKS

Kitsap Peninsula

Only an hour from the heart of Seattle, the Kitsap Peninsula is framed on the east side by Puget Sound and the west by Hood Canal. Historic company towns, naval museums and remote parks make this area a fine retreat from the city. In June and July, Kitsap and Olympic Peninsula visitors should watch the roadsides for the delicate pink blossoms of native rhododendron bushes, which thrive in the understory of the Douglas fir forests.

An interesting loop trip west of Seattle begins in the Navy town of **Bremerton**. You can explore some of the region's history, as well as the remote reaches of southern Puget Sound.

SIGHTS

If you take the ferry or drive to Bremerton, you'll pass by the **Puget Sound Naval Shipyard.** The best way to get here is the Washington State Ferry (cars and walk-ons; one hour) or state footferry (50 minutes) or the passenger-only fast ferry (35 minutes) from Seattle's Colman Dock (Pier 52) through Rich Passage to Bremerton. Although the shipyard is not open for public tours, it's an amazing sight even from a distance. ~ Burwell Street and Pacific Avenue, near the ferry dock, Bremerton; 360-476-7111, fax 360-476-0542.

Bremerton Naval Museum, a half-block north of the ferry dock, looks back to the days of Jack Tar and square-riggers and includes a wood cannon from 1377. ~ 130 Washington Avenue, Bremerton; 360-479-7447, fax 360-377-4186.

Docked along the Bremerton waterfront by the Navy shipyard is the **USS Turner Joy,** a former Navy destroyer where the bridge, engine room and berth areas can be explored on self-guided tours. ~ 360-792-2457, fax 360-377-1020.

In the small town of Keyport, located off Route 308 between Poulsbo and Silverdale, you'll find the **Naval Undersea Museum.** Historical exhibits here focus on the Navy's undersea activities from the Revolutionary War to the present. Diving and defense displays explore such subjects as nautical archaeology and the history of the submarine. There's also an interactive installation on the ocean environment. ~ No. 1 Garnett Way, Keyport; 360-396-4148; www.num.kpt.nuwc.navy.mill.

From Bremerton, Route 3 runs up the eastern side of the Kitsap Peninsula. Turn down Route 305 past Liberty Bay and you'll come to the charming town of **Poulsbo.** "Velkommen til Poulsbo" is an oft-repeated phrase in "Washington's Little Norway." There are some wonderful samples of historic architecture on a **walking tour** of town; the **Greater Poulsbo Chamber of Commerce** can provide a guide map. ~ 19131 8th Avenue Northeast, Poulsbo; 360-779-4848, fax 360-799-3115; www.poulsbo.net/gpcc.

At the **Marine Science Center,** you can learn about the various forms of marine life that inhabit the waters of Southern Puget Sound; they even have touch tanks of friendly sea creatures. Admission. ~ 18743 Front Street Northeast, Poulsbo; 360-779-5549, fax 360-779-8960.

HIDDEN ► A good place to learn about the region's American Indian heritage is the town of **Suquamish.** Chief Seattle and the allied tribes he represented are showcased at the **Suquamish Museum.** There's an outstanding collection of photographs and relics, along with mock-ups of a typical American Indian dwelling and the interior of a longhouse. Two award-winning video presentations are shown in a small theater. Admission. ~ 15838 Sandy Hook Road off Route 305, Suquamish; 360-598-3311, fax 360-598-6295; www. suquamish.nshus/museum.

Chief Seattle's Grave, set under a canopy of dugout canoes in a hillside graveyard overlooking Seattle (his namesake), is just a few miles down Suquamish Way. Follow the road signs.

One of the West's last company towns, **Port Gamble** is a favored visitor stop. Situated on a bluff at the intersection of Admiralty Inlet and Gamble Bay, this century-old community was once owned by the Pope and Talbot lumber firm.

◀ HIDDEN

The oldest running lumber mill in the U.S. (operating since 1853) was closed in 1995. Although all the sawmill workers were

Kitsap Peninsula

0 _____ 10 miles
0 _____ 10 kilometers

N

Whidbey Island

Olympic National Park

Olympic National Forest

Dosewallips River

Dabob Bay

Quilcene

Brinnon

Hood Canal

Holly

Seabeck **I**

Dewatto

Tahuya

Union **J** 106

300

Belfair **A**

Shelton

Lakebay **E**

Hartstine Island

Longbranch **H**

KITSAP PENINSULA

LONGBRANCH PENINSULA

19

104

101

Buck Lake County Park

Hansville

Port Gamble **F**

104

3

Kingston

307

Poulsbo

305

Suquamish **B**

308

Keyport

Silverdale

3

Bremerton

303

Port Orchard

160

Southworth

Bainbridge Island

Illahee **D**

Fort Ward **C**

Manchester **G**

16

302

163

16

Gig Harbor

Vashon Island

Lynnwood   99

Edmonds   104

5

Seattle

520

5

90

99

5

Puget

Hood

Sound

Ferry

Ferry

Ferry

STATE PARKS
- **A** Belfair State Park
- **B** Fay Bainbridge State Park
- **C** Fort Ward State Park
- **D** Illahee State Park
- **E** Jarrell Cove State Park
- **F** Kitsap Memorial State Park
- **G** Manchester State Park
- **H** Penrose Point State Park
- **I** Scenic Beach State Park
- **J** Twanoh State Park

laid off, Pope and Talbot announced that they will keep the town running. The town had long been home to about 150 sawmill workers and their families, who rented homes by the company. Picturesque frame houses, towering elms and a church with Gothic windows and a needle spire give the community a New England look. Don't miss the mock-ups of Captain Talbot's cabin and A. J. Pope's office at the **Port Gamble Historic Museum**. Admission. ~ Route 3, Port Gamble; 360-297-8074, fax 360-297-7455.

Also worth seeing is the **Sea and Shore Museum** on the second floor of the quaint, 1853 **Port Gamble Country Store**. Other historic homes and buildings are occupied by former Pope and Talbot employees but can be seen from the outside; a walking-tour guide can be obtained at the Country Store. ~ Rainier Avenue, Port Gamble; phone/fax 360-297-2426.

HIDDEN ► South of Bremerton is the **Longbranch Peninsula**, a showcase of Southern Puget Sound's outdoor treasures. Quiet coves and lonely forests, dairy farms, funky fishing villages with quiet cafés, shellfish beaches and oyster farmers, a salmon hatchery, fishing piers and wharves all await leisurely exploration. Take Route 16 to Route 302, proceeding west until you reach Key Center. The Key Peninsula Highway, running south from this community, is the main road bringing you to most attractions.

> Looking like a lane in faraway Scandinavia, the main street of Poulsbo is lined with wonderful galleries and boutiques.

To visit the hamlet of **Lakebay** on Mayo Cove, turn east from Peninsula Highway three and a half miles south of Home (the town, not your Home Sweet) onto Cornwall Road and follow it to Delano Road. On the south side of the cove is **Penrose Point State Park** with 152 acres of forest, more than two miles of beaches, hiking trails, fishing, picnicking and camping. ~ 321 158th Avenue K.P.S., Lakebay; 253-884-2514, fax 360-753-1594.

At the end of the highway is another bayside village, **Longbranch**, on the shores of Filucy Bay, one of the prettiest anchorages in these waters.

HIDDEN ► **Harstine Island** (northeast of Shelton via Route 3 and Pickering Road) is connected to the mainland by a bridge, providing auto access to a quintessential Southern Puget Sound island experience.

Many of the island's public beaches are poorly indicated, but **Jarrell Cove State Park** and a marina on the other side of the cove are easily found at the island's north tip. You'll see plenty of boats from both sides of the cove, and at the park you can stroll docks, fish for perch, walk bits of beach or explore forest trails. Main roads loop the island's north end, or head for the far southern tip at Brisco Point near Peale Passage and Squaxin Island. ~ Foot of Wingert Road, off North Island Drive; 360-426-9226.

HIDDEN ► The eastern shore of **Hood Canal** is located a mere mile or two from the western side of the channel, but in character it's worlds apart. Beach access is limited, but views across the canal to the Olympic Mountains are splendid, settlements few and quiet and back roads genuine byways—few tourists ever get here. This is also where the canal bends like a fishhook to the east, which has been nicknamed the "Great Bend."

To see the east shore in its entirety, begin at Belfair, leaving Route 3 for Route 300. At three miles, watch for Belfair State Park on the left. The road now narrows and traffic thins on the way to the modest resort town of Tahuya; shortly beyond, the canal makes its great bend. The road dives into dense forest, bringing you in about 11 miles to a T-junction; bear left, then left again to the ghost town of Dewatto. Take Dewatto Bay Road eastward out of town, then turn north and follow signs 12 miles to a left turn into the little town of **Holly**, or continue north 15 miles more to **Seabeck**, founded in 1856 as a sawmill town and popular today with anglers, scuba divers and boaters.

LODGING

Rooms at Poulsbo's **Holiday Inn Express** are modern and comfortably furnished with big beds, satellite television, individual air conditioning and other basic amenities; a few are equipped with kitchenette or jacuzzi. There is a seasonal outdoor pool and continental breakfast is included. ~ 19801 7th Avenue Northeast, Poulsbo; 360-697-4400, 800-465-4329, fax 360-697-2707; www.hiexpress.com/poulsbowa. MODERATE.

DINING

The family-run **Benson's** offers eclectic Northwest cuisine in a large but intimate dining room. The seasonal menu may include Alaskan scallops with a ginger cream sauce served over angel hair pasta or rosemary-marinated lamb kabobs over curried couscous. Save room for the chocolate mousse torte! ~ 18820 Front Street, Poulsbo; 360-697-3449. MODERATE.

The **New Day Seafood Eatery** features fast and cheap fish and chips (or clams, shrimp, scallops, oysters or chicken and chips). Diners choose from booths inside or picnic tables on the large deck overlooking Liberty Bay and the wharf. ~ 325 Northeast Hostmark Street, Poulsbo; 360-697-3183. BUDGET.

For ice-cream treats, head to the soda fountain at the **Poulsbo Drug Store**. ~ 18911 Front Street Northeast, Poulsbo; 360-779-2737. BUDGET.

SHOPPING

You'll find paintings, pottery, weavings, cards, rosemaling, baskets, and even food products created by local artists at the **Verksted Co-operative Gallery**. ~ 18937 Front Street Northeast, Poulsbo; 360-697-4470. The **Potlatch Gallery** carries a fine selection of prints, glasswork, pottery and jewelry by Northwest artists. ~ 18830-B Front Street Northeast, Poulsbo; 360-779-3377.

Head to **Boehm's Chocolates** for Swiss-European chocolates, truffles and fudge. ~ 18864 Front Street Northeast, Poulsbo; 360-

697-3318. Get your fill of Norwegian strudels, bear claws, breads, pastries and cookies at **Sluys Bakery**. ~ 18924 Front Street Northeast, Poulsbo; 360-779-2798.

BEACHES & PARKS

MANCHESTER STATE PARK This one-time fort overlooking Rich Passage includes abandoned torpedo warehouses and some interpretive displays explaining its role in guarding Bremerton Navy Base at the turn of the 20th century. The park is infamous for its poison oak—stay on the two miles of hiking trails, or try the 3400 feet of beach. The rocks off Middle Point attract divers. Fishing yields salmon and bottomfish. There are picnic areas, restrooms and showers. ~ Located at the east foot of East Hilldale Road off Beach Drive, east of Bremerton; 360-871-4065, fax 503-378-6308.

▲ There are 35 developed sites ($10 per night) plus three walk-in sites ($5 per night); 15 sites with hookups ($15 per night), one group camp with 12 hookups ($15 apiece, $1 per head for tent campers); and two water-trail sites for kayakers ($7 per person); 800-452-5687.

BUCK LAKE COUNTY PARK Near Hansville on the northern tip of the Kitsap Peninsula, picturesque Buck Lake is a good spot for quiet, contemplative fishing or a relaxing summer swim. Trout fishing is excellent on the lake or from the shore. Facilities include restrooms, picnic tables, a baseball diamond, a volleyball court, barbecue pits and a playground. ~ Located on Buck Lake Road; take Route 104 from Kingston to Hansville Road and follow it north; 360-337-4595, fax 360-337-4781.

SALISBURY POINT This tiny, six-acre park with a small stretch of saltwater beach is next to Hood Canal Floating Bridge and gives views of the Olympic Mountains across the canal. Shrimping is popular here. There are restrooms, picnic shelters and a playground. ~ North of Hood Canal Floating Bridge, turn left on Wheeler Road and follow the signs; 360-337-4595.

KITSAP MEMORIAL STATE PARK This 58-acre park four miles south of Hood Canal Floating Bridge has a quiet beach well suited for collecting oysters and clams. Between the canal, beach and playground facilities there's plenty to keep the troops entertained, making this a good choice for family camping. Restrooms, showers, a shelter, tables and stoves, a boat moorage, a playground and volleyball courts are available; some facilities are wheelchair accessible. ~ From Kingston take Route 104 (which turns into Bond Road) to Route 3, then follow it north until you reach the park; 360-779-3205, fax 360-779-3161.

▲ There are 25 sites for tents and RVs ($10 per night; no hookups); 18 sites with hookups ($15 per night); and a trailer dump ($3).

ILLAHEE STATE PARK 🚶🚴🔭🚣🛥️🏊⚓ Wooded uplands and 1700 feet of saltwater shoreline are separated by a 250-foot bluff at this site. A steep hiking trail connects the two park units. On the beach is a wheelchair-accessible fishing pier where anglers can cast for perch, bullhead and salmon or try for shellfish and crabs; at the south end are tide flats for wading. Facilities include a picnic area, restrooms, showers, a baseball field, a play area and horseshoe pits. ~ Located at the east foot of Sylvan Way (Route 306) two miles east of Route 303 northeast of Bremerton; 360-478-6460, fax 360-792-6067.

▲ There are 24 tent/RV sites (no hookups); $10 per night.

TWANOH STATE PARK 🚶🚴🚤🎣🔭🏕️🛥️🏊⚓ With many amenities of a city park, Twanoh's 182 acres also include the forests, trails and camping of a more remote site. A two-mile hiking trail takes you through a thick forest of second-growth conifers next to Twanoh Creek; or explore nearly a half-mile of saltwater beach that attracts divers. Fishing yields cutthroat, salmon and trout. There are picnic areas, restrooms, showers, tennis, horseshoe pits and a concession stand. ~ Eight miles southwest of Belfair on Route 106; 360-275-2222.

▲ There are 25 tent sites ($12 per night) and 22 full hookup sites ($17 per night); closed in winter.

BELFAIR STATE PARK 🚶🚴🚤🏕️ Two creeks flow through this 63-acre park en route to Hood Canal, affording both fresh and saltwater shorelines. Along its 3700 feet of beachfront the saltwater warms quickly across shallow tide flats, but pollution makes swimming here risky; many instead swim in a lagoon with a bathhouse nearby. Shellfish are usually posted off-limits. There are picnic areas, restrooms and showers. ~ Located three miles west of Belfair on Route 300; 360-275-0668.

▲ There are 138 tent sites ($12 per night) and 47 full hookup sites ($17 per night); dump station ($3).

SCENIC BEACH STATE PARK 🚶🚤🔭🏕️🛥️⚓ Well named it is, with glorious views across Hood Canal to the Olympics and north up Dabob Bay. Nearly 1500 feet of cobblestone

---

OLD MAN HOUSE STATE PARK

A day-use-only facility, **Old Man House State Park** was once the site of a longhouse. Check out the interpretive and historical displays. A small, sandy beach overlooks the heavy marine traffic that cruises through Agate Passage. You'll find pit toilet and picnic tables. Closed in winter. ~ On the Kitsap Peninsula north of Agate Pass off Route 305; 360-692-3655, fax 360-337-4781.

beach invites strolls; scuba divers also push off from here. Every year in May, 88 acres of native rhododendrons burst into bloom. Anglers try for salmon and bottom fish at the nearby artificial reef, and there's a boat launch less than a mile from the park. There are picnic areas, restrooms, showers, a play area, a horseshoe pit, a volleyball area and a community center. ~ Located just west of Seabeck on Miami Beach Road Northwest about nine miles northwest of Bremerton; 360-830-5079, fax 360-830-2970.

▲ There are 50 tent/RV sites, no hookups ($11 per night); and two hike- or bike-in sites ($5 per night). Closed in winter.

PENROSE POINT STATE PARK

With more than two miles of saltwater shoreline, this 152-acre park provides some of the most accessible public clamming in Southern Puget Sound. Try the half-mile of sandpit in Mayo Cove exposed at low tide. You can also swim at the park's sandy, shallow-water beaches, hike along two miles of trail, launch a canoe or kayak, fish for bottomfish and salmon, picnic and camp. The entire park closes for the winter. Restrooms, showers, restaurant and grocery store are close by. ~ Located off Delano Road at the foot of 158th Avenue near Lakebay on the Longbranch Peninsula; 253-884-2514, fax 253-884-2526.

▲ There are 83 tent sites (no hookups); $11 per night; 800-452-5687.

Outdoor Adventures

FISHING

Salmon, of course, is the big draw for anglers on Puget Sound. State hatchery programs see to it that the anadromous fish are available year-round, but the months from midsummer to midfall bring the bulk of salmon—and anglers—to these waters. From mid-July to late August, chinook salmon are king; by Labor Day coho take over, until October. Then chum arrive, but since they tend to be plankton eaters they don't bite. Pink salmon return in odd numbered years, in August, and are most plentiful in the Sound north of Seattle, near Everett. Sockeye can be found in Lake Washington from late June to August.

Several charter companies operate fishing trips on the Sound. The cost, which can range from $35 to $80 and up, usually includes everything except lunch and the fishing license (which you can purchase through the charter company).

KITSAP PENINSULA The family-run **Emerald City Salmon Charter** has a 40-foot boat that accommodates up to 12 people for winter weekend and daily summer trips on the Sound. Dad skippers the boat while kids help out as deck hands. ~ 253-630-3150.

KAYAKING & BOATING

If you're in Tacoma, you can fish from a dinghy in Puget Sound off Point Defiance Park.

TACOMA AND OLYMPIA   Located near the tip of the peninsula in Point Defiance Park, the **Boathouse Marina** has three dozen 14-foot dinghies for rent. Most of the time they're rented by anglers, but you can take them out to explore the Sound if you prefer. Also for rent are motors to power the boats. ~ 253-591-5325.

A wide range of rentals including sea kayaks and single kayaks, powerboats, sailboats, sportfishing boats and fishing poles are available from **Rent-a-Boat & Charters**. Nonsailors can charter a sailboat. ~ 8829 North Harborview Drive, Gig Harbor; 253-858-7341.

KITSAP PENINSULA   Kayak rentals and instruction are the specialty of **Olympic Outdoor Center**. A five-day island-hopping tour takes paddlers through the San Juans. Trips include breakfast and dinner. ~ 18971 Front Street, Poulsbo; 360-697-6095.

SCUBA DIVING

Although the water temperature in Puget Sound averages a cool 45° to 55°, diving is quite popular, especially from October through April, when there's no plankton bloom because of reduced sunlight during those months. With several dive clubs in the Seattle-Tacoma area, there are usually many dives scheduled each weekend: a wall dive off Fox Island perhaps, or a shore dive at Three Tree Point (near Federal Way) or Sunrise Beach (near Gig Harbor). Southern Puget Sound and the area around Vashon Island are considered the best places to dive—you'll see starfish, crabs, ling cod, scallops and many more species. Be prepared, however. Because currents are extremely strong south of Seattle you'll need to check the tides and currents carefully before diving. The dive shops listed below can provide details about these hazards as well as information on local dive spots. If you're not an experienced diver, you can arrange lessons with these shops, although it takes several days to complete training for certification. The outfits listed all rent and sell gear and accessories as well as offer a variety of instruction.

Washington State fishers catch more than 1.3 billion pounds of fish and seafood annually, more than half the nation's total edible catch.

TACOMA AND OLYMPIA   In Tacoma, **Lighthouse Diving** takes divers to Canada, the Cayman Islands and other destinations for trips that range from one day to a week. Night dives are available. Lighthouse pros meet divers at designated locations. They use one tank per dive. ~ 2502 Pacific Avenue, Tacoma; 253-475-1316. In Gig Harbor, contact **Tagert's Dive Locker** for diving, camping trips and holiday dives, such as an Easter egg hunt underwater. Night dives are available. Trips are no more than a half day and use two to three tanks per dive. ~ 4021 Harborview Drive; 253-857-3660. **Aquaquest Divers Inc.** has local boat trips and night dives. Trips last from one day to a week. ~ 7824 East River Road, Tacoma; 253-845-5350.

Underwater Sports Inc. offers shore and boat dives as well as dives abroad—both tropical and night dives. They repair gear. Dives are a day long and use two or three tanks. ~ Tacoma: 9606 40th Street Southwest; 253-588-6634. Olympia: 3330 Pacific Avenue Southeast; 360-493-0322.

JOGGING

In Tacoma, the main road through Point Defiance Park, Five Mile Loop, is a spectacular hilly passage through deep old-growth forest, with occasional breakouts offering lovely views of Puget Sound. This is the route used by the Sound-to-Narrows, an early summer 12K that's one of the country's most popular road races.

Olympia's Capitol Lake greenbelt trails pass through pretty woods, and offer great views of the State Capitol Building and the lake itself. A loop would encompass five kilometers or more.

GOLF

Just south of Tacoma is the **Lake Spanaway Golf Course** in Pierce County Park. The 18-hole public course was cut out of a forest, so it's treelined but fairly open. It has a putting green and a pro shop and rents power and pull carts. ~ 15602 Pacific Avenue, Spanaway; 253-531-3660.

TENNIS

Call two or three days in advance to reserve one of the four public hardtop indoor courts (or five racquetball courts) at **Sprinker Recreation Center**. Professionals are available for lessons. Fee. ~ 14824 South C Street at Military Road, Tacoma; 253-798-4000.

RIDING STABLES

Su Dara Riding offers a "tranquil, peaceful" one-hour ride for up to seven people through woodland thick with firs and maples. On a clear day there are views of Mt. Rainier. Su herself says, "We ride rain or shine." ~ Puyallup; 253-531-1569.

BIKING

TACOMA AND OLYMPIA When it comes to bicycling in Tacoma and Pierce County, "things are just getting going," according to one of the city's public works planners. The area does not yet have the extensive network of lanes and trails that they have up in Seattle, but continues to develop its bicycle and pedestrian plan. Meanwhile, the **Pierce County Department of Public Works** puts out a bike route map. ~ 2401 South 35th Street, Tacoma; 253-798-7250. The **Tacoma Wheelman's Bicycle Club** operates a recorded Ride Line. ~ 253-759-2800.

Among the more popular and convenient places to ride in the city is a two-mile lane along the **downtown waterfront**. Beginning at Schuster Parkway and McCarver Street, this multi-use lane (it's separated from traffic, however) extends to Waterview Street along Ruston Way and Point Defiance Park. Within **Point Defiance Park**, a shoulder lane of Five Mile Drive loops around the peninsula. Call the Metropolitan Park District for more information. ~ 253-305-1000.

KITSAP PENINSULA Cyclists find the moderate **Poulsbo–Port Gamble Loop**, with its 20 miles featuring outstanding views of Hood Canal, the Cascade Range and the Olympic Mountains, a worthwhile ride.

Bike Rentals For mountain-bike rentals and repairs in the Tacoma area, contact **Northwest Mountain Bike**. The shop sells accessories, bikes and snowboards and can give you information about the large network of trails near Victor Falls and in Capital Forest, near Olympia. ~ 6304 6th Avenue, Highland Hill; 253-565-9050. On the Kitsap Peninsula, **Mt. Constance Mountain Shoppe** rents and sells full-suspension mountain bikes and accessories, does repairs, and offers occasional bike tours. ~ 1550 Northeast Riddell Road, Bremerton; 360-377-0668.

> For a pleasant bike ride sans cars, head to Point Defiance Park's Five Mile Drive, which is closed to vehicular traffic every Saturday morning until 1 p.m.

HIKING

Nisqually National Wildlife Refuge, Green River Gorge and Point Defiance Park in Tacoma are a hiker's haven. All distances listed for hiking trails are one way unless otherwise noted.

TACOMA AND OLYMPIA A wonderful river-delta walk, **Brown Farm Dike Trail** (5.5 miles), which starts on the Brown Farm Road, loops through the Nisqually National Wildlife Refuge. You may see bald eagles, coyotes, great blue heron, red-tail hawks and a variety of waterfowl such as wood, canvasback and greater scaup ducks, as well as mallards and pintails. Views stretch from Mt. Rainier to the Olympics. You'll also see many of the islands in the south, Steilacoom and the Tacoma Narrows Bridge.

KITSAP PENINSULA Located southwest of Bremerton, **Gold Mountain Hike** (4 miles) is a moderate-to-strenuous climb with a 1200-foot elevation gain. You will survey the twisting waterways of Southern Puget Sound and Hood Canal from a 1761-foot point that also offers vistas from the Olympics to the Cascades and Edmonds to Olympia. The best access is from Holly Road at the trailhead called Wildcat.

Transportation

Route 5 is the main north–south highway connecting Seattle, Tacoma and Olympia. **Route 16** leads north from Tacoma, across the Tacoma Narrows Bridge toward Gig Harbor and farther north toward Bremerton. On Bainbridge Island, the main thoroughfare is **Route 305** that runs northwest across the island and onto Kitsap Peninsula to Poulsbo.

CAR

Ten miles north of Tacoma and 20 miles south of downtown Seattle is **Seattle-Tacoma International Airport**, also known as Sea-Tac, which is served by Aeroflot, Air B.C., Alaska Airlines, Alaska Commuter Service, America West Airlines, American Airlines, Brit-

AIR

ish Airways, Canadian Regional Airlines, China Eastern Airlines, Continental Airlines, Delta Air Lines, EVA (Evergreen) Airlines, Harbor Alaska Commuter Airlines, Hawaiian Airlines, Horizon Air, KLM, Lufthansa, Mark Air, MartinAir Holland Northwest, Morris Air, Northwest Airlines, Reno Air, SAS, Southwest Airlines, Scandinavian Airlines, TWA, United Airlines, United Express, USAir, West Isles Air and several smaller charter airlines. For general information, call 206-431-4444.

Shuttle service to the northern Kitsap Peninsula is available through the **Bremerton-Kitsap Airporter**. ~ 360-876-1737.

BUS

In the Kitsap Peninsula area, **Kitsap Transit** provides routed service in Poulsbo, Bremerton, Kingston and Bainbridge Island; otherwise, you will have to depend on car or taxis for transportation around the peninsula. ~ 360-373-2877.

CAR RENTALS

Rental agencies at Seattle-Tacoma International Airport include **Avis Rent A Car** (800-331-1212), **Budget Rent A Car** (800-527-0700), **Dollar Rent A Car** (800-800-4000), **Hertz Rent A Car** (800-654-3131) and **Thrifty Car Rental** (800-367-2277). **Ace Xtra-Car Rentals** (800-227-5397) offers low rates and shuttle service to the airport.

SIX

Olympic Peninsula and Washington Coast

One of the most spectacular sights for many Pacific Northwest visitors is sitting on the dock of the bay (Seattle's Elliott Bay, that is) watching the sun set behind the stark profile of the Olympic Mountains. The area is even more memorable looking from the inside out.

The Olympic Peninsula is a vast promontory bounded on the east by Puget Sound, the west by the Pacific Ocean and the north by the Strait of Juan de Fuca. With no major city—the largest town is Port Angeles, a community of only 19,000 people—it retains a feeling of country living on the edge of wilderness, which indeed it is.

Olympic National Park, which dominates the peninsula, is a primeval place where eternal glaciers drop suddenly off sheer rock faces into nearly impenetrable rainforest, where America's largest herd of Roosevelt elk roams unseen by all but the most intrepid human eyes, where an impossibly rocky coastline cradles primitive marine life forms as it has done for millions of years. No fewer than five Indian reservations speckle sections of a coast famed as much for its shipwrecks as for its salmon fishing.

South of the national park, the Washington coast extends down the Northwest's finest sand beaches and around two enormous river estuaries, to the mouth of the Columbia River and the state of Oregon. In this region, two towns have become major resort centers: Ocean Shores and Long Beach.

The Washington coast is known for its heavy rainfall, and justifiably so. Although the Olympics are not high by many standards—its tallest peaks are under 8000 feet—they catch huge amounts of precipitation blowing in from the Pacific Ocean. So much snow falls that more than 60 glaciers survive at elevations as low as 4500 feet. Even greater amounts fall on the windward slopes: 140 inches a year and more in the Forks area. Not only does this foster the rapid growth of mushrooms and slugs, but it has also led to the creation of North America's greatest rainforest in the soggy Hoh River valley. Yet a mere 40 miles away as the raven flies, Sequim—in the Olympic rain shadow—is a comparative desert with only about 15 inches of rain per year.

The first residents of the peninsula and coast were tribes like the Makah, Ozette and Quileute, whose descendants still inhabit the area today. A seafaring people noted for their woodcarving, they lived in a series of longhouses facing the sea and are known to have inhabited this region for as long as 2500 years.

Their first contact with Europeans came in 1775, when they massacred a Spanish landing party. Three years later, the ubiquitous British captain James Cook sailed the coast and traded for sea otter furs with Vancouver Island natives; his report opened the gates to the maritime fur trade.

American entrepreneur John Jacob Astor established a fort at the mouth of the Columbia River in 1803, and two years later Meriwether Lewis and William Clark led a cross-country expedition that arrived at Cape Disappointment, on the Washington side of the Columbia, in late 1806. White settlement was at first slow, but by the mid-19th century Port Townsend had established itself as Puget Sound's premier lumber-shipping port, and other communities sprang up soon after.

Olympic National Park was annexed to the national park system in 1938. But long before that, Washingtonians had discovered its natural wonders. A fledgling tourism industry grew, with lodges constructed at several strategic locations around the park, including lakes Crescent and Quinault, Sol Duc Hot Springs and Kaloloch, overlooking the Pacific. Coastal communities were also building a visitor infrastructure, and quiet beach resorts soon emerged.

Today, typical Olympic Peninsula visitors start their tour in Port Townsend, having traveled by ferry and car from Seattle or Whidbey Island, and use Route 101 as their artery of exploration. Port Townsend is considered the most authentic Victorian seacoast town in the United States north of San Francisco, and its plethora of well-preserved 19th-century buildings, many of them now bed and breakfasts, charms all visitors. Less than an hour's drive west, the seven-mile Dungeness Spit (a national wildlife refuge) is the largest natural sand hook in the United States and is famed for the delectable crabs that share its name. Port Angeles, in the center of the north coast, is home to the headquarters of Olympic National Park and is its primary gateway. The bustling international port town also has a direct ferry link to Victoria, Canada, across the Strait of Juan de Fuca.

Neah Bay, the northwesternmost community in the continental United States, is the home of the Makah Indian Museum and Cultural Center and an important marina for deep-sea fishing charters. Clallam Bay, to its east, and La Push, south down the coast, are other sportfishing centers. The logging town of Forks is the portal for visitors to the national park's Hoh Rainforest.

Route 101 emerges from the damp Olympic forests to slightly less moist Grays Harbor, with its twin lumber port towns of Aberdeen and Hoquiam. Though these towns combined have a population of over 25,000, they have limited appeal to travelers, who typically head over the north shore of Grays Harbor to the hotels of Ocean Shores, or down the south shore of the harbor to the quaint fishing village of Westport.

Serene Willapa Bay is another huge river estuary south of Grays Harbor. The resort strip of 28-mile-long Long Beach Peninsula, which provides a seaward dike for the bay, is older and less contrived than the Ocean Shores area. Wildlife refuges, oyster farms and cranberry bogs lend it a sort of 1950s Cape Cod ambience.

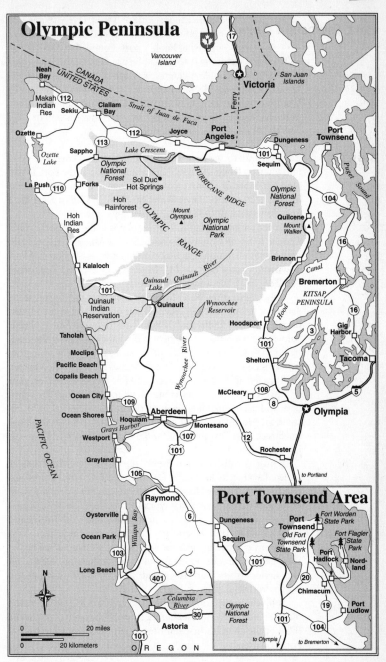

Olympic Peninsula

Vancouver Island

17

CANADA
UNITED STATES

Neah Bay

Makah Indian Res   112

Sekiu   Clallam Bay

Ozette

Ozette Lake

Sappho   112

113   Lake Crescent   Joyce

Strait of Juan de Fuca

Victoria

Ferry

San Juan Islands

Port Angeles   Dungeness   Port Townsend

101

Sequim

Olympic National Forest   Sol Duc Hot Springs

La Push   110   Forks

Hoh Rainforest

HURRICANE RIDGE

Olympic National Forest   104

Quilcene

Mount Walker

Hoh Indian Res

OLYMPIC   Mount Olympus

Olympic National Park

RANGE

Puget Sound

Kalaloch

Quinault Lake   Quinault River

Quinault   Quinault

Brinnon

Bremerton

KITSAP PENINSULA   16

Canal

Hood

Quinault Indian Reservation

Wynoochee Reservoir

Hoodsport

3   Gig Harbor

16

101

Taholah

Moclips

Pacific Beach

Copalis Beach

Wynoochee River

Shelton   Tacoma

5

Ocean City   109   McCleary   108

Ocean Shores

Aberdeen

Hoquiam   Montesano

Grays Harbor   107

Westport   101

12   Rochester

8   Olympia

Grayland

105

to Portland

PACIFIC OCEAN

Raymond   6

Port Townsend Area

Oysterville

Ocean Park   103

Willapa Bay

Long Beach   401   4

N

Columbia River

30

Astoria   101

O R E G O N

0   20 miles

0   20 kilometers

Dungeness

Sequim

101

Port Townsend   Fort Worden State Park

Old Fort Townsend State Park   Fort Flagler State Park

Port Hadlock   Nordland

20

Chimacum   19   Port Ludlow

Olympic National Forest   101   104

to Olympia   to Bremerton

▼▼▼▼▼▼▼▼▼▼▼▼▼▼▼▼
Port Townsend Area

Before either Seattle or Tacoma were so much as a tug on a fisherman's line, Port Townsend was a thriving lumber port. Founded in 1851, it has retained its Victorian seacoast ambience better than any other community north of San Francisco. Much of the city has been designated a National Historic Landmark district, with more than 70 Victorian houses, buildings, forts, parks and monuments. Many of the handsomely gabled homes are open for tours and/or offer bed-and-breakfast accommodations.

SIGHTS

The best way to see **Port Townsend** is on foot. When you drive into town on Route 20, you'll first want to stop at the **Port Townsend Chamber of Commerce** visitors center. Then continue east on Route 20 as it becomes Water Street. ~ 2437 East Sims Way, Port Townsend; 360-385-2722; www.ptguide.com.

At the corner of Madison Street, opposite the city dock, you'll find the **Jefferson County Historical Society Museum** in City Hall, with Victorian antiques, artifacts and hundreds of photos of Port Townsend's early days. ~ 210 Madison Street, Port Townsend; 360-385-1003; www.jchsmuseum.org.

Heading west on Water Street by foot, note the elegant stone and wood-frame buildings on either side of the street, most of them dating from the 1880s and 1890s. Turn right on Adams Street; halfway up the block on the right is the **Enoch S. Fowler Building**, built in 1874, the oldest two-story stone structure in Washington. A former county courthouse, it now houses the weekly newspaper.

Turn left at Washington Street and five blocks farther, on your right, you'll see **The James House**, built in 1889. It has five chimneys and a commanding view of the harbor—and in 1973 became the Northwest's first bed and breakfast. ~ 1238 Washington Street, Port Townsend; 360-385-1238, 800-385-1238; www.jameshouse.com.

Turn right up Harrison Street, then right again at Franklin Street. Two blocks farther, at Franklin and Polk streets, the **Captain Enoch S. Fowler Home**, built in 1860, is the oldest surviving house in Port Townsend and is typical of New England–style homes.

Two more blocks ahead, you will encounter the **Rothschild House**, built in 1868 by an early Port Townsend merchant. Notable for its outstanding interior woodwork, it's maintained by the State Parks Commission for public tours. Admission. ~ Franklin and Taylor streets, Port Townsend; 360-397-8076; www.parks.wa.gov/rothschd.htm.

A block north, **Trinity Methodist Church** (1871) is the state's oldest standing Methodist church. Its small museum contains the Bible of the church's first minister. ~ Jefferson and Clay streets, Port Townsend.

A block east, the 1889 **Ann Starrett Mansion**, now a bed-and-breakfast inn, offers public tours from noon until three. Admission. ~ 744 Clay Street, Port Townsend; 360-385-3205; www. starrettmansion.com.

At Clay and Monroe streets, the **Lucinda Hastings Home** was the most expensive house ever built in Port Townsend when it was erected in 1889 at a cost of $14,000. Turn right here, and return down Monroe to Water Street and your starting point at City Hall.

Get back in your car and drive north on Monroe Street. (The arterial staggers a half-block right at Roosevelt Street onto Jackson Street, then turns right onto Walnut Street.) All roads flow into W Street, the south boundary of **Fort Worden State Park**. Authorized in 1896, it includes officers' row and a refurbished **Commanding Officer's House** (admission), the **248th Coast Artillery Museum** (admission), gun emplacements, a concert pavilion, marine interpretive center and **Point Wilson Lighthouse**. Fort Worden offers stretches of beach that command impressive views of the Cascades and nearby islands. ~ Port Townsend; 360-385-4730; www. olympus.net/ftworden.

If Fort Worden looks familiar, it could be because it was used in the filming of the Richard Gere–Debra Winger movie, *An Officer and a Gentleman*.

On the dock at Fort Worden is the **Port Townsend Marine Science Center**. Of special interest are its four large touch tanks, representing different intertidal habitats, and a "wet lab" where creatures like starfish, anemones and sea cucumbers can be handled by curious visitors. Closed Monday. Admission. ~ Port Townsend; 360-385-5582; www.olympus.net/ptmsc, e-mail ptmsc@olympus.net.

Visitors driving to Port Townsend typically cross the one-and-a-half-mile **Hood Canal Floating Bridge** on Route 104 from the Kitsap Peninsula. Located 30 miles southeast of Port Townsend, it is the world's only floating bridge erected over tidal waters and one of the longest of its kind anywhere. Constructed in 1961, the bridge was washed away during a fierce storm in February 1979, but was rebuilt in 1982.

Traveling south from Port Townsend, Route 20 joins Route 101 at Discovery Bay. Twelve miles south of the junction is the town of **Quilcene** on the Hood Canal, a serpentine finger of Puget Sound. The town is especially noted for its oyster farming and processing and is the location of a state shellfish research laboratory (not open to the public). The **Mount Walker Observation Point**—five miles south on Route 101, then another five miles on a gravel road that starts at Walker Pass—offers a spectacular view of the Hood Canal and surrounding area. On a clear day, you can see Seattle and the Space Needle.

LODGING   **The James House** claims to have been the Pacific Northwest's first bed and breakfast. Just a few steps from shops and restaurants at the foot of the bluff that stands behind lower downtown, it dates from 1889, though it's only been a bed and breakfast since 1973. The house is unmistakable for its five chimneys; inside, the floors are all parquet. Most of the 13 rooms have private baths. There are a fireplace and a library, and a full breakfast is served. Save a few moments to enjoy the English gardens with an impressive view of the water. Kids over 12 are welcome. ~ 1238 Washington Street, Port Townsend; 360-385-1238, 800-385-1238, fax 360-379-5551; www.jameshouse.com, e-mail info@jameshouse.com. MODERATE TO ULTRA-DELUXE.

For those less than enthralled with bed and breakfasts, the **Palace Hotel** provides historic accommodation in a former seafarers' bordello. Though nicely renovated, this is a bit rustic: After checking in at the main lobby you must climb a long flight of stairs (or two) to your room. There are 15 guest chambers, each with antiques recalling the red-light flavor of the past. Three of the rooms, including the madam's former room, even have kitchenettes. ~ 1004 Water Street, Port Townsend; 360-385-0773, 800-962-0741, fax 360-385-0780; www.olympus.net/palace. MODERATE TO DELUXE.

The renowned **Ann Starrett Victorian Mansion Bed and Breakfast Inn**, a National Historic Landmark built in 1889, is a classic mansion in Victorian style. High on a bluff overlooking downtown Port Townsend and Puget Sound, it combines diverse architectural elements—frescoed ceilings, a free-hung spiral staircase, an eight-sided dome painted as a solar calendar, the requisite gables and dormer window—into a charming whole. The 11 guest rooms all have private baths and are furnished with antiques, of course. The gourmet breakfast menu changes daily. ~ 744 Clay Street, Port Townsend; 360-385-3205, 800-321-0644, fax 360-385-2976; www.starrettmansion.com. MODERATE TO ULTRA-DELUXE.

With so many heritage choices, few visitors actually opt for a motel stay. If you do, check out **The Tides Inn**, along the waterfront at the south end of town. Among the 21 units are five efficiencies and nine with hot tubs; most units have balconies overlooking the bay. ~ 1807 Water Street, Port Townsend; 360-385-0595, 800-822-8696, fax 360-379-1115; www.olympus.net/tides inn. MODERATE TO DELUXE.

For students and backpackers, there are two **youth hostels** in eastern Jefferson County. The first is at **Fort Worden State Park**, open year-round. ~ Port Townsend; 360-385-0655; www.olympus.net/ftworden. BUDGET.

The other hostel is at **Fort Flagler State Park**, open mid-March through September. ~ Located three miles north of Nordland; 360-385-1288, www.parks.wa.gov/ftflaglr.htm. BUDGET.

Author Picks

◀◀◀

CHAPTER FAVORITES

I love time travel, and one of the most powerful places to do it is the dimly lit longhouse inside the **Makah Cultural and Research Center**, where the recorded sounds of ceremonial chanting transport visitors back to the world of the ancient whale hunters. *page 164*

After the daytrip traffic has died down for the evening, I find that the remote setting of **Kalaloch Lodge**, on a bluff high above the crashing surf, makes for the ultimate seaside escape in the Pacific Northwest. *page 166*

I've seen Willapa Bay oysters on the menus at gourmet restaurants throughout the Northwest. The best place I can imagine to try them is at the source—**The Shoalwater Restaurant**, located right on the shore of Willapa Bay in Washington's oldest hotel. *page 184*

One of the most unforgettable hikes I've experienced is the **Hoh River Trail**, which wends through miles of lush, primeval rainforest teeming with deer on its way up the side of Mount Olympus. (Afterwards, I felt like a very tired Greek god.) *page 195*

South of town about 20 miles, **Port Ludlow Resort and Conference Center** is one of the Northwest's premier family resorts. It boasts a championship golf course, tennis courts, swimming pools, a marina, hiking and bicycling trails and 1500 acres of land. There are 180 suites with fireplaces, kitchens and decks and a restaurant with marvelous views of water and mountains. ~ 200 Olympic Place, Port Ludlow; 360-437-2222, 800-732-1239, fax 360-437-2482; www.portludlow.com. MODERATE TO DELUXE.

DINING

For an evening of fine dining, it would be hard to top the **Manresa Castle**. Located in an 1892 hilltop inn that overlooks the town and bay like a German castle on the Rhine River, it combines an elegant restaurant and an Edwardian pub. The menu offers regional and seasonal specialties, everything from curry chicken and bouillabaisse to tiger prawns. Sunday brunch. Closed Sunday through Tuesday in winter. ~ 7th and Sheridan streets, Port Townsend; 360-385-5750, fax 360-385-5883. MODERATE TO DELUXE.

With a great location offering spectacular views, the **Surf Waterfront Café** complements its surroundings with pleasant blue-and-white contemporary decor and marine artwork. Fresh, simply prepared local seafood, particularly salmon, clams, mussels and oysters, is the specialty. ~ 106 Taylor Street, Port Townsend; 360-385-2992, fax 360-385-7106. MODERATE.

Ask locals where to eat, and chances are they'll recommend the **Fountain Café**. You'll probably have to stand in line for a seat, but the wait will be worth it. Occupying the ground floor of a historic building (is there anything else in downtown Port Townsend?), the Fountain serves outstanding seafood and pasta dishes, including oysters as you like 'em. Soups and desserts are homemade. The decor is in keeping with the eclectic penchant of many young local artists. ~ 920 Washington Street, Port Townsend; 360-385-1364. MODERATE.

> Port Townsend shops feature the work of talented local painters, sculptors, weavers, potters, poets and writers.

Breakfasts draw full houses at the **Salal Cafe**. Huge omelettes and various seafood and vegetarian recipes get *oohs* and *ahs*, as do the burgers and meat dishes. Lunch features gourmet home-style cooking, along with pastas and sandwiches. No dinner Tuesday or Wednesday in summer. ~ 634 Water Street, Port Townsend; 360-385-6532. BUDGET.

HIDDEN ▶

It's on a back street in Port Townsend. On Friday and Saturday nights a vibes player in the corner provides soft jazz and Caribbean rhythms. Not much makes sense about **Khu Larb Thai**; nonetheless, its fare is probably the best Thai food in Washington State. Curries are rich and flavorful; pad thai, usually mundane, is interesting; mussel hot pots are divine. The rich soups, especially the seafood concoctions, are practically enough for a meal by themselves. And the black rice pudding is an unusual treat. Come early for a table on weekend nights. Closed Monday. ~ 225 Adams Street, Port Townsend; 360-385-5023. BUDGET TO MODERATE.

Some say the **Shanghai Restaurant** serves the best Chinese food this side of Vancouver's Chinatown. Forget the view of the RV park across the street, and enjoy the spicy Szechuan and northern Chinese cuisine. ~ Point Hudson, Port Townsend; 360-385-4810, fax 360-385-0660. BUDGET.

HIDDEN ▶

The **Chimacum Café**, nine miles south of Port Townsend, is a local institution. This is food like grandma should have made—country-fried chicken dinners, baked ham and so forth, followed, of course, by homemade pies brimming with fresh fruit. Breakfast, lunch and dinner are served. ~ 9253 Rhody Drive, Chimacum; 360-732-4631. BUDGET.

SHOPPING   Port Townsend offers the most interesting shopping on the peninsula with its array of galleries, antique and gift shops, bookstores, gourmet restaurants and cafés and all-purpose emporiums. Proprietors have paid particular attention to historical accuracy in restoring commercial buildings. Many of the shops feature the work of talented local painters, sculptors, weavers, potters, poets and writers.

If you're looking for antiques, try the **Port Townsend Antique Mall** or any of the many other shops along the 600 through 1200 blocks of Water or Washington streets. ~ Antique Mall: 802 Washington Street, Port Townsend; 360-385-2590.

Among the many fine galleries for contemporary arts and crafts are **Ancestral Spirits Gallery**, which features Inuit and Northwest Coast tribal artwork. ~ 701 Water Street, Port Townsend; 360-385-0078. **Artisans on Taylor** specializes in handwoven textiles and hand-formed glass beads. ~ 236 Taylor Street, Port Townsend; 360-379-8098.

NIGHTLIFE

Live blues, jazz, opera and folk music accompany dinner at **Lanza's** on the weekend. Closed Sunday and Monday. ~ 1020 Lawrence Street, Port Townsend; 360-379-1900.

BEACHES & PARKS

FORT WORDEN STATE PARK 🚶 🚲 🚤 🎣 ⚓ A 433-acre estate right in Port Townsend, this turn-of-the-20th-century fort includes restored Victorian officers houses, barracks, theater, parade grounds and artillery bunkers. A beach and a boat launch are on Admiralty Inlet, at the head of Puget Sound. Try the dock or beach for salmon fishing. Restrooms, picnic areas, tennis courts and lodging are found here. ~ The entrance is located on W Street at Cherry Street, at the northern city limits of Port Townsend; 360-385-4730, fax 360-385-7248.

▲ There are 80 sites with RV hookups; $16 per night. Reservations, by mail or in person, are strongly recommended year-round.

KAH TAI LAGOON NATURE PARK 🚶 🚲 This midtown park, which features 50 acres of wetlands and 35 acres of grasslands and woodlands, is a great place for birdwatching: more than 50 species have been identified here. There are two and a half miles of trails, a play area for kids, interpretive displays, restrooms and picnic areas. ~ Located on 12th Street near Sims Way in Port Townsend; 360-385-2722, fax 360-379-3804.

OLD FORT TOWNSEND STATE PARK 🚶 🚲 ⚓ Decommissioned in 1895 when Indian attacks on Port Townsend (the town) were no longer a threat, the fort site has seven miles of trails and a beach on Port Townsend (the inlet). You can fish from the shore. You'll find restrooms and picnic areas. Closed October through May. Fee. ~ Located on Old Fort Townsend Road, three miles south of the town of Port Townsend off Route 20; 360-385-3595, fax 360-385-7248.

▲ There are 40 sites; $10 per night.

FORT FLAGLER STATE PARK 🚶 🚲 🚤 🎣 ⚓ 🛥 The long-abandoned fort building, which dates from 1898, is a minor attraction here: bigger is the saltwater beach on Admiralty Inlet, popular for clamming, beachcombing and fishing for salmon, halibut, sole, crab and shellfish. There are also a boat launch, hiking trails, restrooms, picnic areas and lodging. Closed December through February. ~ Located on north tip of Marrowstone Island, eight miles northeast of Hadlock off Route 116; 360-385-1259, fax 360-379-1746.

▲ There are 116 developed sites for tents or RVs; prices range from $11 to $16 per night. To reserve a spot, call 800-452-5687.

DOSEWALLIPS STATE PARK 🏃 🚴 ⚓ 🛶 At the mouth of the Dosewallips River on the Hood Canal, a long, serpentine arm of Puget Sound, this 425-acre park is especially popular among clam diggers and oyster hunters during shellfish season. There are a mudflat beach, hiking trails, restrooms, showers and picnic areas. ~ Located on Route 101 in Brinnon, 37 miles south of Port Townsend; 360-796-4415, fax 360-796-3242.

▲ There are 87 developed sites and 40 RV sites with hookups; $10 to $15 per night. For reservations, call 800-452-5687.

OLYMPIC NATIONAL FOREST 🏃 🚴 🏇 ⚓ 🛶 🛥 🚤 🛶 Surrounding Olympic National Park on its east, south and northwest sides, this national forest provides ample recreational opportunities, including good fishing for trout and, in some areas, for rock cod and salmon in the forest's many lakes and rivers. It includes five wilderness areas on the fringe of the park. There are restrooms and picnic areas. Dogs and hunting are allowed in the national forest, but not in Olympic National Park. Some areas of the park and some campgrounds close periodically due to weather. ~ Numerous access roads branch off Route 101, especially south of Sequim, and between Quilcene and Hoodsport, on the east side of the Olympic Peninsula; 360-956-2300, fax 360-956-2330.

▲ There are 19 campgrounds throughout the forest. Camping costs up to $14. Some spots are free.

▼▼▼▼▼▼▼▼▼▼▼▼
Port Angeles Area

The northern gateway to Olympic National Park as well as a major terminal for ferries to British Columbia, the Port Angeles area is one of northwest Washington's main crossroads. Sequim on Route 101, 31 miles west of Port Townsend, and nearby Port Angeles are two of the peninsula's more intriguing towns. On the Strait of Juan de Fuca at the foot of the Olympic Mountains, this region often may be dry when it's pouring rain just a few miles south.

SIGHTS

The town of **Sequim** (pronounced "Squim") is graced with a climate that's unusually dry and mild for the Northwest: it sits in the Olympic rain shadow. A major attraction just north of town is the **Olympic Game Farm**, whose animals—lions, tigers, bears, buffalo and many others—are trained for film roles. Driving tours of the farm are available year-round; walking tours, including a studio barn, are offered during the summer. Admission. ~ 1423

Ward Road, Sequim; 360-683-4295, fax 360-681-4443; www. olygamefarm.com.

In the Sequim–Dungeness Valley area, the **Museum and Art Center** preserves the native and pioneer farming heritage of Sequim and showcases the work of local artists. ~ 175 West Cedar Street, Sequim; 360-683-8110.

For visitor information, contact the **Sequim–Dungeness Valley Chamber of Commerce Visitors Center**. ~ 1192 East Washington Street, Sequim; 360-683-6690.

North off Route 101, the Dungeness Valley is dotted with strawberry and raspberry fields. Weathered barns left over from the area's dairy farming days are still visible. Pay a visit to the **Cedarbrook Herb Farm**, where 300 different varieties of herbs and spices fill the air with a marvelous (but undefinable!) aroma and inspire many a gourmet chef to go on a culinary buying spree. ~ 1345 Sequim Avenue South, Sequim; 360-683-7733, fax 360-681-3040; www.lavanderfarms.com.

> The New Dungeness Lighthouse was the first lighthouse in the Puget Sound– Strait of Juan de Fuca area.

Opposite the mouth of the Dungeness River is one of the Olympic Peninsula's most remarkable natural features: the **Dungeness Spit**, almost seven miles long and the largest natural sand hook in the United States. A short trail within the adjacent **Dungeness Recreation Area** provides access to this national wildlife refuge. The spit and the surrounding bay and estuary are teeming with wildlife, including seabirds, seals, fish, crabs and clams. At the end of the spit, the **New Dungeness Lighthouse** rises 63 feet above the sea. Established in 1857, the lighthouse is now on the National Register of Historic Places. Visitors who brave the five-and-a-half mile walk out along the spit will be rewarded with an in-depth tour of the facilities.

Seventeen miles west of Sequim on Route 101 is the fishing and logging port of **Port Angeles**, the Olympic Peninsula's largest town. A major attraction here is the **City Pier**. Adjacent to the ferry terminal, it boasts an observation tower, promenade decks and a picnic area. ~ Port Angeles; 360-417-6254.

The **Arthur D. Feiro Marine Life Center**, where visitors can observe and even touch samples of local marine life, is also found at the City Pier. Call ahead for hours. Admission. ~ Port Angeles; 360-417-6254.

As the gateway to Olympic National Park, Port Angeles is home to national park headquarters. At the **Olympic National Park Visitor Center**, you'll find an excellent slide show and exhibits on the natural and human history of the park. ~ 3002 Mount Angeles Road, Port Angeles; 360-452-0330; www.nps.gov/olym/home.htm.

The **Museum of Clallam County** divides its contents between the federal building at First and Oak streets (exhibits) and the Lincoln School at Eighth and C Streets (genealogical information and county archival research information). Closed Saturday and Sunday in winter. ~ Port Angeles; 360-452-2662.

For tourist information, contact the **North Olympic Peninsula Visitor & Convention Bureau.** ~ 338 West 1st Street, Port Angeles; 360-452-8552; www.olympicpeninsula.org.

LODGING

You'll feel good right down to your cockles—as well as your steamer clams, butter clams and horse clams—after shellfishing on the saltwater beach outside the **Sequim Bay Resort**. The eight fully equipped housekeeping cottages here are suitable for vacationing families and shoreline lovers. There are no pets allowed in the cottages. There are also guest laundry facilities and hookups for RVs. ~ 2634 West Sequim Bay Road, Sequim; 360-681-3853. BUDGET.

HIDDEN ▶

Just a spit from the Spit—Dungeness, that is—is the **Groveland Cottage**, by the coast north of Sequim. The early 20th-century building has four carpeted rooms with art, Indian-style antique decor and private baths. There is also a private cottage with a queen-size bed and private bath. The rooms may be simple, but service is not: coffee is delivered to your room in anticipation of the four-course gourmet breakfast. The accent overall is on comfort. They also rent 17 vacation cottages in the area. ~ 4861 Sequim-Dungeness Way, Dungeness; 360-683-3565, 800-879-8859, fax 360-683-5181; www.northolympic.com/groveland. MODERATE.

Perhaps the nicest motel-style accommodation in these port communities is the **Doubletree Hotel**. A modern tan building that extends along the Strait of Juan de Fuca opposite the ferry dock, it offers rooms with private balconies overlooking the water. A private strand of beach and swimming pool beckon bathers. ~ 221 North Lincoln Street, Port Angeles; 360-452-9215, 800-222-8733, fax 360-452-4734; www.portangeleshotel.com. MODERATE TO DELUXE.

Situated on the water with spectacular views of the San Juan Islands, the **Domaine Madeleine Bed and Breakfast** excels in both comfort and hospitality. There are five rooms at this charming inn, including a honeymoon cottage. There's the Renoir Room with impressionist art and feather beds; the Monet Room with Monet prints and a jacuzzi; and the Ming Room, with 19th-century antiques, a jacuzzi and a large private balcony. All rooms have fireplaces and collections of French perfumes. Four rooms have jacuzzis for two. Relax in front of the 14-foot-high basalt fireplace or try your hand at the handcrafted harpsichord. The full gourmet breakfast is elegantly presented—don't miss it. Gay-friendly. ~ 146 Wildflower Lane, Port Angeles; 360-457-4174, fax 360-457-3037; www.domainemadeleine.com. DELUXE TO ULTRA-DELUXE.

Victoria, across the strait on Vancouver Island, is said to be "more British than the British"—but the same slogan could almost apply to **The Tudor Inn**. Host Jane Glass serves a traditional English breakfast and afternoon tea in the restored Tudor-style home. Most of their antique collection is Old English, and the well-stocked library will steer you to books on the United Kingdom. All five bedrooms have private baths; one has a gas fireplace and small balcony. ~ 1108 South Oak Street, Port Angeles; 360-452-3138; www.tudorinn.com, e-mail info@tudorinn.com. MODERATE TO DELUXE.

DINING

El Cazador is a casual, family-run restaurant with red and green table linens, whitewashed walls and Mexican artwork. What sets it apart is its use of fresh seafood in traditional Mexican dishes that consistently win local "best of" awards. The burrito Veracruz stuffed with baby shrimp is a standout. ~ 531 West Washington Street, Sequim; 360-683-4788. BUDGET.

If retired physicist Tom Wells and his Cambodian-born wife, Lay Yin, aren't off studying a solar eclipse somewhere around the globe, you'll find them at the **Eclipse Café**. Yin's culinary touch dominates: Southeast Asian taste tempters stand out. This one's for hungry adventurers. Breakfast and lunch only. Closed Wednesday through Friday. ~ 139 West Alder Street, Sequim; 360-683-2760. BUDGET.

◄ HIDDEN

The undisputed winner in the northern Olympic Peninsula fine-dining sweepstakes is **C'est Si Bon**. The decor is modern and dramatic, with handsome oil paintings and full picture windows allowing panoramas of the Olympic Range. The cuisine, on the other hand, is classical French: tournedos with crabmeat and a shallot sauce, coquilles St. Jacques, veal Normande with apples and calvados. There are French wines and desserts, too. Dinner only. Closed Monday. ~ 23 Cedar Park Drive, four miles east of Port Angeles; phone/fax 360-452-8888. DELUXE.

The Dungeness crab was the first commercially harvested shellfish on the Olympic coast.

A New England reader raved about the clam linguine at the charming **Bella Italia**. In addition to a variety of pasta, this intimate, candlelit eatery whips up Tuscan steak, cioppino and veal Marsala. It also has an extensive wine selection. ~ 117-B East 1st Street, Port Angeles; 360-457-5442, fax 360-457-6112. MODERATE TO DELUXE.

Port Angeles Crabhouse, located in the Doubletree Bayshore Inn, offers sweeping waterfront views in a casually elegant decor of etched glass and tapestry-covered booth seating. Simple and straightforward seafood dishes such as cracked Dungeness crab and grilled salmon are the specialties. ~ 221 North Lincoln Street, Port Angeles; 360-457-0424, fax 360-452-4734. MODERATE TO ULTRA-DELUXE.

Practically next door is the **First Street Haven**, one of the best places around for quick and tasty breakfasts and lunches. Have a homemade quiche and salad, along with baked goods and the house coffee, and you'll be set for the day. Breakfast and lunch only. ~ 107 East 1st Street, Port Angeles; 360-457-0352, fax 360-452-8502. BUDGET.

SHOPPING   **Mad Maggie's Etta Street Salon** is a woman's clothing boutique that doubles as a hair salon. ~ 131 East Washington Street, Sequim; 360-683-5733.

NIGHTLIFE   You didn't come to this part of the state for its nightlife, and that's good. What little there is usually exists only on Friday and Saturday nights.

The **Port Angeles Crabhouse Lounge** in the Doubletree Bayshore Inn features daily drink specials. ~ 221 North Lincoln Street, Port Angeles; 360-457-0424.

BEACHES & PARKS   **SEQUIM BAY STATE PARK** Shellfish (clams, oysters and crabs) as well as fishing for salmon and halibut are the main attractions at this park on Sequim Bay, sheltered from rough seas by two spits at its mouth and from heavy rains by the Olympic rain shadow. There's a beach; you'll also find restrooms and picnic areas. ~ Located on Route 101, four miles east of Sequim; 360-683-4235, fax 360-681-5054.

▲ There are 60 tent sites, 26 RV sites and 3 hiker/biker sites; $10 to $15 per night. For reservations, call 800-452-5687.

DUNGENESS RECREATION AREA The Dungeness Spit is a national wildlife refuge, but a recreation area trail provides access. Marine birds and seals are among the impressive wildlife to be seen; the Dungeness crab is internationally famous as a fine food. There are restrooms, showers and picnic areas. ~ Located at the base of the Dungeness Spit, five miles west of Sequim on Route 101, then four miles north on Kitchen-Dick Road; phone/fax 360-683-5847.

▲ There are 66 sites; $10 per night February through September.

HIDDEN ►   **SALT CREEK RECREATION AREA** One of the finest tidepool sanctuaries on the Olympic Peninsula is this three-mile stretch of rocky beach. Starfish, sea urchins, anemones, mussels, barnacles and other invertebrate life can be observed . . . but not removed. Anglers will find rockfish. Restrooms, picnic areas, playground and hiking trails are all here. ~ Located three miles north from Joyce (or 15 miles west from Port Angeles) on Route 112, then another three miles north on Camp Hayden Road; 360-928-3441, fax 360-417-2395.

▲ There are 92 sites; $8 to $10 per night.

The Olympic Peninsula's main attraction —in fact, the reason most tourists come here at all—is Olympic National Park. Rugged, glaciated mountains dominate the 1400-square-mile park, with rushing rivers tumbling from their slopes. The rainier western slopes harbor an extraordinary rainforest, and a separate 57-mile-long coastal strip preserves remarkable tidepools and marvelous ocean scenery. Wildlife in the park includes the rare Roosevelt elk, as well as deer, black bears, cougars, bobcats, a great many smaller mammals and scores of bird species. Besides the main part of the park, which encompasses the entire mountain wilderness in the center of the peninsula and can be entered from the north or west, Olympic National Park includes a separate Coastal Unit spanning more than 50 miles of Pacific headlands and beaches.

Olympic National Park

There are no lack of facilities throughout the park: picnic areas, hotels, restaurants and groceries. For general information on the park, call the **Olympic National Park Visitor Center**. ~ 360-452-0330.

SIGHTS

The most direct route into the park from Port Angeles is the Heart of the Hills/Hurricane Ridge Road. It climbs 5200 feet in just 17 miles to the **Hurricane Ridge Lodge**, where there are breath-

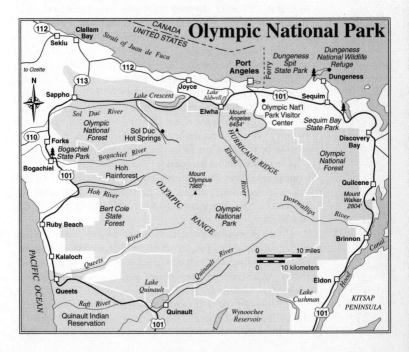

Olympic National Park

taking views to 7965-foot Mt. Olympus, the highest peak in the Olympic Range, and other glacier-shrouded mountains. Visitors to Hurricane Ridge can dine in the day lodge, picnic, enjoy nature walks or take longer hikes. In winter, enjoy the small downhill ski area here and many cross-country trails.

Twenty miles west of Port Angeles on Route 101 is **Lake Crescent**, one of three large lakes within park boundaries. Carved during the last Ice Age 10,000 years ago, it is nestled between steep forested hillsides. A unique subspecies of trout lures many anglers to its deep waters. There are several resorts, restaurants, campgrounds and picnic areas around the lake's shoreline. From National Park Service–administered Lake Crescent Lodge, on the southeast shore, a three-fourth-mile trail leads up Barnes Creek to the beautiful **Marymare Falls**. ~ 360-928-3211, fax 360-928-3253; www.olypen.com/lakecrescentlodge.

The Ozette Loop Trail weaves past 56 petroglyphs that depict various aspects of historic Makah life.

West of Lake Crescent, the Sol Duc River Road turns south to **Sol Duc Hot Springs**, 14 miles off of Route 101. Long known to the Indians, the therapeutic mineral waters were discovered by a pioneer in 1880 and like everything else the white man touched, soon boasted an opulent resort. But the original burned to the ground in 1916 and today's refurbished resort, nestled in a valley of old-growth Douglas fir, is more rustic than elegant. The springs remain an attraction. Sol Duc is a major trailhead for backpacking trips into Olympic National Park; also located here is a ranger station. ~ 360-327-3583, fax 360-327-3593; www.northolympic.dom/solduc, e-mail pamsdr@aol.com.

Forks, with over 3000 people, is the largest town between Port Angeles and Hoquiam. (It's also Washington's rainiest town, with well over 100 inches a year.) Steelhead fishing, river rafting and mushroom gathering are major activities here, but the one most evident to visitors is the timber industry. Some days, in fact, there seem to be more log trucks on the roads than passenger cars.

The **Forks Timber Museum** is filled with exhibits of old-time logging equipment and historical photos, as well as pioneer and Indian artifacts. Interpretive trails, gardens and a logger memorial are next to the visitors center. ~ Route 101 South, Forks; 360-374-9663.

On the coast 14 miles west of Forks is the 800-year-old Indian fishing village of **La Push**, center of the **Quileute Indian Reservation**. Sportfishing, camping and beach walking are popular year-round. An abandoned Coast Guard station and lighthouse here are used as a school for resident children. ~ 360-374-6163.

A national park road eight miles west of Forks branches off the La Push Road and follows the north shore of the Quileute River five miles to **Rialto Beach**, where spectacular piles of driftwood often accumulate. There are picnic areas and campgrounds here, and a trailhead for hikes north up the beach toward Cape Alava.

On the west side of the national park are three more major points of entry. The **Hoh Rainforest** is 19 miles east of Route 101 via the Hoh River Road, 13 miles south of Forks. For national park information here, call the **Forks Ranger Station** (360-374-5450). There's a less well-known rainforest at the end of the **Queets River Road**, 14 miles off Route 101, 17 miles west of Quinault. Finally, **Quinault Lake**, on Route 101 at the southwestern corner of Olympic National Park, is the site of several resorts and campgrounds, including the venerable Lake Quinault Lodge. Watersports of all kinds are popular at this glacier-fed lake, surrounded by old-growth forest.

The **Hoh Indian Reservation** is 25 miles south of Forks, off Route 101. Of more interest to most visitors is the **Kalaloch Lodge**, 35 miles south of Forks on Route 101. A major national park facility, it affords spectacular ocean views at the southernmost end of the park's coastal strip. ~ Kalaloch Lodge: 157151 Route 101; 360-962-2271; www.visitkalaloch.com.

The **Olympic National Park Coastal Unit** includes some 3300 square miles of designated marine sanctuary both above and below water level. Although most of the 50-mile seacoast is unreachable by road, trails lead down to six diverse beaches from Route 101 between Kalaloch and Ruby Beach. Here you'll find broad, log-strewn expanses of sand, gravel stretches great for beachcombing, and rocky tidepools teeming with tiny marine life.

LODGING

The rustic **Log Cabin Resort** is a historic landmark on the shores of gorgeous Lake Crescent along Route 101. Budget-watchers can stay in the main lodge; more upscale are the lakeshore chalets and cabins. There is also an RV park with full hookups on Log Cabin Creek. The handsome log lodge has a restaurant and a gift shop; all manner of boats are rented at the marina. Closed October through March. ~ 3183 East Beach Road, 21 miles west of Port Angeles; 360-928-3325, fax 360-928-2088; www.logcabinresort. net. BUDGET TO MODERATE.

The **Sol Duc Hot Springs Resort** is another historic property, this one was originally built in 1910 around a series of hot sulphur pools 12 miles south of Route 101. The 33 cabins (six with kitchens) were rebuilt in the mid-1980s and now have indoor plumbing! The best plunge, however, after a day of hiking or fishing, remains the water in three ceramic natural mineral spring pools, kept between 98 and 104 degrees and cleaned nightly. There is also a full-size swimming pool. Camping sites and RV hookups are available. The resort is closed October through April. ~ Sol Duc Hot

The Peninsula's Northwest Coast

Much less traveled than Route 101, Route 112 runs from near Port Angeles to Neah Bay on the northwest tip of the Olympic Peninsula. The drive takes about one and a half hours each way. Allow an additional one and a half to two hours to see the Makah Cultural and Research Center. You may wish to make this an all-day excursion by adding a side trip to Lake Ozette, one of the most hidden spots you can reach by road in Olympic National Park.

THE NORTHWEST COAST From Port Angeles, follow Route 101 west for five miles, then turn off to the right on Route 112. For much of its length, this narrow two-lane highway runs within sight of the Strait of Juan de Fuca and partly traces the water's edge. Travel 46 miles to the sister communities of **Clallam Bay** and **Sekiu** (pronounced "C-Q"). These are prime sportfishing grounds for salmon and huge bottomfish, especially halibut. Check out the wonderful tidepools north of Clallam Bay at **Slip Point**. Just west of Sekiu, at the mouth of the Hoko River, visitors can view the remains of a 2500-year-old Makah Indian fishing village at the **Hoko Archaeological Site**.

NEAH BAY Continue for 18 more miles past Sekiu to the highway's end at Neah Bay, the administrative center of the Makah Indian Reservation. This rather bleak little village has a few motels and a commercial fishing fleet, and visitors can book charter-fishing excursions from the harbor. Beyond the town, roads continue to stormswept beaches on Cape Flattery, strewn with driftwood and shipwrecks. Neah Bay's touristic centerpiece, the **Makah Cultural and Research Center** houses finds from the Oz-

Springs Road, 44 miles west of Port Angeles; 360-327-3583, fax 360-327-3593; www.northolympic.com/solduc, e-mail pamsdr@aol.com. MODERATE.

The hamlet of Sekiu flanks Route 112 on the protected shore of Clallam Bay, on the Strait of Juan de Fuca. The lone waterfront hotel here is **Van Riper's Resort and Charters**. Family owned and operated, it's a cozy getaway spot. More than half of the 16 rooms have great views of the boats on the picturesque strait. ~ 280 Front Street, Sekiu; 360-963-2334, fax 360-963-2354; www.seiku.com. BUDGET TO DELUXE.

The Cape Motel and RV Park has eight motel rooms and two cottages; five have kitchens. Six months of the year, an RV Park with restrooms is also open. ~ Bayview Avenue, Neah Bay; phone/fax 360-645-2250. BUDGET.

ette Dig at Cape Alava, about 20 miles down the Pacific coast. Few relics remain from the ancient culture of the Northwest Coast tribes because their wooden structures and implements rotted away quickly in the damp climate. Ozette, however, was buried 500 years ago by a mudslide that preserved it from the elements until archaeologists discovered it in the 1970s. The artifacts found there and exhibited in an atmospheric long-house setting at the cultural center include baskets, log canoes, clothing, wood carvings and whaling harpoons. Admission. ~ Bay View Avenue; 360-645-2711, fax 360-645-2656; www.makah.com.

LAKE OZETTE   Returning from Neah Bay on Route 112, two miles before you reach Sekiu a paved secondary road turns off to the south (right) and goes 20 miles to Lake Ozette, the northernmost part of Olympic National Park's Coastal Unit. The largest of the park's three lakes, it is separated from the ocean by a strip of land just three miles wide. Several trails lead from here to the sea, including the Indian Village Trail, which leads to the Ozette Dig at Cape Alava.

SAPPHO   Back on Route 112, six miles east of Clallam Bay Route 113 turns off to the south (right) and goes nine miles through the forest to join Route 101 at Sappho. Here you face a choice: If you turn east (left), you'll return to Port Angeles, a distance of 45 miles through Olympic National Forest and Olympic National Park, passing **Lake Crescent** and **Mary-mare Falls** (page 162) and the road to **Sol Duc Hot Springs** (page 162). If you turn west (right), Route 101 will take you through Forks to the turnoff for the **Hoh Rainforest** (page 167) and past that to the beaches of the **Olympic National Park Coastal Unit** (page 163), a total distance of 53 miles.

The main population center on the Olympic Coast, and the nearest to the Hoh Rainforest, is the lumber town of Forks. Among several low-priced bed and breakfasts here is the **River Inn on the Bogachiel**, an A-frame chalet on the banks of the Bogachiel River two-and-a-half miles from town. Two bedrooms share a bath and sundecks; one has a private bathroom and stairs leading to the hot tub. You can fish from the shore or relax in the hot tub while keeping your eyes open for elk, deer and river otter. Full breakfast. Closed in September. ~ 2596 West Bogachiel Way, Forks; 360-374-6526, fax 360-374-6590. MODERATE.

◄ HIDDEN

Much nearer to shops and restaurants is the **Miller Tree Inn**. A quiet and comfortable farm homestead on three acres, it has six attractive rooms (two with half-baths) that practice an "open-house" policy not common among bed and breakfasts: children and pets are welcome! And visitors love the fresh farmhouse breakfasts. ~ 654 Division Street, Forks; 360-374-6806, fax 360-374-6807; www.northolympic.com/millertree. MODERATE.

Sixteen miles west of Forks in the Quileute Indian Reservation, surrounded by the coastal strip of Olympic National Park, is the **La Push Ocean Park Resort**. The driftwood-speckled beach is just beyond the lodgings, which fall into four categories: moderate to ultra-deluxe cabins with fully supplied kitchenettes and fireplaces; older moderate-priced townhouse units with balconies overlooking the beach; 20 budget-priced motel units with either full kitchens or kitchenettes; and rustic, budget-priced A-frames with wood stoves (haul your own fuel from the woodshed) and toilets (showers are in a communal washroom). ~ 700 Main Street, La Push; 360-374-5267, 800-487-1267, fax 360-374-4153; www.lapushw. com. BUDGET TO ULTRA-DELUXE.

Forks also has a youth hostel, complete with the cosmopolitan atmosphere one would expect. The **Rain Forest Hostel**, like other lodgings of its ilk, offers dorm bunks and community bathrooms and kitchen. The common room is a bonus with its fireplace and library. There is also one room for a couple and one room for a family. ~ 169312 Route 101 North, 23 miles south of Forks; 360-374-2270; www.hostels.com/rainforest. BUDGET.

Back in Olympic National Park, one of the most picturesque spots found on the Washington coastline is the **Kalaloch Lodge**. Accommodations here include eight lodge units, ten motel units, 20 log cabins with kitchenettes (but no utensils provided) and 18 units atop the bluff, six of which are duplexes. The lodge has a dining room and lounge overlooking the Pacific Ocean, as well as a general store, gas station and gift shop. ~ 157151 Route 101, 35 miles south of Forks; 360-962-2271, fax 360-962-3391. DELUXE TO ULTRA-DELUXE.

If you're planning a stay in the corner of Olympic National Park that includes beauteous Lake Quinault, consider the **Lake Quinault Lodge**—especially if you can get a lakefront room in the historic cedar-shingled lodge itself. The huge building arcs around the shoreline, a totem-pole design on its massive chimney facing the water. Antiques and wicker furniture adorn the main lobby, constructed in the 1920s. There is also a sun porch, dining room and bar. There are nice rooms in a newer wing, but they lack the lodge's historic ambience. You can rent boats in the summer, hike year-round or relax in the pool or sauna. ~ 345 South Shore Road, Quinault; 360-288-2571, fax 360-288-2901; www.visitlakequinault.com. MODERATE TO ULTRA-DELUXE.

An alternative lodging on the lake is the **Rain Forest Resort Village**, with 11 deluxe-priced cabins (some with kitchens and whirlpool bathtubs, all with fireplaces), 16 moderately priced motel rooms and 31 RV spaces (budget). Here, you'll find most of the

The Hoh Rainforest

No matter where you go on this earth, there's only one Hoh Rainforest. It's said to be one of the only coniferous rainforests in the world. Graciously spared the logger's blade, it's been undisturbed since time began. In other words, it's a natural wonder to be embraced and cherished.

Reached by traveling 13 miles south from Forks on Route 101, then 19 miles east on Hoh River Road, this is the wettest spot in the contiguous 48 states. In fact, wet isn't the word: even the air drips like a saturated sponge, producing over 30 inches of fog drip in the summer. The average annual precipitation due to rainfall is 145 inches, more than 100 inches of which fall between October and March. But temperatures at this elevation, between 500 and 1000 feet, rarely fall below 40° in winter or rise above 85° in summer. The legacy of this mild climate is dense, layered canopies of foliage.

The forest floor is as soft and thick as a shag carpet, cloaked with mosses, bracken ferns, huge fungi and seedlings. Hovering over the lush rug are vine maple, alder and black cottonwood, some hung with moss, stretching wiry branches to taste any slivers of sunlight that may steal through the canopy. Above them, Douglas fir, Sitka spruce, Western hemlock, Western red cedar and other gigantic conifers rise 200 to 300 feet, putting a lid on the forest. In all, over 300 plant species live here, not counting 70 epiphytes (mosses, lichens and such).

Some compare this environment to a cathedral. Indeed, the soft light is like sun filtered through stained glass, and the arching branches could pass for a vaulted apse. To others, it's simply mystical. The ancient coastal Indians would have agreed.

Though there are similar rainforests in Washington, the rainforest ecology is most conveniently studied at the **Hoh Rainforest Visitor Center** and on the nature trails that surround it. ~ 360-374-6925; www.nps.gov/olym. The **Hoh River Trail** extends for 18.5 miles to the river's source in Blue Glacier, on the flank of Mt. Olympus, but the rainforest can be appreciated by most visitors on one of two loop hikes that are both about a mile long. About three-fourths of a mile in, you'll see enormous old-growth Douglas fir, spruce and hemlock, some over nine feet in girth and at least 500 years old. At about one mile, the trail drops down to Big Flat, the first of several grassy open areas. The winter grazing of Roosevelt elk, whose survival was a major reason for the creation of Olympic National Park, has opened up the forest floor. Keep your eyes open, too, for wildlife. Besides the elk, you may spot river otter or weasel. Black bears and cougars also inhabit these forests. Bald eagles and great blue heron feed on the salmon that spawn seasonally in the Hoh.

amenities of the lodge, including restaurant and lounge, boat rentals and general store, but you don't have to pay for the atmosphere. ~ 516 South Shore Road, Quinault; 360-288-2535, 800-255-6936, fax 360-288-2957. MODERATE TO DELUXE.

DINING

The best choice for dining in the park is the **Log Cabin Resort.** Enjoy the view of beautiful Lake Crescent, where anglers dip their lines for the unique crescenti trout, a subspecies of rainbow trout that may wind up on your platter in the restaurant. Northwest cuisine is a specialty. ~ 3183 East Beach Road, 21 miles west of Port Angeles; 360-928-3325, fax 360-928-2088. MODERATE.

There's another dining room at the **Sol Duc Hot Springs Resort,** just behind the hot sulphur springs. As at the Log Cabin, the food is solid Northwest fare, including some vegetarian dishes and Dungeness crab from the north Olympic Coast. Closed October through April. ~ Sol Duc Hot Springs Road, 44 miles west of Port Angeles; 360-327-3583, fax 360-327-3593. MODERATE.

A mile high in the Olympic Range, 17 miles south of Port Angeles, the **Hurricane Ridge Lodge** frames glaciers in the picture windows of its coffee shop. Come for the view, but the standard American fare served here isn't half-bad either. Open daily mid-May through September, weekends mid-December to April. ~ Hurricane Ridge Road; 360-928-3211. MODERATE.

Sunsets from the **Kalaloch Lodge,** high on a bluff overlooking the ocean in the national park's coastal strip, can make even the most ordinary food taste good. Fortunately, the fresh salmon and oysters served here don't need the view for their rich flavor. A lounge adjoins the dining room. Breakfast, lunch and dinner. ~ 157151 Route 101, 35 miles south of Forks; 360-962-2271, fax 360-962-3391. MODERATE TO DELUXE.

The restaurant at the park's **Lake Quinault Lodge** faces another gorgeous lake surrounded by lush cedar forests. As you've come to expect along this coast, the seafood is excellent. Breakfast and dinner year-round; lunch in summer. ~ 345 South Shore Road, Quinault; 360-288-2900, fax 360-288-2901. DELUXE.

FLATTERY WILL GET YOU NOWHERE, BUT THE VIEW'S TERRIFIC

A winding, scenic coastal drive to the end of Route 112 climaxes at **Cape Flattery,** the northwesternmost corner of the contiguous United States. The road at times runs within feet of the water, providing spectacular blufftop views of the Strait of Juan de Fuca and Tatoosh Island—a great location for whale watching between March and May. A short trail leads to the shore. Beach hikers can find some of the last wilderness coast in Washington south of here.

Other than the national park lodges, pickings are slim in the restaurant department along this stretch of highway. A mile north of Forks, the **Smoke House Restaurant** serves a superb alder-smoked salmon. You can also get generous portions of other seafood and meats, plus a salad bar and homemade desserts. ~ Route 101 at La Push Road; 360-374-6258. MODERATE.

For authentic Northwest Indian crafts, you won't do better than the gift shop at the **Makah Cultural and Research Center** on the Makah Indian Reservation near Cape Flattery at the end of Route 112. ~ Bay View Avenue, Neah Bay; 360-645-2711.

SHOPPING

OLYMPIC NATIONAL PARK This spectacular national park, 922,626 acres in area and ranging in elevation from sea level to nearly 8000 feet, contains everything from permanent alpine glaciers to America's lushest rainforest (the Hoh) to rocky tidepools rich in marine life. Wildlife includes goats in the mountains, elk in the rainforest, steelhead and trout in the rivers and colorful birds everywhere. Three large lakes—Crescent (near Port Angeles), Ozette (on the coast) and Quinault (on the southwestern edge)—are especially popular visitor destinations. There are restrooms, picnic areas, hotels, restaurants and groceries. ~ Route 101 circles the park. The numerous access roads are well marked; 360-452-4501, fax 360-452-0335 (Port Angeles); ranger stations in Forks (360-374-5450), Quilcene (360-765-3368) and Sol Duc (360-327-3534).

▲ There are 17 campgrounds; $10 to $12 per night.

BEACHES & PARKS

BOGACHIEL STATE PARK Not far from the Hoh Rainforest, this eternally damp park sits on the Bogachiel River, famous for its salmon and steelhead runs. Hiking and hunting in the adjacent forest are popular activities, although this park is more of a campsite than a day-use area. Facilities include restrooms, showers and limited picnic areas. ~ Located on Route 101 six miles south of Forks; 360-374-6356.

▲ There are 34 standard sites, six RV hookups and two primitive sites; $5 for primitive sites, $10 to $15 for other sites.

A six-mile-long, 6000-acre peninsula, Ocean Shores was a cattle ranch when a group of investors bought it for $1 million in 1960. A decade later, its assessed value had risen to $35 million. Today, it would be hard to put a dollar figure on this strip of condominium-style hotels and second homes, many of them on a series of canals. The main tourist beach destination on the Grays Harbor County coastline, it's located along Route 115 three miles south of its junction with Route 109.

Ocean Shores– Pacific Beach

SIGHTS

Folks come to **Ocean Shores** for oceanside rest and recreation, not for sightseeing. One of the few "attractions" is the **Ocean Shores Interpretive Center** four miles south of the town center near the Ocean Shores Marina, which has exhibits describing the peninsula's geological formation and human development. Open daily from April through October; open the rest of the year by appointment only. ~ Point Brown Avenue, Ocean Shores; 360-289-4617.

The Ocean Shores Peninsula has 23 miles of interconnecting freshwater canals and lakes.

The 22-mile beach that parallels Routes 115 and 109 north to Moclips is an attraction in its own right. Beyond Moclips, however, the coastline gets more rugged. Eight miles past Moclips, the **Quinault Indian National Tribal Headquarters** in the village of Taholah, on the Quinault Indian Reservation, offers guided fishing trips on reservation land and tribal gifts in a small shop. ~ Taholah; 360-276-8215.

LODGING

The nearest ocean beach area to the Seattle-Tacoma metropolitan area, Ocean Shores' condominiums and motels are frequently booked solid during the summer and on holiday weekends, even though prices can be high. At other times, it can be downright quiet . . . and inexpensive.

Like almost every other lodging on this stretch of shoreline, **The Polynesian Resort** is as close to the water as you can get—a good mile trek across the dunes to the high-tide mark. The four-story building has 71 guest rooms ranging from motel units to three-bedroom penthouse suites. It has a restaurant, lively lounge, indoor pool and spa, outdoor games area and indoor game room popular with families. ~ 615 Ocean Shores Boulevard Northwest, Ocean Shores; 360-289-3361, 800-562-4836, fax 360-289-0294; www.v-v-a.com. MODERATE TO ULTRA-DELUXE.

Across the street from the Polynesian is Ocean Shores' largest property, with 83 units, and one of its least expensive: **Linde's Landing**. Basic sleeper units are small, but kitchen units (many with fireplaces) are good-sized. Rooms have televisions and phones; everyone can use the sauna and indoor and outdoor pools. ~ 648 Ocean Shores Boulevard Northwest, Ocean Shores; 360-289-3323, 800-448-2433, fax 360-289-3320; www.lindeslanding.com. BUDGET TO DELUXE.

Neighboring units at **The Grey Gull** are fewer in numbers (37), but they're all studios or suites with fireplaces, microwave ovens, VCRs and private decks or balconies. The Gull has an outdoor pool and jacuzzi guarded by a wind fence. ~ 647 Ocean Shores Boulevard, Ocean Shores; 360-289-3381, 800-562-9712, fax 360-289-3673; www.thegreygull.com. DELUXE.

The **Caroline Inn** offers four bi-level townhouse suites with great views, just steps from the water. The decor follows a *Gone With the Wind* theme in soft rose colors. The rooms are furnished with sleigh beds and other antiques. Each suite offers all the comforts of home and then some: fireplaces, jacuzzis, complete kitchens and living areas with entertainment centers. ~ 1341 Ocean Shores Boulevard, Ocean Shores; 360-289-0450, fax 360-289-9682. DELUXE.

One of few accommodations away from "the strip" is the **Discovery Inn,** a condo motel close to the Ocean Shores Marina near the cape's southeast tip, five miles from downtown. Rooms are built around a central courtyard with a seasonal pool. There is an indoor jacuzzi and family game room. A private dock on Ocean Shores' grand canal encourages boating and fishing. ~ 1031 Discovery Avenue Southeast, Ocean Shores; 360-289-3371, 800-882-8821, fax 360-289-7977. BUDGET TO MODERATE.

North up the coast from frenetic Ocean Shores are numerous quiet resort communities and accommodations. At Ocean City, four miles north, the **Pacific Sands Motel** is one of the top economy choices on the coast. There are just nine units, but they're well kept; seven have kitchens and three have fireplaces. The extensive grounds include a nice swimming pool, playground, picnic tables and direct beach access across a suspension bridge. ~ 2687 Route 109, Ocean City; 360-289-3588. BUDGET.

◄ HIDDEN

The **Iron Springs Resort** has 28 units in 28 cottages built up a wooded hill and around a handsome cove at the mouth of Boon Creek. The beach here is popular for razor clamming, crabbing and surf fishing; the cottages are equally popular for their spaciousness and panoramic views. All have kitchens and fireplaces. There are an indoor pool, playground and gift shop. ~ 3707 Route 109, Copalis Beach; 360-276-4230, fax 360-276-4365; www.iron springsresort.com. MODERATE.

Ocean Crest Resort may be the most memorable accommodation on this entire stretch of beach. It's built atop a bluff, so getting to the beach involves a 132-step descent down a staircase through a wooded ravine. But the views from the rooms' private balconies are remarkable, and all but the smallest rooms have fireplaces and refrigerators. There are exercise facilities with a swimming pool, jacuzzi and weight room open to all guests free of charge. ~ Sunset Beach, Route 109, Moclips; 360-276-4465, 800-684-8439, fax 360-276-4149; www.ohwy.com/wa/o/ocecrere. htm. MODERATE TO DELUXE.

Mariah's provides a spacious, relaxing cedar dining room with a domed ceiling and skylights. Specialties include honey-baked salmon, prime rib and chicken baked with artichoke hearts. Dinner only. ~ 615 Ocean Shores Boulevard, Ocean Shores; 360-289-3315, fax 360-289-0294. BUDGET TO DELUXE.

DINING

The **Home Port Restaurant** is appointed like the private garden of a sea captain home from the waves. Steaks, seafood and pasta dominate the menu. ~ 857 Point Brown Avenue opposite Shoal Street, Ocean Shores; 360-289-2600. MODERATE.

Numerous Ocean Shores restaurants appeal to more casual diners. **Flipper's Fish Bar** has excellent fish-and-chips. Closed Monday through Thursday from September through February. ~ Chance a la Mer at Ocean Court, Ocean Shores; 360-289-4676. And the **Sand Castle Drive-in**, north of Chance a la Mer, is the in-spot for hamburgers, with interesting variations such as the oyster burger and the clam burger. ~ 788 Point Brown Avenue, Ocean Shores; 360-289-2777. BUDGET.

A bit of Manzanillo on the Washington coast, **Las Maracas** feels like the tropics with its bright tropical colors and profusion of plants. All the usual Mexican specialties are on the menu, but the best bets are the fajitas, crab and prawn enchiladas and seafood chimichangas. ~ 729 Point Brown Avenue, Ocean Shores; 360-289-2054, fax 360-289-2045. BUDGET TO MODERATE.

Authentic Irish pub fare is dished up at **Galway Bay Irish Restaurant and Pub** where you can ward off the coastal chill with Irish stew, beef sautéed in Guinness, and chicken and mushroom pasties. The pub decor is authentic, with wainscoted walls adorned with Irish prints and memorabilia. Breakfast, lunch and dinner. ~ 676 Ocean Shores Boulevard, Ocean Shores; 360-289-2300, fax 360-289-3129. BUDGET TO MODERATE.

SHOPPING The most interesting galleries in Grays Harbor County are, not surprisingly, in the beach communities. For oil paintings, watercolors and textile crafts, make sure to seek out **The Cove Gallery**. ~ Route 109, Iron Springs; 360-276-4360. The **Gallery Marjuli** exhibits recent works by local artists. ~ 865 Point Brown Avenue, Ocean Shores; 360-289-2858.

NIGHTLIFE In Ocean Shores, at the Polynesian Hotel, **Mariah's** is a nice place to enjoy a nightcap. ~ 615 Ocean Shores Boulevard, Ocean Shores; 360-289-3315.

TRIBAL AND GOURMET

For a gourmet Continental dinner in spectacular surroundings, check out the **Ocean Crest Resort**. Attentive service and superb meals (with a focus on seafood and Northwest regional cuisine), amid an atmosphere of Northwest Indian tribal art, only add to the enjoyment of the main reason to dine here: the view from a bluff, through a wooded ravine, to Sunset Beach. Breakfast, lunch and dinner. ~ Sunset Beach, Route 109, Moclips; 360-276-4465, fax 360-276-4149. MODERATE TO ULTRA-DELUXE.

The **Legend Inn** is a sports bar and tavern with a big-screen TV, karaoke, some live bands, pool tables, an extensive burger menu and some 18 brews on tap. ~ 105 Chance a la Mer, Ocean Shores; 360-289-3095.

OCEAN CITY STATE PARK 🚶🚴🐎⛵🏄🏖️🚗 This North Beach park, stretching for several miles along the Pacific coastline, offers a dozen access points. There are clamming and surf fishing (in season), horseback riding on the beach (but not on the dunes or soft sand), surf kayaking in summer, kite flying when the wind blows, birdwatching especially during migratory periods, and beachcombing year-round. Swimming is not recommended because of undertow and riptides. This flat, sandy beach is the same broad expanse that stretches 22 miles north to Pacific Beach. You can drive on some sections of the beach! You'll find restrooms and picnic areas. ~ Located off Route 115 and Route 109 north of Ocean Shores; campground is two miles north of Ocean Shores off Route 115; 360-289-3553, fax 360-289-9059.

BEACHES & PARKS

▲ There are 178 sites, 29 with RV hookups; $12 and $17 per night. For reservations, call 800-452-5687 in summer only.

PACIFIC BEACH STATE PARK 🚶🏖️ Broad, flat and sandy North Beach, extending 22 miles from Moclips (just north of Pacific Beach) to the north jetty of Grays Harbor at Ocean Shores, is the *raison d'être* of the entire park. Beachcombing, kite flying, jogging and (in season) surf-perchfishing and razor-clam digging are popular activities. Swimming is not recommended because of undertow and riptides. Facilities are limited to restrooms and picnic areas. ~ Located along Route 109 in Pacific Beach; 360-276-4297, fax 360-289-9059.

▲ There are 64 sites, 33 with electric hookups; $10 to $15 per night. For reservations, call 800-452-5687 in summers only.

▼▼▼▼▼▼▼▼▼▼▼▼

Grays Harbor Area

Industrial towns are not often places of tourist interest. The twin cities of Aberdeen and Hoquiam, on the northeastern shore of the broad Grays Harbor estuary, are an exception. A historic seaport, a rich assortment of bird life and numerous handsome mansions built by old timber money make it worthwhile to pause in this corner of Washington.

Aberdeen has about 16,750 people, Hoquiam around 9000, and the metropolitan area includes some 33,000. Wood-products industries provide the economic base; in fact, more trees are harvested in Grays Harbor County than in any other county in the United States. Boat building and fisheries, both more important in past decades, remain key businesses.

SIGHTS

For information on the region, check with the **Grays Harbor Chamber of Commerce**. ~ Duffy Street at Route 101, Aberdeen; 360-532-1924, 800-321-1924; www.graysharbor.org.

If you're coming down Route 101 from the north, it's wise to follow the signs and make your first stop a guided tour of **Hoquiam's Castle**. A stately, 28-room hillside mansion built in 1897 by a millionaire lumber baron, it has been fully restored with elegant antiques like Tiffany lamps, grandfather clocks and a 600-piece, cut-crystal chandelier. With its round turret and bright red color, the house is unmistakable. Open weekends only in winter. Admission. ~ 515 Chenault Avenue, Hoquiam; phone/fax 360-533-2005; www.hoquiamscastle.com.

Also in Hoquiam is the **Arnold Polson Museum**. Built in the early 1920s by a pioneer timber family and furnished with pieces donated by Hoquiam and Grays Harbor County residents, the 26-room home represents the history of the area. It is surrounded by native trees and the Burton Ross Memorial Rose Gardens. Open weekends only in winter. Admission. ~ 1611 Riverside Avenue at Route 101, Hoquiam; phone/fax 360-533-5862.

A couple miles west of Hoquiam on Route 109, at Bowerman Basin on Grays Harbor, next to Bowerman Airfield, is the **Grays Harbor National Wildlife Refuge**, one of four major staging areas for migratory shorebirds in North America. Although this basin represents just two percent of the intertidal habitat of the estuary, fully half of the one million shorebirds that visit each spring make their stop here. April and early May are the best times to visit. ~ 360-753-9467, fax 360-534-9302.

A major attraction in neighboring Aberdeen, just four miles east of Hoquiam on Route 101, is the **Grays Harbor Historical Seaport**. Craftspersons at this working 18th-century shipyard have constructed a replica of the *Lady Washington*, the brigantine in which Captain Robert Gray sailed when he discovered Grays Harbor and the Columbia River in 1783. There are also two 18th-century longboat reproductions, as well as informational and hands-on exhibits. Visitors can stay and watch the shipbuilders at work or go for a sail on the *Lady Washington*. Call 24 hours ahead for schedules. Open summers only. ~ 813 East Heron Street, Aberdeen; 360-532-8611, fax 360-533-9384; www.ladywashington.org.

A few blocks west, the **Aberdeen Museum of History** offers exhibits, dioramas and videos of regional history in a 1922 armory. Displays include several re-created early 20th-century buildings: a one-room school, a general store, a church, a blacksmith's shop and more. Closed Monday and Tuesday from June through Labor Day and weekdays the rest of the year. ~ 111 East 3rd Street, Aberdeen; 360-533-1976.

Route 105 follows the south shore of Grays Harbor west from Aberdeen to the atmospheric fishing village of **Westport**, at the estuary's south head. Perhaps the most interesting of several small museums here is the **Westport Maritime Museum**, housed in a Nantucket-style Coast Guard station commissioned in 1939 but decommissioned in the 1970s. Historic photos, artifacts and memorabilia help tell the story of a sailor's life. The museum also has exhibits of skeletons of marine mammals (including whales), a beachcombing exhibit, a children's discovery room and tours of the Grays Harbor lighthouse. Closed Friday through Sunday in winter. Admission. ~ 2201 Westhaven Drive, Westport; phone/fax 360-268-0078; www.westportwa.com/museum.

Other spots of interest in Westport include the **Westport Aquarium**, with tanks of fish and other ocean creatures. Admission. ~ 321 Harbor Street, Westport; 360-268-0471. Also in town is **Shellflair**, featuring displays of sea shells, crustacea and fossils. Closed in winter. Admission. ~ 102 South Forest Street, Westport; 360-268-9087.

There's considerable character at the **Lytle House Bed & Breakfast**, a three-story Victorian hillside mansion. Each of the eight guest rooms, six of which have private bathrooms with clawfoot tubs, has a different theme, such as nautical (Harbor View room) and equestrian (Esquire). Guests choose a full gourmet breakfast from a menu offered the previous night. The house hosts murder-mystery parties by guest appointment. ~ 509 Chenault Street, Ho-

LODGING

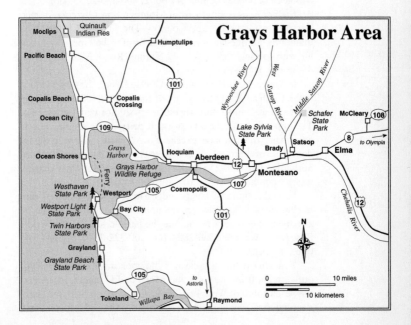

quiam; 360-533-2320, 800-677-2320, fax 360-533-4025; www. lytlehouse.com. MODERATE TO DELUXE.

Like any regional center, the twin cities of Aberdeen and Hoquiam have a strip of look-alike motels along Route 101. Though it's hard to choose one above another, the **Olympic Inn Motel** is notable for its modern, spacious rooms. Decor in the 55 units is simple but pleasant. ~ 616 West Heron Street, Aberdeen; 360-533-4200, 800-562-8618, fax 360-533-6223; www.wa-accommodations.com. MODERATE TO ULTRA-DELUXE.

Just southeast of Aberdeen, the **Cooney Mansion** is located in a secluded wooded area on a golf course with an adjoining tennis court and park. A National Historic Landmark built in 1908 by a lumber baron, its interior was designed to show off local woods. Now a bed and breakfast, it has nine bedrooms, five with private baths, as well as a jacuzzi, sauna, sundeck and exercise room. Full lumber baron's breakfast included. ~ 1705 5th Street, Cosmopolis; phone/fax 360-533-0602; www.cooneymansion.com. MODERATE TO ULTRA-DELUXE.

The Whitney Gardens in Brinnon, on Route 101, boast an extensive collection of rhododendrons, Washington state's official flower.

East of Aberdeen in the county seat of Montesano is the **Abel House**. This stately 1908 home has five bedrooms, two with private baths. There are also a game room and reading room and an exquisite English garden. A full breakfast, afternoon tea and dessert are included in the room rate. ~ 117 Fleet Street South, Montesano; phone/fax 360-249-6002, 800-235-2235. MODERATE.

Farther east—halfway from Montesano to Olympia, in fact, but still in Grays Harbor County—**The Old McCleary Hotel** maintains antique-laden rooms that seem to be especially popular with touring bicyclists. ~ 42 Summit Road, McCleary; 360-495-3678. BUDGET.

In Westport, at the mouth of Grays Harbor, the largest motel is the **Château Westport**. Many of the 108 units have balconies and fireplaces, and a third are efficiency studios with kitchenettes. The upper floors of the four-story property, easily identified by its gray mansard roof, have excellent ocean views. Dip into the indoor pool and hot tub. ~ 710 West Hancock Avenue, Westport; 360-268-9101, 800-255-9101, fax 360-268-1646; www.chateau westport.com. MODERATE TO ULTRA-DELUXE.

For value-hunters, **The Islander Motel & RV Park** offers simple but clean and spacious motel units. Fifty-seven RV spaces are also available, some overlooking the harbor. ~ 421 East Neddie Rose Drive, Westport; 360-268-9166, 800-322-1740, fax 360-268-0902. MODERATE.

You can catch a fish, clean it and cook it for dinner all without straying from the **Grayland Motel and Cottages**, located on the beach south of Westport. The grounds offer a fish- and clam-cleaning shed, children's play area, motel units and self-contained cottages with tiled kitchens, pine furnishings and small living/dining areas. ~ 2013 Route 105, Grayland; 360-267-2395, 800-292-0845. BUDGET TO MODERATE.

It's a comfort to know that Grays Harbor has a few memorable restaurants to go with its memorable accommodations.

DINING

When chef Pierre Gabelli moved to the Washington coast from Italy, it was only natural that he should open the **Parma Ristorante Italiano**. Dine on gourmet pastas like gnocchi and tortelli d'Erbetta, as well as a handful of outstanding meat dishes. Best of all are the homemade desserts. Closed Sunday and Monday. ~ 116 West Heron Street, Aberdeen; 360-532-3166. MODERATE.

◄ HIDDEN

Bridges Restaurant is a handsome, garden-style restaurant with one dining room and a banquet room that's actually a greenhouse. As the size of its parking lot attests, it's very popular locally, for its lounge as well as its cuisine. Local seafood, steaks, chicken and pasta highlight the menu. ~ 112 North G Street, Aberdeen; 360-532-6563, fax 360-532-5490. MODERATE.

For historic flavor, you needn't look further than **Billy's Bar and Grill**. Named for an early 20th-century ne'er-do-well notorious for mugging loggers and shanghaiing sailors, Billy's boasts an ornate century-old ceiling, huge antique bar and wall murals that are colorful if not downright bawdy. This is the place to settle back with a burger and a beer and soak up the past. ~ 322 East Heron Street, Aberdeen; 360-533-7144, fax 360-532-5490. BUDGET TO MODERATE.

Elsewhere in the area, the **Hong Kong Restaurant** is surprisingly authentic for a town so far removed from China! It has chop suey and egg foo yung, yes, but it also has egg flower soup, *moo goo gai pan* and other tastes from the old country. Closed Monday. ~ 1212 East 1st Street, Cosmopolis; 360-533-7594. BUDGET TO MODERATE.

There aren't many restaurant choices in McCleary, but if you appreciate a good old-fashioned hamburger, head for **M & M Burger House**. An authentic 1950s burger stand with drive-up service and a tiny inside dining area, the M & M makes burgers to order with heated buns, quality beef and a variety of toppings. Some other specialties are homemade soups and fries, fresh salads and soda fountain treats. ~ 301 Simpson Avenue, McCleary; 360-495-3822. BUDGET.

For a sampling of creations by regional artisans visit the **Pacific Center of the Arts and Crafts**, which features pottery, original art, prints and gift items. ~ 1767 Route 105, Grayland; 360-267-1351.

SHOPPING

Folks in the Grays Harbor area show a predilection for **Sidney's Casino**, where a deejay spins discs Friday and Saturday. ~ 512 West Heron Avenue, Aberdeen; 360-533-6635 or 360-533-0296 (bar).

NIGHTLIFE

Also check out the Victorian bar at **Billy's Bar and Grill**. ~ 322 East Heron Street, Aberdeen; 360-533-7144. The posh lounge at **Bridges Restaurant** is also a happenin' spot for drinks. ~ 112 North G Street, Aberdeen; 360-532-6563.

BEACHES & PARKS

LAKE SYLVIA STATE PARK Visitors can circumambulate this narrow, forest-enshrouded lake on a two-mile hiking trail. Also here are trout fishing (from a non-motorized boat or from shore), a swimming beach and boat rentals in season. There are restrooms, picnic areas and groceries. ~ Located two miles north of Montesano off Route 12, via North 3rd Street; 360-249-3621, fax 360-586-4272.

▲ There are 35 sites; $11 per night. Open summer only.

SCHAFER STATE PARK Once a family park for employees of the Schafer Logging Company, this tranquil 119-acre site on the East Fork of the Satsop River is still popular with families. This heavily forested park is ideal for picnics, hikes and fishing. You can fish for rainbow trout, cutthroat trout, salmon and steelhead in the river. Swimmers may find the water too cold. You'll find restrooms and picnic areas. ~ West 1365 Schafer Park Road, 12 miles north of Elma, off Route 12 via Brady; 360-482-3852, fax 360-586-4272.

▲ There are 42 sites, six with hookups; $10 to $15 per night. Open summer only.

WYNOOCHEE LAKE RECREATION AREA Originally an Army Corps of Engineers project, now run by Tacoma Power, this four-and-a-half-mile-long lake was created in 1972 by a water-supply and flood-control dam on the Wynoochee River. The visitors center has interpretive displays. A 12-mile trail winds around the lake, past a beach and designated swimming area. Trout fishing, waterskiing, swimming (the water is cold, though), horseback riding (on the roads only) and wildlife watching are also popular. Restrooms and picnic areas are the only facilities. ~ Located off Route 12 about 35 miles north of Montesano on West Valley Road. Take a left on Forest Service Road 22 and a right on Forest Service Road 2294; 360-877-5254, fax 360-352-2569.

▲ There are 46 developed sites and ten primitive sites in the Coho campground; $8 and $12 per night. Closed December through April.

WESTHAVEN & WESTPORT LIGHT STATE PARKS Westhaven State Park, which occupies the southern headland at the mouth of Grays Harbor, is a great place for watching birds and wildlife, including harbor seals and whales during migratory periods. Surfing is excellent here (try the jetty) and there are yearly competitions. Surfers and swimmers should be very careful of riptides. Westhaven is adjacent to Westport Light State Park, from which you can see a historic lighthouse that's warned coastal ships of the entrance to Grays Harbor since 1897. There's a multiuse paved trail connecting the two parks that's open for hiking, bicycling, inline skating and other nonmotorized forms of transportation. You can fish for salmon, ocean perch, codfish and Dungeness crab from the shores of both parks or the jetty of Westhaven. There are restrooms and picnic areas. ~ Both parks are close to downtown Westport; Westhaven is about one and a half miles from downtown on East Yearout Drive; Westport Light is a half mile from downtown at the end of Ocean Avenue; 360-268-9565, fax 360-268-0732.

> Grays Harbor National Wildlife Refuge is the last place to be flooded at high tide and the first to have its mudflats exposed, giving the avians extra feeding time.

TWIN HARBORS STATE PARK 🚶 🚴 🏄 🛶 The Washington coast's largest campground dominates this 168-acre park. It also includes the Shifting Sands Nature Trail with interpretive signs for dunes explorers. Beachcombing, kite flying and clamming are popular activities on the broad, sandy beach. There's fishing in the surf or from a boat (which you can charter at Westport) for cod, salmon, ocean perch and Dungeness crab, but swimming is not recommended because of riptides. You'll find restrooms and picnic areas. ~ Located along Route 105, four miles south of Westport and four miles north of Grayland; 360-268-9717, fax 360-268-0372.

▲ There are 307 sites, three of which are for campers with disabilities, 49 with RV hookups; $11 and $16 per night. Closed November through February. Call 800-452-5687 for reservations.

GRAYLAND BEACH STATE PARK 🚶 🛶 This 400-acre park is broad and flat and ideal for surf fishing, clam digging, beachcombing, kite flying and other seaside diversions. Swimming is discouraged due to riptides. You'll find restrooms, groceries and restaurants in Grayland. ~ Located on Route 105, one mile south of Grayland; 360-267-4301, fax 360-268-0372.

▲ There are 60 sites with full RV hookups; $16 per night. Call 800-452-5687 for reservations.

This region is the largest "unpopulated" estuary in the continental United States. Its pristine condition makes it one of the world's best places for farming oysters. From Tokeland to Bay Center to Oysterville, tiny villages that derive their sole income from the shelled creatures display mountains of empty shells as evidence of their success. Begin your visit on Route 105 south from Westport, then head east along the northern shore of Willapa Bay.

Long Beach–Willapa Bay

SIGHTS

Thirty-three miles from Westport, Route 105 rejoins Route 101 at **Raymond**. This town of 3000, and its smaller sister community of **South Bend** four miles south on Route 101, are lumber ports on the lower Willapa River.

You'll find murals—43 of them, to be exact—on walls from Ocean Shores to the Columbia River, Elma to Ilwaco. Chambers of commerce and other visitor information centers have guide pamphlets. But no mural is larger than the 85-foot-wide painting of an early logger on the **Dennis Company Building**. The company's outdoor display of old-time farm equipment is across the street. ~ 5th Street, Raymond.

Attractions in South Bend include the **Pacific County Museum**, with pioneer artifacts from the turn of the century. ~ 1008 West Robert Bush Drive, South Bend; 360-875-5224.

Also have a look at South Bend's 1911 **Pacific County Courthouse**, noted for its art-glass dome and historic foyer wall paintings. ~ 300 Memorial Drive off Route 101, South Bend; 360-875-9300.

The **Long Beach Peninsula**, reached via Route 101 from South Bend (43 miles), has had a significant flow of vacationing Northwest urbanites for over a century. But its economy is more strongly founded in fish processing and cranberry growing. Information is available from the **Long Beach Peninsula Visitor Bureau**. ~ Route 101 and Route 103, Seaview; 360-642-2400; www.funbeach.com.

Route 103, which runs north–south up the 28-mile-long, two-mile-wide peninsula, is intersected by Route 101 at **Seaview**. The town of **Long Beach** is just a mile north of the junction.

Long Beach's principal attraction is a 2300-foot-long wooden **boardwalk**, South 10th to Bolstad streets, elevated above the dunes, enabling folks to make an easy trek to the high-tide mark. The beach, incidentally, is open to driving on the hard upper sand, and to surf fishing, clamming (in season), beachcombing, kite flying and picnicking everywhere.

Kite flying is a big thing on the Washington coast, so it's no accident that the **World Kite Museum and Hall of Fame** is in Long Beach. The museum has rotating exhibits of kites from around the world—Japanese, Chinese, Thai and so on—with displays of stunt kites, advertising kites and more. Call ahead for hours. Admission. ~ 3rd Street Northwest at Route 103, Long Beach; 360-642-4020; www.worldkitemuseum.com.

The **Pacific Coast Cranberry Museum** provides a historic view of the West Coast cranberry industry. Exhibits include hand tools, cranberry boxes, labels, pickers, sorters and separators. ~ 2907 Pioneer Road, Long Beach; 360-642-5553.

During the peak blooming season in May, the **Clarke Rhododendron Nursery** is a dazzling place to view rhododendrons and azaleas in all their splendor. ~ 15600 Sandridge Road, Long Beach; 360-642-2241.

North of Long Beach ten miles is **Ocean Park**, the commercial hub of the central and northern Long Beach Peninsula. Developed as a Methodist camp in 1883, it evolved into a small resort town.

Older yet is **Oysterville**, another three miles north via Sandridge Road. Founded in 1854, this National Historic District boasts the oldest continuously operating post office in Washington (1858) and 17 other designated historic sites. Get a walking-tour pamphlet from the **Old Church** beside the Village Green. ~ Territory Road, Oysterville.

South of Seaview just two miles on Route 103 is **Ilwaco,** spanning the isthmus between the Columbia River and the Pacific Ocean.

Local history is featured at the impressive **Ilwaco Heritage Museum.** A series of galleries depicts the development of southwestern Washington from early Indian culture to European voyages of discovery, from pioneer settlement to the early 20th century. Closed Sunday in winter. Admission. ~ 115 Southeast Lake Street, Ilwaco; 360-642-3446.

About eight miles southeast, a short distance before Route 101 crosses the Columbia River to Astoria, Oregon, **Fort Columbia**

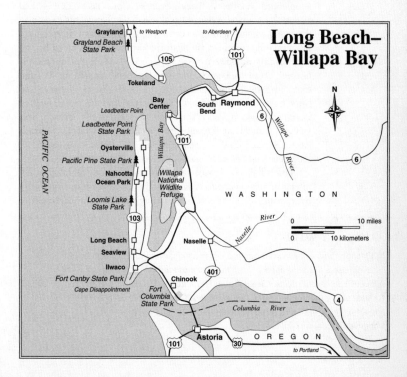

State Park is a highly recommended stop for history buffs. Two buildings at the site are museums: the **Fort Columbia Interpretive Center**, exhibiting artifacts of early-20th-century military life in a former coastal artillery post, and the **Columbia House**, which the Daughters of the American Revolution have restored to depict the everyday lifestyle of a military officer of the time. The state park is open summer only. ~ Route 101, Chinook; 360-777-8221.

LODGING

Possibly the most delightful accommodation anywhere on the Washington coast is the **Shelburne Country Inn**. The oldest continually operating hotel in the state, it opened in 1896 and is still going strong. Fifteen guest rooms are furnished with Victorian antiques and fresh flowers. All have private baths and most have decks. A hearty country breakfast is served in the morning, as well as freshly baked cookies upon arrival. ~ 4415 Pacific Way, Seaview; 360-642-2442, 800-466-1896, fax 360-642-8904; www.the shelburneinn.com. DELUXE TO ULTRA-DELUXE.

HIDDEN ▶

Another one-of-a-kinder, but for very different reasons, is **The Sou'wester Lodge, Cabins and Tch! Tch!** It's a place much beloved by youth hostelers who, well, grew up. Proprietors Leonard and Miriam Atkins have intentionally kept the accommodation simple and weathered. They advertise it as a B&MYODB—"bed and make your own damn breakfast." Kitchen rights extend to the living room, including the fireplace and library. Sleeping options include rooms in the historic lodge, cedar-shingled housekeeping cabins, a dozen-or-so vintage TCH! TCH! RVs and mobile homes ("Trailer Classics Hodgepodge") and an area for RVs and tent campers. The historic lodge draws an artistic clientele and often hosts cultural events such as poetry readings or evenings of chamber music. It also is the closest lodging to the ocean in Seaview, separated from the water only by protected wetlands. ~ Beach Access Road, 38th Place, Seaview; 360-642-2542; www.souwester lodge.com, e-mail info@souwesterlodge.com. BUDGET TO DELUXE.

The Whale's Tale Motel and Bookshop in central Long Beach offers amazingly economical one- and two-bedroom suites with living rooms and full kitchens. Though the accommodations are

CATCH THE WAVE

In October and early November, the cranberry harvest takes precedence over all else on the peninsula. Most fields are owned by local farmers who sell much of their crop to Ocean Spray. The **Pacific Coast Cranberry Research Foundation** offers free self-guided tours of the cranberry bogs during harvest, and other times by appointment. ~ Pioneer Road, Long Beach; 360-642-2891.

plain and a little frayed around the edges, guests enjoy the use of a recreation hall with a ping pong table, pool table, hot tub, sauna and exercise equipment, as well as free use of a rubber boat, fresh-water fishing gear and metal detector. ~ P.O. Box 418, Long Beach, WA 98631; 360-642-3455, 800-559-4253, fax 360-642-2626; www.thewhalestale.com. BUDGET.

Numerous beachfront cabin communities speckle the shoreline of the Long Beach Peninsula north from the towns of Ilwaco and Seaview. One of the best is the **Klipsan Beach Cottages**. Each of the ten cottages, in a lovely wooded setting eight miles north of the town of Long Beach, has a kitchen and fireplace or wood-burning stove (with free firewood). There is also a two-bedroom and a three-bedroom unit. Closed in early January. ~ 22617 Pacific Highway, Ocean Park; 360-665-4888, fax 360-665-3580. MODERATE TO DELUXE.

A yellow, fairytale-like Victorian perched on the edge of Willapa Bay, **Caswell's on the Bay** offers five antique-furnished rooms with garden or water views. Unwind in the fireplace-warmed parlor or the book-filled library; refreshments are served daily in the sun room. If you're quiet on the covered deck, you might spy deer roaming the three-acre grounds. Full breakfast included. ~ 25204 Sandridge Road, Ocean Park; 360-665-6535, 888-553-2319, fax 360-665-6500; www.caswellsinn.com. MODERATE TO ULTRA-DELUXE.

Shakti Cove is a located just five minutes from the water. Ten rustic cabins all are fully equipped with kitchens and sleep up to four guests. The units are furnished with queen-size beds, older couches and feature eclectic decor. Pets are welcome. Gay-friendly. ~ 253rd Place and Park Avenue, Ocean Park; 360-665-4000, fax 360-665-6000; www.shatkicove.com. MODERATE.

A hideaway on a pristine stretch of beach near Ocean Park, **Coast Watch Bed & Breakfast** has two suites where unobstructed views of dunes and the sea take center stage. Each suite has a queen-size bed and sitting area and is decorated in subtle earth tones and wicker furnishings. A private walking trail leads to the beach. Breakfasts of fresh fruit and muffins are served in the suite. Call ahead for directions. ~ P.O. Box 841, Ocean Park, WA 98640; 360-665-6774; www.willapabay.org/~kmj/cw. MODERATE.

Willapa Bay oyster lovers frequent the beds near the north end of the Long Beach Peninsula, and this is where they'll find the **Moby Dick Hotel**. An 11-room bed-and-breakfast inn that first opened its doors in 1930, it maintains a country nautical atmosphere, with rambling grounds, its own vegetable garden and oyster farm. A fireplace, bayside pavilion, sauna and piano beckon on rainy days. Dinners feature visiting chefs in summer. ~ Sandridge Road near Bay Avenue, Nahcotta; 360-665-4543, fax 360-665-6887; www.nwplace.com/mobydick.html. MODERATE.

◀ HIDDEN

The Inn at Ilwaco blends its elements in a unique manner: Housed in a 1928 building that was once the Ilwaco Presbyterian Church, it's a bed and breakfast and wedding chapel! Nine guest rooms with private baths and a two-bedroom suite with two baths occupy the old Sunday school wing. And yes, you can get married here in the sanctuary. ~ 120 Williams Street Northeast, Ilwaco; 360-642-8686, 888-244-2523, fax 360-642-8642; www.longbeach lodging.com. MODERATE TO ULTRA-DELUXE.

DINING

HIDDEN ►

For a unique dining experience, visit the **Blue Heron Inn**, on an off-the-beaten-track peninsula that juts into Willapa Bay 12 miles south of South Bend just off Route 101. Oysters, of course, are a specialty at this café-tavern; they even serve them for breakfast, along with other seafood omelettes. The fish market here also sells fresh crab and smoked salmon. ~ Bay Center Road at 2nd and Bridge streets, Bay Center; 360-875-5130. MODERATE.

Expensive, but worth it. Everything is exquisite in **The Shoal-water Restaurant**, one of Washington's most highly acclaimed country restaurants. From the seafood mousseline to the mussel chowder, the country rabbit sausage to the sautéed Willapa Bay oysters with a Thai-style wild mushroom sauce and the creative preparations of the day's fresh catches, a meal here is one to savor. The turn-of-the-20th-century ambience adds an element of comfort. ~ Shelburne Inn, 4415 Pacific Way, Seaview; 360-642-4142, fax 360-642-8826. MODERATE TO ULTRA-DELUXE.

Opposite the restaurant entrance is **The Heron & Beaver Pub**, with light meals produced by the same kitchen as the Shoalwater Restaurant. ~ Shelburne Inn, 4415 Pacific Way, Seaview; 360-642-4142. MODERATE.

Owned and operated by the former chef and manager of the renowned Shoalwater Restaurant, the **42nd St. Café** is fast making its own reputation. Hand-cut ravioli sauced with sun-dried tomato cream, iron skillet fried chicken, pot roast with vegetables and other down-home fare are prepared with a gourmet hand. The café is located in a converted army barracks. The dining room is bright and casual with blue and green cloth napery, candles and fresh flowers. Breakfast, lunch and dinner. ~ Route 1 at 42nd Street, Seaview; 360-642-2323, fax 360-642-3439. BUDGET TO MODERATE.

My Mom's Pie Kitchen has great pies—from wild blackberry to chocolate almond to sour-cream raisin. The small menu also offers clam chowder, curry chicken salad and meatloaf sandwiches, and the chicken-almond pot pie is a mouth-watering delight. Lunch only. Closed Sunday through Tuesday and December through May. ~ 1113 Pacific Avenue Southwest, Long Beach; 360-642-2342. BUDGET.

Mountains of oyster shells surround **The Ark Restaurant and Bakery**, located near the north end of the Long Beach Peninsula on oyster-rich Willapa Bay. In fact, the casual, relaxed restaurant has its own oyster beds—as well as an herb and edible-flower garden and a busy bakery. Nearby are cranberry bogs and forests of wild mushrooms. All these go into the preparation of creative dishes like pan-fried salmon with wild mushrooms, sun-dried tomatoes and balsamic crème sauce, the scallop sautée with ginger, cilantro, coconut milk and lemongrass and the Ark all-you-can-eat oyster feed, a decades-old tradition. Dinner Tuesday through Sunday; Sunday brunch. Call ahead for winter hours. ~ 270 3rd Street and Sandridge Road, Nahcotta; 360-665-4133, fax 360-665-5043. MODERATE TO DELUXE.

The **Corral Drive In** claims its Tsunami is the world's largest hamburger—and who's to argue with a five-pounder on a 15-and-a-half-inch bun? Not only is it huge (better have the whole family along), it's actually quite good. The place also has regular burgers, fries, milkshakes and such. ~ North Pacific Highway and 95th Street North, Long Beach; 360-642-2774. BUDGET.

◀ HIDDEN

SHOPPING

There's wonderful bric-a-brac at **Marsh's Free Museum**, from world-famous Jake the Alligator Man, an authentic shrunken head and freaks-of-nature stuffed animals to antique jewelry. ~ 409 Pacific Avenue South, Long Beach; 360-642-2188.

The souvenir most typical of beach recreation here, perhaps, would be a colorful kite. Look for them in Long Beach at **Ocean Kites** located at 511 Pacific Avenue South (360-642-2229) and **Long Beach Kites** at 104 Pacific Avenue North (360-642-2202).

Noted watercolorist Eric Wiegardt displays his work at the **Wiegardt Studio Gallery**. ~ 2607 Bay Avenue between Route 103 and Sandridge Road, Ocean Park; 360-665-5976.

NIGHTLIFE

The Lightship Restaurant has the Long Beach Peninsula's only ocean-view restaurant from its third-story loft; come for a sunset drink. ~ Nendel's Edgewater Inn, 409 Southwest 10th Street, Long Beach; 360-642-3252. Quiet beers are best quaffed at **The Heron & Beaver Pub** in the Shelburne Inn. ~ 4415 Pacific Way, Seaview; 360-642-4142.

MANNA FROM HEAVEN

Dining at **The Sanctuary** is a sacred ritual to some folks. And well it should be: The restaurant occupies the premises of the historic Methodist Episcopal Church of Chinook (1906–1978). Few renovations have been made to the building, although wine is taken much more often than during communion, and sundaes can sometimes be sinful. The varied menu includes Swedish meatballs and fish cakes, steaks and fresh seafood. Dinner only. Call ahead for hours. ~ Route 101 and Hazel Street, Chinook; 360-777-8380; www.seattleintheround.com/sanctuary. MODERATE.

BEACHES
& PARKS

LOOMIS LAKE STATE PARK 🏃 ⚓ Situated south of Klipsan Beach, this day-use park offers ocean beach access with good fishing from the shore and good clamming on the beach. Swimming is not recommended. Facilities include restrooms and picnic areas. ~ Located on Park Road off Route 103 (Pacific Way), four miles south of Ocean Park; 360-642-3078, fax 360-642-4216.

PACIFIC PINES STATE PARK 🏃 ⚓ This day-use park offers beach access for various activities, like beachcombing, kite flying, jogging, surf fishing and razor clam digging in season. You can drive on the uppermost sand, but be sure it's hard-packed; more than one car owner has needed a tow after getting bogged in the sand. There are restrooms and picnic areas. ~ At 274th Place off Park Avenue, a mile north of Ocean Park; 360-642-3078, fax 360-642-4216.

LEADBETTER POINT STATE PARK 🏃 🚲 ⚓ Shifting dunes and mudflats, ponds and marshes, grasslands and forests make this northern tip of the Long Beach Peninsula an ideal place for those who like to observe nature. As many as 100 species of migratory birds stop over here. There are numerous hiking trails. Surf fishing is popular, but riptides discourage swimming. You'll find pit toilets, restrooms and picnic areas. ~ Located three miles north of Oysterville on Stackpole Road, via Route 103 and Sandridge Road; 360-642-3078, fax 360-642-4216.

Leadbetter Point State Park was originally named Low Point in 1788; it was renamed in 1852.

FORT CANBY STATE PARK 🏃 🚲 🛶 🚣 🚤 ⚓ The point where the Columbia River meets the Pacific Ocean has been a crossroads of history for two centuries. The Lewis and Clark expedition arrived at this dramatic headland in 1805 after 18 months on the trail. Two 19th-century lighthouses—at North Head on the Pacific and at Cape Disappointment on a Columbia sandbar—have limited the number of shipwrecks to a mere 200 through 1994. The fort was occupied from the Civil War through World War II. Today, the 1800-acre park contains the Lewis and Clark Interpretive Center (with exhibits and a multimedia program), numerous forest, beach and clifftop trails, a boat launch, a swimming beach, fishing (in the surf, from the jetty or from a boat), summer interpretive programs, lighthouse tours, restrooms, picnic areas and groceries. ~ Located two and a half miles southwest of Ilwaco on Route 101; 360-642-3078, fax 360-642-4216.

▲ There are 250 sites, 90 with RV hookups; $11 to $16 per night. For reservations, call 800-452-5687.

Southwest Washington

Heading east from the coast via Route 401 and Route 4, you'll want to take the cutoff south to the circa 1905 **Grays River Covered Bridge**. Continue east another 17 miles to Skamokawa, a town that's hard to pronounce and easy to visit. The site of an

Indian village that dates back two thousand years, this lumber town is on the Lewis and Clark Trail. Local Skamokawa Vista Park is a good spot to watch traffic on the Columbia River shipping channel. At **Redman Hall,** an 1894 schoolhouse has become a riverlife interpretive center. Step inside the three-story landmark to learn more about this 19th-century riverfront town now on the National Register of Historic Places. Closed Monday and Tuesday. ~ 1394 West Route 4, Skamokawa; 360-795-3007.

To the east, you won't want to miss the **Julia Butler Hansen National Wildlife Refuge.** A sanctuary for the Columbian white-tailed deer, this waterfront refuge is also a place to spot elk and migratory birds. ~ Route 4, Cathlamet; 360-795-3915.

The refuge is next door to Cathlamet, a historic logging town. Begin your visit at the **Wahkiakum County Museum.** The collection is strong on community artifacts, victrolas, dolls and railway equipment. Closed Monday in summer and Monday through Wednesday in winter. Admission. ~ 65 River Street, Cathlamet; 360-795-3954.

▼▼▼▼▼▼▼▼▼▼▼▼▼

Outdoor Adventures

SPORT-FISHING

Despite charter operators' complaints that government restrictions hinder their operations, the Strait of Juan de Fuca is still one of the nation's great salmon grounds, with chinook, coho and other species running the waters during the summer months. From April to September, halibut is also big in these waters—literally: one local operator holds the state record, 268 pounds. Bottomfish like ling cod, true cod, red snapper and black bass round out the angling possibilities.

OLYMPIC COAST   When **Big Salmon Charters** isn't breaking state records for halibut (288 pounds), it runs half-day charters for salmon and bottomfish. The store also sells bait and rents tackle. ~ Bay View Avenue (or Front Street), Neah Bay; 360-645-2374.

Herb's Motel runs six-hour trips in the Strait of Juan de Fuca for salmon, halibut, ling cod and bottomfish, accommodating up to six people. The resort provides bait and tackle. ~ Sekiu; 360-963-2346.

GRAYS HARBOR AREA   **Deep Sea Charters** operates six boats for one-day bottomfish charters, and for overnight tuna charters. The price includes bait and tackle. ~ Across from Float 6, Westport; 360-268-9300.

Neptune Charters runs one-day trips for salmon, bottomfish and halibut and two-day trips for tuna, as well as leading whale-watching expeditions. The store sells bait and tackle. ~ 2601 Westhaven Drive, across from Float 14; 360-268-0124.

LONG BEACH–WILLAPA BAY   At the mouth of the Columbia River, Ilwaco is another center for deep-sea fishing. Salmon and sturgeon are caught near the river mouth, while tuna, rockfish, cod and sole are in deeper waters. **Seabreeze Charters** arranges day charters, operating four boats that each carry up to 16 people. Large engines cut down run times for deep-bottom trips. ~ 185 Howerton Way Southeast, Ilwaco; 360-642-2300.

RIVER FISHING

It's not just the fish—salmon, steelhead, trout—that attract anglers to the mountain streams flowing from the Olympic Mountains. Spectacular scenery and glimpses of eagles, deer, elk and other wildlife sweeten the deal.

PORT ANGELES AREA An hour or two away are several destinations for river fishing: the Sol Duc, Bogachiel, Hoh, Queets and Calawah rivers.

OLYMPIC COAST The lower Quinault River is not "overpacked" with fishermen—yet—partly because nontribal people may not fish rivers on the reservation without a Quinault guide. Contact the **Quinault Indian Nation Fish and Game Department** to receive information about available guides for drift boat or walk-in fishing. ~ 1214 Aalis Street, Taholah; 360-276-8211 ext. 227. Between Forks and La Push, **3-River Resort & Guide Service** operates two 16-foot drift boats for two anglers (plus guide) on the Sol Duc, Bogachiel and Hoh rivers (another "quiet" spot). The eight-hour trips are for salmon and steelhead. Tackle and lunch are included. ~ 7764 La Push Road, Forks; 360-374-5300.

SHELL FISHING

Before you start digging up clams or other shellfish, please remember that just like other forms of fishing, a license is required for this activity. You can pick one up at tackle shops and other locations that sell fishing licenses. Recreational harvesting of shellfish is permitted on public beaches, but you should double-check, because much of the state's tideland is privately owned. Generally, shellfishing is permitted year round; razor clams and oyster harvests are restricted by season and location. Call the **Washington State Department of Fish and Wildlife** for information. ~ 360-902-2700. You must also check with the Health Department's **Red Tide Hotline** to find out which waters are unhealthy for shellfish harvesting. ~ 800-562-5632 from inside Washington; 360-753-5992 from outside the state.

HIDDEN ▶

One of the best spots in the state is at the west end of the Hood Canal Bridge. The **Shine Public Tidelands** and **Hood Spit Tidelands** are both easily reached and offer healthy clam and oyster populations in season. The oyster beds at Hood Spit are especially bountiful; it's a hike from the access point, about a mile along the beach, but worth it. Please note that all oysters must be shucked on the beach, and their shells left where you found them. (Seed oysters are attached to mature shells.) ~ Access is off Port Ludlow Road, a half mile north of State Route 104, just after it exits the Hood Canal Bridge.

The Elwha River flows from the Olympic Mountains into the Strait of Juan de Fuca. Along the way, there are some Class II whitewater rapids—not quite a thrill ride, but enough excitement for good family fun (it's the only commercially rafted whitewater on the peninsula). Besides that, there's plenty of wildlife to see— elk, osprey, bald eagles, deer, harlequin ducks—as well as a view of a glacier. **Olympic Raft and Kayak Service** runs a couple of trips daily, each lasting about two and a half hours. The service rents canoes and sea kayaks, but the trips down the Class II Elwha and Class I Hoh rivers are on rafts. Both beginning and experienced rafters can partake. ~ 239521 Route 101 West, Port Angeles; 360-452-1443, 888-452-1443; www.raftandkayak.com.

RIVER RUNNING

Experienced or novice, kayakers who paddle around a mountain lake, through coastal marshlands or under sea cliffs will be rewarded not only with good exercise but also with the opportunity to observe abundant wildlife in a wilderness setting. Companies offering guided tours generally operate during the warmer months (May through September). But think about this: Many kayakers swear the best time to paddle is in the rain.

KAYAKING

PORT TOWNSEND AREA   Nearby Bird Island is a popular half-day sea-kayaking destination for the guided tours operated by **Kayak Port Townsend**. Trips, for up to nine people, can be extended to full day or longer. Rentals available. ~ 435 Water Street at Monroe Street, Port Townsend; 360-385-6240; 877-578-2252; www.kayakpt.com.

Port Townsend is a sea-kayaking center; call **Sport Townsend** where you can buy backpacks and kayaks. ~ 1044 Water Street, Port Townsend; 360-379-9711. **Olympic Outdoor Center** offers three-hour sea-kayaking tours on Saturday. The center also rents canoes and kayaks and offers classes. ~ 18971 Front Street, Poulsbo; 360-697-6095; www.kayakproshop.com.

PORT ANGELES AREA   For kayak rentals and sales in Port Angeles, try **Sound Bikes and Kayaks**. ~ 120 East Front Street, Port Angeles; 360-457-1240.

DIGGIN' IN

Folks who like to shellfish will be happy in Washington. There are clams (littleneck, butter, Manila and razor), scallops, oysters (Willapa Bay is famous for its oysters), mussels and crab (Dungeness Spit, north of Sequim, is the home of the renowned Dungeness crab). Then, of course, there's that Northwest oddity, the geoduck (say "gooey-duck"), whose huge foot cannot fit within its shell. See "Shellfishing" for information on this popular activity.

You may have Lake Aldwell all to yourself, aside from the waterfowl nesting along its shores, when you join a two-hour guided tour of this clear blue lake. **Olympic Raft and Kayak Service** uses the more stable sea kayaks for these lake tours. The service also offers a four-hour trip in the saltwater Freshwater Bay just west of Port Angeles, which teems with bald eagles, otters and endangered marbled murrelets. All tours have guides. ~ 239521 Route 101 West, Port Angeles; 360-452-1443, 888-452-1443; www.raftandkayak.com.

GRAYS HARBOR AREA   **Resonance Canoe and Kayak** will give you a lighter composite paddle to use on its guided tours (which often include lunch) of the sloughs and marshes fed by several rivers in the Grays Harbor area and along the coast. A favorite kayaking spot of owner Jeff Beard is the Black River, so-called for the tea-colored water (a high tannin content) of this slow-moving stream east of Elma. Paddling on the Black, which feeds into the Chehalis River, is like skimming over a carpet of vegetation. Beard manufactures, sells and rents kayaks and offers classes to individuals who may want to set out on their own. ~ 409 East Market Street, Suite B, Aberdeen; 360-532-9176; www.resonance.cc.

KITE FLYING

Several miles of wide, flat beach make the beaches at Ocean Shores and Long Beach ideal kite-flying spots. A nationally sanctioned kite-flying festival in June brings some of the sport's best fliers to Ocean Shores; the same month, competing stunt kites fill the sky over Long Beach. In August, Long Beach hosts the weeklong Washington State International Kite Festival, said to be the biggest kite festival in the country (about 100,000 people attend). You don't have to be up to championship standards, though, to buy a kite and fly it or to visit a museum about kite flying.

OCEAN SHORES–PACIFIC BEACH   Pick up a kite and some tips on how to fly it at **Ocean Shores Kites**. Besides dozens of different kites, the store sells windsocks and other wind toys (Frisbees, etc.). ~ Shores Mall, 120 Chance a la Mer, Ocean Shores; 360-289-4103.

LONG BEACH–WILLAPA BAY   The beach is about 200 yards away from **Long Beach Kites**, where you can buy a variety of kites as well as windsocks and flags. ~ 104 Pacific Highway North, Long Beach; 360-642-2202. Also in Long Beach is the **World Kite Museum and Hall of Fame**, which has probably the largest collection of Chinese and Japanese kites outside Asia. ~ 3rd Street Northwest at Route 103; 360-642-4020.

WHALE WATCHING

California gray whales and humpbacks head back up to Alaskan waters between March and May. Orcas, or killer whales, are frequently seen in the waters of the Strait of Juan de Fuca, and we

Return of the Monster Slayers

Makah, the tribal name of Neah Bay's native people, means "generous food"—and no wonder! For 2000 years, the main protein in the Makah diet was the meat of the gray whale. Men of the tribe would chase one of the 35-ton leviathans in canoes, harpoon it, and kill it by stabbing it repeatedly with spears as it towed them through the open ocean. So vital was whaling to the Makah culture that in their 1855 treaty the U.S. government guaranteed their right to hunt whales forever—the only treaty ever made by the United States that contains such a guarantee. Thereafter, the tribe also sold whale oil to non-Indian settlers and became the wealthiest Indians in the Northwest. (They are now among the poorest.) They had to stop in the 1920s after the whales nearly disappeared from coastal waters due to industrial whaling.

In recent years, since the California gray whale population has recovered and the whales have been removed from the endangered species list, the Makah intend to hold new whale hunts on a limited scale, still in traditional hand-carved log canoes but using a specially designed rifle—hopefully a single carefully aimed shot at the same instant the harpoon is thrown—as a more humane alternative to spears. Meat from the whales would be divided among the 1800 tribal members, storing any excess in tribal freezers. Under the supervision of the National Marine Fisheries Service, the tribe is allowed to take up to 20 migrating adult whales without calves in a five-year period. After nearly five years of planning the hunt and practicing the use of the harpoon and rifle, and a year of ceremonial purification, tribal hunters killed their first whale in May 1999.

Makah whaling is the subject of one of the biggest animal rights controversies in the Northwest. Opponents interpret the language of the Makah treaty as allowing whaling only as long as non-Indians were also hunting whales, before the present international ban. They also fear that despite federal prohibitions the tribe might find the Japanese importers' $1 million offer for a single whale an irresistible temptation. Tribal leaders say whaling is a matter of cultural preservation, discipline and pride. They claim that many of the tribe's health problems may come from the loss of their traditional whale meat diet and point out that the indigenous Chukotki people of Russia's Pacific coast have been "harvesting" about 165 gray whales a year for the last 40 years, yet the whale population continues to grow. Escalating with each whale hunt, the dispute is unlikely to be resolved soon.

land-based mammals can't seem to get enough of the spectacle. Many fishing charter operators convert to whale-watching cruises during these months.

GRAYS HARBOR AREA Two-and-a-half-hour cruises generally head offshore toward the whales' migration path, but occasionally the whales wander into Grays Harbor and the boats never get out to sea. In Westport, contact **Ocean Charters** for whale-watching trips. ~ Across from Float 6; 360-268-9144, 800-562-0105. In the same harbor, **Deep Sea Charters** offers more of the same. ~ Across from Float 6; 360-268-9300, 800-562-0151. From Westport, there's a number of specialty whale-cruise operators.

SKIING

The only skiing on the Olympic Peninsula is **Hurricane Ridge Ski Area**, 17 miles south of Port Angeles, in Olympic National Park. Here skiers will find a few downhill runs and several cross-country trails starting from the visitors center. There are two rope tows and a T-bar lift on site. The Hurricane Hill Road cross-country trail (1.5 miles one way) is probably the easiest of the area's six trails; the most challenging is the Hurricane Ridge Trail to Mt. Angeles, a steep three-mile route that's often icy. Rentals of downhill, cross-country and snowshoeing equipment are also available. Open December through March, weekends only. Contact the **Olympic National Park Visitor Center**. ~ 3002 Mt. Angeles Road, Port Angeles; 360-452-0330, for road conditions 360-452-0329.

RIDING STABLES

On the Olympic Peninsula, it's possible to saddle up for a guided mountain ride through forests of towering trees or a ride along the beach at sunset.

OCEAN SHORES–PACIFIC BEACH The year-round guided rides at **Nan-Sea Stables** stick to the hilly, wooded property (but never follow paved trails). The half-hour to one-hour rides take small groups past ponds and forest or along the beach; the one-and-a-half-hour sunset rides go on the beach (by reservation only); and a three-hour day camp in summer that provides grooming, saddling, riding lessons and a trail ride is great for kids and beginners. ~ 255 State Route 115, Ocean Shores; 360-289-0194.

LLAMA TREKKING

Llama lovers will be delighted to accompany an Andean pack animal into the Olympics, thanks to **Kit's Llamas**. ~ 5494 Southeast Burley-Olalla Road, Olalla; 253-857-5274. **Wooley Packer Llama Company** leads one to seven night trips into the Olympic National Rain Forest. ~ 5763 Upper Hoh Road, Forks, WA 98331; 360-374-2243.

GOLF

Bay views, ocean views, mountain views—take your pick. They're part and parcel with the courses in this region, all of which rent power carts, push carts and clubs.

PORT TOWNSEND AREA   The public 18-hole **Chevy Chase Golf Club** is set in the woods above Discovery Bay. It is a fairly flat course, although it can get a bit mushy after winter rains. ~ 7401 Cape George Road, Port Townsend; 360-385-0704. The public, double-teed, nine-hole **Port Townsend Golf Club** is located in town. It's considered the driest winter course in the area (it gets only 17 inches of rain), with rolling terrain, small greens and a driving range. ~ 1948 Blaine Street, Port Townsend; 360-385-4547. *Golf Digest* has named the semiprivate 27-hole **Port Ludlow Golf Course** designed by Robert Muir Graves one of the best in the country. Although housing flanks one section, the spectacular views of Ludlow Bay and abundant wildlife prompt comments like "Amazing" and "It's like golfing in a national park" from local duffers. ~ 751 Highland Drive, Port Ludlow; 360-437-0272, 800-455-0272.

For biking, hiking, canoeing and country life, you can't beat Puget Island, a bucolic retreat just minutes from Cathlamet connecting Washington to Oregon via ferry.

PORT ANGELES AREA   Although the 18-hole private **Sunland Golf and Country Club** goes through a housing development, it's well treed and fairly flat. Call for reciprocal play times. ~ 109 Hilltop Drive, Sequim; 360-683-6800. **Dungeness Golf & Country Club** offers a semiprivate, 18-hole course. The number-three hole, called "Old Crabbie," has ten contracts guarding the crab-shaped green. ~ 1965 Woodcock Road, Sequim; 360-683-6344.

OCEAN SHORES–PACIFIC BEACH   The front nine of the municipal **Ocean Shores Golf Course** has a links-like layout in the dunes; the back nine wanders into the trees. ~ 500 Canal Drive Northeast at Albatross Street, Ocean Shores; 360-289-3357.

GRAYS HARBOR AREA   An old farming tract turned into a public 18-hole golf course in the early 1920s, **Oaksridge Golf Course** is very flat. It's pretty wet in the winter, but drains fast. The front nine is long. ~ 1052 Monte–Elma Road, Elma; 360-482-3511.

Except along the southwestern shore areas, bicycling this part of Washington requires strength and stamina. There's spectacular beauty here, but there's also lots of rain and challenging terrain.

BIKING

PORT TOWNSEND AREA   Recreational bicyclists will probably enjoy a ride through **Fort Worden State Park**, which overlooks the Strait of Juan de Fuca, in Port Townsend.

OLYMPIC COAST   A recommended road tour is the 85-mile **Upper Peninsula Tour** from Sequim to Neah Bay. The 55-mile trip down Route 101 from **Port Angeles to Forks** is also recommended. A paved six-mile trail loops the Port Angeles waterfront. The trail is flat, mostly following the shoreline, with picnic tables and other stopping spots along the way. On a clear day, you can see across the strait to Victoria.

OCEAN SHORES–PACIFIC BEACH One of the area's gentlest biking opportunities is the 14-mile **Ocean Shores Loop** from North Beach Park. For a map, call the Ocean Shores Chamber of Commerce, 360-289-2451.

GRAYS HARBOR AREA The 69-mile **Aberdeen-Raymond-Westport** loop on Routes 101 and 105 is worth a long ride. A new paved trail has been built in Westport along the beach. It runs for a mile and a half between two small state parks.

LONG BEACH–WILLAPA BAY The 42-mile **Seaview-Naselle** loop in Pacific County is popular.

Bike Rentals In Port Townsend, rent mountain bikes, tandems, running strollers, bike trailers and road bikes at **Port Townsend Cyclery**. ~ 100 Tyler Street, Port Townsend; 360-385-6470. In Port Angeles, rent hybrids and mountain bikes at **Sound Bikes and Kayaks**. ~ 120 East Front Street, Port Angeles; 360-457-1240. **Westport Family Fun Center** rents cruisers (with the wide tires for beach riding). ~ 1600 North Montesano Street, Westport; 360-268-0700.

HIKING

All distances listed for hiking trails are one way unless otherwise noted.

PORT TOWNSEND AREA Mount Walker Trail (2 miles) ascends the Olympics' easternmost peak (2804 feet) through a rhododendron forest. The view from the summit, across Hood Canal and the Kitsap Peninsula to Seattle and the Cascades, is unforgettable. The trailhead is one-fifth mile off Route 101 at Walker Pass, five miles south of Quilcene.

PORT ANGELES AREA Dungeness Spit Trail (5.5 miles) extends down the outside of the longest natural sandspit in the United States, and back the inside. The spit is a national wildlife refuge with a lighthouse at its seaward end. The trail begins and ends at the Dungeness Recreation Area.

OLYMPIC NATIONAL PARK Olympic National Park and adjacent areas of Olympic National Forest are rich in backpacking opportunities. Most trails follow rivers into the high country, with its peaks and alpine lakes. **Obstruction Point Trail** (7.4 miles) leads from the Deer Park Campground to Obstruction Point, following a 6500-foot ridgeline.

The **West Fork of the Dosewallips-Anderson Pass** trail (9 miles) starts at the Dosewallips Ranger Station on the park's eastern boundary, follows the Dosewallips River to its source in the Anderson Glacier, then goes down the East Fork of the Quinault to the Graves Creek Campground.

Seven Lakes Basin Loop (22.5 miles) has several trail options, starting and ending at Sol Duc Hot Springs.

Hoh River Trail (17.5 miles) wanders through North America's most famous rainforest from the Hoh Ranger Station, to Glacier Meadows, at the base of the Blue Glacier on 7965-foot Mt. Olympus, the park's highest point.

Coastal areas of the Olympic Peninsula have hiking trails as well. **Cape Alava Loop** (11 miles) crosses from the Ozette Ranger Station to Cape Alava; follows the shoreline south to Sand Point, from which there is beach access to shipwreck memorials farther south; and returns northeast to the ranger station. Prehistoric petroglyphs and an ancient Indian village can be seen en route.

GRAYS HARBOR AREA Wynoochee Lake Shore Trail (12 miles) circles this manmade reservoir in Olympic National Forest north of Montesano.

Shifting Sands Nature Trail (.5 mile) teaches visitors to Twin Harbors State Park, south of Westport, about plant and animal life in the seaside dunes.

LONG BEACH–WILLAPA BAY Along the southwestern Washington coast there are few inland trails, but the long stretches of flat beach appeal to many walkers. **Leadbetter Point Loop Trail** (2.5 miles) weaves through the forests and dunes, and past the ponds, mudflats and marshes, of the wildlife sanctuary/state park at the northern tip of the Long Beach Peninsula. Accessible from Oysterville, it's of special interest to birdwatchers.

The Trail of the Ancient Cedars (3.2 miles) goes through an important grove of old-growth red cedar, some as large as 11 feet wide and 150 feet tall, on Long Island. You must find your own boat access to Long Island. The Willapa Bay National Wildlife Refuge provides an interpretive brochure of the trail called the Long Island brochure. ~ Milepost 24, Route 101; 360-484-3482.

IN MEMORIAM

Much of the Olympic coastline remains undeveloped. Hikers can wander along the high-water mark or on primitive trails, some wood-planked and raised above the forest floor. Offshore reefs have taken many lives over the centuries since European exploration began, and two memorials to shipwreck victims are good destinations for intrepid hikers. Nine miles south of Ozette, the **Norwegian Memorial** remembers seamen who died in an early-20th-century shipwreck. Six miles farther south, and about three miles north of Rialto Beach opposite La Push, the **Chilean Memorial** marks the grave of 20 South American sailors who died in a 1920 wreck.

Transportation

CAR

Route 101 is the main artery of the Olympic Peninsula and Washington coastal region, virtually encircling the entire land mass. Branching off Route 5 in Olympia, at the foot of Puget Sound, it runs north to Discovery Bay, where Route 20 turns off to Port Townsend; west through Port Angeles to Sappho; then zigzags to Astoria, Oregon, and points south. Remarkably, when you reach Aberdeen, 292 miles after you start traveling on 101, you're just 36 miles from where you started!

Traveling from Seattle, most Olympic Peninsula visitors take either the Seattle–Winslow ferry (to Route 305) or the Edmonds–Kingston ferry (to Route 104), joining 101 just south of Discovery Bay. From Tacoma, the practical route is Route 16 across the Narrows Bridge. From the north, the Keystone ferry to Port Townsend has its eastern terminus midway down lanky Whidbey Island, off Route 20. Northbound travelers can reach the area either through Astoria, on Route 101, or via several routes that branch off Route 5 north of Portland.

AIR

William R. Fairchild International Airport, near Port Angeles, links the northern Olympic Peninsula with major cities throughout the United States and western Canada via Horizon Air Lines. ~ 360-417-3433.

FERRY

Washington State Ferries serves the Olympic Peninsula directly from Whidbey Island to Port Townsend and indirectly across Puget Sound (via the Kitsap Peninsula) from Seattle and Edmonds. ~ 206-464-6400. The Black Ball Transport offers direct daily service between Port Angeles and Victoria, B.C. ~ 360-457-4491. Victoria Rapid Transit provides foot-passenger service mid-May through October. ~ 360-452-8088. Some smaller cruise lines may make stops in Port Angeles.

CAR RENTALS

In Port Angeles, Budget Rent A Car can be found at or in town. ~ 800-527-0700. In Forks, there is Dan Wilder Auto Center. ~ 800-927-9372.

PUBLIC TRANSIT

For local bus service in the northern Olympic Peninsula, including Port Angeles and Sequim, contact Clallam Transit System in Port Angeles. ~ 360-452-4511. Port Townsend, Sequim and eastern Jefferson County are served by Jefferson Transit. ~ 360-385-4777. The Grays Harbor Transportation Authority offers bus service to Aberdeen, Ocean Shores and the surrounding region. ~ 360-532-2770.

Bus service between Raymond, Long Beach and Astoria, Oregon, is provided by the Pacific Transit System. ~ 360-642-9418.

SEVEN

Northern Puget Sound and the San Juan Islands

"Every part of this land is sacred to my people. Every shining pine needle, every sandy shore, every mist in the dark woods, every clearing and humming insect is holy in the memory and experience of my people. . . . We are part of the earth and it is part of us. The perfumed flowers are our sisters; the deer, the horse, the great eagle, these are our brothers. The rocky crests, the juices in the meadows, the body heat of the pony, and man—all belong to the same family." This was part of Chief Seattle's poignant reply when, in 1854, the "Great White Chief" in Washington pressed to purchase some of the land around Puget Sound then occupied by several Northwest Indian tribes. And those sentiments still ring true today as the natural beauty and appeal of Northern Puget Sound and the San Juan Islands remain undiminished.

This awe-inspiring land supported the American Indians, providing for all their needs with verdant woods full of deer and berries and crystal waters full of salmon, letting them live in peaceful coexistence for hundreds of years. Even the weather was kind to them here in this "rain shadow," shielded by the Olympic and Vancouver mountain ranges.

Things slowly began to change for the Northwest Indian tribes and the land with the arrival of Juan de Fuca in 1592, who came to explore the coastline for the Spanish. The floodgates of exploration and exploitation weren't fully opened, however, until Captain George Vancouver came in 1792 to chart the region for the British, naming major landmarks such as Mt. Baker, Mt. Rainier, Whidbey Island and Puget Sound after his compatriots.

Establishment of trade with the American Indians and the seemingly inexhaustible quantity of animals to supply the lucrative fur trade drew many pioneers. Before long, industries such as logging, mining, shipping and fishing began to flourish, supporting the early settlers (and still supporting their descendants today).

Geologists who have studied the record say that a now long-disappeared continent moving eastward out of the Pacific Ocean eons ago collided with, or "docked" against, the Puget Sound mainland, laying the foundation for the multiplicity of land forms—islands, estuaries, mountains, coastlines—that characterize the northern Puget Sound region today.

The geographical layout of the 172 islands of the San Juan Archipelago made for watery back alleys and hidden coves perfect for piracy and smuggling, so the history of the area reflects an almost Barbary Coast–type of intrigue where a man could get a few drinks, a roll in the hay and be shanghaied all in one night. Chinese laborers were regularly brought in under cover of night to build up coastal cities and railroads in the 1800s. This big money "commodity" was replaced by opium and silk, and then booze during Prohibition.

Smuggling has since been curbed, and while things are changing as resources are diminished, logging and fishing are still major industries in the region. However, current booms in real estate and tourism are beginning to tilt the economic scale as more and more people discover the area's beauty.

The area referred to as Northern Puget Sound begins just beyond the far northern outskirts of Seattle, where most visitors first arrive, and extends northward up the coast to the Canadian border. Coastal communities such as Everett, Bellingham and Blaine tend to be more commercial in nature, heavily flavored by the logging and fishing industries, while other small towns such as La Conner and Mt. Vernon are still very pastoral, dependent on an agriculturally based economy. When heading east from Mt. Vernon, for every mile traveled toward the Cascade Mountains, the average annual rainfall increases by one inch. Consequently, springtime along this stretch of land is particularly lovely, especially in the Skagit Valley when the fields are ablaze in daffodils, iris and tulips. The world's biggest single grower of tulip bulbs—Washington Bulb Company—is based in the Skagit Valley.

Of the 172 named islands of the San Juans, we concentrate on the four most popular. These also are very pastoral, with rich soil and salubrious conditions perfectly suited to raising livestock or growing fruit. The major islands are connected to the mainland by bridges or reached by limited ferry service, an inhibiting factor that helps preserve the pristine nature here.

Although it's not considered part of the San Juans, serpentine Whidbey Island, with its thick southern tip reaching toward Seattle, is the largest island in Puget Sound. Situated at Whidbey's northern tip is Fidalgo Island, home of Anacortes and the ferry terminal gateway to the San Juans. Lopez is by far the friendliest and most rural of the islands, followed closely by San Juan, the largest and busiest. Shaw Island is one of the smaller islands, and lovely Orcas Island, named after Spanish explorer Don Juan Vincente de Guemes Pacheco y Padilla Orcasitees y Aguayo Conde de Revilla Gigedo (whew!) rather than orca whales, is tallest, capped by 2400-foot Mt. Constitution.

The ferry system is severely overtaxed during the busy summer season when the San Juans are inundated with tourists, making it difficult to reach the islands at times and absolutely impossible to find accommodations if you haven't booked months in advance. The crowds drop off dramatically after Labor Day, a pleasant surprise since the weather in September and October is still lovely and the change of seasonal color against this beautiful backdrop is incredible.

Stretched along the fertile coastline between the Canadian border and the outer reaches of Seattle, communities along Northern

▼▼▼▼▼▼▼▼▼▼▼▼▼▼▼▼
Northern Puget Sound

Puget Sound are dependent on agriculture, logging and fishing, so the distinct pastoral feel of the area is no surprise. Verdant parks and vista spots taking in the beauty of the many islands not far off-shore head the list of sightseeing musts here. But islands and shore-lines are just part of the scenic and geographic mix in this region, which also includes rivers and delta wetlands, forests and pictur-esque farmlands.

As you drive north from Seattle along Route 5, you'll cross a series of major rivers issuing from the Cascade Mountains. In order, you'll pass the Snohomish River (at Everett), the Stillaguamish (not far

SIGHTS

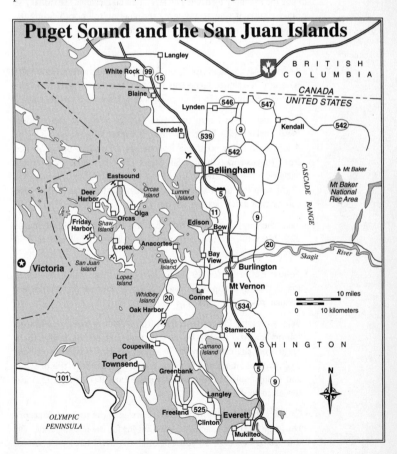

Puget Sound and the San Juan Islands

Text continued on page 202.

Three-Day Weekend

Island-hopping to the San Juans

The trip through the San Juan Islands is the longest and most beautiful cruise the Washington State Ferries network has to offer. It's not expensive, but in recent years, as both tourism and population in the Puget Sound area have grown enormously, the San Juan ferries have become so overburdened that even island residents have a hard time getting home during the summer months and on sunny weekends. If visiting during the off-season is out of the question, the best strategy is to arrive in Anacortes the afternoon before, sleep early and get in line for the ferry by dawn. The ferry schedule changes seasonally so obtain a current one at any ferry terminal or toll booth. Study the San Juan Island schedule carefully—it's complicated.

DAY 1
- Leaving Seattle, head north on Route 5 to **Edmonds** (Exit 189), where a 30-minute ferry trip will take you to **Kingston** on the Olympic Peninsula (16 to 20 sailings daily from 5:50 a.m. to 1 a.m.).

- Drive eight miles north on Route 104 for a look at picturesque, New England–like **Port Gamble** (Chapter Five, pages 137–38). Another 25 miles north via Routes 104, 19 and 20 brings you to **Port Townsend** (Chapter Six, pages 150–51), a quaintly Victorian village on the northwest tip of the peninsula. Along the way, you might stop for lunch at the **Chimacum Café** (page 154), or you can catch a quick bite on the ferry.

- Take the ferry across to Keystone on **Whidbey Island** (pages 222–24), a 30-minute trip (ten sailings daily from 7:45 a.m. to 9:30 p.m.).

- Follow Route 20 for 40 miles up the northern half of Whidbey Island, visiting **Coupeville** (page 224), yet another picture-perfect historic town, along the way.

- Before crossing **Deception Pass** from Whidbey Island to **Fidalgo Island** (pages 233–34), be sure to walk out on the bridge for a magnificent seascape view. You've almost reached today's destination, so if you have time and feel like stretching your legs, the beaches and hiking trails of **Deception Pass State Park** (page 232) are the place to do it.

- Crossing the bridge, drive another six miles to the town of **Anacortes** (page 233) and check into your lodging for the evening. Dine out, then go to bed early so you can catch the dawn ferry well rested.

DAY 2 • Be at the Anacortes ferry dock no later than (yawn!) 5:15 a.m. to catch the first ferry of the day to **Orcas Island** (page 244). Otherwise you can expect to wait in line for *at least* three hours to get on another one. The trip to Orcas Island takes about one hour with intermediate stops at Lopez and Shaw islands; there are 10 to 12 sailings daily from 5:45 a.m. to 9:15 p.m. or later; vehicles for Orcas load 20 minutes before sailing.

• Have breakfast on the ferry or upon arrival on Orcas Island.

• Check into your accommodations and buy food for a picnic lunch.

• Head for **Moran State Park** (page 247), the largest and finest park in the Washington State Parks system. Take in the view from the top of Mount Constitution, the highest point in the San Juans. Then take your pick of many hiking possibilities.

• By mid-afternoon you may be ready for a nap.

• For dinner this evening, try a seafood feast at **The Deer Harbor Inn** (page 246).

DAY 3 • It's not quite as critical to catch the first ferry from Orcas to **San Juan Island** (pages 239–40) because any of the ferries, which run from 7:25 a.m. to 9:50 p.m. or later, is likely to unload as many vehicles at Orcas as are waiting to load. The trip to Friday Harbor takes about 30 minutes.

• Visit the **Whale Museum** (page 250).

• Take a driving tour around San Juan Island. On opposite sides of the island you'll find the sites of two historic forts of **San Juan Island National Historical Park** (pages 239–40), where U.S. and British armies faced off in the anticlimactic "Pig War" over control of the San Juans. Several coastal beaches and parks along the way offer opportunities for picnicking and wildlife viewing. You may even see bald eagles or orca whales.

• As evening nears, catch a ferry back to Anacortes. The trip takes one to one and a half hours, depending on whether the ferry makes intermediate stops, and there are eight or nine sailings daily from 6 a.m. to 7:45 p.m.

• Back in Anacortes, you're less than an hour away from Seattle via Route 5.

from Stanwood), the Skagit (at Mt. Vernon/Burlington) and the Nooksack (Bellingham). The lower reaches of these streams offer wetlands and wildlife to see, fishing villages to poke around in, a vital agricultural heritage in the Skagit and Nooksack valleys, and small towns by the handful.

If you plan to catch the Mukilteo ferry to Clinton on Whidbey Island, be sure to allow enough time to visit the historic **Mukilteo Lighthouse** built in 1906. There are picnic tables above a small rocky beach cluttered with driftwood and a big grassy field for kite-flying adjacent to the lighthouse in little Mukilteo State Park. Open April through September, weekend afternoons only. ~ Mukilteo; 425-513-9602.

In Everett you'll find your best vantage point from the dock behind **Marina Village**, a sparkling complex of upscale shops, microbreweries and restaurants located in the second-largest marina on the West Coast. ~ 1728 West Marine View Drive, Everett.

In summer, a free pontoon boat ride will shuttle you from the 10th Street boat launch to picturesque **Jetty Island** for guided nature walks, birdwatching, campfires, a hands-on "Squirmy, Squiggly and Squishy" program to teach children about small marine animals and one of the only warm saltwater beaches on the Sound. For reservations, call 425-257-8300, fax 425-257-8325.

The **Firefighter's Museum** offers a storefront display of antique early-20th-century firefighting equipment. The collection is set up for 24-hour, through-the-window viewing. ~ 13th Street Dock, Everett.

The **Everett Area Chamber of Commerce** can provide you with more information. ~ 11400 Airport Road, Everett; 425-438-1487; www.everettchamber.com.

On the hillside above the marina, ornate **mansions** of the lumber barons that once ruled the economy here line Grand and Rucker streets from 16th Street north. None are open to tour, but a slow drive up and down these avenues will give you a feel for the history of the city.

On the south side of town you can take a **Boeing Everett factory tour**, which showcases the Boeing airplane company and the Everett product line, the 747, 767 and 777. It starts with a video about how airplanes are built, then takes visitors through the largest building in the world by volume (472,000,000 cubic feet). Visitors will see airplanes in various stages of pre-flight and flight-testing. Children must be 50 inches tall. Tours are weekdays, on a first-come, first-serve basis; fee. Groups of ten or more people may make a reservation. ~ Tour Center, State Road 526, Everett; 800-464-1476, fax 425-342-7787; www.boeing.com.

HIDDEN ►   Visitors to **Biringer Farm** can not only pick fresh summer strawberries, fall pumpkins and Christmas trees, they can get a good look at how a farm operates. Kids can ride a trolley-train;

adults can learn about gardening; the whole family can ride a tractor-drawn trolley to the fields. But the prime reason to visit remains the incomparable fresh berries. Watch carefully for direction signs off Route 5 north of downtown Everett. ~ 4625 40th Place, Everett; 425-259-0255.

Just west of Route 5, in the delta of the Stillaguamish River, the small farming town of **Stanwood** hides its main street away, signing it 271st Street. Many tourists never discover its shops and pubs, ethnic restaurants and bakery specializing in "lefse," popular among the descendants of pioneer Scandinavian farmers.

A few miles west, across a bridge on Route 532, lies **Camano Island**, not one of the famous San Juans, but boasting three bed-and-breakfast inns (at last count) and blessed with one magnificent public park, 134-acre **Camano Island State Park**. Located midway down the island's west shore, the park offers splendid forest and beach trails and sweeping views across Saratoga Passage to Whidbey Island. Also on the island is a wonderful art gallery. Called **"History of the World—Part IV,"** the name suggests the owners' whimsical way with art. Jack Gunter is quickly earning a reputation as a painter and folk artist, but prefers to describe himself as a creator of "pseudo naive surrealistic narrative art." You'll find plenty to chuckle over here—wry paintings, entertaining sculpture, playful art glass and Karla Matzke's American pop art. Open weekends only. ~ 3311 South East Camano Drive, Camano Island; 360-387-5225; www.historyoftheworldpt4.com.

Someday, the Skagit Valley may become as famous as the well-known tourist attractions that surround it. But for now, out-of-state visitors tend to speed through this 25-mile-wide floodplain, missing its beauty as they hurry to or from the San Juan Islands, the Olympic Peninsula, Whidbey Island, North Cascades National Park, or Vancouver and Victoria, B.C.

Alas, they're missing something special. **Skagit Valley**, about halfway between Seattle and Vancouver (and an hour's drive or so from either city via Route 5) is very likely the most glorious union of countryside and seashore in the Northwest. It's centered on the largest, most pristine river delta on Puget Sound, whose sweeping estuary—an important stop on the Pacific Flyway—nurtures an extraordinary diversity of marine life and waterfowl. With topsoil up to several feet deep, the Skagit is the world's third-most fertile river delta, according to Skagitonians to Preserve Farmland.

Nowadays, big-city folk from both sides of the border flock to the Skagit to explore the valley's country roads and small towns, especially historic La Conner (see "Walking Tour"). They come to pedal a bike or stroll a beguiling stretch of coast, to boat

SCENIC SKAGIT VALLEY

The Skagit Valley has become a year-round retreat for city visitors, as nourishing to the soul in winter as it is inspiring to the adventurous spirit in summer. Indeed, artists and writers have been gathering in the Skagit for decades, including members of the famed "Northwest School" beginning in the 1930s— Mark Tobey, Morris Graves, Kenneth Callahan, Clayton James, Guy Anderson and many others. They were drawn by the Skagit's enchanting blend of meandering river levees and farm fields, bayous and bays, nearby islands and distant misty mountains, along with the extraordinary quality of the valley's ever-changing light.

and fish for salmon in season. To watch in winter for the delta's treasure of hawks and eagles, snow geese and trumpeter swans. To marvel at blooming tulips that paint the valley in vivid colors every April and herald the return of spring.

Other visitors from Seattle and Vancouver, seeking respite from urban life, come to unwind in the Skagit's delightful country inns and bed-and-breakfast homes. Here, you can sprawl before a roaring fire with a good book in hand. Or idle away a Sunday morning over a splendid country breakfast. Or just stare in silent reverie from a farmhouse veranda across open fields to the sea.

Today, the Skagit is gateway both to Whidbey Island and the San Juans (westward on Route 20 from Route 5), and to the North Cascades (Route 20, eastbound). The valley is a travelers' crossroads, with adventures enough for a month of sightseeing. You won't find a better place to begin than picturesque La Conner.

Mt. Vernon, situated on the broad banks of the Skagit River, has done little to capitalize on its superior riverside location. But it does claim the liveliest "main street" in the valley. The true main street is signed as 1st Street here; it is lined with a variety of vintage architecture in both brick and wood dating to the turn of the century. Preservation or recycling of old buildings is in full swing.

Don't miss **The Granary** (360-466-3190), which includes **Scott's Bookstore & Card** (360-336-6181) and the adjoining **Calico Cupboard Restaurant** (360-336-3107). Here, too, is the valley's land trust, **Skagitonians to Preserve Farmland** (360-336-3974), where you can learn how concerned citizens are working to save farmlands and the valley's agricultural heritage. ~ 1st and Division streets, Mt. Vernon.

Across railroad tracks just to the west is the old **Condensary Building**, now remodeled into offices.

South of Division Street, but still on 1st Street, is the Uptowne Centre. The **Deli Next Door** (360-336-3886) serves appetizing organic vegetarian fare.

Stroll south on 1st and you'll find more old buildings housing vintage books and records, handcrafts from around the valley, jewelry, art and outdoor gear, and the 1926 **Lincoln Theater** (now an art film house; 360-336-2858). Several more eateries and coffee bars also compete for your patronage.

Each spring, the fields of the Skagit Valley are alive with color as the tulips and daffodils begin to appear. **The Skagit Valley Tulip Festival Office** provides a guide to the festival that runs the first three weeks of April; the guide lists events and includes a tour map of the fairs, children's activities and display gardens. ~ 117 North 1st Street, Suite 4, Mt. Vernon; 360-428-5959, fax 360-428-6753; www.tulipfestival.org.

There are interesting gardens to view year-round. The prettiest is **RoozenGaarde** with display gardens and a great little gift shop.

WALKING TOUR
La Conner

Built on pilings above the bank of Swinomish Channel, La Conner got its start in the 1880s as a market center for farmers in the Skagit Flats. Now a historic district, this small village of fewer than 800 people is easy to explore on foot and, with its many well-preserved homes and buildings, offers a glimpse of turn-of-the-20th-century life.

SKAGIT COUNTY HISTORICAL MUSEUM   Park your car at the **La Conner Chamber of Commerce**. ~ Morris Street between 3rd and 4th streets; 360-466-4778, 888-642-9284, fax 360-466-0204; www.la conner-chamber.com. Walk a short distance up 4th Street to the top of the hill to visit the Skagit County Historical Museum, where you'll find a collection of automobiles, farm and fishing equipment, vintage clothing, household furnishings and photographs. Exhibits in the south wing focus on how early settlers made their living and include a Northwest Coast Indian display. Admission. ~ 501 4th Street; 360-466-3365, fax 360-466-1611; e-mail histmuseum@co.skagit.wa.us.

GACHES MANSION   From the museum, head south along 4th Street, which turns a corner and becomes Calhoun Street. Follow Calhoun downhill toward the channel for two blocks to the Gaches Mansion. This grand Victorian home was built in 1891 by a local merchant who wanted the

~ 1587 Beaver Marsh Road, Mt. Vernon; 360-424-8531; www.tulips.com.

West of Mount Vernon, across the channel from the Swinomish Indian Reservation, **La Conner** (see "Walking Tour" above) is in the running for the title of quaintest little seaside town in the Puget Sound area.

Burlington, the next city north of Mt. Vernon, is famous for a different sort of shopping. Bargain-hunters from Seattle and Vancouver come to seek out the discount designer merchandise at Pacific Edge Outlet Center. Neighboring Cascade Mall offers a more classic array of mall shops.

For the perfect counterpoint to the sort of creeping suburbanism encountered in Burlington, drop in on the small communities of **Bay View, Edison** and the town of **Bow**. This trio of country hamlets (located in the northern valley across Route 20) are treasures of the old way of life and are rarely discovered by the average tourist. Here, you'll see century-old farmhouses rising behind white picket fences, boatworks (some still active) that finest house in town. The former site of the town's art museum, it has been restored with period furnishings and is open to the public Friday through Sunday afternoons. The mansion also houses the **La Conner Quilt Museum**, the Pacific Northwest's only quilt museum. Closed Monday and Tuesday, and January and February. Admission. ~ 703 2nd Street South; phone/fax 360-466-4288.

MAGNUS ANDERSON CABIN   Stroll a block south of the Gaches Mansion to see the Magnus Anderson Cabin next to city hall. The oldest structure in Skagit County, the 1869 cabin was moved here from a solitary location on the north fork of the Skagit River to save it from decay. ~ 2nd and Douglas streets.

MUSEUM OF NORTHWEST ART   Walk one more block west to 1st Street, then proceed north. This time-capsule waterfront street has been gentrified with boutiques, galleries and restaurants yet still retains a palpable air of history. Seven blocks up the street you'll find the Museum of Northwest Art, which exhibits the works of regional painters and sculptors, presenting a cohesive look at the distinctive school of visual arts that has developed in the Skagit Valley—an often surrealistic blend of Northwest Coast Indian and Asian motifs. Admission. ~ 121 South 1st Street; 360-466-4446, fax 360-466-7431; www.museumofnwart.org. Walking three blocks up Washington Street and five blocks south on 3rd Street will bring you back to the chamber of commerce and your car.

once turned out fishing boats, country taverns alive with the rustic merriment of farmers, loggers, truck drivers and dairymen. Here, too, are a smattering of art galleries, antique shops, country cafés and upscale eateries.

Located just north of Bay View, **Padilla Bay National Estuarine Research Reserve** is the place to find bald eagles, great blue herons and dozens of other species of waterfowl and raptors. The interpretive center offers exhibits on the region's natural and maritime history. ~ 10441 Bay View–Edison Road, Bay View; 360-428-1558, fax 360-428-1491; www.inlet.geol.sc.edu/pdb/home.html.

For a view-rich and slow-paced alternate to Route 5 that will take you north to Bellingham, opt for **Chuckanut Drive** (Route 11), a signed exit from the freeway just north of Burlington. The "drive" takes you north through gorgeous farmlands, in and out of the village of Bow in a twinkling, and then along the rocky and precipitous shoulder of the Chuckanut Mountains overlooking the San Juan Islands (you can stop and savor the scene from numerous pullouts). The drive continues all the way to the funky 1880s brick town of **Fairhaven**, now a suburb of Bellingham. This slightly counterculture community is a treasure of refurbished brick Victorians housing shops, galleries, artists' studios and bohemian eateries. Most are concentrated around 11th Street and Harris Avenue.

But Fairhaven also boasts the **Bellingham Cruise Terminal**, southern terminus for ferries of the Alaska Marine Highway (foot of Harris Avenue). The terminal presents dynamite views over the harbor, a seafood restaurant (Barnacles; 360-647-5072) and a variety of shops. Here, too, the sightseeing vessel *Victoria Star* (360-738-8099) is moored for daily departures in summer through the San Juan Islands to Victoria, B.C. After hours of sightseeing in Victoria, enjoy a dinner of fresh salmon served on the return trip to the San Juans.

Another boating operator also serves the San Juans. **San Juan Island Shuttle Express** departs daily in summer from Bellingham Cruise Terminal for sightseeing cruises to Orcas Island and Friday Harbor on San Juan Island. ~ 360-671-1137; www.orcawhales.com.

Early growth in **Bellingham** centered around the industries of mining and logging. To this day, the city retains an industrial nature with thriving ports that are home to a large fishing fleet and, more recently, the Alaska Marine Highway Ferry System terminal, tempered by a firm agricultural base. Perhaps it is because of this outward appearance that visitors are often amazed at the array of cultural arts and international dining experiences to be enjoyed here.

Bellingham has two noteworthy museums. The first is the **Whatcom Children's Museum**, which has several hands-on exhibitions to delight the kids (ages 2–10). Closed Monday. Admission. ~ 227 Prospect Street, Bellingham; 360-733-8769; www.what commuseum.org.

Just down the street, the red-brick Victorian architecture of the **Whatcom Museum** is as interesting as the fine collections of contemporary American art, Northwest art and regional history featured inside. It's also a good point to start a walking tour of the many outdoor sculptures scattered around downtown. Closed Monday. Admission for special shows. ~ 121 Prospect Street, Bellingham; 360-676-6981; www.whatcommuseum.org.

A Sculpture Walk route guide is available at the museum or from the **Bellingham/Whatcom County Visitor and Convention Bureau**. ~ 904 Potter Street, Bellingham; 360-671-3990; www. bellingham.org.

At the **Maritime Heritage Center** you can tour the hatchery, watch fish make their way up the ladder (recommended in October and November), learn about the life cycle of salmon, or just toss a line (with the proper license) into the abutting creek for steelhead or chinook salmon. ~ 1600 C Street, Bellingham; 360-676-6806.

No visit to Bellingham is complete without a trip to the **Big Rock Garden**, a serene Japanese garden with plantings, a patio and deck areas where visitors can sit and take it all in. ~ 2900 Sylvan Street at Illinois Avenue, Bellingham; 360-676-6985, fax 360-647-6367; www.cob.org.

The **T.G. Richards & Co. building** is the oldest brick building still standing in the state, dating from 1858. Its bricks came around Cape Horn from Philadelphia. ~ 1308 E Street, Bellingham.

Don't miss the opportunity to stroll through the grounds of **Western Washington University** on the Western Sculpture Tour

◄ HIDDEN

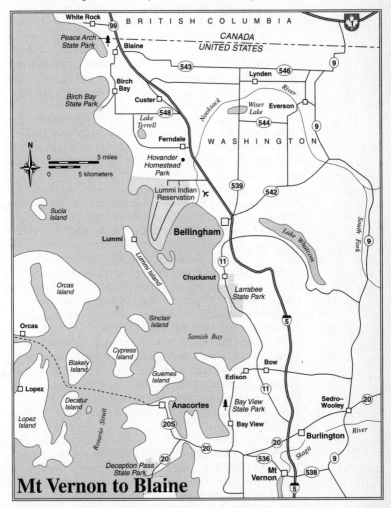

Mt Vernon to Blaine

to enjoy the many fountains, sculptures and rich variety of architecture to be found on this green campus. Brochures are available at the visitors information center on campus or at the Western Gallery. ~ McDonald Parkway, Bellingham; 360-650-3963; www.wwu.edu.

The Darigold plant in Lynden produces some 340,000 pounds of non-fat dry milk a day and is the largest powdered milk factory in the U.S.

Immediately adjacent to the campus is **Sehome Hill Arboretum**, 165 acres laced with six miles of hiking trails and fern-lined footpaths under a cool green canopy of moss covered trees; only the hum of traffic and the view from the observation tower remind you that you are in the city rather than some forest primeval. ~ 25th Street, Bellingham; 360-676-6985, fax 360-647-6367.

The **Nooksack River Valley** located east of Bellingham is a treasure of rolling green dairy pastures, berry fields, Christmas tree farms and charming small towns, like Lynden. Settled by Dutch dairymen more than a century ago, **Lynden** and its main street (Front Street) offer a colorful collection of storefronts looking as if they were plucked right out of Amsterdam, including a windmill hotel. A beguiling array of import shops proffers wooden shoes, Delft tiles, kitchenware and other goods from Holland. Several eateries also specialize in Dutch fare. Festivals such as Sinterklaas (Santa Claus) in December and Holland Days in May also reflect the rich Dutch heritage.

The **Lynden Pioneer Museum** tells the story of early Dutch and Northern European settlers. The five galleries that comprise the museum are filled with life-size replicas of street scenes of Lyndon from days gone by. Don't miss the Fred K. Polinder buggy collection. Closed Sunday. Admission. ~ 217 Front Street, Lynden; 360-354-3675, fax 360-354-4632; www.lyndenpioneermuseum.com.

Just outside of town begin several superb bike routes that follow winding and picturesque country roads, one of which brings you to a first-rate winery, **Mt. Baker Vineyards**, famous for its excellent German-style white wines. ~ 4298 Mt. Baker Highway, Everson; 360-592-2300, fax 360-592-2526.

Hovander Homestead Park features a 19th-century farmhouse and handsome Victorian residence (open summers only). Laced by the Nooksack River, the 720-acre park also includes **Tennant Lake**, where you'll find a boardwalk leading out over the lake and a fragrance garden with braille signs. There's also an interpretive center. Admission. ~ 5299 Nielsen Road, Ferndale; 360-384-3444.

To see the largest collection of original log homes in the state, stop by **Pioneer Park**. Each of the 12 buildings is a minimuseum. You'll see a post office, a stagecoach inn, a granary, a veteran's museum, a schoolhouse and a residence. Look for the little log church. Closed Monday and from October through April. ~ 1st Avenue at Cherry Street, Ferndale; 360-384-6461; www.ci.ferndale.wa.us.

Another site in the Northern Puget Sound area worth taking in is **Peace Arch State Park**. The large, white arch, flanked by American and Canadian flags, is surrounded by bountiful formal gardens and symbolizes the ongoing friendship between the two neighboring countries. The park is meticulously groomed, and spills across the international boundary. ~ Follow the signs to the park off Route 5, Exit 276, Blaine; 360-332-8221.

In addition to its outstanding waterfront location, the friendly 26-room **Marina Village Inn** is loaded with special touches. The spacious harborside rooms have sunken sitting areas with custom sleeper sofas, cushioned seats built into large bay windows and personal telescopes for viewing Whidbey, Hat and Jetty islands. Some rooms have private decks and jacuzzi tubs. Reservations are required. ~ 1728 West Marine View Drive, Everett; 425-259-4040, 800-281-7027, fax 425-252-8419. MODERATE TO DELUXE.

LODGING

La Conner and the Skagit Valley now boast several bed and breakfasts and two first-class inns. One of them is the **La Conner Channel Lodge**, a handsome luxury inn, the only hostelry in town on the Swinomish Channel. Each of its 40 rooms looks out to the channel and the ceaseless parade of fishing boats and pleasure craft. Continental breakfast. ~ 205 North 1st Street, La Conner; 360-466-1500, fax 360-466-1525; www.laconnerlodging.com. DELUXE.

The **Wild Iris** is the newest inn hereabouts, on the edge of town overlooking farm fields and mountains. Each of its 19 rooms is decorated individually in bold and fearless strokes. Many rooms feature a jacuzzi spa and a fireplace. Breakfast fare is generous and varied, a hallmark of this inn's overall attention to quality. ~ 121 Maple Avenue, La Conner; 360-466-1400, fax 360-466-1222; www.wildiris.com, e-mail info@wildiris.com. MODERATE TO ULTRA-DELUXE.

Next door to the Wild Iris, the **Heron** offers the same views in smaller, cozier style, with ten rooms. ~ 117 Maple Avenue, La Conner; 360-466-4626, fax 360-466-2831. MODERATE TO ULTRA-DELUXE.

The Hotel Planter, originally built in 1907, is right in the thick of things when it comes to shopping and dining in downtown La Conner. The 12 rooms have sunlights, light paint and carpeting, floral chintz comforters and pine furnishings. There's also a jacuzzi under the gazebo on the garden terrace out back. ~ 715 1st Street, La Conner; 360-466-4710, 800-488-5409, fax 360-466-1320. MODERATE TO DELUXE.

Opened in 1977, **La Conner Country Inn** was the first inn in these parts. It's still a favorite with long-time visitors, partly because several of its 28 rooms are so affordable. It's also close to shops and restaurants. Continental breakfast. ~ 107 2nd Street South,

La Conner; 360-466-3101, fax 360-466-5902; www.laconner lodging.com. MODERATE.

Katy's Inn is one of the oldest homes in town, built by a sea captain in 1822, and appeals strongly to history-minded folk. Evenings mean tea, cocoa and just-baked cookies. Its five rooms bear names such as the Rose Room, which overlooks the rose garden from the wraparound porch; the Lilac Room, decorated in white wicker and purple shades; Ashley's Room; the Garden Room, which overlooks dahlias and gardens; and the Captain's Suite, which has its own entrance and overlooks the orchard, a pond and waterfall. All rooms come with bathrobes, two have private baths, and an outside gazebo houses a hot tub. Full brunch is provided and can arrive at your door on a silver tray. ~ 503 South 3rd Street, La Conner; 360-466-3366, 800-914-7767; e-mail katysinn@juno.com. MODERATE TO DELUXE.

In a home loaded with a lifetime's collection of art, **Art's Place Bed & Breakfast** offers a one-room guest house with balcony bedroom, jacuzzi bath. ~ 511 Talbot Street, La Conner; 360-466-3033. MODERATE.

About half a mile east of town, the **Rainbow Inn** is surrounded by farm fields. This classic Craftsman built in 1908 offers eight guest rooms and oodles of old-fashioned charm. Full breakfast. ~ 12757 Chilberg Road, La Conner; 360-466-4578, 888-266-8879, fax 360-466-3844. MODERATE.

A Dutch Colonial farmhouse with five guest rooms and a suite, the **Ridgeway Farm Bed and Breakfast** sits amid daffodil and tulip fields, just right for spring visits. Views also include the mountains and Chuckanut Bay. Hot-air balloons take flight from the farm, as do two Cessna 172s for one-hour scenic flights over the San Juans. Full breakfast. ~ 14914 McLean Road, about four miles northeast of La Conner; 360-428-8068, 800-428-8068, fax 360-428-8880; www.placestostay.com/lacon-ridgewayfarm. MODERATE TO ULTRA-DELUXE.

White Swan Guest House offers accommodations in a country setting. The rooms are country casual and there's a superb collection of samplers spread across the house. The English country garden features a big orchard where you're welcome to pick your own apples and plums as well as pears. A separate cottage offers kitchen facilities. Country continental breakfast and homemade chocolate chip cookies are included. ~ 15872 Moore Road, Mt. Vernon; 360-445-6805; www.thewhiteswan.com. MODERATE TO DELUXE.

Built in 1914, the **Benson Farmstead Bed and Breakfast** is a four-room charmer in the heart of "north valley" farms. All rooms have private baths and queen beds. Some guests come for the homemade desserts, big farm breakfasts and cozy rooms full of country

Author Picks

CHAPTER FAVORITES

Although Mukilteo may seem a little off the beaten path, I'll take the detour just to dine at **Charles at Smugglers Cove**. After all, how often do you get a chance to enjoy a seafood feast at Al Capone's house? *page 215*

One of my favorite places to slog along with a shovel and bucket in search of clams is the long sand spit **Semiahmoo Park**, a stone's throw from the Canadian border. In the park's picnic area you can watch for bald eagles or whales while you steam the clams and eat them. *page 222*

And then there's the awesome view from the bridge at **Deception Pass**,

a choice spot to put my wide-angle camera lens to the test—especially at sunset. *page 225*

Why paint a building just one color when you can paint a mural on it? One of the best examples I've seen is in the otherwise unremarkable town of **Anacortes**, where some 40 buildings have been decorated with giant reproductions of historical photographs. *page 233*

After a day of hiking or biking on Orcas Island, I can hardly wait to sink into a hot mineral bath, followed by a steamy sauna, at **Doe Bay Village Resort**. *page 245*

---

antiques. Others come for the chance to stay on a working farm that's been in operation for more than eight decades. Still others stay for the proximity to some of the state's best country bicycling. Or perhaps they seek the English garden and the garden of flowers filled with antique machinery. ~ 10113 Avon-Allen Road, Bow; 360-757-0578, 800-441-9814. MODERATE.

South Fork Moorage is one of those true hideaways (dare we ◀ HIDDEN
say, "unique") that travelers yearn to discover. The "moorage" is comprised of two houseboats floating in the usually placid waters of the South Fork of the Skagit River adjacent to a wildlife reserve. Bring your canoe, kayak or raft, and the owner will shuttle you up to Burlington for a lazy float back to the moorage. Or paddle across the river to an island full of wildlife. Or just sprawl like Huck Finn on the docks for a picnic as you watch the peaceful river unspool before you. No river shacks these—the Tea House is decorated in Japanese style, and the Karma boasts leaded, stained-glass windows and a fireplace. Both houseboats have fully equipped kitchens and are outfitted as housekeeping cabins; each can accommodate up to four persons. And yet the prices are only moderate! Small pets are allowed for a fee. ~ 2187 Mann Road, Fir Island, Conway; 360-445-4803. MODERATE.

HIDDEN ►   As you might guess from the name, **Schnauzer Crossing** is presided over by a delightful pair of schnauzers. Choose from a spacious garden suite with fireplace, garden sitting room, jacuzzi tub and double shower, a smaller lakeview room done in iris motif or a cottage perfect for families or couples seeking romantic seclusion. Well-thought-out amenities in each room include thick terry robes for the trip to the hot tub in the Japanese garden. Gourmet breakfast included. ~ 4421 Lakeway Drive, Bellingham; 360-733-0055, 800-562-2808, fax 360-734-2808; www.schnauzer crossing.com. MODERATE TO ULTRA-DELUXE.

Tucked into the rose garden near the north end of picturesque Chuckanut Drive is the **Hostelling International—Bellingham**. You'll find this your typical hostel environment: men's and women's dorms, showers and laundry facilities. All the action of the Fairhaven district is within walking distance. Closed December and January; reservations required in winter. ~ 107 Chuckanut Drive, Bellingham; 360-671-1750; www.washingtonhos tels.org. BUDGET.

Boeing means big. The largest aerospace, electronic and computer business in the U.S. employs more than 100,000 people in the Puget Sound area alone.

Dutch Village Inn Hotel is a local landmark. Besides several conventional motel-style rooms, it also offers six rooms in the colorful windmill tower (ask for the "windmill rooms"). All rooms boast Dutch decor and artifacts, and some present views across the Nooksack River Valley. A big Dutch breakfast is included in the room rates. Also available are seven full RV hook-ups, $13. ~ 655 Front Street, Lynden; 360-354-4440, fax 360-354-3390. MODERATE.

Built in 1888 as the town hotel, the **Century House Bed and Breakfast** is a restored four-room guesthouse decorated with antiques from its previous incarnation. The third-floor suite commands sweeping views of the Nooksack Valley and the Cascades. ~ 401 South B.C. Avenue, Lynden; 360-354-2439, 800-820-3617. MODERATE.

Slater Heritage House Bed and Breakfast is a handsomely restored 1904 Victorian surrounded by lovely well-tended gardens bursting with Northwest ornamentals. There are four guest rooms with private baths and antique furnishings. Full breakfast. ~ 1371 West Axton Road, Ferndale; 360-384-4273, 888-785-0706, fax 734-758-7256; www.bedandbreakfast-wa.com, e-mail info@bedandbreakfast-wa.com. MODERATE.

Housed in the old Blaine Air Force Base a few miles from the Canadian border, the **Hostelling International—Birch Bay** provides 40 beds in bare shared or private rooms. Pluses here include a sauna and the hostel's proximity to Birch Bay State Park. Closed October through April. ~ 7467 Gemini Street, Blaine; 360-371-2180; e-mail bbhostel@az.com. BUDGET.

There is something for everyone at the sumptuous **Inn at Semiahmoo**, located on the tip of the sandy spit stretched between Semiahmoo Bay and Drayton Harbor. History buffs will enjoy browsing through the inn's collection of early photography, romantics will delight in a walk on the beach or a leisurely sunset meal in one of the restaurants or lounges, and sports fanatics will flip over the array of activities, including charter boats, parasailing and jet skiing. The 196 guest rooms are spacious and nicely appointed; some rooms have decks or patios, and others have fireplaces. ~ 9565 Semiahmoo Parkway, Blaine; 360-371-2000, 800-770-7992, fax 360-371-5490; www.semiahmoo.com. ULTRA-DELUXE.

The **Willows Inn** was built in 1910 by the grandparents of the current owners. Today, it offers a honeymoon cottage amid flower gardens and a two-bedroom guesthouse. The cottage has a private deck with a fantastic view, and the guesthouse offers a fireplace and jacuzzi. Both have full kitchens. Views here are outstanding— west and northwest across other San Juan Islands to Vancouver, British Columbia. Continental breakfast in suite or self-catered. ~ 2579 West Shore Drive, Lummi Island; 360-758-2620; www. lummi-island.com/willows. DELUXE TO ULTRA-DELUXE.

DINING

◀ HIDDEN

The history of **Charles at Smugglers Cove** is as good as the food, making it doubly worth the drive out to Mukilteo. This red-brick mansion-turned-restaurant was purportedly owned at one time by Mafia kingpin Al Capone. Today the owners traffic in fresh seafood and steaks with French flair; their bouillabaisse, châteaubriand, rack of lamb, prawns in tarragon butter and baked Alaska are outstanding, and the setting in the elegant dining rooms or on the sheltered deck is splendid. Closed Sunday. ~ 8340 53rd Avenue West, Mukilteo; 425-347-2700, fax 425-531-8981. DELUXE.

Anthony's Home Port is the spot for seafood when it comes to waterfront dining in Everett. Prime picks on the seasonal menu include Whidbey Island mussels, grilled steak and prawns, Dungeness crab cakes, pan-fried scallops sprinkled with gremolatta, and six varieties of fresh oysters. Their four-course Sunset Dinner (served from 4:30 to 6 p.m.) is a bargain and includes everything from appetizer to dessert. You can dine alfresco on the deck or pick a spot in the considerably less breezy dining room or lounge. ~ 1725 West Marine View Drive, Everett; 425-252-3333, fax 425-252-7847. MODERATE.

The **Lighthouse Inn** on the waterfront in nearby La Conner dishes out extra-large servings of primarily seafood and pasta. Favorites include lobster, fresh barbecued fish, clam strips and prime rib, with fish and chips and burgers thrown in to please the little ones. The simple nautical decor leaves something to be desired, but the fresh flowers and dim lamps on the tables lend a slight air of romance. ~ 512 1st Street South, La Conner; phone/ fax 360-466-3149. MODERATE.

Best bet for breakfast or lunch in La Conner is the **Calico Cupboard** at the south end of the main drag, where they serve hearty and wholesome baked goods, soups, salads, sandwiches and vegetarian fare as good for the heart as for the taste buds. Don't be surprised if there is a line to get in to this modest café. ~ 720 1st Street South, La Conner; 360-466-4451, fax 360-466-2181. BUDGET.

Palmer's Restaurant and Pub is not on the waterfront, but may just be the best restaurant in town nevertheless. All dishes on the wide-ranging Continental menu (seafood, pasta, chicken, beef) are served with distinctive Northwest and European flair. All ingredients are fresh and, when possible, local. ~ 205 East Washington Street, La Conner; 360-466-4261, fax 360-466-3270. MODERATE TO DELUXE.

HIDDEN ▶ Few tourists ever discover **Yaw's Marina Cafe & Pub**, located off the beaten shopping track in the marina just north of town. But local anglers and working folk know it well. The lack of tourist attention means you get good café food at budget prices. The café opens for breakfast at 7 a.m. (for fishermen and boat builders), and also serves lunch and dinner. Specialties are burgers and sandwiches. ~ 612 North 2nd Street, La Conner; 360-466-0331, fax 360-466-2410. BUDGET.

The Norwegian proprietors of the **Farmhouse Inn**, a large restaurant with country decor dominated by heavy oak tables and chairs, believe in serving solid, old-country-style portions of meat and potato classics—fried chicken and french fries, roast turkey with mashed potatoes and gravy, rib-eyes and baked potatoes—along with a hearty selection of daily baked goods like their famous pies thrown in for good measure. The lunch buffet and children's menu are great bargains. Breakfast, lunch and dinner. ~ 1376 La Conner–Whitney Road, outside of Mt. Vernon; 360-466-4411, fax 360-466-4413. BUDGET TO MODERATE.

HIDDEN ▶ The drive to **Chuckanut Manor Bed & Breakfast** near Bow is one of the most scenic in Washington. Chuckanut Drive winds along the coast between Bellingham and Mt. Vernon, overlooking Samish Bay. Not surprisingly, the restaurant's fare centers on expertly prepared seafood—oysters, salmon and halibut. Closed Monday. ~ 3056 Chuckanut Drive, Bow; 360-766-6191, fax 360-766-8515. MODERATE TO DELUXE.

The **Archer Ale House**, tucked in the basement of one of Fairhaven's historic Victorians, is a smoke-free English-style pub that's considered one of the country's best Belgian beer bars by *All About Beer* magazine. The main fare is upscale pub grub (check out the pizza) and an array of microbrewery and imported beers. ~ 1212 10th Street, Fairhaven; 360-647-7002. BUDGET.

The **Colophon Cafe** shares a building—and an intellectual/bohemian ambience—with a neighboring bookstore. The café is known for its homemade soups (including a wonderfully spicy African peanut soup) and its sinfully rich desserts. ~ 1208 11th Street, Fairhaven; 360-647-0092, fax 360-676-1742. BUDGET.

There are cows everywhere—from the pictures on the walls to the salt and pepper shakers—at the **Colophon Restaurant**, which shares a historic brick building with Village Books. Don't look for beef on the menu, though. Instead, you'll find café fare by a master chef. Soups are the specialty; try the African peanut soup. There are also salads, big sandwiches and quiche, as well as smoked salmon and hummus platters for grazers. ~ 1208 11th Street, Fairhaven; 360-647-0092, fax 360-676-1742. BUDGET.

In addition to coffees and teas, the coffee shop in **Tony's Coffees and Teas** serves up fresh daily soups, salads, sandwiches and pastries to an eclectic crowd of regulars. It's almost too bohemian, but the bagels with cream cheese and sprouts, Greek salad and cocoa mocha make it worth the trip. ~ 1101 Harris Avenue, Bellingham; 360-738-4710, fax 360-715-3866. BUDGET.

> The Skagit Valley's farmlands, estuaries and tide flats attract several species of hawks and is one of the best places in all of North America to go "hawkwatching."

The tables at **Café Toulouse** are always full, a testament to the quality breakfast, lunch and dessert selections served here. Favorites include fresh fruit pancakes, curried chicken salad, roast pork with mint jelly or smoked turkey with cranberry-apple cream cheese sandwiches. You will also find pizzas and calzones from their wood-fire stove, and many selections from the fresh daily dessert board accompanied by piping espresso or latte to finish the meal. ~ 114 West Magnolia Street, Crown Plaza Building, #102, Bellingham; 360-733-8996. BUDGET.

At the **Boundary Bay Brewery**, bare woodplank floors and simple wooden tables and chairs create an unpretentious setting for "Northwest pub fusion food." What's that, you ask? In this case, it means casually eclectic offerings such as a tasty portobello mushroom and eggplant sandwich. Wash it down with a sampler of small glasses of all five beers and ales they make in plain sight on the premises. ~ 1107 Railroad Avenue, Bellingham; 360-647-5593, fax 360-671-5897. BUDGET.

Dutch Mother's Restaurant is "the" place in Lynden for traditional (that's to say, hearty) Dutch cuisine such as pot roast, meatloaf, beef cutlet, sausage and perogies. Friday night is prime-rib night, Saturday is country buffet night, and Gordon Lautenbach plays accordion on weekends. Waitresses sport Dutch dress and often can be overheard speaking Dutch with locals. ~ 405 Front Street, Lynden; 360-354-2174, fax 360-354-2987. BUDGET TO MODERATE.

For Mexican dining, try **Chihuahua**. Decorated with Mexican murals, paintings and parrot sculptures, the dining room offers booth and table seating. There's also dining in an enclosed patio. Popular specialties are fajitas, carne asada and a wide variety of combination plates. ~ 5694 3rd Avenue, Ferndale; 360-384-5820, fax 360-380-6706. BUDGET TO MODERATE.

For romantic waterfront dining, it's hard to beat the Inn at Semiahmoo's elegant dining room, **Stars**. Soft piano music fills the room as diners feast on deluxe-priced mixed seafood plank roast (salmon, halibut, sea scallops, red potatoes and vegetables), Dungeness crabcakes, parmesan-crusted sea scallops and other rich entrées. For lighter fare, try the livelier, budget-priced **Packers Oyster Bar** just down the corridor for chilled garden gazpacho soup, a salmon sandwich, shrimp caesar salad or homestyle burgers. ~ 9565 Semiahmoo Parkway, Blaine; 360-371-2000, fax 360-371-5490. BUDGET TO ULTRA-DELUXE.

Just north of the ferry dock and across the street from The Beach Store Café is the only public access beach on Lummi Island.

Near the ferry landing and offering gorgeous water views, **The Beach Store Café** is the only place on Lummi Island where visitors can find deli quality picnic supplies and lunches to go. But it's also a terrific little restaurant where everything is homemade, where herbs, lettuce and other produce is grown in its own garden or elsewhere on the island. Seafood, a specialty, is also local—crab, salmon, halibut. The café serves lunch and dinner, along with weekend brunch during the busy tourist season. Closed Monday through Wednesday. ~ 2200 South Nugent Road, Lummi Island; phone/fax 360-758-7406, 360-758-2233. BUDGET TO MODERATE.

SHOPPING Antique hounds will want to make the quick 15-minute trip east of Everett to Snohomish, home to **Star Center Antique Mall**, a five-level mall with over 178 dealers and dozens of other antique shops to browse through. ~ 829 2nd Street, Snohomish; 360-568-2131.

In Everett, the **Everett Public Market** is the prime browsing spot for antiques as well as Northwest arts and crafts. The market also houses a natural foods co-op that offers organically grown fruits and vegetables. ~ 2804 Grand Avenue, Everett; 425-252-1089.

Shopping is a major drawing card of little La Conner, with most of the boutiques and galleries concentrated along 1st and Morris streets. Focus on **Earthenworks** for fine art. ~ 712 1st Street, La Conner; 360-466-4422. **The Scott Collection** also has a selection of fine art. ~ Pier 7 Building on 1st Street, La Conner; 360-466-3691. Stop by **Bunnies by the Bay** for collectibles and unique gifts. ~ 617 East Morris Street, La Conner; 360-466-5040.

The Wood Merchant features handcrafted gifts and custom furniture by Northwest woodworkers. ~ 709 South 1st Street,

La Conner; 360-466-4741. Richard Gilkey paintings as well as arts and crafts from around the world are sold at **Janet Huston Gallery**. ~ 413 Morris Street, La Conner; 360-466-5001.

The historic **Tillinghast Seed Company** has been in business for over 100 years. Besides a variety of seeds for sale, there are a flower shop, a garden store, kitchen supplies, a Christmas attic and a nursery. ~ 623 East Morris Street, La Conner; 360-466-3329. At **Go Outside**, the owners' remarkable taste is reflected in an appealing collection of garden tools, clothing and art selected with great care. ~ 111 Morris Street, La Conner; 360-466-4836.

Don't miss **Cascade Candy**—it produces first-class truffles and other chocolate concoctions at about half the price of similar candy-makers in Seattle or Vancouver, B.C. ~ 605 South 1st Street, La Conner; 360-466-2971.

Between the communities of Bay View and Edison lies **Merritt Apples, Inc.**, an orchard proving that western Washington apples (Gravenstein and Jonagold) are serious and tasty rivals to the more famous Red Delicious of Yakima and Wenatchee. A shop open in autumn offers samples of apples and cider, and sells jam and country crafts. ~ 8914 Bay View–Edison Road, Bow; 360-766-6224.

The best shops and galleries in Bellingham are generally located in the Fairhaven District.

Artwood is a co-op gallery of fine woodworking by Northwest artists. ~ 1000 Harris Street, Bellingham; 360-647-1628. Try **Inside Passage** for gifts of the Pacific Northwest. ~ 355 Harris Street, Suite 103, Bellingham; 360-734-1790.

Dutch Village Mall is a collection of 12 shops specializing in imported Dutch lace, foodstuffs, wooden shoes and the like. The "mall" is built around a 150-foot-long canal to re-create a typical Dutch street scene. ~ 655 Front Street, Lynden; 360-354-4440.

Everett's **Club Broadway Entertainment Center** offers several after-hours options under one roof, including a sports bar, dance club, jazz club and Top-40 bar. Enjoy live classic rock on weekends, live comedy shows and murder-mystery dinners. Cover. ~ 1611 Everett Avenue, Everett; 425-259-3551. Things are jumping at **Anthony's Home Port**, with great happy-hour prices and a nice sheltered deck overlooking the marina. ~ 1725 West Marine View Drive, Everett; 425-252-3333.

NIGHTLIFE

The **La Conner Pub and Eatery**, housed in a waterfront structure that was at one time Brewster's Cigar Store, is the primary watering hole in La Conner and does a booming business through the wee hours of the morning. There are six microbrews on tap. ~ 702 1st Street, La Conner; 360-466-9932.

There are a half-dozen other country taverns scattered across the Skagit Valley, well known to locals but nearly unknown to tourists, which also serve up terrific burgers, microbrewery ales and bitters and weekend jazz and dancing. The **Conway Pub and Eatery** is best for burgers. ~ 1667 Spruce Street, Conway; 360-445-4733. The **Old Edison Inn** is also very popular. ~ 5829 Cains Court, Edison; 360-766-6266.

HIDDEN ► You'll find great happy-hour specials and the best sunset views in the little bar of **Le Chat Noir**. ~ 1200 Harris Avenue, Sycamore Square, Suite 306, Fairhaven; 360-733-6136.

BEACHES & PARKS

MUKILTEO STATE PARK A swath of beach adjacent to the Whidbey Island–Mukilteo Ferry facilities on Puget Sound, Mukilteo State Park is a day-use-only facility known primarily as a prime salmon-fishing spot with public boat launch (fee). Noble little Elliott Point Lighthouse, also known as Mukilteo Lighthouse, on the tip will keep shutterbugs happy; it's also a fine spot for beachcombing or picnicking while waiting for the ferry to Whidbey Island. There are restrooms, picnic grounds and floats. Fee for boat launch. ~ Take the Mukilteo exit off Route 5 and follow the signs to the ferry; 425-353-2923, fax 360-652-1785.

CAMANO ISLAND STATE PARK There are a handful of tiny beachfront pocket parks and boat ramps scattered around Camano Island. For instance, Kama Beach State Park nearby is an old 1930s fishing resort. But there's just one true park, Camano Island State Park, and it's a real stunner, boasting the finest stretch of shoreline in this part of Puget Sound. Here is well over a mile of enchanting beach to wander, in view of the Olympic Mountains rising to the west. Anglers fish for clams, salmon, perch, bottomfish, flounder, sole and rock cod. You can find camping facilities and places to picnic; forest and beach hiking and nature trails; and plenty of opportunities for swimming, but cold water. ~ From Stanwood, drive west on Route 532 for five miles, then follow signs to West Camano Drive and the park; phone/fax 360-387-3031.

▲ There are 87 sites (no hookups); $10 per night.

BAY VIEW STATE PARK This tiny park on the north side of the town of Bay View overlooks the **Padilla Bay National Marine Research Reserve**, an ecological pocket of 11,600 acres of marsh and tidelands tucked between the north Skagit Valley at Bay View and March Point. The Breazeale Padilla Bay Interpretive Center, half a mile north on Bay View–Edison Road, is a good place to get better acquainted with the many forms of wildlife that inhabit the area. A nature trail winds through parts of the wildlife habitat area just beyond the center. Restrooms, showers, fireplaces, picnic tables and shelter, and a kitchen are some of the facilities here. Day-use fee, $3. ~ Exit 230 off Route 5 in Burlington, follow Route 20 west to Bay View–Edison Road.

Turn right, then follow the signs to the park; 360-757-0227, fax 360-757-1029.

▲ There are 90 sites (RV hookups available); $11 to $16 per night. For reservations, call 800-452-5687.

LARRABEE STATE PARK 🚶🚲🏇 ⚓🛶🛥️🚤 This 2683-acre park on Samish Bay offers nine miles of hiking trails, including two steep trails to small mountain lakes (Fragrance and Lost lakes), and a stretch of beach with numerous tidepools for views of the local marine life. There's good freshwater fishing for trout in either of the mountain lakes and crabbing, clamming and saltwater fishing in Chuckanut and Samish bays. You'll find restrooms, showers, picnic tables and shelters, barbecue grills and kitchens. ~ Located seven miles south of Bellingham on scenic Chuckanut Drive (Route 11); 360-676-2093, fax 360-676-2061.

▲ There are 59 tent sites and 26 sites with hookups; $11 to $16 per night. For reservations, call 800-452-5687.

TEDDY BEAR COVE 🏊 This secluded, narrow stretch of white   ◄ HIDDEN
sand bordered by thick trees just south of the Bellingham city limits is a public beach that lacks facilities—and the water is very cold in case you're thinking of swimming. The beach area curves out around the shallow cove, like a thumb jutting out toward Chuckanut Bay. ~ There's a well-signed parking lot along Chuckanut Drive, Route 11, at the intersection of California Street. The trail to the beach is marked with signs at the parking lot and meanders down a steep bank for 100 yards or so from the road; 360-733-2900, fax 360-676-1180.

> In 1903, 110 shingle mills operated in Whatcom County, a testament to the one-time productivity of the region's forests.

WHATCOM FALLS PARK 🚶🚲 This popular park sprawls across 241 acres along the tumbling waters of Whatcom Creek. It's just the place to discover cooling breezes on a hot summer day as you stroll next to the woodland-bordered stream. There are hiking trails, waterfalls, fishing ponds and a hatchery, picnic shelters and barbecue pits. ~ 1401 Electric Avenue, five miles east of the Maritime Heritage Center; 360-676-6985, fax 360-647-6367.

BIRCH BAY STATE PARK 🚶⚓🛶🏊🚤 The highlight of this 192-acre park with 6000 feet of shoreline is the warm, shallow bay, which is suitable for wading up to half a mile out in some spots. The bay is bordered by a mile-long stretch of driftwood and shell-strewn beach edged by grassland. Swimming, clamming, crabbing and fishing for salmon are excellent here. The camping area is inland in a stand of old-growth cedar and Douglas fir; nestled in the lush greenery it's hard to tell that the park sits in the shadow of Arco's Cherry Point Refinery. Birdwatchers frequent the park to visit the marshy estuary at the south border that attracts over 100 varieties of birds. Facilities include restrooms, fireplaces, picnic tables, shelters, trails and an underwater park; some facilities for the disabled. ~ Eight miles south of Blaine off Birch Bay; 360-371-2800, fax 360-371-0455.

▲ There are 167 sites here, 20 with RV hookups; $11 to $16 per night. For reservations in summer, call 800-452-5687.

SEMIAHMOO PARK 🚲 🏊 This long, slender spit dividing Semiahmoo Bay and Drayton Harbor is a favorite among beach lovers, who can comb sandy, narrow beaches on both sides of the spit, and of birdwatchers who come here to observe bald eagles, loons, herons and others supported by this protected, nutrient-rich habitat. You'll encounter outstanding clamming on both sides of the spit. Kite flying is also ideal here. The spit was once home to the Semiahmoo Indians and later the site of a fish cannery; the history of both are reviewed in the park's museum. Restrooms, picnic tables, fire pits and a bike path are found here. ~ Located near Blaine. Take the Birch Bay–Lynden Road exit west off Route 5, turn north onto Harbor View Road then west onto Lincoln Road, which becomes Semiahmoo Parkway and leads into the park; 360-733-2900, fax 360-676-1180.

▼▼▼▼▼▼▼▼▼▼

Whidbey Island

Whidbey Island, stretching north to south along the mainland, is the longest island in the continental United States aside from Long Island. This slender, serpentine bit of land is covered in a rolling patchwork of loganberry farms, pasturelands, sprawling state parks, hidden heritage sites and historic small towns. The artistic hamlet of Langley near Whidbey's southern tip is a current hot spot for weekend escapes from Seattle.

SIGHTS

Most of the sights in **Langley** are concentrated along 1st and 2nd streets, where falsefront shops house small galleries, boutiques and restaurants. There's a lovely stretch of public beach flanked by a concrete wall adorned in Northwest Indian motifs just below **Seawall Park** (look for the totem pole on 1st Street), and a wonderful bronze statue by local artist Georgia Gerber above a second stairwell leading down to the beach.

In the spring months, you'll find a colorful tulip display at **Holland Gardens**. During the balance of the year come to see the beautiful floral displays that make this small garden a local favorite. ~ Corner of Southeast 6th and Ely streets, Oak Harbor.

Beautiful greenery typifies Whidbey Island, and two Greenbank area establishments offer visitors a close look at cultivating the landscape. The famous **Meerkerk Rhododendron Gardens** feature hundreds of varieties of these showy bushes—with 2000 species spread across 53 acres—which find Whidbey's climate one of the best on earth. Magnolia, maple and cherry trees add to the

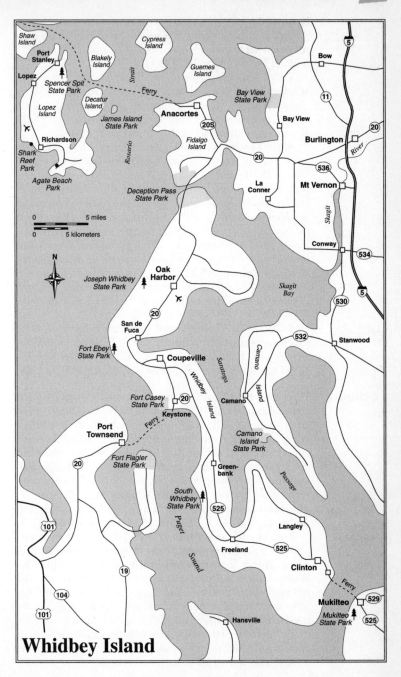

Whidbey Island

beauty of this spot, which is also a test garden. April and May are the peak months for blooms. The nursery has rhodies for sale from the end of March through May. Admission. ~ Just off Route 525 south of Greenbank; 360-678-1912.

Only a few wine grapes ripen in Puget Sound's cool climate; **Whidbey Island Vineyard & Winery** specializes in clean, crisp vintages, such as Madeleine Angevine and Siegerrebe, that are rarely grown elsewhere. Closed Tuesday and Wednesday. ~ 5237 South Langley Road; 360-221-2040, fax 360-221-4941.

Ebey's Landing National Historical Reserve, the first such reserve in the country, lies midway up Whidbey Island. The reserve takes in 19,000 acres that include Fort Ebey and Fort Casey state parks and the historic town of Coupeville, where falsefront buildings line Front Street above the wharf. Here you'll find **Alexander Blockhouse** (Alexander and Front streets) and **Davis Blockhouse** (Sunnyside Cemetery Road), built by early settlers for protection against possible Indian attacks, and a good collection of pioneer agricultural artifacts and historical displays in the **Island County Historical Museum** (908 Northwest Alexander Street, Coupeville; 360-678-3310). Admission. Reduced winter hours. ~ Ebey's Landing National Historical Reserve, P.O. Box 774, Coupeville, WA 98239; 360-678-6084; www.nps.gov/ebla.

Built in 1901, **Admiralty Head Lighthouse** at Fort Casey State Park features an interpretive center offering history on the region's military past. You'll also enjoy excellent views of Puget Sound. ~ 1280 Engle Road, Coupeville; 360-679-7391, fax 360-678-2246.

LODGING

There are some 17 hotels on the island, mostly motel-style and clustered around Oak Harbor. But the big draw on Whidbey has always been bed-and-breakfast inns, around 60 of them at last count. Your choices run the gamut from log cabins on the beach to posh retreats tucked into the forest. Many Whidbey Island bed and breakfasts offer only a single room, and come and go with regularity. Others have been in business for decades. For a comprehensive list, contact the **South Whidbey Visitor Information and Accommodation Referral Service**. ~ P.O. Box 403, 208 Anthes, Langley, WA 98260; 360-221-6765, fax 360-221-6468.

HIDDEN ►

The beautiful **Inn at Langley** has perfected the fine art of hospitality at a polished property worthy of its magnificent waterfront setting. With a decorator's color palette taken directly from the beach, rooms in shades of gray, cream, tan and brown accented by lots of natural wood are elegant, presenting a delicate balance of modern art and furnishings, and are decked out with every possible amenity (fireplace, jacuzzi, Krups coffee set and large deck to take advantage of the view). A serene oriental garden set in front of the grand dining room is an added touch. If you can afford the tariff, this is the most luxurious selection available on the island.

Continental breakfast. ~ 400 1st Street, Langley; phone/fax 360-221-3033; www.innatlangley.com. ULTRA-DELUXE.

Whidbey Inn overlooks Saratoga Passage and boasts six rooms with a view. On the main shopping street, this long-established bed and breakfast also is close to shopping and other attractions. Although the rooms are not huge, they feel more cozy than cramped, and large antique-decorated suites with fireplaces also are available. Full breakfast is delivered to your room. ~ 106 1st Street, Langley; phone/fax 360-221-7115, 888-313-2070; www.whidbey inn.com. MODERATE TO DELUXE.

Garden Path Bed and Breakfast, one of the older establishments in town, presents two luxurious and private suites decorated by the designer-owner with original art from the Northwest and around the world. ~ 111 1st Street, Langley; 360-221-5121, fax 360-221-6050. MODERATE TO ULTRA-DELUXE.

Ashendon Manor is a typical country house built by the owner —from Twickenham, England—on ten acres of woods and pasture. The large inn includes six guest rooms, all decorated with European pine furnishings and each with an open fireplace. Guests can relax in an English pub, reading room, or music room. ~ 5023 Langley Road, Langley; 360-221-2334, fax 360-221-8503. MODERATE TO DELUXE.

Country Cottage of Langley sits on two acres of handsomely landscaped garden with an English country feel and oodles of lawn for endless games of croquet. Despite the country feel, this bed and breakfast is still within easy walking distance of downtown Langley. Choose from two rooms attached to the farm house built in the 1920s, a refurbished bungalow with a wraparound porch to capture water views, and a third cottage (formerly a creamery), also circa 1920. Three rooms feature jacuzzis. Antiques from various periods and materials decorate all the rooms. Full breakfast. ~ 215 6th Street, Langley; 360-221-8709, 800-713-3860, fax 360-221-5865; www.acountrycottage.com. MODERATE TO ULTRA-DELUXE.

Gallery Suite overlooks Saratoga Passage and includes a bedroom, parlor, kitchen and great views from a private deck. Fur-   ◄ HIDDEN

DECEPTION PASS BRIDGE

Spanning the "Grand Canyon of Puget Sound," **Deception Pass Bridge** links Whidbey with Fidalgo Island. Most visitors just drive slowly by, taking in the sights. But if you want a little more excitement, stroll out onto the bridge for vertigo-inducing views—straight down into the swift, churning currents of Deception Pass. You can also walk down to the shore on the footpaths of Pass Island to watch the streaming waters up close and personal.

nished with contemporary pieces and an antique Japanese chest, this inn is convenient to good shopping and restaurants in early-20th-century Langley. Gay-friendly. ~ 302 1st Street, Langley; 360-221-2978, fax 360-331-8549. BUDGET.

Though it's inland a few miles from Langley, Lone Lake offers its own special sense of solitude and repose. A 100-acre lake that offers excellent swimming in the summer, Lone Lake is great for trout fishing, birdwatching, canoeing or just sitting quietly on the dock watching evening fall. **Lone Lake Cottages & Breakfast** offers two spacious cottages with kitchens, a tiny houseboat and a lake-front suite—all with jacuzzis and fireplaces. Many birds—exotic birds inside the main house's aviary, and ducks, pheasant, peacocks, quail and swans—populate the premises. Canoes, rowboats and bikes are available free for guest use. Continental breakfast. ~ 5206 South Bayview Road, Langley; phone/fax 360-321-5325; www.lonelake.com. DELUXE.

HIDDEN ▶

Though it's only a few miles north of downtown Langley, the **Log Castle Bed and Breakfast** somehow feels like a retreat hidden away on a gorgeous, sandy beach far from everything. This colossal log home crowned by an eight-sided turret was hand-built by the owner over the years. The four rooms are warm and inviting, with private baths and comfortable furnishings, and private decks with grand views. Full breakfast. ~ 4693 East Saratoga Road, Langley; 360-221-5483, fax 360-221-6249; www.thelog castle.com. MODERATE TO DELUXE.

From a hot tub on the deck of **Eagles Nest Inn**, you can gaze east across Saratoga Passage and Camano Island to Mt. Baker and the Cascades. Guests come to enjoy the very rural setting, soak up the pampering country hospitality, and take long strolls on a nearby cobbled beach. Four traditional rooms and a honeymoon cottage offsite. Full breakfast. ~ 4680 Saratoga Road, Langley; phone/fax 360-221-5331; www.eaglesnestinn.com. MODERATE TO DELUXE.

Home By The Sea Guest Cottages gives guest a choice of locales. The Sandpiper Suite is a quintessential sandy beach property next to a bird sanctuary, while the French Road Farm Cottage sits inland amid tall timber on ten acres that include a vineyard and perennial gardens. Both cottages have feather beds, kitchens and jacuzzis, and come with a complimentary breakfast basket on the first morning. Though the address is Clinton, Home By The Sea is actually closer to Langley. ~ 2388 East Sunlight Beach Road, Clinton; 360-321-2964, fax 360-321-4378; www.frenchroadfarm. com. ULTRA-DELUXE.

Cliff House is an architecturally stunning two-story structure of wood and sweeping panes of glass set on a wooded bluff overlooking Admiralty Inlet. Guests have the run of the entire two-bedroom house, with its open central atrium, wonderful gourmet kitchen, sunken sitting area with fireplace and wraparound cedar deck with large jacuzzi. There is also a separate small cottage with one bedroom. ~ 727 Windmill Drive, Freeland; 360-331-1566; www.cliffhouse.net, e-mail wink@whidbey.com. ULTRA-DELUXE.

Steeped in history, **Colonel Crockett Farm Bed and Breakfast Inn** is a five-room inn perched on a 40-acre rise above Crockett Lake, a 200-acre haven for waterfowl and wildlife watchers just a mile from the ferry to Port Townsend. This is a historic Puget Sound crossroads, and the inn (built between 1852 and 1855 by Colonel Walter Crockett) is reputedly the oldest continuously used home on the island. The colonel's political life stretched back to President Andrew Jackson. Three acres of grounds and gardens feature antique trees and shrubbery more than a century old. Inside, you'll find faux-marble fireplaces, an enclosed sunporch, Victorian antiques throughout, including three large bed-sitting rooms with private baths, and a library with 2000 volumes—but no radios or televisions. Full breakfast buffet. ~ 1012 South Fort Casey Road, Coupeville; 360-678-3711, fax 360-678-3707; www.crockettfarm. com. MODERATE.

> Of Washington State's nearly 400 bed-and-breakfast inns, almost 50 are on Whidbey Island.

The **Captain Whidbey Inn**, a well-preserved and maintained log inn on Penn Cove, is a fine example of the type of Northwest retreat all the rage 50 years ago and now coming back into fashion. This walk into the past offers several cozy, antique furnished rooms that share two baths and waterfront views; more recent additions to the property include two rows of spacious, pine-paneled rooms with baths and a few private cottages with fireplaces. A full breakfast is served in the dining room where the wooden floors creek nostalgically and the massive stone fireplace chases away the chill. This is one of only a handful of waterside accommodations in the region; to enjoy the water fully, arrange for an afternoon sail with Captain John Colby Stone, the third-generation descendant of the original innkeeper. Full breakfast. ~ 2072 West Captain Whidbey Inn Road, Coupeville; 360-678-4097, 800-366-4097, fax 360-678-4110; www.captainwhidbey. com. MODERATE TO ULTRA-DELUXE.

The **Victorian Bed and Breakfast** dates to 1889, with two rooms in the house, plus a cottage of similar vintage out back that once housed a pioneer dentist's office. Children and pets are welcome in the cottage. ~ 602 North Main Street, Coupeville; 360-678-5305; www.whidbeyvictorianbandb.com. MODERATE.

Within walking distance of shops and restaurants, the **Inn at Penn Cove** is actually a pair of elegant century-old Victorian homes converted into bed and breakfasts. Together, they offer six spacious rooms, some fitted with gas fireplaces, one suite with double jacuzzi; most have views over Penn Cove. Each house boasts plenty of antiques. Full breakfast and afternoon tea. ~ 702 North

Main Street, Coupeville; 360-678-8000, 800-688-2683; www. whidbey.net/penncove. MODERATE TO DELUXE.

The **Coupeville Inn** has a French mansard–style roof that adds a touch of class to this otherwise straightforward two-story inn with a condo unit (subject to availability) that sleeps up to five. Breakfast featuring homemade muffins is included in the room rates. Of the two dozen rooms, most have balconies, about half have water views. Possibly the best motel value on the island, given the free continental breakfast and excellent location. ~ 200 Northwest Coveland Street, Coupeville; 360-678-6668, 800-247-6162, fax 360-678-3059. MODERATE TO DELUXE.

The **Auld Holland Inn** is a reasonably priced roadside motel with flair, from the flowering window boxes on the European exterior to the immaculately clean, antique-filled rooms. Some rooms have fireplaces and princess canopied beds. For those seeking budget prices, there are 24 mobile home units with two or three bedrooms tucked behind the full-sized windmill housing the motel's office. If you're looking for more luxury, there are six deluxe-priced units furnished with jacuzzis and fireplaces. Continental breakfast. ~ 33575 Route 20, Oak Harbor; 360-675-2288, 800-228-0148, fax 360-675-2817. BUDGET TO DELUXE.

DINING

Since 1989, **Cafe Langley** has served Mediterranean favorites such as spanikopita, moussaka, dolmades and lamb shish kabobs along with fresh seafood (Penn Cove mussels, grilled salmon and halibut), pastas and steaks. The atmosphere here is airy Mediterranean, with stucco-like walls, exposed beams and an assortment of exotic fish etched on a glass partition. There are often people waiting in the park across the street for a table in this popular café. Closed Tuesday in winter. ~ 113 1st Street, Langley; 360-221-3090, fax 360-221-8542. MODERATE TO DELUXE.

The **Doghouse Tavern** is the place to go for great ribs, burgers, fish-and-chips and chowder. A totem on the side of this waterfront building points the way to their separate family dining room in case you've got the kids along. ~ 230 1st Street, Langley; 360-221-9825. BUDGET TO MODERATE.

BURGERS AND STARS

Toby's Tavern serves up a cheeseburger that was rated tops by actress Kathleen Turner, who starred in the film *War of the Roses*, which was filmed partly in and around Coupeville in 1989. Good fish-and-chips, Penn Cove steamed mussels and an upscale atmosphere add a touch of class to this waterfront watering hole. ~ 8 Northwest Front Street, Coupeville; 360-678-4222. BUDGET TO MODERATE.

The chef provides a floor show as well as fine cuisine at the **Inn at Langley**. The dining area is a huge country kitchen where gleaming copper pots and pans hang from the ceiling and each table has a view of the culinary action. Served on weekend nights only, the dinners consist of five courses emphasizing regional flavors such as duck breast with loganberries or baked salmon with apples, leeks and chanterelles. ~ 400 1st Street, Langley; phone/fax 360-221-3033. ULTRA-DELUXE.

The **Sapori Café** provides a homey atmosphere with its blue glass, flowers, cinnamon-colored walls and burgundy-mauve trim. The mostly vegetarian fare is simple and tasty, with an emphasis on hearty soups and scones in flavors ranging from raspberry-almond to spinach and feta cheese. A gallery room showcases local artists. Breakfast and lunch. ~ 197 2nd Street, Langley; 360-221-3211, fax 360-221-8182. BUDGET.

The **Star Bistro Cafe and Bar,** a trendy little café with art deco decor, is a popular meeting spot for lunch, dinner and drinks. Their pastas, salads and Northwest wines are particularly good, fresh mussels are always available and the grilled pesto King salmon on a french roll is inventive and tasty. On a calm day you can dine alfresco on the second-floor heated deck with a great view of the Saratoga Passage. No dinner on Monday. ~ 201½ 1st Street, Langley; 360-221-2627, fax 360-221-5853. MODERATE.

Award-winning **Rosi's Garden** serves a blend of Northwest and gourmet Italian cuisine. On the menu you'll find Penn Cove mussels, garlic-and-black-pepper-crusted prime rib, halibut florentine and poached salmon in hollandaise. Save room for the decadent desserts. Seating in the front room of this historic Victorian is very limited, so reservations for dinner, the only meal they serve, are highly recommended. There is live classical music Wednesday and Friday nights. ~ 606 North Main Street, Coupeville; 360-678-3989. MODERATE TO DELUXE.

Christopher's specializes in "creative contemporary cuisine" with a menu that changes seasonally. The emphasis is on fresh, local fare, especially seafood, and runs the gamut from superb Penn Cove mussels, to beef and chicken, vegetarian dishes, and pasta; regional wines and microbrews are also available. ~ 23 Front Street, Coupeville; 360-678-5480, fax 360-678-1827. BUDGET TO DELUXE.

Splendid views across Penn Cove are the chief attraction at **Captain's Galley**, a seafood and prime rib house. Live music is featured on Friday and Saturday nights along with the hearty fare. There's karaoke on Wednesday night. ~ 10 Front Street, Coupeville; 360-678-0241. BUDGET TO DELUXE.

At **Kasteel Franssen**, lace table dressings, antiques, tapestries and fine-art reproductions of Rembrandt and other masters set a romantic European tone well suited to this Northwest French restaurant. Special dishes include ostrich in pinot noir–shallot tarragon demi-glace, Ellensburg rack of lamb and specials that feature venison, pheasant and other wild game. Dinner only. ~ 33575 Route 20, Oak Harbor; 360-675-0724, fax 306-675-2817. MODERATE TO DELUXE.

SHOPPING   There's plenty to keep shoppers and browsers busy on Whidbey Island, especially in artsy Langley and historic Coupeville. The best art galleries are concentrated in Langley. **Museo** specializes in art glass made by local Whidbey Island artists. ~ 215 1st Street, Langley; 360-221-7737. The **Gaskill/Olson Gallery** showcases bronzes, paintings, sculpture and pottery. ~ 302 1st Street, Langley; 360-221-2978. **Soleil** carries Nambé ware, double-sided aluminum-alloy pieces by Arthur Court, silver, bone, pewter and glass jewelry, candles, stationery, photo albums and soaps. ~ 308 1st Street, Langley; 360-221-0383. The **Hellebore Glass Gallery** has fine handblown glass and a studio where you can watch glassblowers work. ~ 308 1st Street, Langley; 360-221-2067.

Another noteworthy shop in town is **The Star Store**, a modern mercantile selling fun clothing and housewares. ~ 201 1st Street, Langley; 360-221-5222. You can also browse the two shops of **Whidbey Island Antiques**. ~ 2nd Street and Anthes Avenue, Langley; 360-221-2393.

Blackfish Gallerio offers women's clothing with handpainted designs on raw silk. Check out the gallery for Northwest photography, jewelry, handwovens and pottery, all made by Northwest artists. ~ 111 Anthes Street, Langley; 360-221-1274.

There's an array of charming shops in the revitalized waterfront district of Coupeville. You'll find wonderful antiques and collectibles at **Elk Horn Trading Company**. ~ 15 Front Street, Coupeville; 360-678-2250. Fine imported clothing and jewelry from Scotland and Ireland are the specialties at **Tartans and Tweeds**. ~ 4 Front Street, Coupeville; 360-678-6244. Nautical gifts, artifacts and sportswear can be found at **Nautical 'N' Nice**. ~ 22 Front Street, Coupeville; 360-678-3565.

Just three miles south of Coupeville is **Salmangundi Farms**, which specializes in estate liquidations, tag sales and auctions. It's listed in the National Historic Register and filled with antiques and old farm equipment. Open weekends only. ~ 19162 South Route 20; 360-678-5888.

NIGHTLIFE   **Hong Kong Gardens** has a pool table and occasional deejays. ~ 4643 East State Highway 525, Clinton; 360-341-2828.

For local color in a friendly tavern try the cozy pub in the **Captain Whidbey Inn**, where the walls are adorned with university pennants and business cards. ~ 2072 West Captain Whidbey Inn Road, Coupeville; 360-678-4097.

Or drop by **Toby's Tavern**, where they filmed the bar scene from the movie *War of the Roses*. ~ 8 Northwest Front Street, Coupeville; 360-678-4222.

SOUTH WHIDBEY STATE PARK 🏃 🛶 ⤴ There are 340 acres with 4500 feet of rocky shoreline to explore in this lovely state park. Hikers here will enjoy the one-and-a-quarter-mile loop trail through an old-growth stand of fir and cedar. Anglers seek silver salmon, and climbing is popular. Black-tailed deer, bald eagles and osprey are among the many creatures here. Only the hardy will venture into the cold waters of Admiralty Inlet for a dip. There are restrooms, showers, picnic tables, shelter and fireplaces. ~ Take Route 525 nine miles north of Clinton to Bush Point Road, which after six miles becomes Smuggler's Cove Road; 360-331-4559, fax 360-331-5202.

BEACHES & PARKS

▲ There are 53 standard sites, one with electric and water hookups, and three primitive ones (campsites on the wooded bluff above the beach are very secluded); $10 to $15 per night. Closed December through February. For reservations, call 800-452-5687.

FORT CASEY STATE PARK 🏃 🎣 🏔 🚤 ⤴ History buffs and children will enjoy exploring the military fortification of this 137-acre park. While most of the big guns are gone, you'll still find panoramic views of the Olympic Mountains across the Strait of Juan de Fuca from the top of the concrete bunkers built into the escarpment. Wild roses and other flowers line the paths to the museum housed in pretty Admiralty Head Lighthouse and the beach-side campground that overlooks the Keystone Harbor ferry terminal. Scuba enthusiasts swarm to the underwater trail through the park's marine wildlife sanctuary off Keystone Harbor, and anglers try for salmon and steelhead. Facilities include restrooms, showers, picnic tables, fireplaces and an underwater marine park. ~ At Coupeville turn south off Route 20 onto Engle Road and follow the Keystone Ferry signs to the park; phone/fax 360-678-4519.

> In Deception Pass State Park, you'll find beaver dams and muskrats at Cranberry Lake's south shore.

▲ There are 35 sites; $10 to $11 per night.

FORT EBEY STATE PARK 🏃 🚲 🛶 🎣 🏔 🚤 ⤴ The massive guns are long gone from this coastal World War II fortification, but there are still bunker tunnels and pillboxes to be explored. The picturesque beach at Partridge Point is the hands-down favorite of the islanders; at low tide it's possible to walk the five-mile beach stretch to Fort Casey. Anglers cast a rod for bass and salmon on Lake Pondilla. There are restrooms, showers, picnic tables, fireplaces and nature trails. ~ From Route 20 turn west onto Libbey Road, then south onto Hill Valley Drive and follow the signs; 360-678-4636, fax 360-678-2982.

▲ There are 50 sites; $10 to $11 per night. The secluded campsites under a canopy of Douglas fir are much nicer than the crowded sites at nearby Fort Casey. Closed November through March. For reservations, call 800-452-5687.

JOSEPH WHIDBEY STATE PARK 🚶 🚲 This small park has remained a secluded treasure, known only to locals, until recently signed on Route 20. Famous for its mile or so of sandy beach, it is just right for sunset strolls or picnics with views westward across Admiralty Inlet to the Olympic Mountains. There's no overnight camping. Closed October through March. ~ Located three miles west of Oak Harbor on Swantown Road; 360-678-4636, fax 360-678-2982.

OAK HARBOR CITY BEACH PARK 🚶 🚲 ⛵ 🛶 🏖 ⚓ 🚤
🚤 🛶 A full-scale windmill and an A-6 Intruder, first used in Vietnam and donated by the Navy, are just two of the features of this day-use park on Oak Harbor Bay next to the sewage processing plant (not a deterrent, believe it or not). A sandy beach slopes down from the lighted walking path bordering expansive green fields suitable for flying kites or playing frisbee. Anglers will find salmon, bottomfish and bass. There are two wading pools in summer and a protected swimming area. There are bathhouses, picnic tables, ball fields, tennis and volleyball courts and a playground. ~ Located in downtown Oak Harbor off Pioneer Parkway, east of Route 20; watch for the windmill; 360-679-5551, fax 360-679-3902.

▲ An RV park with 56 full hookups and hot showers can be accessed at Beeksma Drive or City Beach Street. An overflow area has campsites with no hookups.

DECEPTION PASS STATE PARK 🚶 🚲 ⛵ 🛶 🏖 ⚓ 🚤
🛶 The most popular state park in Washington, it encompasses over 4800 acres laced with eight and a half miles of hiking trails through forested hills and wetland areas and along rocky headlands. There are several delightful sandy stretches for picnics or beachcombing. Breathtaking views from the 976-foot steel bridge spanning the pass attract photographers from around the world. There's swimming on Cranberry Lake in the summer and flyfishing for trout on Pass Lake. Facilities include restrooms, showers, bathhouses, picnic tables, kitchens, shelters, fireplaces, a concession stand, an environmental learning center and an underwater park. ~ Take the Mukilteo ferry to Whidbey Island and follow Route 525 and Route 20 to the park on the northern tip of the island; 360-675-2417, fax 360-675-8991.

▲ There are 235 sites (83 with hook-ups) at Deception Pass and 16 at Bowman Bay; $16 to $17 per night. For reservations, call 800-452-5687.

A two-hour drive northwest of Seattle, Anacortes on Fidalgo Island is a good place to enjoy folk art, ride a charming excursion train and see impressive murals.

Fidalgo Island

Quiet inns and waterfront restaurants make this town a pleasant retreat.

But Anacortes is only the beginning of adventures on this charming island. Often called the first of the San Juans, Fidalgo is actually linked to the mainland by the Route 20 bridge over Swinomish Channel in the Skagit Valley, and to Whidbey Island by another bridge. Access is easy. Nevertheless, you can still find quiet beaches and parks to explore. Lonely trails wind through an enormous forest reserve to superb viewpoints. A mini "Lake District" clusters more than half a dozen splendid lakes. And a marvelous resort complex—Scimitar Ridge Ranch—combines a working Northwest horse ranch and a deluxe campground that includes covered wagons outfitted for camping.

Because of its ferry terminal, **Anacortes** is known as "the gateway to the San Juans," but don't just zip on through because there's plenty to see and do here. One of the best ways to get acquainted with the city and its history is to make a walking tour of downtown to view the 40 life-size murals attached to many of the historical buildings. As part of the **Anacortes Mural Project**, these murals are reproductions of early-20th-century photographs depicting everyday scenes and early pioneers of the town. A tour map of the murals is available from the **Anacortes Chamber of Commerce**. ~ 819 Commercial Avenue, Anacortes; 360-293-3832; www.anacorteschamber.com.

SIGHTS

In front of the Anacortes History Museum there's a highly amusing (but non-functional) drinking fountain with varying levels suited for dogs, cats, horses and humans, which was donated to the city by the Women's Temperance Union.

Another reminder of earlier days is the **W. T. Preston**, a drydocked sternwheeler that once plied the waters of the Sound breaking up log jams. ~ 7th Street and R Avenue, Anacortes; 360-293-1916; www.anacorteshistorymuseum.org.

At the **Anacortes History Museum**, you'll find an entertaining collection of memorabilia from Fidalgo and Guemes islands. Closed Tuesday and Wednesday. ~ 1305 8th Street, Anacortes; 360-293-1915, fax 360-293-1929; www.anacorteshistorymuseum.org.

Even if you don't plan to stay in Anacortes at the **Majestic Hotel**, stop by for a 360-degree view of Fidalgo and surrounding islands from the fantastic cupola above fourth-floor suites and ogle the amazing skylight and collection of art and antiques. ~ 419 Commercial Avenue, Anacortes; 360-293-3355, fax 360-293-5214; www.majesticinn.com.

◀ HIDDEN

The **Anacortes Community Forest Lands** is a 2200-acre treasure of fishing and swimming lakes, wildlife wetlands, and tall conifers climbing the slopes of 1270-foot Mt. Erie, about five miles south of downtown Anacortes. Some 20 miles of foot trails offer days of wandering. For maps, stop at the Anacortes Chamber of Commerce. ~ 819 Commercial Avenue, Anacortes; 360-293-3832, fax 360-293-1595.

In the late 1800s, the bustling city of Anacortes was also referred to as the "Magic City," "Liverpool of the West" and "New York of the West."

You can also simply drive to the top of Mt. Erie and enjoy a series of vista points carved into its rocky summit that look out in all directions of the compass from the Cascades to the Olympics, across the San Juans, over Skagit Bay to Whidbey and all the way to Mt. Rainier.

Within the park and all around it are a handful of lakes—Heart, Erie, Campbell, Whistle, Cranberry, Pass. You can swing past Campbell Lake and Pass Lake (good fishing) on Route 20 between Anacortes and Deception Pass. And you can visit Heart and Erie (picnicking, fishing) from Mt. Erie Road leading into the park. Whistle and Cranberry (good fishing) are reached by foot trail.

LODGING

At the **Holiday Motel** one of the only motels that keeps its prices low even during high season, you get what you pay for. Aging rooms are very basic but tidy, with nicked furnishings in both the cramped bedroom and separate sitting room. ~ 2903 Commercial Avenue, Anacortes; phone/fax 360-293-6511. BUDGET.

HIDDEN ►

A lot of care and expense went into the painstaking renovation of the historic 1889 McNaught Building, now the **Majestic Hotel** which specializes in European elegance, from the plush feather bedding and antique furnishings of each highly individual guest room to the warm and inviting mahogany-paneled library and grand English garden. Guests are treated to a gourmet continental breakfast each morning. ~ 419 Commercial Avenue, Anacortes; 360-293-3355, 800-588-4780, fax 360-293-5214; www.majesticinn.com. MODERATE TO ULTRA-DELUXE.

At the **Nantucket Guest House Inn** the proprietress was welcoming weary travelers into her home long before bed and breakfasts came into fashion. Each of the comfortable guest rooms is furnished in lovingly polished family antiques and cozy quilts; of the seven rooms, five have private baths. There is even a spa. ~ 3402 Commercial Avenue, Anacortes; 360-293-6007, 888-293-6007, fax 360-299-4339; www.whidbey.com/nantucket. MODERATE TO DELUXE.

DINING

Gisela's Bridgeway Cafe serves a mix of German and American cuisine. In addition to the traditional hand-breaded oysters and prawns, grilled burgers and mouth-watering pies that have kept the original Bridgeway in business for over 50 years, the current owners now serve schnitzel and German sausages. Look for this unpretentious roadside establishment located on the hill four miles north of Deception Pass. Closed Monday and Tuesday. ~ 1541 Route 20, Anacortes; 360-293-9250, fax 360-299-3112. BUDGET TO MODERATE.

Although it's not particularly well-decorated or romantic, **La Petite** is the only dinner spot in town fancy enough to have table-cloths. The fare here is solid Dutch gourmet, with often repeated favorites such as *gemarinerde de lam* (marinated lamb in herbs and red wine) and *kippige knoflok* (chicken breast over parmesan pasta). The traditional Dutch breakfast of egg cup, thinly sliced ham and cheese, and piping hot loaves of bread draws a crowd. Closed Monday. ~ 3401 Commercial Avenue, Anacortes; 360-293-4644, fax 360-293-4544. DELUXE.

Potted plants, taped classical music and tablecloths soften the rough edges of **Charlie's**, a hash house overlooking the ferry terminal and water. Captive diners, here during the long wait for the ferry, choose from soups, salads, sandwiches and seafood at lunch and pasta, steak and seafood for dinner. ~ 5407 Ferry Terminal Road, Anacortes; 360-293-7377, fax 360-293-6124. MODERATE TO ULTRA-DELUXE.

SHOPPING

At the fascinating and fun **Bunnies by the Bay** you can tour the workshop where they create designer stuffed animals (not taxidermy) to complement any decor scheme. ~ 3115 V Place, Anacortes; 360-293-8037. The same business also has a retail outlet store at 2320 Commercial Avenue as well as one in La Conner.

Most of the great shops on Fidalgo Island are scattered along Anacortes' Commercial Avenue. **Left Bank Antiques**, housed in two floors of a renovated church, absolutely bulges with American and European antiques and architectural items. ~ 1904 Commercial Avenue, Anacortes; 360-293-3022.

◄ HIDDEN

The historic **Marine Supply and Hardware** is packed to the rafters with nautical antiques and memorabilia. ~ 202 Commercial Avenue, Anacortes; 360-293-3014.

Resist the temptation to buy smoked salmon to take home until you visit **SeaBear Smokehouse**, which has been producing authentic smoked salmons since 1957. Not only does the smokehouse sell smoked salmon, smokehouse chili and smoked salmon chowder, it also offers tours Tuesday through Saturday. Pose with a salmon, learn to fillet, or just taste the goods. ~ 605 30th Street, Anacortes. Take 22nd Street east toward the Anacortes Marina, turn right onto T Avenue and you'll find the warehouse in an industrial complex a block down on the right; 360-293-4661; www. seabear.com.

▼▼▼▼▼▼▼▼▼▼
Lopez Island

Life on pastoral Lopez Island is slow and amiable; residents wave to everyone and are truly disappointed if you don't wave back. Lopez didn't earn its nickname as the "Friendly Island" for nothing. Even better, it remains much less developed than San Juan and Orcas islands.

SIGHTS

The history of the island is well mapped out at the **Lopez Historical Museum** with its exhibit of pioneer farming and fishing implements, stone, bone and antler artifacts and fairly large maritime collection. While you're here, pick up a historical landmark tour guide to the many fine examples of Early American and American Indian architecture scattered around the island. Closed October through April. ~ 28 Washburn Place, Lopez Village; 360-468-2049.

Stroll out to **Agate Beach Park** on MacKaye Harbor Road to watch the sunset. Another good sunset view spot is **Shark Reef Park** on Shark Reef Road, where you might see some harbor seals, heron and, if you're lucky, a whale or two.

Shaw Island is one of only four of the San Juan Islands that can be reached by ferry, but most visitors to the San Juans miss it. You need to stay on the ferry from Anacortes and get off at Shaw, one stop beyond Lopez Island. Those who do make the trip are in for a treat. Stop by the general store near the ferry landing for picnic supplies before heading out to **South Beach County Park** on Squaw Bay Road, two miles to the south.

Afterward, continue east along Squaw Bay Road, turn north on Hoffman Cove Road and make your way to the picturesque little red schoolhouse. Park by the school and cross the street to see the **Shaw Island Historical Museum**, a tiny log cabin housing a hodgepodge of pioneer memorabilia. Open limited hours on Tuesday, Thursday and Saturday. ~ Schoolhouse Corner; 360-468-4068.

LODGING

The **Lopez Islander**, once a dog-eared motel, is turning upscale with new owners and a major-league improvement program. All of the 28 rooms have been refurbished and two suites have been added (moderate to deluxe). The marina has been upgraded (new floats and piers, a seaplane dock). An ambitious outings program for guests includes opportunities to bike, boat and fish. ~ Fisherman Bay Road, Lopez Village; 360-468-2233, 800-736-3434, fax 360-468-3382; www.lopezislander.com. MODERATE TO DELUXE.

Edenwild, the newest addition to the scant list of lodgings on the island, is a two-story Victorian. The eight guest rooms are pretty, with blond-wood floors, claw-foot tubs and antique furnishings; three rooms have romantic fireplaces, one is handicapped accessible and four have views of Fisherman's Bay or San Juan Channel. Included in the room rates is breakfast, served in the sunny dining nook or on the delightful garden terrace. Apéritifs and truffles are served in the rooms. ~ Lopez Village; 360-468-3238, fax 360-468-4080; www.edenwildinn.com. DELUXE TO ULTRA-DELUXE.

You might feel a bit like Little Red Riding Hood as you bound up a footpath to your cabin at **Lopez Farm Cottages**, nestled in an ancient cedar grove teeming with wildlife. Thankfully, only an inviting queen-size bed—not a wolf—awaits. These light and airy efficiencies feature a contemporary design with fireplaces, kitchens, decks and plenty of windows; an outdoor spa is an additional amenity. In the morning, continental breakfast arrives at your doorstep in a basket. ~ Fisherman Bay Road, Lopez Island; 360-468-3555, 800-440-3556, fax 360-468-3966; www.lopezfarm cottages.com. DELUXE.

◄ HIDDEN

The best bet on Lopez Island is the **Inn at Swifts Bay**, a delightful bed and breakfast in an elegant Tudor home. Posh best describes the interior, with a comfortable mix of modern, Williams Sonoma–style furnishings and antique reproductions adorned in crocheted antimacassars and needlepoint pillows. There are two rooms sharing one bath, as well as three suites with private entrances and baths; each room has a gas-lit fireplace. A hot tub, an exercise studio and a sauna are on the premises. The leisurely gourmet breakfast is without a doubt the most delicious morning repast available in the islands. Gay-friendly. ~ Port Stanley Road; 360-468-3636, fax 360-468-3637; www.swiftsbay.com. MODERATE TO ULTRA-DELUXE.

◄ HIDDEN

> Both the general store and ferry landing on Shaw Island are operated by Franciscan nuns.

The **Lopez Lodge** above Lopez Video in the village has three no-frills, motel-like rooms with a shared bath across the hall. One room has a private bath and kitchenette. ~ 360-468-2500, 800-472-3311, fax 360-468-3314. MODERATE TO DELUXE.

The **Island Farm House** offers a more cozy and comfortable room (with bath) overlooking a pasture and pond, as well as a private cabin near the main house. ~ Route 2, Box 252, Hummel Lake Road; 360-468-2864. BUDGET TO MODERATE.

The **Bay Cafe** has an imaginative menu of ethnic cuisine featuring fresh Northwest products. There are always daily specials to choose from, with often-repeated favorites like scallops in Thai curry; chargrilled orange-ginger-sesame-glazed boneless half breast of duck and wild Mexican prawns with Asian risotto cakes; and aged tenderloin of beef with toasted walnuts, gorgonzola butter and grilled portobellos. Reservations are essential, especially during summer. Closed Tuesday in fall; Monday through Wednesday in winter. ~ Lopez Village Road; 360-468-3700, fax 360-468-4000. MODERATE TO DELUXE.

DINING

Set off to one side within the **Lopez Island Pharmacy** is an old-fashioned, red, white and black soda fountain, the best spot for lunch on Lopez, recently recognized by the *Chicago Tribune*. Grab a booth or a stool at the bar and order a sandwich, bowl of soup or chili or slice of pie to go with your phosphate, malt, float or other fountain treat. Closed Sunday. ~ Lopez Village; 360-468-4511. BUDGET.

Located next to the Lopez Village Market in a handsome Cape Cod–style building with weathered shingles and a terrace overlooking the water, **Gail's** uses fresh ingredients, including herbs and vegetables from the chef's garden, to create dishes bearing both Northwest and Pacific Rim influences. For the last four years the restaurant has won *Wine Spectator*'s Award of Excellence. Among the menu highlights are steamed halibut wrapped in bok choy with black bean sauce, Thai curried prawns and salmon barbecued over alderwood. Dinner served year-round; breakfast and lunch served September through May. Closed Sunday. ~ 360-468-2150; e-mail gails@pacificrim.net. MODERATE TO DELUXE.

The **Islander Lopez Restaurant** is a true waterfront restaurant, looking west across Fisherman Bay to spectacular evening sunsets. In summer, ask for a table on the outdoor dining patio. Specialties of the house include an award-winning clam chowder, cajun chicken and a daily fresh sheet of local seafood—salmon and halibut, for example. Breakfast is available on weekends. ~ Fisherman Bay Road, Lopez Village; 360-468-2234, fax 360-468-3382. BUDGET TO DELUXE.

SHOPPING   For the most part, shopping here is limited to establishments in Lopez Village. **Archipelago** sells cotton T-shirts and women's casual apparel. ~ 360-468-3222. **Islehaven Books and Borzoi** stocks an admirable selection of new books and regional music. ~ 360-468-2132. For fine art, visit **Chimera Gallery**, the cooperative showcase for prints, paintings, weaving, pottery, handblown glass and jewelry produced by local artists. ~ 360-468-3265.

BEACHES & PARKS   **SPENCER SPIT STATE PARK** 🚶 🚲 ⚓ 🦞 🏖️ 🛶 This long stretch of silky sand on Lopez Island encloses an intriguing saltwater lagoon. The mile-long beach invites clamming, crabbing, shrimping, bottom fishing, wading and swimming during warm summer months. Facilities include restrooms, beach firepits and picnic shelters. ~ Take the ferry from Anacortes to Lopez Island, then follow the five-mile route to the park on the eastern shore of the island; 360-468-2251, fax 360-468-3176.

▲ There are 35 sites here, ten of which are walk-in only; $11 per night. Call 800-452-5687 for reservations. Closed December and January.

San Juan Island, the namesake of the archipelago, is a popular resort destination centered around the town of Friday Harbor. This 20-mile-long island has a colorful

San Juan Island

past stemming from a boundary dispute between the United States and Great Britain. The tension over who was entitled to the islands was embodied in American and British farmers whose warring over, get this, a pig, nearly sent the two countries to the battlefield. When an American farmer shot a British home-steader's pig caught rooting in his garden, ill feelings quickly es-calated. Fortunately, cooler heads prevailed so that what is now referred to as the "Pig War" of 1859 only resulted in one casu-alty: the pig.

The history of this little-known war is chronicled through inter-pretive centers in the **San Juan Island National Historical Park**, which is divided into English Camp and American Camp. Lo-cated on West Valley Road at the north end of the island is

SIGHTS

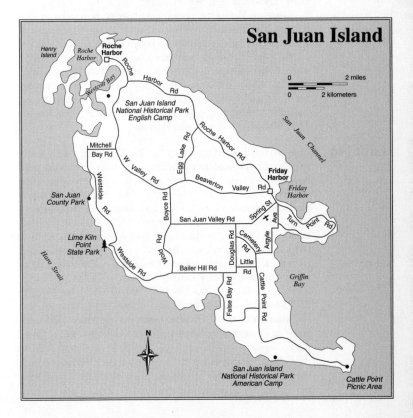

English Camp, which features barracks, a formal garden, cemetery, guardhouse, hospital and commissary left intact. **American Camp,** on Cattle Point Road at the south end of the island, is where the officers and laundress' quarters, and the Hudson Bay Company Farm Site remain. ~ 360-378-2240, fax 360-378-2615.

San Juan Historical Museum is a charming early-20th-century frame building that gathers within its walls a good collection of American Indian baskets and stone implements, an antique diving suit, period furniture and clothing. A great place to learn about the region's maritime history, the museum also features an excellent collection highlighting the region's proud past. Closed Monday through Wednesday. ~ 405 Price Street, Friday Harbor; phone/fax 360-378-3949.

HIDDEN ►

Oyster lovers and birdwatchers should make the trip down the dusty road to **Westcott Bay Sea Farms,** where they'll find saltwater bins of live oysters and clams and an array of birds attracted to the oyster beds that stretch out into the bay. ~ 4071 Westcott Drive, Friday Harbor; 360-378-2489, fax 360-378-6388.

Afterglow Vista is the mausoleum of one of the region's wealthy families. The structure itself is fascinating; an open, Grecian-style columned complex surrounds six inscribed chairs, each containing the ashes of a family member, set before a round table of limestone. A seventh chair and column have obviously been removed, some say as part of Masonic ritual, others believe because a member of the family was disinherited or because the seventh member considered life unending. ~ Roche Harbor Resort, 4950 Reuben Tarte Memorial Drive, Roche Harbor.

LODGING

Conveniently located one and a half blocks from the ferry terminal, **Harrison House Suites** provides home-away-from-home comfort in five spacious suites. The suites, set in a turn-of-the-20th-century Craftsman and a 1930s cottage, sleep from two to fourteen guests and include private baths and kitchens. Most have sundecks, while one features a wood stove and upright piano. In addition, laundry facilities are available. For those without the luxury of an in-room whirlpool, relax in the outdoor hot tub. Transportation from the ferry can be provided by request. Continental breakfast is complimentary; full gourmet breakfast costs extra. ~ 235 C Street, Friday Harbor; 360-378-3587, 800-407-7933, fax 360-378-2270; www.san-juan-lodging.com. MODERATE TO ULTRA-DELUXE.

Named for its view, **Olympic Lights** is a remodeled 1895 farmhouse set on five grassy, breeze-tossed acres overlooking the Olympic Peninsula across the Strait of Juan de Fuca. Guests kick off their shoes before heading up to the cream-carpeted second floor with four comfortably appointed, pastel-shaded rooms sharing two baths; a fifth room on the ground floor has a private bath.

You'll find no frilly, Victoriana clutter here, just a peaceful night snuggled under down comforters topped off by a farm-fresh breakfast. ~ 4531-A Cattle Point Road, Friday Harbor; 360-378-3186, fax 360-378-2097; www.olympiclightsbnb.com. MODERATE.

If you've dreamed of life on the water, you'll appreciate the **Wharfside Bed and Breakfast,** a 60-foot, two-masted sailboat with two guest rooms. The forward stateroom with a double bed and two bunks feels cozy, while the aft stateroom with queen bed is a little roomier. The rates include a three-course breakfast. Pets and children are welcome. ~ Port of Friday Harbor; 360-378-5661, 800-899-3030; www.slowseason.com. MODERATE.

Friday's is a renovated bed and breakfast with 11 individually decorated rooms, all with down comforters and wildlife art. You can stay in the Rose Room and watch the sunset or the Orca Room and soak in the private jacuzzi. The most popular is the Eagle Cove Room, with its private jacuzzi, kitchen and balcony. And all this romance is conveniently located in the heart of Friday Harbor. Continental breakfast. ~ 35 1st Street, Friday Harbor; 360-378-5848, 800-352-2632, fax 360-378-2881. MODERATE TO ULTRA-DELUXE.

Believe it or not, Friday Harbor was named after an early 1800s settler named Joe Friday.

Overlooking Griffin Bay and surrounded by fruit orchards and lush gardens, **Duffy House** is a lovely 1920s Tudor farmhouse offering country-cozy accommodations. Its five antique-appointed rooms are outfitted with queen beds, private baths and views of the bay or the Olympic Mountains. Keep an eye out for majestic bald eagles tending their nests on the grounds of this tranquil B&B. Transportation can be provided from the ferry or the airport. Full breakfast. ~ 4214 Pear Point Road, Friday Harbor; 360-378-5604, 800-972-2089, fax 360-378-6535, www.duffhouse.bnb.com. MODERATE TO DELUXE.

Set in the rolling West Valley near British Camp National Park and surrounded by a working ranch, **States Inn** is a bit of Sleepy Hollow in San Juan. Each of the ten rooms has a decor that hints at its namesake state—tiny Rhode Island comes closest, with shells and brass dolphins on the fireplace mantle, various renditions of ships on the walls and copies of the New England publication *Yankee* to peruse. The friendly and informative innkeeper and the multicourse country breakfasts make up for the slight sulphur odor of the tap water. The inn is also disabled-accessible, hard to find in the islands. Full breakfast. ~ 2039 West Valley Road, Friday Harbor; 360-378-6240, fax 360-378-6241; www.statesinn.com, e-mail info@statesinn.com. MODERATE TO ULTRA-DELUXE.

Roche Harbor Resort has something for everyone. You can check in to the 1886 **Hotel de Haro,** where gingerbread trim, parlor beds, antiques and a roaring fireplace bring back memories of the good old days. In addition to this three-story, 20-room establishment, nine former workers' cottages have been converted into two-bedroom units, ideal for families. The cottages are convenient to the swimming pool. For contemporary lodging, choose one- to three-room condominiums. ~ Roche Harbor Resort, 4950 Reuben Tarte Memorial Drive, Roche Harbor; 360-378-2155, 800-451-8910, fax 360-378-6809; www.rocheharbor.com, e-mail roche@rocheharbor.com. MODERATE TO ULTRA-DELUXE.

DINING

HIDDEN ►

From the patio and dining room at **Roberto's**, you can look down at the ferries while enjoying Southern Italian and traditional Basque dishes (from the Basque region of France, influenced by French and Spanish cultures). Menu items include polenta, oxtail stew, veal cutlets and chicken San Fermin. The restaurant also features a cellar full of exceptional wines. Closed Monday. ~ 1st and A streets, Friday Harbor; 360-378-6333, e-mail lrichter@island.net. MODERATE TO DELUXE.

Another welcome addition to Friday Harbor is **The Blue Dolphin**, an unpretentious diner serving hearty portions of home-cooked breakfast favorites like biscuits and gravy, eggs Benedict, blueberry pancakes and chicken-fried steak. ~ 185 1st Street, Friday Harbor; 360-378-6116. BUDGET.

Among the best restaurants on the island, the rustic look and rural setting of the **Duck Soup Inn** hardly hints at the creative, though somewhat limited, bill of fore. Several seafood and beef options are available, but why not try the inn's namesake—Southwest duck stew seasoned with chipotle chiles, lime and cilantro? For starters, there are appetizers such as Westcott Bay manila clams steamed in a vindaloo curry broth, as well as fine Northwestern wines. Dinner only. ~ 50 Duck Soup Lane, Friday Harbor; 360-378-4878; www.ducksoupinn.com. DELUXE.

SHOPPING

Most of the shops are located within blocks of Friday Harbor, giving you plenty to do while waiting for the ferry. In Sunshine Alley, **Dolphin Art** (360-378-3531) sells original screenprint art on cotton sportswear. ~ 165 Front Avenue.

Art lovers visiting Friday Harbor will want to stop by several galleries. **Waterworks Gallery** features a collection of contemporary eclectic Northwest art in media such as glass, pottery, oil and watercolor. ~ Spring and Argyle streets, Friday Harbor; 360-378-3060. **Garuda & I** carries an amazing selection of ethnic arts, beads, crafts, musical instruments as well as jewelry from Indian, Asian and local artisans. ~ 60 1st Street, Friday Harbor; 360-378-3733. The **Sunshine Gallery** offers locally produced sculptures, watercolors, ceramics and jewelry. ~ Spring Street, Friday Harbor; 360-378-5819.

On San Juan Island, **Herb's Tavern** is the local sidle-up-to-the-bar joint with pool tables. ~ 80 1st Street, Friday Harbor; 360-378-7076. You'll find pool tables, a dart board and six TVs at **Haley's Bait Shop**, a smoke-free sports bar and grill. ~ 175 Spring Street, Friday Harbor; 360-378-4434. The **Roche Harbor Resort Lounge** has weekend dancing to live music in the summer. ~ 248 Reuben Memorial Drive, Roche Harbor; 360-378-2155.

NIGHTLIFE

SAN JUAN COUNTY PARK Orca whales frequently pass by the rocky shoreline of this ten-acre park on the western edge of San Juan Island. Because of its location on Smallpox Bay, the park is a haven for kayakers and scuba divers who enjoy the easy waters in the shallow bay or the more challenging shelf that drops steeply off about 80 feet out. Swimming is good in the shallow, protected bay; fishing is fair for bottomfish, rockfish, salmon and crab. There are restrooms, picnic tables and fire pits. ~ On Westside Road just north of Lime Kiln Point State Park; phone/fax 360-378-2992.

BEACHES & PARKS

▲ There are 20 standard sites ($18 per night), two mooring buoys with potable water ($8 per night) and one site for groups ($3 per person, nine-person minimum). For reservations, call 360-468-4413.

LIME KILN POINT STATE PARK Situated on a rocky bluff overlooking Haro Strait, this is the prime whale-watching spot on San Juan Island. A footpath takes you to picturesque Lime Kiln Lighthouse, listed on the National Register of Historic Places. Restrooms, picnic tables and interpretive displays are found here. There is no drinking water for the public. ~ Located off Westside Road on the western shore of San Juan Island; 360-378-2044.

Lime Kiln Point State Park is named for an early lime kiln operation, with remnants of old structures still visible to the north of the lighthouse.

CATTLE POINT PICNIC AREA Though it takes a precarious scramble down a rocky ledge to reach it and picnic tables on the bluff above lend little privacy, this gravelly half-moon is arguably the prettiest public beach on San Juan Island. Anglers will find bottomfish and salmon. Facilities include picnic tables, shelter, restrooms, interpretive signs and a nature trail. ~ Follow Cattle Point Road through American Camp and on to the southern tip of the island. ~ 360-856-3500, fax 360-856-2150.

FOURTH OF JULY BEACH This secluded, sandy crescent is where the locals head when they're looking for privacy. There are often bald eagles nesting in the nearby trees, a poignant sign of this aptly named stretch. The shallow, little bay area extends out a long way and is suitable for wading on hot days. Anglers can try for bottomfish and salmon. There are pit toilets, picnic tables and a fenced grassy area off the parking lot suitable for frisbee. Large groups should call American Camp for a permit (360-378-2902). ~ Located on the northeastern edge of American Camp; 360-378-2240, fax 360-378-2615.

Orcas Island

Trendy, artsy-crafty and lovely to look at, Orcas Island is a resort that caters to everyone from backpackers to the well-to-do. A nature sanctuary pocketed with charming towns, the island also boasts more sun than some of its neighbors.

SIGHTS

One of Orcas Island's leading landmarks is Rosario Resort. Even if you're not planning to stay here during your trip, make sure to

HIDDEN ► visit **Moran Mansion** for a fantastic evening show that includes music performed on a 1910 Steinway grand piano and an amazing pipe organ along with entertaining narration and slides of life on the island in the early 1900s. ~ 1 Rosario Way, Eastsound; 360-376-2222, fax 360-376-3680; www.rosarioresort.com.

Of the many small historical museums in the San Juans, the **Orcas Island Historical Museum** is our favorite. Six interconnected log cabins of prominent early settlers house a fine assemblage of relics and antiques, American Indian art and local contemporary art that maps the history and growth of industry on the island. Closed Monday and from October through April. Admission. ~ North Beach Road, Eastsound; 360-376-4849; www.sanjuanweb.com/orcashistoricalmuseum.

HIDDEN ► **Madrona Point,** a pretty madrone tree–dotted waterside park saved from condo development by the Lummi Indians and local residents, is a fine spot for a picnic. It's at the end of the unmarked road just past Christina's Restaurant in Eastsound. No dogs allowed.

LODGING

A stay at **Turtleback Farm Inn** is like stepping into the much-loved story *The Wind in the Willows*, surrounded as it is by acres of forest and farm tracts full of animals as far as the eye can see. Rooms in this lovely, late-19th-century farmhouse vary in size and setup, but all 11 rooms have a charming mix of contemporary and antique furniture, cozy quilts and antique fixtures in private baths. Full breakfast. ~ Route 1, Box 650, Eastsound, WA 98245; 360-376-4914, 800-376-4914, fax 360-376-5329; www.turtlebackinn.com. MODERATE TO ULTRA-DELUXE.

HIDDEN ► One of Orcas Island's best-kept secrets is Doug and Jeri Smart's **Little House on the Farm,** a no-host home for rent that looks so homey passersby just assume the Smarts live in it. The house nicely accommodates four people who have the run of it, from the two bedrooms with queen-size beds to the reading room, full kitchen, stone fireplace in the living room and jacuzzi. Decorated with Victorian country furnishings, the house sits on 27 acres of fenced pastures and woodlands complete with grazing horses. Carriages are on display in the yard. ~ Eastsound; 360-376-5306, 877-376-9423; www.walkinghorsefarm.com/lodging.htm. ULTRA-DELUXE.

The **Outlook Inn** is right in Eastsound, overlooking the bay and close to the town's many shops and restaurants. A classic turn-of-the-20th-century maritime inn, it's been restored, with light pine and fir floors and wood furnishings helping bring in the light off the harbor. There are 16 deluxe suites. The inn's restaurant serves hearty, maritime-style breakfasts, with salmon and oyster omelets typical. ~ Main Street, Eastsound; 360-376-2200, 888-688-5665, fax 360-376-2256. MODERATE TO ULTRA-DELUXE.

It's not unusual to find semi-tame deer roaming around the ample grounds of **Rosario Resort**, tucked away on Cascade Bay on the east side of the horseshoe of Orcas Island. The motel-style rooms scattered along the waterfront or perched on the hillside overlooking the bay are clean and comfortable, and many have been recently renovated to imitate the original state of the resort. ~ 1 Rosario Way, Eastsound; 360-376-2222, 800-562-8820, fax 360-376-3680. ULTRA-DELUXE.

Accommodations at the funky **Doe Bay Village Resort** range from bunk houses to rustic cabins to tents with 33 units total. There are shared central bathrooms, a community kitchen and a small café on the grounds of this large retreat along with a splendid three-tiered sauna and three mineral baths perched on a covered deck. ~ Star Route 86, Olga; 360-376-2291, fax 360-376-5809; www.doebay.com. BUDGET TO MODERATE.

La Famiglia, an inviting, wood-paneled restaurant decorated with local prints, has been the preferred choice of islanders since opening in 1976. The lunch and dinner menus feature Italian classics with island flair—pasta primavera with salmon, seafood linguine, Orcas Island oysters and steamer clams in garlic and wine. There

DINING

SOUND BITE

With thousands of miles of tidal coastline, Puget Sound and the San Juan Islands once boasted some of the best sportfishing opportunities in North America. These days, the fish—especially salmon—are in great peril from various abuses. For the present, there are still five varieties of Pacific salmon (chinook, coho, chum, pink and sockeye), and anglers can also try for cod, flounder, halibut, ling, rockfish, sea perch, squid and sturgeon. Scuba divers often concentrate their efforts on harvesting abalone, crab, octopus, shrimp and squid, while shellfishers are rewarded with butter and razor clams. Clamming and fishing licenses are required and are available in sporting goods stores.

is even pizza to please the younger set. Closed Monday in winter. ~ A Street, Eastsound; phone/fax 360-376-2335. MODERATE TO DELUXE.

Bilbo's Festivo specializes in Tex-Mex fare. A margarita or cerveza on the tiled garden patio surrounded by adobe walls rounds out the experience. Bilbo's serves dinner only, but opens **La Taqueria**, a lunch outlet in the courtyard, during the summer months. ~ North Beach Road, Eastsound; 360-376-4728, fax 360-376-3692. BUDGET TO MODERATE.

The Deer Harbor Inn, tucked away in an expanse of orchard grove peering out over Deer Harbor and the Olympic Range, is where locals come for that special night out. The daily menu is chalked on the board; rock cod, coho salmon and choice steaks are prime picks. For diners on the deck, this is a great spot to watch the sunset. Dinner only; reservations recommended. ~ Deer Harbor Road, Deer Harbor; 360-376-4110, fax 360-376-2237. MODERATE TO DELUXE.

SHOPPING   You'll find several interesting shops in Eastsound. **Darvill's Rare Print Shop** carries antique maps, etchings and fine prints and has a connected bookstore. ~ 296 Main Street; 360-376-2351. Charts, maps, local music and original T-shirts can be found at **Gulls & Buoys Gifts**. ~ Horseshoe Highway; 360-376-2199.

An 1866 cabin houses **Crow Valley Pottery & Gallery**, a long-established studio that got its start making ceramic wind bells inspired by Northwest tribal arts. It has expanded to represent numerous island artists and craftspeople working in art glass, metal sculpture, watercolors, jewelry, pastels and more. ~ 2274 Orcas Road, Eastsound; 360-376-4260; www.crowvalleypottery.com.

HIDDEN ►   Don't spend all your time and money in Eastsound because you won't want to miss **Orcas Island Pottery**, the oldest existing craft studio on Orcas. You can watch potters at work through the windows of the studio. ~ Off West Beach Road; 360-376-2813. An intriguing spinning and weaving shop, **The Naked Lamb** is also on West Beach Road. ~ 360-376-4606.

Monkey Puzzle Curiosities carries a curious selection of boutique items—jewelry and clothing, both elegant and casual—by several island designers, plus Tibetan books, videos and imports. ~ 432 North Beach Road; 360-376-2275; www.monkeypuzzle. com, e-mail monkey@rockisland.com.

The Right Place has pottery strewn about the garden and in the showroom. ~ Off Enchanted Forest Road; 360-376-4023.

HIDDEN ►   At a bend in Horseshoe Highway as you reach Olga is **Orcas Island Artworks**, the cooperative art gallery showcasing fine arts, handicrafts and furniture all produced by local hands. ~ 360-376-4408. Tucked away in the attic is **Temenos Books and Music**, with metaphysical books, crystals, incense and world music ranging from meditational to Celtic to Jimi Hendrix. ~ 360-376-5645.

Moran Lounge is the place to go for live entertainment and great sunsets. ~ Rosario Resort, 1 Rosario Way, Eastsound; 360-376-2222. For convivial pub action, step into the **Lower Tavern** and amuse yourself with darts and pool. Beer and wine only. ~ Prune Alley and Main Street, Eastsound; 360-376-4848.

NIGHTLIFE

MORAN STATE PARK 🚶🚴 🛶⛵🏊🚤 Washington's fifth-largest park consists of 5000 verdant acres flanked by 1800 feet of saltwater shoreline and crowned by sweeping Mt. Constitution. There are miles of forest trails connecting the four mountain lakes, numerous waterfalls and five campgrounds. There is fishing for rainbow, cutthroat and kokanee trout on several lakes, with boat rentals available. Facilities include restrooms, showers, kitchen shelters and picnic tables. ~ Located near Eastsound, accessible by state ferry from Anacortes; 360-376-2326, fax 360-376-2360.

BEACHES & PARKS

The view from the stone tower at the peak of Mt. Constitution takes in the San Juans, Mt. Baker and Vancouver, B.C.

▲ There are 135 developed sites and 15 primitive sites; $11 per night; reservations are recommended. For reservations, call 800-452-5687 mid-May to mid-September.

OBSTRUCTION PASS STATE PARK 🛶🚤 This primitive, heavily forested locale on the southeastern tip of Orcas Island is tricky to get to, so the crowds are kept to a minimum, a reward for those who care to search it out. The area has a hiking trail, several free campsites and a beach with cold water for brave swimmers. Anglers will find bottomfish and rockfish. There are vault toilets, picnic tables, three mooring buoys and trails. ~ From the town of Olga follow Doe Bay Road east, turn right on Obstruction Pass Road and keep right until you hit the parking area. From there it's a half-mile hike to the campground; 360-856-3500, fax 360-856-2150.

◀ *HIDDEN*

▲ There are nine free primitive sites; hike-in only.

OTHER PARKS Many of the smaller islands are preserved as state parks including **Doe, Jones, Clark, Sucia, Stuart, Posey, Blind, James, Matia, Patos** and **Turn**. They are accessible by boat only and in most cases have a few primitive campsites, nature trails, a dock or mooring buoys off secluded beaches, but no water (except Jones, Stuart and Sucia, in season) or facilities except for composting toilets. Costs are $5 for mooring buoys, $5 for camping, $8 for boats under 26 feet and $11 for boats over 26 feet to dock overnight. Washington watertrail sites cost $7 per night and must be reached by a human-powered beachable watercraft. One vessel that carries passengers to any of the 16 islands in the San Juans is the Island Commuter Services, which leaves from Bellingham or Friday Harbor. ~ 888-734-8180.

Outdoor Adventures

BOATING

Spending time on the water is a part of daily life here, and certainly something that visitors should not miss. In fact, many of the 100-plus islands of the San Juans are accessible only by boat. Rental options are numerous; on the mainland, contact **Fairhaven Boatworks** for kayaks, rowboats and sailboats. Closed Monday. ~ 501 Harris Avenue, Bellingham; 360-647-2469.

In the islands, try **North Isle Sailing**, which offers sea cruises around Whidbey, the San Juans and Canada. Trips last from a half day to a week. ~ 1856 North Swantown Road, Oak Harbor; 360-675-8360. **Penmare Marine Co.** rents 15- to 60-foot yachts. ~ 2011 Skyline Way, Anacortes; 360-293-4839.

In February 1996, San Juan County outlawed jet skis. Locals complained that the serenity of the San Juans was disrupted by the incessant buzzing of cityfolk zipping around on their waterfront.

Sailboat charters are offered by **Kismet Charters**, which tailors tours for groups of six to last from one day to a week. ~ P.O. Box 111, Lopez Island, WA 98261; 360-468-2435; www.rockisland.com/~sail kismet. Captain Ken McDonald of **Viking Cruises** has been leading tours since 1979 aboard his wooden-hulled custom-built boat, which holds 49 people. Choose form a wide variety of trips including a two-and-a-half-hour Skagit Bay float and crabfeast. In winter, consider taking a birdwatching tour to see the more than 200 species that flock to the islands. ~ 109 North 1st Street, La Conner; 360-466-2639; www.viking cruises.com.

SPORT-FISHING

Catching some salmon is the hoped-for reward when you head out on a fishing charter through Northern Puget Sound and the San Juan Islands. As a bonus, you're also likely to encounter seals, eagles and whales as you sail past islands wooded with red-bark madrone trees.

In winter, of course, the temperature on the water can get chilly and the water a bit choppy. All the charter fishing services listed here provide boats with heated, enclosed cabins to keep you comfortable. Charter fees include bait and tackle, but do not include a fishing license or food and drink.

NORTHERN PUGET SOUND **Jim's Salmon Charter** specializes in arranging full-day trips to fisheries in the San Juan and Canadian islands for groups of no more than four people. Jim has more than three decades of experience. Bait and tackle are included. ~ Marine Drive, Blaine Marina; 360-332-6724.

In Everett, Gary Krein is president of the Charter Boat Association of Puget Sound and owner of **All Star Charters**. He operates a 28-foot fiberglass-bottom boat that can carry up to six people each, and encourages "angler participation" on his full-day trips (two daily in summer, one in winter). The boat comes fully equipped with electronic fishfinding equipment that seeks out the salmon and bottomfish. Bait and tackle are included. ~ Port of Everett; 425-252-4188, 800-214-1595; allstarfishing.com.

Mike Dunnigan is the skipper of **Sea Hawk Salmon Charters.** He runs year-round, exclusive eight-hour charters for up to four people to fish for salmon, bottomfish and halibut. Bait and tackle are included. ~ Skyline Marina, Anacortes; 360-424-1350.

SAN JUAN ISLANDS   Trophy Charters will pick anglers up from the other islands before heading out on a four- to six-hour fishing trip seeking salmon and bottomfish in a 29-foot bayliner that holds six. Captain Monty runs a fast boat (up to 30 mph), so travel time is reduced. He also runs sailing boats to the Caribbean for three-day to week-long trips. ~ Friday Harbor; 360-378-2110.

Several rivers in the area—the Snohomish, Skykomish, Skagit and Sauk, for example—provide year-round catches, notably steelhead and all species of salmon except sockeye (it's not permitted to take this fish from rivers). **Washington Fishing Adventures** Service specializes in full-day, highly personalized fishing trips on a 16-foot driftboat or a 22-foot jetboat for a maximum of five people. Ken Elsea tries to help anglers both catch fish and sharpen their skills. His jet boat lets him take anglers onto sections of rivers inaccessible to boats with conventional motors. Bait and tackle are included. ~ Marysville; 360-653-5924.

RIVER FISHING

For nonadventurers who want an outdoor experience that's a lot of fun but not extremely challenging, a guided water excursion in a sea kayak may be just the thing. No previous kayaking experience is necessary to join one of these groups for a paddling tour on the gentle waters of Chuckanut Bay, with its sandstone formations near Bellingham; of sea caves around Deception Pass State Park on Whidbey Island; or off San Juan Island, where you are likely to see whales, seals and other marine wildlife. Unless noted, the operators listed here generally offer a regular schedule of excursions from April–May to September–October. Cost for a sea kayak excursion ranges from $30 to $60. Most operators can also arrange overnight or longer trips.

KAYAKING

NORTHERN PUGET SOUND   Moondance Sea Kayaking Adventures leads half-day to three-day trips to nearby locations such as Chuckanut Bay, Cypress Island and Clark's Point (where you'll see a fossil of the entire trunk of a palm tree). A slightly longer trip to sea caves occasionally heads down to Deception Pass State Park, where the wave action is rougher. ~ Bellingham; 360-738-7664.

LOPEZ ISLAND   Lopez Kayaks offers morning and afternoon sea-kayaking tours in double kayaks for eight people to MacKaye Harbor, which is also popular with seals. If you have

Text continued on page 252.

Whale Watching in the San Juan Islands

Here in the waters of the San Juan archipelago there are three resident pods, or extended families, of *Orcinus Orca*, otherwise known as "killer" whales. Because they are so frequently and easily spotted in the protected waters, these gentle black and white giants have been carefully studied by scientists since 1976.

Their research is documented at the **Whale Museum**, where you can learn more about whales. A photo collection with names and pod numbers will help you identify some of the 100 or so resident orcas, distinguished by their grayish saddle patches and nicks, scars or tears in the dorsal fins and tails. Displays and videos explain the difference between breaching, spyhopping, tail-lobbing and other typical orca behavior and the many vocalization patterns that scientists can only guess at the significance. Admission. ~ 62 1st Street North, Friday Harbor; 360-378-4710, 800-946-7227, fax 360-378-5790; www.whale-museum.org.

The Whale Museum also has an orca adoption program set up to help fund the ongoing research and all sorts of whale-related educational material, art and souvenirs available in their gift shop. They operate a 24-hour hotline (800-562-8832) for whale sightings and marine mammal strandings as well.

From May to September you can often see the whales from shore when they range closest to the islands to feed on migrating salmon. The best shoreline viewing spots are **Lime Kiln Point** on San Juan Island or **Shark Reef Park** on Lopez Island. Sightings drop dramatically in the winter as the pods disperse from the core area in search of prey.

If you want to get a closer look, put on your parka and sunglasses, grab your binoculars and camera and climb aboard one of the **wildlife cruises** that ply the waters between the islands. Even if you don't see any orca during the trip, you will almost certainly spot other interesting forms of wildlife such as sleek, gray minke whales, Dall's porpoises (which look like miniature orca), splotchy brown harbor seals, bald eagles, great blue heron, cormorants or tufted puffin.

Mosquito Fleet Enterprises offers full-day whale-watching tours on cruisers that hold form 68 to 149 people. The boats leave the Everett Marina from April to October. ~ 1724 West Marine View Drive, Everett; 425-252-6800.

Deer Harbor Charters offers four-hour whale-watching tours from April to October on a 36-foot boat that carries 20 people from Deer Harbor Resort or on a 47-foot boat that carries 30 people from Rosario Resort. Both boats have a naturalist guide. ~ P.O. Box 303, Deer Harbor, WA 98243; 360-376-5989, 800-544-5758; www.deerharborcharters.com.

Island Mariner Cruises boasts a high success rate for spotting whales: 94 percent for whales and 85 percent for orcas. It's no wonder the naturalist has worked there for 15 years and they use more spotting services—including a plane—than any other on the island. Enjoy day-long nature and whale watching expeditions with commentary on the history, flora and fauna of the San Juans as you cruise through the islands on a boat designed for whale-watching that holds 100 people. ~ 5 Squalicum Esplanade, Bellingham; 360-734-8866.

Western Prince Cruises has similar naturalist-accompanied wildlife tours on a half-day basis. Boats include a 46-footer that holds 30 people and a 28-footer that holds six people. ~ Friday Harbor; 360-378-5315, 800-757-6722; www.orcawhalewatch.com.. **Viking Cruises** offer full-day tours to Deception Pass from La Conner. Their three-day excursion to Rosario Resort in Eastsound combines a crabfeast and pipe-organ concert with whale-watching trips. The captain claims an 80 percent success rate for spotting whales. ~ 109 North 1st Street, La Conner; 360-466-2639; www.vikingcruises.com. You can also try **San Juan Boat Tours Inc.** for a three-hour whale-sighting excursion aboard fast boats. ~ Friday Harbor; 360-378-3499.

Happy spotting!

experience, you can also rent a kayak for your own use without joining a tour or buy your own vessel, accessories or related books. ~ 2845 Fisherman Bay Road; 360-468-2847.

SAN JUAN ISLAND   Since the waters just off the west side of San Juan Island are in the main whale-migration corridor, your chances of seeing whales are good. If not, there's plenty of other wildlife to view, notably seals and bald eagles. (The highest density of bald-eagle nestings in the lower 48 states is in the San Juan Islands.) There are also kelp forests, jutting cliffs, sea caves and rocky outcroppings. A biologist or scientist accompanies the day excursions led by **Sea Quest Kayak Expeditions** for groups of four to twelve. There are also camping trips lasting from two to five days that go through primary orca viewing areas. ~ Friday Harbor; 360-378-5767. **Crystal Seas Kayaking** escorts up to eight people on morning or afternoon sunset excursions. Paddlers will see eagles, seals and whales. ~ Friday Harbor; 360-378-7899.

> The greatest concentration of wintering bald eagles can be found at the Skagit River Bald Eagle Natural Area.

ORCAS ISLAND   **Osprey Tours** brings a different, historical twist to half-day and full-day sea-kayaking tours. Following the Alaskan Eskimo tradition, owner Randy Monge makes these wood-frame kayaks with bifurcated (T-shaped) bows, which, he says, split the water and provide lift going through waves. Monge also gives each kayaker an Aleutian whale-hunter's hat, shaped like a conical visor that resembles a bird's beak. The hats helped disguise Aleutian hunters and, acting like a hearing aid, collected sound. ~ West Beach; 360-376-3677. For lessons or tours contact **Shearwater Sea Kayak Tours**, which offers half-day to five-day guided tours. Shearwater has also sold accessories and clothing since 1982, making it the oldest outfitter on the islands. ~ P.O. Box 787, Eastsound, WA 98245; 360-376-4699.

SCUBA DIVING   The protected waters of Puget Sound hold untold treasures for the diver: craggy rock walls, ledges and caves of this sunken mountain range and enormous forests of bull kelp provide homes for a multitude of marine life. Giant Pacific octopus thrive in these waters, as do sea anemones and hundreds of species of fish.

"Within 15 minutes of Friday Harbor on San Juan Island, there are hundreds of great dive spots," says one local diver who grew up in the area. The west side of San Juan Island and the south side of Lopez Island are particular favorites, largely because the absence of silt means the water is cleaner and therefore clearer. There are also lots of ledges along these rocky coasts, which abound with exceptional wall-dive spots. Acres of bull kelp forests, with their teeming marine life, are also popular dive spots. But just as these waters hold great beauty, they can also be treacherous with tremendous tidal changes and strong currents.

NORTHERN PUGET SOUND Washington Divers, Inc. offers complete rental and diving services, including a full schedule of diving activities year-round, from one-day trips to month-long excursions. A one-day dive charter to the San Juan Islands is the most popular trip. In the summer, extended daylight hours make it possible to make up to three dives during the six- to seven-hour trip. The shop also runs night dives and a free "come along" beach dive at least two weekend days a month. Scuba certification classes (open water) are also available. ~ 903 North State Street, Bellingham; 360-676-8029.

WHIDBEY ISLAND Besides air fills, diving lessons and rental of wetsuits and other equipment, **Whidbey Island Dive Center** offers half- to full-day dive charters using two tanks per dive. One popular spot for experienced divers is under the bridge at Deception Pass State Park, where currents reach seven knots—"a diving rush." For the less experienced, the charter to the diving sanctuary off Keystone Jetty is an excellent spot to view marine life. The Dive Center also teaches all types of certification. ~ 1050 Northeast 7th Avenue #1, Oak Harbor; 360-675-1112.

SAN JUAN ISLAND **Emerald Seas Aquatics** is a full-service dive shop, retail and rental. It specializes in daily half-day charters, guaranteeing you at least two dives using one tank per dive, in different locations during the trip. One might be a vertical wall dive, another may be in a grotto filled with marine life. Groups are kept small—two to six people. Open-water certification classes are also available. ~ 2-A Spring Street Landing, Friday Harbor; 360-378-2772, 800-942-2507; www.emeraldseas.com. **Underwater Sports Inc.** offers full-day chartered trips to the islands, night dives, rentals, open-water certification, classes and air fills. ~ 205 East Casino Road, Everett; 425-355-3338.

Many of the public parks and tidelands in north Puget Sound offer clamming opportunities in season. Licenses are necessary, and it's imperative to check first with the **Red Tide Hotline**. Shellfish poisoning can be deadly. ~ 800-562-5632.

Beaches in the immediate Seattle area are often polluted as well; most outlying beaches are safe until late summer. For information on seasons, licenses and limits, call the **Washington Department of Fish & Wildlife**. ~ 1111 Washington Street, 360-902-2200. Most sporting goods and fishing supply stores sell licenses.

One of the best beaches is on Whidbey Island. **Double Bluff State Tidelands** is a long beach stretch looking south across Useless Bay. This is a fine place for a walk; the beach stretches two miles to the headland, and the southern exposure means it's warm on almost any sunny day.

SHELL-FISHING

◄ *HIDDEN*

It's also a top-notch spot during low tides to dig for steamer clams and for the native Washington butter clam, which is excellent for steaming or chowder. Clams and mussels are available year-round, but there are no oysters. ~ At the end of Double Bluff Road, turn west off State Route 525 about ten miles west of Clinton, a mile north of the Langley turnoff.

RIDING STABLES

Saddle up for a gentle, leisurely ride around an 85-acre ranch or take in the scenic beauty of the San Juan Islands.

NORTHERN PUGET SOUND A year-round operation, **Lang's Pony and Horse Farm** takes up to 20 riders on a leisurely guided trail ride (half-hour to one-hour) around the hilly and wooded ranch, which is about 30 miles south of Bellingham. The farm also offers a Mom's Camp so mothers can ride in tranquility, as well as summer camps and riding lessons. Call for reservations. ~ 21463 Little Mountain Road, Mt. Vernon; 360-424-7630.

WHIDBEY ISLAND Put on jeans and a pair of sturdy leather shoes (leave your Birkenstocks and sneakers at home) for a guided trail ride through the hilly, wooded **Madrona Ridge Ranch**. Please call ahead (evenings are best) to arrange a one-and-a-half-hour ride; groups are limited to only three people at a time. Riding lessons are available for all ages, but the trail rides are for teens and adults only. Nonriders can enjoy nature walks and the nearby beach. ~ Madrona Way, Coupeville; 360-678-4124.

ORCAS ISLAND You'll have to call ahead for an appointment to ride one of Jeri Smart's Tennessee walking horses at **Walking Horse Country Farm**. These horses can walk fast and keep their backs flat for a smooth ride. Allow one hour for instruction before the hour-long guided ride, which takes in the farm's hilly woodlands and ponds. Only six riders at a time; reservations necessary. ~ Eastsound; 360-376-5306; www.walkinghorsefarm.com.

GOLF

Award-winning design, lush scenery and the Northwest's only par-5 to an island green are among the distinctions of golf courses in this part of the state.

NORTHERN PUGET SOUND **Dakota Creek** was named Washington's most challenging 18-hole course by the Pacific Northwest Golf Association. This public course, carved out of a mountain, is quiet, well maintained and hilly. ~ 3258 Haynie Road, Custer; 360-366-3131.

The 18th hole at **Homestead Golf Course** is the Northwest's only par-5 to an island green. The public course is flat, but has lots of water. ~ 115 East Homestead Boulevard, Lynden; 360-354-1196.

A good choice is the **Walter E. Hall Memorial Golf Course,** an 18-hole public facility with well-kept grounds, a restaurant and

cart rentals. ~ 1226 West Casino Road, Everett; 425-353-4653.
The 18-hole **Kayak Point Golf Course** has an 18-hole putting
course, a driving range, a full-service restaurant and lounge, and
cart, shoe and club rentals. ~ 15711 Marine
Drive, Stanwood; 360-652-9676. **Overlook Golf
Course**, a nine-hole public course with a view of
Big Lake, offers club and cart rentals. ~ 523 Route
9, Mt. Vernon; 360-422-6444.

Useless Bay is so named
because it's too shallow
to provide anchorage
for any but
small boats.

There's a hilly front nine at **Lake Padden Municipal
Golf Course**, located in Lake Padden Park. It's a tight,
densely treed public course. ~ 4882 Samish Way, Bellingham; 360-676-6989. **Sudden Valley Golf and Country
Club** is an 18-hole semiprivate course that sits on a lake. There
are cart rentals, a driving range and a snack shop. ~ 2145 Lake
Whatcom Boulevard, Bellingham; 360-734-6435.

The most expensive course (up to $90 greens fees) in the area
is the semiprivate **Semiahmoo Golf and Country Club**. It's ranked
as one of nation's best resort courses and was designated as a sec-
tional qualifying course for the 1997 U.S. Open. The 18-hole,
par-72 course was designed by Arnold Palmer; hole number 4
has a scenic view of Mt. Baker and the valley beyond. ~ 8720
Semiahmoo Parkway, Blaine; 360-371-7005.

The **Avalon Golf Club** has the hottest new links around the
Sound. The 27-hole public course will keep you busy for a while.
You can rent carts, too. ~ 19345 Kelleher Road, Burlington; 360-
757-1900.

FIDALGO ISLAND **Similk Beach Golf Course** is a public 18-hole
facility that rents carts. ~ 1250 Christiansen Road, Anacortes;
360-293-3444.

LOPEZ ISLAND The nine-hole **Lopez Island Golf Course** is a
private, flat course. ~ Airport Road, Lopez Island; 360-468-2679.

SAN JUAN ISLAND It's only nine holes, but the **San Juan Golf
and Country Club** "plays like 18." Private, but open to the public, the course is set on a wooded, rolling tract next to Griffin
Bay. Cart rentals are available. ~ 2261 Golf Course Road, Friday
Harbor; 360-378-2254.

ORCAS ISLAND For a distinctive, lesser-known golf experience,
try the **Orcas Island Golf Club**, a quaint, challenging 18-hole public course. The regular nine alternates tees on the back nine to
make play a little more interesting. The pro shop and clubhouse
are like a touch of Scotland, and wildlife abounds. ~ Horseshoe
Highway, Eastsound; 360-376-4400.

◄ *HIDDEN*

No need to leave your racquet at home with so many public
courts to take advantage of. In Everett, you'll find six lighted
courts at **Clark Park**. ~ 2400 Lombard Street. Or try the courts

TENNIS

at **Fairhaven Park** in downtown Bellingham. ~ 107 Chuckanut Drive; 360-676-6985.

On Whidbey Island, you can use the four lighted courts at **Coupeville High School** at South Main Street or the four clay courts at **Oak Harbor City Park** at 1501 City Beach Street. On Fidalgo Island, try the six courts at **Anacortes High School facility**. ~ 20th Street and J Avenue. Though **Lopez High School** is your only option on Lopez Island, the school has two hardtop courts and is building four more. ~ Center Road. On San Juan, try the four courts at the **Friday Harbor High School** at Guard Street or head out to the **Roche Harbor Resort** at Roche Harbor Road.

BIKING

For bicycling in the Bellingham area, the best map is "Bicycling in Bellingham and Whatcom County," which outlines trails according to traffic volume, surface status (gravel, paved, etc.) and hill difficulty; it also categorizes trails as City Ride, City Trail or Country Ride. The map is available in many bicycle stores and during the summer from the **Bellingham/Whatcom County Convention and Visitors Bureau**. ~ 904 Potter Street, Bellingham; 360-671-3990, 800-487-2032.

If you plan to bike on the San Juan Islands, it's important to remember that the islands' narrow roads don't have special lanes or other provisions for cyclists. Lopez Island is probably the best bet for the occasional bicyclist: you'll be able to bike long, flat country roads, rather than the steeper, twisting roads of some of the other islands. You can rent a bike on the island or in Anacortes before ferrying over for the day.

The hardy cyclist might prefer a 20-mile hilly and winding route around San Juan Island or 16 miles of steep, twisting roads beginning at the ferry landing on Orcas Island.

For bike trails here and in other parts of the state, contact the **Washington Department of Transportation** to request a route map and informative brochure, or call 360-705-7277 for the Bicycle Hotline. ~ P.O. Box 47393, Olympia, WA 98504-7393.

NORTHERN PUGET SOUND Some of the best country bike routes in the state can be found in the **Skagit and Nooksack valleys**. Use the backroads east, northeast and southeast of La Conner to fashion loop tours from a few miles to over 20. Or, head for the north Skagit Valley and create a route using backroads starting in Bow on Chuckanut Drive, and heading west to Edison, south to Bay View, west over Bay View Ridge to Chuckanut Drive, then north back to Bow.

Do the same in the slightly hillier Nooksack Valley, beginning in Lynden and circuiting Sumas, Everson and Nooksack, before returning to Lynden.

There's great bike riding on often-overlooked Lummi Island.

The **Waterfront Loop** in Everett takes you past the majestic old homes of early lumber barons and through the Everett Marina Village.

Bellingham offers several bike routes, some arduous, some easy, all highlighting the scenery and history of the area. One is the moderate **Interurban Trail** (also known as the Chuckanut Trail). The seven-mile trail, which follows an old trolley route, begins at the Fairhaven Parkway and ends at Larrabee State Park. The best of the bunch is the fairly easy, 45-minute **Lake Padden Loop** in Lake Padden Park. It connects to a series of trails on **Mt. Galbraith**, a local hot spot for mountain biking.

There are no designated bike lanes along the dusty rural roads of Mt. Vernon, but you'll see rich fields and quiet lanes for miles.

WHIDBEY ISLAND Those looking for a long-distance ride will enjoy the 50-mile Island County Tour, which begins at Columbia Beach on Whidbey Island and continues on to Deception Pass at the northern tip of the island. This trip is moderately strenuous, with high traffic on a good portion of the ride, but the spectacular views of the Strait of Juan de Fuca and the Saratoga Passage are reward enough.

LOPEZ ISLAND The easiest and most popular bike route here is the **Lopez Island Perimeter Loop**, 32 miles of gently rolling hills and narrow, paved roads passing by Fisherman's Bay, Shark Reef Park, MacKaye Harbor and Agate Beach on the west side of the island and Mud Bay, Lopez Sound and Shoal Bay on the east side.

SAN JUAN ISLAND The slightly difficult, 30-mile **San Juan Island Loop** leads along hilly, winding roads through Friday Harbor, Roche Harbor, San Juan Island National Historical Park and along the San Juan Channel.

ORCAS ISLAND The **Horseshoe Route** is by far the most difficult island bike route, with 16 miles of steep, twisting roads beginning at the ferry landing in Orcas, continuing through Eastsound, then on to Olga. An alternative route for the very hardy starts in Olga, passes through Moran State Park and ends in Doe Bay, with a possible challenging 3.5-mile sidetrip up and back down Mt. Constitution.

Bike Rentals For mountain-bike sales and repairs in the Northern Puget Sound region, contact **The Bicycle Center**. ~ 4718 Evergreen Way, Everett; 425-252-1441. For year-round mountain-bike rentals, sales and repairs in the Bellingham area, try **Fairhaven Bicycle and Ski**. ~ 1103 11th Street, Bellingham; 360-733-4433. North of Bellingham, rent a mountain or hybrid bike at **Semiahmoo Marina** for a leisurely ride around the adjacent resort or golf course. ~ 9540 Semiahmoo Parkway, Blaine; 360-371-5700.

If you're planning a trip out to the San Juan Islands and you'd like to ferry a bike over with you, call ahead to reserve a mountain or 21-speed bike at **Ship Harbor Inn Bicycle Rental**. A lock, tool kit, patch kit and water bottle come with the cost of the rental (and you can keep the water bottle). ~ 5316 Ferry Terminal Road, Anacortes; 360-293-5177.

Most people coming to Lopez Island who want to bicycle bring their own bikes. Otherwise, head for **Bike Shop on Lopez**, which is open year-round for rentals of hybrids, mountain bikes, ten speeds, touring bikes and children's bikes. The shop also sells accessories and bike parts, offers repairs and will even deliver a bike to any location on the island, including the ferry landing. ~ Lopez Village; 360-468-3497.

Lopez Bicycle Works also rents, repairs and sells mountain bikes, touring bikes and hybrids and will let you drop off the bike at the ferry landing when you leave for the day. ~ Fisherman's Bay Road; 360-468-2847.

For bike rentals on San Juan Island, contact **Island Bicycles**, which offers mountain bikes, cross bikes, seven-speeds and two tandems, as well as bike sales and repairs. ~ 380 Argyle, Friday Harbor; 360-378-4941.

Rent, buy or repair mountain bikes and hybrids on Orcas Island at **Dolphin Bay**, which also offers custom tours for 10 to 30 people. ~ Ferry Landing; 360-376-3093. Mountain bikes, road bikes, tandems, bike trailers and trail-a-bikes can be found for sale or rent at **Wildlife Cycles**, which also does repairs and offers tours. The half-day tours around the island include lunch, are limited to no more than six in a group and are arranged by sign-up. ~ North Beach Road, Eastsound; 360-376-4708.

Velocity Bikes on Whidbey Island offers a wide variety of mountain bikes, hybrids, trailers, tandems and children's bikes to rent. They also sell bikes and accessories. ~ 5603½ South Bay View Road, Langley; 360-321-5040.

HIKING

All distances listed for hiking trails are one way unless otherwise noted.

NORTHERN PUGET SOUND   On the **Langus Riverfront Park Nature Trail** (2.5 miles) in Everett, hikers are likely to spot red-tailed hawk or gray heron as they make their way through towering spruce, red cedar and dogwood trees along the banks of the Snohomish River, past Union Slough and on toward Spencer Island, a protected haven for nesting ducks.

The Padilla Bay National Estuarine Reserve (360-428-1558) in the tiny community of Bay View (about six miles west of Burlington) offers the best hikes in the area. The **Padilla Bay Shore Trail** (2.3 miles) is a bicycle/pedestrian path with views of the estuary, mudflat, sloughs and tidal marsh. The Breazeale Interpretive Center is one mile north of the Shore Trail. Binoculars and trail guides can be checked out at the center to aid your exploration of the forest and meadow along the **Upland Trail** (.8 mile).

There are several good choices for hikes in Bellingham. The **Interurban Trail** (6 miles) begins near the entrance to Larrabee State Park and hugs the crest above Chuckanut Drive overlooking the bay and the San Juan Islands. Chuckanut Drive passes the rose gardens of Fairhaven Park on its way into the revitalized Fairhaven District of the city.

There are 5.9 miles of rolling trails through the lush **Sehome Hill Arboretum**, crowned by views of Mt. Baker and the San Juans from the observation tower at the summit. Since no motorized boats are allowed on **Lake Padden**, the path (3 miles) around the glistening lake and through some of the park's 1008 acres is both peaceful and rejuvenating.

In Birch Bay State Park in Blaine, the gently sloping **Terrell Marsh Trail** (.5 mile) winds through a thickly wooded area of birch, maple, red cedar, hemlock and fir, home to pileated woodpeckers, bald eagle, ruffed grouse, blue heron, muskrats and squirrels, and on to Terrell Marsh, the halfway point on the loop, before passing back through the forest to the trailhead.

WHIDBEY ISLAND   The most picturesque hikes on Whidbey Island are found in and around Fort Ebey State Park. The **Ebey's Landing Loop Trail** (3.5 miles) has some steep sections on the bluff above the beach, but carry your camera anyway to capture the views of pastoral Ebey's Prairie in one direction and Mt. Rainier and the Olympic Mountains framed by wind-sculpted pines and fir in the other. Trimmed in wild roses, the trail swings around Perego's Lagoon and back along the driftwood-strewn beach. Be aware that the trail passes over some private property.

The **Partridge Point Trail** (3.5 miles) in Fort Ebey State Park climbs through a mix of coastal wildflowers on a windswept bluff

EASY GOING OUTINGS

A variety of intriguing guided hiking, biking and van tours of the Skagit Valley, Cascade Mountains, San Juans and Whidbey Island are available from **Easy Going Outings**. The owner is a master at creating bike routes that combine first-class scenery with easy terrain on lesser-traveled back roads. For hiking tours, the trails are typically short, scenic and easy enough for anyone in sound health to enjoy. Deluxe day tours by luxury van may include visiting artists in their home studios, organic farmers and other grassroots entrepreneurs, all sorts of wildlife, or simply touring back roads and little-known corners of the region. ~ 1460 Augusta Lane, Burlington; 360-757-3062.

rising 150 feet above the water with wide views of Port Townsend, Admiralty Inlet, Protection Island and Discovery Bay. A fenced path at the southern end drops down the headland to the cobbly beach below.

There are numerous trails to choose from in Deception Pass State Park. Locals prefer **Rosario Head Trail** (.3 mile) on the Fidalgo Island side, stretching over the very steep promontory between Rosario Bay and Bowman Bay with sweeping views of the San Juans, Rosario Strait and the Strait of Juan de Fuca, and continuing on the **Lighthouse Point Trail** (1.5 miles), which extends farther along the rocky bluff, past the lighthouse and into a dense stand of fir and cedar. On the Whidbey Island side of the bridge, climb the steep switchback on **Goose Rock Perimeter Trail** (3.5 miles) and you might see great blue heron on Coronet Bay, then follow the path down under the bridge next to the swirling waters of the pass and on to quiet North Beach to see the totem pole located at West Point where North and West beaches converge. Heartier hikers might want to tackle the **Goose Rock Summit Trail** (.5 mile), with an altitude gain of some 450 feet for an unparalleled view of Deception Pass and the Cascades.

Close to five million vehicles a year cross the U.S./Canada border at Blaine, Washington, making this the West Coast's busiest northern border station.

FIDALGO ISLAND In Anacortes, your best bet is to head for the **Washington Park Loop Road** (3 miles), located on Fidalgo Head at the end of Sunset Avenue four miles west of downtown. Rewarding views on this easy, paved path with a few moderate slopes include incredible glimpses of the San Juan Islands, Burrows Pass and Burrows Island. You'll also find quiet, cool stretches through dense woods and access to beaches and romantic, hidden outcroppings suitable for a glass of champagne to toast the breathtaking sunsets.

LOPEZ ISLAND On Lopez, ideal hiking choices include the **Shark Reef Park Trail** (.5 mile), a mossy path that meanders through a fragrant forest area and along a rock promontory looking out over tidal pools, a large kelp bed, a jutting haul out spot for seals and across the channel to San Juan Island. Spencer Spit State Park's **Beach Trail** (2 miles) travels down the spit and around the salt marsh lagoon alive with migratory birds; at the end of the spit is a reproduction of a historic log cabin built by early settlers, a fine spot for a picnic or brief rest stop with a nice view of the tiny islands offshore.

SAN JUAN ISLAND Two of the best hiking alternatives on San Juan are the established hiking trails of the San Juan Island National Historical Park. The **Lagoon Trail** (.5 mile) in American Camp is actually two trails intertwined, starting from a parking area above Old Town (referred to on maps as First) Lagoon and passing through a dense stand of Douglas fir connecting the lovely, protected cove beaches of Jakle's Lagoon and Third Lagoon. The highlight of the short but steep **Mt. Young Trail** (.75 mile) in English Camp are the plates identifying the many islands dotting the waters as far as the eye can see. If you want a closer view of the water, you can take the flat, easy **Bell Point Trail** (2 miles), also in English Camp, which runs along the edge of the coast.

ORCAS ISLAND   Unless you plan to spend an extended period of time here, there's little chance of covering the many hiking trails that twist through Moran State Park on Orcas Island connecting view spots, mountain lakes, waterfalls and campgrounds. The **Mountain Loop** (3.9 miles) is fairly easy and takes in sights such as drooping log cabins and a dam and footbridge at the south end of Mountain Lake. For a little more challenge, try a section of the two-part **Twin Lakes Trail**: one part (2.2 miles) heads up the valley at the north end of Mountain Lake; the other (3.7 miles) takes you from the summit of Mt. Constitution along a rocky ledge to Twin Lakes and the Mountain Lake Campground, with occasional views through the thick trees. If you're a waterfall lover, take the **Cascade Creek Trail** (4.3 miles) from the south end of Mountain Lake past Cascade and Rustic falls and on to Cascade Lake.

Transportation

Route 5, also known as the Pacific Highway, parallels the Northern Puget Sound coastline all the way up to the Canadian border. **Route 20** from Burlington takes you into Anacortes, the main jump-off point for ferry service to the San Juan Islands. **Route 16** leads from Tacoma across The Narrows and onto the Kitsap Peninsula where it connects to **Route 3** skirting the Sinclair Inlet and continuing north to Port Gamble.

CAR

Visitors flying into the Northern Puget Sound area usually arrive at either **Bellingham International Airport** (360-671-5674) or the much larger and busier **Seattle-Tacoma International Airport** (see Chapter Two for further information). Carriers serving the Bellingham airport include Casino Express, Horizon Airlines, West Isle Air with service to the San Juan Islands, and United Express.

AIR

Charter and regularly scheduled commuter flights are available into the tiny **Friday Harbor Airport** through Harbor Airlines, Island Air and West Isle Air. ~ 360-378-4724. Small commuter airports with limited scheduled service include **Anacortes Airport**, **Eastsound Airport** and **Lopez Airport**; all are served by West Isle Air.

Washington State Ferries, which are part of the state highway system, provide transportation to the main islands of the San Juans—Lopez, Orcas, Shaw and Friday Harbor on San Juan—departing from the Anacortes Ferry Terminal (Ferry Terminal Road; 800-843-3799 in Washington). Schedules change several times per year, with added service in the summer to take care of the

FERRY

heavy influx of tourists. The system is burdened during peak summer months, so arrive at the terminal early and be prepared to wait patiently (sometimes three hours or more) in very long lines if you plan to take your car along; walk-on passengers seldom wait long. ~ 206-464-6400.

San Juan Island Shuttle Express runs between Bellingham and the San Juan Islands. ~ 355 Harris Avenue, Bellingham; 360-671-1137.

BUS

Greyhound Bus Lines (800-231-2222) provides regular service into Bellingham, Everett and Mt. Vernon. Stations are in Bellingham at 401 Harris Avenue in Fairhaven Station, 360-733-5251; in Everett at 1503 Pacific Avenue, 425-252-2143; and in Mt. Vernon at 1101 South 2nd Street, 360-336-5111.

The **Bellingham/Sea-Tac Airporter** provides express shuttle service between Bellingham, Mt. Vernon, Stanwood, Anacortes, Marysville, Oak Harbor and the Sea-Tac airport. ~ 360-380-8800.

TRAIN

Amtrak offers service into Everett on the Puget Sound shoreline via the "Empire Builder," which originates in Chicago and makes its final stop in Seattle before retracing its route. West Coast connections through Seattle on the "Coast Starlight" are also available. ~ 2900 Bond Street, Everett; 800-872-7245.

CAR RENTALS

At the Bellingham International Airport, you'll find **Avis Rent A Car** (800-331-1212), **Budget Rent A Car** (800-527-0700), **Hertz Rent A Car** (800-654-3131) and **National Car Rental** (800-328-4567).

Less expensive local rental agencies include the **Inn at Friday Harbor Rentals** (360-378-4351) and **U-Save Auto Rental** (360-293-8686) in Anacortes.

PUBLIC TRANSIT

Whatcom Transportation Authority provides public transit in Lynden, Bellingham, Blaine, Birch Bay, Ferndale and Gooseberry Point. ~ 360-676-7433. **Skagit Transit** services the Mt. Vernon, Sedro Woolley, Anacortes and Burlington areas. ~ 360-757-4433. In Everett you can get just about anywhere for 75 cents via **Everett Transit**. ~ 425-353-7433. **Island Transit** covers Whidbey Island, with scheduled stops at Deception Pass, Oak Harbor, Coupeville, the Keystone Ferry, Greenbank, Freeland, Langley and the Clinton Ferry. ~ 360-678-7771. In smaller towns like La Conner and Mt. Vernon and on most of the islands there are no public transportation systems set up; check the Yellow Pages for taxi service.

TAXIS

A cab company serving the Bellingham International Airport is **City Cab, Inc./Yellow Cab** (360-733-8294). For service from the Friday Harbor Airport contact **San Juan Taxi Service** (360-378-3550). **Triangle Vans** (360-293-3979) serves the Anacortes Airport.

EIGHT

The Cascades
and Central Washington

Perhaps without even realizing it, many Americans have a burning image of this region. For it was here, in the Cascade Range, that Mt. St. Helens blew its top in 1980. But the area has a lot more going for it than one hyperactive mountaintop. Indeed, think of the Cascades and Central Washington as one wild place for anyone who loves the outdoors.

The Cascade Range contains some of the most beautiful mountain scenery in the United States, much of it preserved by two major national parks, several national recreation areas and numerous wilderness areas that make this a major sports haven. There are also glaciers galore; 318 are in the North Cascades National Park alone. Thousands of miles of trails and logging roads lace the Cascades, leading to mountaintop lookout towers, old gold mines, lakes, streams and gorgeous sights.

The hand of man has done little to alter the Cascades. Not until 1952 did a highway cross the state north of Route 2. And when the North Cascades Highway (Route 20) was completed, it was with the understanding that it would be closed during the heavy snows, usually from October until May. Thus, most of the Cascades are still wild and remote, seen and experienced by humans but not transformed by them.

The range, about 700 miles long, begins at the Fraser River in southern British Columbia and extends southward through Washington and Oregon and into California just beyond Lassen Peak. The most dominant features of the Cascades are its 15 volcanoes. Washington lays claim to five, with Mt. Rainier the granddaddy at 14,411 feet. Most peaks are under 10,000 feet, and Harts Pass, the highest pass in the state, is only 6197 feet.

Although the range is not a comparatively high one, it served as an effective barrier to exploration and development until well into the 20th century. The pioneers who came over the Oregon Trail avoided it, choosing instead to go down the Columbia River to the Cowlitz River, travel up to present-day Toledo, then move overland to Puget Sound at Tumwater and Olympia.

Mining has always been part of the Cascades story. Although no major gold strikes have been found, several smaller ones have kept the interest alive, and there's probably never been a day since the mid-1870s when someone wasn't panning or sluicing in the mountains.

The range supports a wide variety of plants and wildlife because it has so many climatic zones. Naturalists have given names to eight distinct ones: Coastal Forest Zone, Silver Fir Zone, Sierran Mixed-Conifer Zone, Red Fir Zone, Subalpine Zone, Alpine Zone, Interior Fir Zone and Ponderosa Pine Zone. Each zone has its own community of plants, animals and birds.

Although most of the range is under the stewardship of the Forest Service, which by law has to practice multiple-use policies, most people think of the Cascades as their very own. It is used by mushroom hunters, hikers, runners, birdwatchers, anglers, hunters, photographers, painters, skiers, horse riders, loggers and miners. Whichever of these apply to you, enjoy.

▼▼▼▼▼▼▼▼▼▼▼▼
North Cascades

Extending from the Canadian border south into the Mt. Baker–Snoqualmie National Forest, the North Cascades region has over 300 glaciers, valleys famous for their spring tulip fields and some of the best skiing in the Pacific Northwest. Backroads wind through old logging towns past mountain lakes to unspoiled wilderness areas. The North Cascades National Park forms the core of this realm that includes Rainy and Washington passes, two of the Cascades' grandest viewpoints.

SIGHTS

Beginning at the northernmost approach, **Route 542** enters the Cascades from Bellingham, a pleasant, two-lane, blacktop highway that is shared by loggers, skiers, anglers and hikers. Much of the route runs through dense forest beside fast streams and with only rare glimpses of the surrounding mountains. The road deadends just beyond the Mt. Baker day-use lodge for skiers. In clear weather you will see 9127-foot **Mt. Shuksan**, one of the most beautiful peaks in the Cascades. It can't be seen from any other part of the range, but it probably appears on more calendars and postcards than its neighbor Mt. Baker or even Mt. Rainier.

The **Mt. Baker** ski slopes usually open in November and run all the way into April, making for the longest ski season of any area in Washington. During summer the mountain is popular with day hikers and backpackers. Several hiking trails wind through high alpine meadows dotted with wildflowers in the Heather Meadows area. ~ Heather Meadows Visitors Center; 360-856-5700, fax 360-856-1934.

Mt. Baker was named by George Vancouver on April 30, 1792, in honor of James Baker, a lieutenant on his ship. It was first climbed on August 17, 1868, by a party of four led by an experienced alpinist named Edward T. Coleman. Although it is listed as an active volcano and occasionally steam is seen rising from it, Mt. Baker hasn't erupted for nearly 10,000 years.

Washington Cascades Area

Route 20, one of America's premier scenic routes, goes through the North Cascades National Park and along the way provides hiking trails, roadside parks, boat launches and one of the more unusual tours in the Cascades, the **Seattle City Light Skagit Tours.** This four-hour tour tells how Seattle built three dams on the Skagit to produce its electricity. The tour begins with a ride up the side of a mountain on an antique railway lift to a tour boat, which takes you up Diablo Lake to Ross Lake and the powerhouse. The ride lasts 25 minutes and covers four and a half miles. After a thorough tour of the powerhouse and control room, guests are taken to the cookhouse for an all-you-can-eat chicken dinner. Reservations are required. Tours run mid-June through August and weekends in September. Admission. ~ 206-684-3030, fax 206-233-1642; www.ci.seattle.wa.us/light/tours.

Because the highway is enclosed by the Ross Lake National Recreation Area, new development is virtually nonexistent, and the small company towns of Newhalem and Diablo look frozen in the pre–World War II days. **Ross Lake,** created by the hydroelectric project, is a fjordlike lake between steep mountains that eventually crosses over into British Columbia.

When driving on Route 20, be forewarned: No gasoline is available between Marblemount and Mazama, a distance of more than 70 miles, and there are few places to buy groceries. Fill your tank and bring your lunch.

Ross Lake on the Skagit River was formed by Ross Dam. Diablo Dam was built a short distance downstream, creating the much smaller Diablo Lake. Stairstepped below Diablo is Gorge Lake, created by Gorge Dam. Ross Lake is an international body of water because its backwaters cross the border into Canada, and when the timber was being cleared before the lake was formed, the work was done via a road in from British Columbia.

Another way to reach Route 20 is over what is locally known as the **Mountain Loop Highway,** a favorite weekend drive for years before Route 20 was completed across the mountains. The Mountain Loop begins in Granite Falls with Route 92, which goes along the South Fork of the Stillaguamish River past the one-store towns of Robe, Verlot and Silverton. The road is crooked and slow driving because it follows the river route closely. It is always closed in the winter and sometimes landslides close it for much of the summer. Near the old mining town of Monte Cristo, the road turns north along the Sauk River and emerges in the logging town of Darrington. Here you can drive due north to catch Route 20 at Rockport or turn west on Route 530 and return to Route 5.

Route 20 plunges into the Cascades and goes over two passes —**Rainy Pass,** 4860 feet, and **Washington Pass,** 5477 feet—before descending into the Methow Valley. Stop at each viewpoint and turnout for stunning views of the region. One viewpoint above

Ross Lake shows miles of the long, narrow lake, and another just beyond Washington Pass gives a grandstand view of the jagged mountains behind the pass.

The only way to visit the resort town of **Stehekin**, at the tip of Lake Chelan, is by boat, plane or hiking. Most visitors take the trip up the lake on the **Lady of the Lake**, the tour-mail-supply boat for Stehekin and points between. The schedule allows you three and a half hours in Stehekin, and you can buy lunch either on the boat or at the Stehekin landing. Reservations suggested. Admission. ~ 509-682-4584, fax 509-682-8206; www.ladyofthelake.com.

The best way to get to Stehekin, though, is also an incomparably scenic way to see Lake Chelan and its surroundings. **Chelan Airways** has been flying the lake for more than a half-century, and its experienced floatplane pilots not only give passengers the best views, they know every nook and cranny of the lake and all the stories that accompany them. Round-trip passage is not too expensive, but it's worth a flight just to see the sights even if you don't stay "uplake." ~ 1328 West Woodin Avenue (one mile west of Chelan on Route 97A); 509-682-5555, fax 509-682-5065 (call first).

The nearest public lodging to Mt. Baker is the **Snowline Inn**, a condominium complex with 40 units. Half of these are studios for up to four people, and half have sleeping lofts, which accom-

LODGING

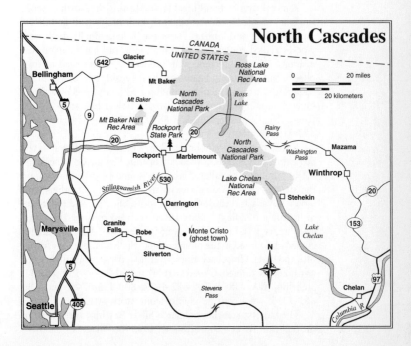

modate three to five people. The rustic, two-story inn is set back amid evergreens, 17 miles from the top of the mountain. All units have full baths, linens and kitchenettes (some with microwaves); some also have bunk beds. ~ 10433 Mt. Baker Highway, Glacier; 360-599-2788, 800-228-0119, fax 360-599-2772; e-mail show lineinn @telcomplus.net. MODERATE.

The **Glacier Creek Lodge** earns its description of rustic. It is a motel with nine units and 12 blue-and-white cabins. In addition to a hot tub, there is a large lobby with an espresso bar and a few café tables. The cabins are one or two bedrooms, with bath, double bed, bedside table and tired furniture. The motel units are so small there's no room for a table. ~ 10036 Mt. Baker Highway, Glacier; 360-599-2991, 800-719-1414, fax 360-599-1048. BUDGET TO ULTRA-DELUXE.

One of the larger lakeside resorts is **Baker Lake Resort**, 20 miles north of Concrete on Baker Lake Road. It is a mixture of RV sites and nine rustic cabins on the lake. Four of the cabins have bathrooms and showers, a refrigerator, dishes and cooking utensils, but guests must bring their own linen and towels. Boating and fishing are popular on the lake; boat rentals are available. Open seven days a week in the summer and only on weekends in the winter. ~ 46110 East Main Street, Concrete; 360-853-9007, fax 425-462-2063. BUDGET TO MODERATE.

A motel with bed-and-breakfast ambience, the **North Cascade Inn** is a vintage Northwest cedar-shake hostelry with an adjoining restaurant and lounge. There are 14 individually decorated, wood-paneled rooms, some with antique and hand-carved furnishings. All rooms come with modern comforts such as telephones and televisions. Guests can have breakfast or dinner in the restaurant or on an adjoining outdoor patio adorned by a three-tiered fountain and dozens of hanging flower baskets. ~ 44618 Route 20, Concrete; 360-853-8870, 800-251-3054, fax 360-853-7123. BUDGET.

Rustic reigns in remote Stehekin. The most outdoorsy is the **Stehekin Valley Ranch**, owned and operated by the Courtneys, the major family in the valley. The ranch is nine miles from town, up the Stehekin River Valley. Guests are housed in tent cabins with wooden walls and canvas-covered roofs. Showers and toilets are in the main building. Guests are encouraged to bring their own sleeping bags and towels to save $5 per person. All meals are included and served in the dining room, which has split logs for tables and seats. Horseback rides, river float trips, scenic flights and day hikes are offered. Closed October to mid-June. ~ P.O. Box 36, Stehekin, WA 98852; 509-682-4677, 800-536-0745, fax 509-682-9253; www.courtneycountry.com. MODERATE.

The fanciest Stehekin lodging is **Silver Bay Inn**, at the head of the Stehekin River a short distance from the village. In the own-

Author Picks

CHAPTER FAVORITES

I'm awestruck by the constantly changing mountain landscapes as the **Lady of the Lake** cruise makes its way from Chelan to Stehekin—as deep as you can get in the North Cascades without a long trek. *page 267*

I can't decide whether the drive along Route 97 from **Wenatchee** to **Leavenworth** and **Cashmere** is more fun in spring, when apple and cherry blossoms scent the air, or fall, when stands selling fresh-picked fruit line the roadway. *pages 279, 280, 283*

And then there are those wonderful Aplets and Cotlets they make at **Liberty Orchards** in Cashmere—

every Northwesterner's favorite confection. *page 282*

When I want to spend a pricey night in the lap of luxury, I can't think of a more dramatic setting to do it in than the clifftop **Salish Lodge at Snoqualmie Falls**, whether watching the falls from the lounge or relaxing by the fireplace in my room. *page 288*

Seeing the seedlings of a mighty forest slowly but surely being reborn from the volcanic ash along Windy Ridge in **Mount St. Helens National Volcanic Monument** always makes my heart sing. *page 301*

ers' home there are two rooms with private baths and one large suite that includes a private bath, a soaking tub and two decks. Guests can rent the entire house, or two can rent the back of the house, which has a kitchenette and a deck overlooking the river. Outside are two cabins that will sleep six and are complete with kitchens and dishwashers. Closed mid-October to mid-May. ~ 10 Silver Bay Road, Stehekin, WA 98852; 509-682-2212, 800-555-7781, fax 509-687-3142; www.silverbayinn.com. DELUXE TO ULTRA-DELUXE.

A popular place along the Mt. Baker Highway is **Milano's Market and Deli**, a combination small restaurant and deli. With its black-and-white tile floor and café tables, it offers a hearty supply of soups, salads, fresh pasta dishes and homemade desserts. This is a good place to have a picnic lunch made up. If the weather is right, the deck is open for outside dining. ~ 9990 Mt. Baker Highway, Glacier; 360-599-2863. MODERATE.

DINING

A mile east of Glacier, near the Snowline Inn, is a much larger restaurant with more of a rural flavor. **The Chandelier** is built in the chalet style and divided into two sections with a large fireplace in the entrance hall. To the left is a large bar with the obligatory big-screen television set and wooden chairs and tables. The restaurant serves straightforward American food, large burgers, steaks, seafood, barbecued chicken, fresh strawberry pie and home-made cheesecakes. You can also have them make up box lunches for day trips. Closed Monday, except during ski season. ~ 10453 Mt. Baker Highway, Deming; 360-734-3336, fax 360-734-4058. BUDGET TO MODERATE.

The town of Concrete, home to the Portland Cement Company, was formerly known as "Minnehaha," "Baker" and, most appropriately, "Cement City."

On the western edge of Concrete, **North Cascade Inn** has established a local reputation for good, plain American food (steaks, chops, seafood) and delicious pie (made by a local woman especially for the restaurant). The exterior is decorated with farm and logging equipment, but the interior decor is softened a bit with antique furnishings and decorations. There's also a full-service bar. ~ 44618 Route 20, Concrete; 360-853-8771, 800-251-3054, fax 360-853-7123. BUDGET.

SHOPPING If you're in Concrete on Saturday during the summer months, hit the **Saturday Market** in the **North Cascades Visitor Center** on Route 20 for arts and crafts and baked goods. ~ 360-853-7042.

For nostalgic atmosphere as well as the largest variety of goods in town, take a stroll through the **Concrete Department Store**. With its wooden floors and counters, it has remained almost unchanged since the 1920s and has been used as a backdrop for several Hollywood films. Closed Sunday. ~ 45880 Main Street, Concrete; 360-853-8700.

Potter Stephen Murray is known for his wood-fired ceramic dinnerware that comes in a variety of lustrous glazes. Individual pieces are sold at his **Sauk Mountain Pottery** store east of Concrete. ~ 50303 Route 20, Concrete; 360-853-8689.

NIGHTLIFE The Cascades isn't the place to go for stellar nightlife. After a day traipsing around in the mountains, most people return to town tired and only want to eat and go to bed. Consequently, only the busiest areas even have live music.

Near Mt. Baker, the **Chandelier** has dancing and occasional live music on weekends. ~ 10453 Mt. Baker Highway, Deming; 360-734-3336, fax 360-734-4058.

PARKS **MT. BAKER–SNOQUALMIE NATIONAL FOREST** 🏃🚴🐎🎿 🏕️🚶⛷️🛶🚤⛵ This 1.7-million-acre forest begins at the Canadian border and goes south along the western slopes of the Cascades to Mt. Rainier National Park. It is dominated on the north by the inactive volcano, 10,778-foot Mt. Baker. Another inactive volcano, 10,568-foot Glacier Peak, lies in the middle of the forest. The Forest Service controls the land for the ski areas at Crystal Mountain, Mt. Baker, Stevens Pass and Snoqualmie Pass. Its best-known wilderness area is Alpine Lakes Wilderness, but it also includes the Glacier Peak, Noisy Diobsud, Boulder River, Henry M. Jackson, Clearwater, Norse Peak and Mt. Baker Wilderness areas. Within the forest is excellent fishing for rainbow trout in Baker Lake and many other streams and lakes. There are picnic areas, restrooms and showers. Parking fee, $3 to $5 per day. ~ Four east–west highways cross the national forest: Routes 90, 20, 2 and 410; 425-775-9702, fax 425-744-3255; www.fs.fed.us/r6/mbs.

▲ Camping is permitted (unless otherwise posted) along the highways, trails and the Pacific Crest Trail, as well as at established campsites. Most of the 40-plus campgrounds are primitive with pit toilets and vary from walk-in to drive-in sites; RV sites are available. Roughly 60 percent of sites are by reservation only (800-280-2267, fax 916-414-8410); $7 to $12 per night.

ROCKPORT STATE PARK 🧍 🚲 ⛟ 🛥 ⛴ This park is essentially a large campground in a grove of old-growth Douglas fir. Most of the camping areas are shielded from one another by thick undergrowth. It is within easy walking distance of the fish-laden Skagit River, which makes it popular with steelheaders. There are picnic areas, restrooms, showers and five miles of footpaths. ~ Located on Route 20 one mile west of Rockport;   phone/fax 360-853-8461.

▲ There are 50 RV sites with hookups, eight walk-in sites and four three-sided Adirondack shelters; $10 to $15 per night.

HOWARD MILLER STEELHEAD COUNTY PARK 🧍 🚲 🏇 ⛟ ⛴ 🛥 ⛴ One of the most popular parks on the Skagit River for steelheaders and travelers alike, this county park covers 93 acres and has exhibits of a historic cabin, an old river ferry and dugout canoe. Anglers will find salmon and trout, and birders will enjoy bald-eagle watching from December to February. The clubhouse is a popular hangout for local anglers. Facilities include picnic areas, volleyball court, playground, clubhouse, restrooms, showers and trailer dump. ~ Located in the middle of Rockport at the junction of Routes 20 and 530; 360-853-8808.

▲ There are ten tent sites ($12 per night) and 50 RV sites with partial hookups ($16 per night). Reservations, 360-853-8808, fax 360-853-7315.

NORTH CASCADES NATIONAL PARK COMPLEX 🧍 🏇 🏇 ⛴ 🛶 ⛟ 🛥 ⛴ Covering 505,000 acres in the north central part of the state, this park is divided into two units. The northern unit runs from the Canadian border to **Ross Lake National Recreation Area**. The southern unit continues on to the **Lake Chelan National Recreation Area**. Much of its eastern boundary is the summit of the Cascade Range, and the western boundary is the Mt. Baker–Snoqualmie National Forest. It is the most rugged and remote of the national parks in Washington and has the fewest roads. All visitor facilities and roads in the northern portion are inside the Ross Lake National Recreation Area. On the southern end, the Lake Chelan National Recreation Area covers the heavy-use area on the north end of the lake, including the village of Stehekin. Try for rainbow trout in Ross Lake, steelhead in the Skagit River downstream from Newhalem and rainbow and eastern brook trout in high lakes. There's a visitors center in Newhalem and rangers sometimes lead nature walks from the Colonial Creek and Newhalem campgrounds. Picnic areas, restrooms and nature walks are located here. ~ Only Route 20 goes through North Cascades National Park, and it is closed in winter, generally from mid-November to April; 360-856-5700, fax 360-856-1934.

▲ There are over 400 campsites at four campgrounds. You can camp year-round at Goodell Creek. Some sites in the four campgrounds are free; others cost up to $10 per night. The adjacent Okanogan Forest has more sites, including the popular Lone Fir and Early Winter campgrounds.

▼ ▼ ▼ ▼ ▼ ▼ ▼ ▼ ▼
Methow Valley

The scenery changes quickly and dramatically once you have crossed Washington Pass into the Methow Valley. Located along Route 20 between Mazama and Pateros, this region includes the tourist center of Chelan, gateway to one of the state's most popular lake-resort areas.

SIGHTS

As you descend the east slope of the Cascades, the thick, fir forest gives way to smaller pine with almost no underbrush. The mountains become bare, and you can see for miles. And by the time you arrive in **Winthrop**, you will wonder if you are in Colorado or Wyoming because the small town is all falsefronts, saloon doors, hitching rails and wooden porches.

The **Shafer Museum** is in the cabin built by town founder Guy Waring in 1897 and has exhibits from the valley's early days, including a stagecoach and antique automobiles. Open weekends and some weekdays from May through September. ~ One block up the hill off Route 20, Winthrop; 509-996-2712, www.methow.com/~jtonseth, e-mail jtonseth@methow.com.

HIDDEN ►

There are several areas around Winthrop worth driving to, including 6197-foot **Harts Pass** a short distance from town. This is the highest point to which you can drive in Washington and is only an hour's drive on a gravel Forest Service road. The views from the summit are spectacular.

Not long after driving south on Route 153, the last of the timbered mountains are left behind, and the Methow Valley flattens into a series of irrigated ranches with broad hayfields. The valley is gaining popularity with people from Puget Sound looking for more space, so houses are beginning to line the low hills on both sides.

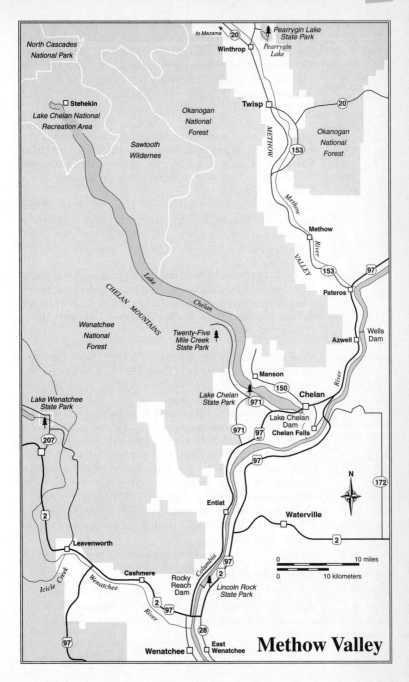

Methow Valley

When you reach the **Columbia River** at Pateros, the landscape is one of basaltic cliffs on both sides of the river. Instead of a fast-flowing river there is a chain of lakes behind dams all the way past Wenatchee. Route 97 hugs the west side of the Columbia, then splits off onto 97A at Chelan Falls and swings away from the river to go through the resort town of Chelan, which sits at the end of **Lake Chelan**. The two highways meet again at Wenatchee.

The lake is a remnant of the Ice Ages. Scoured out of the mountains by glaciers, it is one of the deepest lakes in the region, more than 1500 feet deep in at least one area, which places its bed at 400 feet below sea level. It is 55 miles long but quite narrow, and the mountains rising from its shores give it the appearance of a Norwegian fjord.

Chelan is a small town that has been given over almost entirely to apples and tourism. Woodin Avenue is the main drag and the lakefront is lined with resorts, but the small-town atmosphere remains intact, so a farmer can come to town and still buy a two-by-four or a cotter pin.

The **Lake Chelan Museum** displays American Indian artifacts, early farming and orchard equipment. One room depicts a miner's cabin, and another shows a typical country kitchen. Limited hours October through May. ~ Woodin Avenue and Emerson Street, Chelan; 509-682-5644.

LODGING　If you want to get up close and personal with the North Cascades, head for the **Freestone Inn and Cabins**. The 15 cabins sit across the highway from the Forest Service/National Park Service information center at the foot of the mountains. Small and widely spaced apart, each cabin is heated with a propane fireplace and there are fire pits outside. Electric heaters warm the bathrooms. All cooking utensils are provided. In the inn, all 21 rooms have fireplaces. The inn has one hot tub, the cabins have another. The Nordic Center offers cross-country ski rentals in the winter and mountain-bike rentals in the summer for adventurers who want to explore the Methow Valley Nordic Ski Trails—a 175-kilometer network of trails running through the property. ~ 17798 Route 20, Mazama; 509-996-2355, 800-639-3809, fax 509-996-3907; www.freestone inn.com. ULTRA-DELUXE.

ORCHARDS, ORCHARDS EVERYWHERE

Chelan has some of the best orchards along the eastern slopes of the Cascades. If you take a drive northwest of town on Route 150 to Manson, you will see thousands of acres of apple orchards climbing up the sun-baked hills from the lake.

The most elaborate place in the Methow Valley, and one of the best resorts in the Pacific Northwest, is **Sun Mountain Lodge**. Built at the 3000-foot level atop a small mountain, this low-rise, stone-and-timber resort gives a 360-degree view of the Cascades, Pasayten Wilderness, Okanogan Highlands and Methow Valley. The 115 units are spread over three buildings atop the mountain and down the road in thirteen rustic, cozy cabins. The resort has just about everything: several miles of hiking trails that become cross-country ski trails in the winter, two pools, three hot tubs, an exercise room, the largest string of saddle-and-pack horses in the state, mountain-bike rentals, canoe and sailing on the lake, heli-skiing and tennis. It also has a great restaurant. Rooms feature bentwood furniture, a fireplace (only the suites have real-wood fireplaces), coffee, the thickest and softest towels and robes you can hope for and no television. ~ Patterson Lake Road, Winthrop; 509-996-2211, 800-572-0493, fax 509-996-3133; www.sun mountainlodge.com. ULTRA-DELUXE.

Right in the heart of Western-themed Winthrop you'll find the **Trail's End Motel** with its tall false front and wooden porch. The 12 units, which have VCRs (you can choose from among 50 free videos), are simply furnished, and big windows look down onto Main Street. In season, the area's oldest irrigation canal runs behind the motel. A bookstore anchors one end of the building. A full breakfast is provided. ~ 130 Riverside Avenue, Winthrop; 509-996-2303, fax 509-996-2303. MODERATE.

On the south edge of Winthrop is the **Virginian Resort**. Located on the high bank of the Methow River, the riverfront rooms in this 39-unit motel have balconies. Cedar was used extensively, and most units retain the pleasant aroma. There are also seven cabins, which are a bit more expensive, but several have fireplaces and room enough for six. Kitchens are large and equipped with microwaves. Offsite, the resort also rents the **Westar Lodge**, which sleeps 27 and includes a full-service kitchen and a couple of secluded acres on the Chewuch River. Also available is a two-bedroom cottage that sleeps eight and has a full kitchen. ~ 808 North Cascades Highway, Winthrop; 509-996-2535, 800-854-2834, fax 509-996-2483; www.methow.com/~virgnian. MODERATE TO DELUXE.

The oldest and most reliable resort in Chelan is **Campbell's Resort**, which has been in business since 1901. With 173 rooms, it is still growing along the lakeshore in the heart of town. It has two heated pools, an outdoor jacuzzi, good beach and boat moorage. The larger rooms have kitchenettes and one king or two queen beds, and are decorated in soft pastels or earth tones. ~ 104 West Woodin Avenue, Chelan; 509-682-2561, 800-553-8225, fax 509-682-2177; www.campbellsresort.com. DELUXE TO ULTRA-DELUXE.

One of the most complete resorts inside the Chelan city limits is **Darnell's Resort Motel**, a few blocks southwest of the city center on Route 150. It has a heated pool and hot tub, putting greens, lighted tennis courts, swimming beach, boats and bicycle rentals, waterskiing, volleyball, badminton and conference rooms. The resort is divided into two three-story buildings. All rooms have balconies with views of the lake. All units are suites; some have two bedrooms, and the larger units have sleeping lofts. The penthouse suites have two fireplaces and private jacuzzi. ~ 901 Spader Bay Road, Chelan; 509-682-2015, 800-967-8149, fax 509-682-8736; www.chelan.com/motels. DELUXE TO ULTRA-DELUXE.

Mary Kay's Romantic Whaley Mansion is actually a bed and breakfast. This white Edwardian house trimmed in dark green has six rooms decorated with antiques from the family collection. A footstool has antlers for legs; ribbons and garlands of artificial flowers are everywhere. The guest rooms, on the second and third floors, are decorated with flowered wallpaper and have old-fashioned beds and private baths, TVs and VCRs with a selection of free movies. There is also a full library for sitting. In addition to a gourmet breakfast that includes hand-dipped chocolates, Mary Kay will sing with the player piano accompanying her. Gay-friendly. ~ 415 3rd Street, Chelan; 509-682-5735, 800-729-2408, fax 509-682-5385; www.lakechelan.com. MODERATE TO DELUXE.

On the eastern edge of Chelan is the clean and comfortable **Apple Inn Motel** with white stucco walls and black wood trim. The 41 rooms are small and clean; some have kitchenettes. The heated outdoor pool is open in the summer, and a hot tub is open year-round. ~ 1002 East Woodin Avenue, Chelan; 509-682-4044, fax 509-682-3330. BUDGET.

DINING

The dramatic **Sun Mountain Lodge Dining Room** garners statewide attention. The room is cantilevered with views down into the Methow Valley and Winthrop 1000 feet below. All seats here have a view. The food is wonderful. The menu features seafood and creatively prepared grilled or roasted meats. ~ Sun Mountain Lodge, Patterson Lake Road, Winthrop; 509-996-2211, fax 509-996-3133. MODERATE TO ULTRA-DELUXE.

One of Winthrop's most trendy restaurants is the oddly named **Duck Brand Cantina** in the hotel of the same name. The menu reflects an effort to please several palates, including Mexican, Continental, American and vegetarian. The restaurant is divided into two areas: a dining room with several old, oak tables and hanging greenery, and a deck overlooking Winthrop's sole street. ~ 248 Riverside Avenue, Winthrop; 509-996-2192, fax 509-996-2001. BUDGET TO MODERATE.

Decorated in rustic western style with wooden tables, hardwood floors, and elk heads mounted on the walls, **Three Fingered Jack's Saloon and Restaurant** offers fresh meats and vegetables, homemade soups, salads and desserts. The New York steaks are cut in-house in this family-run establishment. Try the vegetarian mixed grill with risotto or the fettuccine with garlic parmesan sauce. ~ 176 Riverside Avenue, Winthrop; phone/fax 509-996-2411. MODERATE TO DELUXE.

Although Campbell's Resort is so large it overwhelms some people, it is hard to find a better place in the area for a good meal than the resort's **Campbell House**. The large room seats about 130 and is pleasantly decorated in Early American furnishings with walls covered with an eclectic collection of prints, documents and paintings. The menu is large: prime rib, medallions of pork, prawns Provençal, the catch of the day and a variety of pasta. Open weekends only in winter. ~ 104 West Woodin Avenue, Chelan; 509-682-2561, fax 509-682-2177. BUDGET TO MODERATE.

Winthrop adopted a Wild West theme years ago, and it has revitalized the sawmill town and surrounding area into one of the state's most popular destinations.

A few doors down from Campbell's on the lakefront is **Peter B's Bar & Grill**. It has two floors—with open-air seating on the top level—and specializes in lunches of sandwiches (some are purely vegetarian), soups and salads. Dinner offers a series of specials throughout the week, seafood, steak and several pastas. ~ 114 East Woodin Avenue, Chelan; 509-682-1031. BUDGET TO DELUXE.

SHOPPING

Art is popular, and quite often very good, in Winthrop, especially at **Hildabob's Gallery**, where you will find paintings, sculpture and handknit apparel. Closed January to mid-April. ~ 231 Riverside Avenue, Winthrop; 509-996-3279. Other artwork, some by nationally known artists such as Richard Beyer, is usually on exhibit in the public rooms at **Sun Mountain Lodge**. ~ Patterson Lake Road, Winthrop; 509-996-2211. For photographs by the area's best-known photographer, Bob Spiwak, try **Winthrop Mountain Sports**. ~ 257 Riverside Drive, Winthrop; 509-996-2886.

Art is also a growth industry in the Chelan area. **Wapato Studio** features watercolors, oils and sculpture by local artists, as well as custom framing. Closed Sunday during winter. ~ 108 East Woodin Avenue, Chelan; 509-682-2423.

However, the apple is king in Chelan, and the **Harvest Tree** is a mail-order store with more than 1000 apple gift items, packaged apples and other Northwest-produced foods. ~ 109 East Woodin Avenue, Chelan; 509-682-3618.

NIGHTLIFE

In Winthrop the **Winthrop Palace** offers live rock and rhythm-and-blues music most nights during summer. Cover on occasion. ~ 918 Riverside Avenue, Winthrop; 509-996-2245.

Not much happens in Chelan after dark, which may be fine if you're planning to wake up in time to catch the *Lady of the Lake* cruise in the morning. If you simply must go out, your best bet may be the **Ruby Theatre**, a small but historic pink theater that presents double-feature movies and weekend matinees. ~ 135 East Woodin Avenue, Chelan; 509-682-5016.

Seven miles west of Chelan, the Colville Indian Reservation operates the **Mill Bay Casino**, with blackjack, roulette, craps, mini baccarat and 400 slot machines. ~ 455 Wapato Lake Road, Manson; 509-687-2102.

Also in Manson, the **Sports Bar at Tim's** has live entertainment and dancing Thursday through Saturday. ~ 76 West Wapato Way, Manson; 509-687-3035.

PARKS **PEARRYGIN LAKE STATE PARK**

This is a popular park for travelers in RVs because it is close to Winthrop and has a sandy beach on a small lake surrounded by mountains. Anglers will find rainbow trout off the fishing dock. Facilities include picnic areas, restrooms and showers. Closed November through March. ~ Located four miles northeast of Winthrop on Bear Creek Road; 509-996-2370.

Winthrop's town hall was originally the Duck Brand Saloon, built in 1891.

▲ There are 30 RV hookup sites and 53 tent or RV sites and two ADA-accessible sites, one with hookups, one without; $11 to $16 per night. Reservations, 800-452-5687, fax 503-378-6308.

LAKE CHELAN STATE PARK

This is a favorite park for youths yearning for sunshine, and in July and August the shoreline looks more like California than Washington with its broad, sandy beach (great swimming) and play area. Because it has docks and launching areas for skiers, it is equally popular with powerboaters and waterskiers. Anglers fish for rainbow trout, kokanee and king salmon, burbot, lake trout and bass as far away from the powerboats as possible. There are picnic tables, restrooms and showers. Closed in winter except weekends and holidays. ~ Located nine miles west of Chelan on Route 971; 509-687-3710, fax 509-378-6447.

▲ There are 111 tent sites and 34 RV hookup sites; $11 to $16 per night. Reservations (800-452-5687, fax 503-378-6447) highly recommended for summer.

TWENTY-FIVE MILE CREEK STATE PARK

More remote than Lake Chelan State Park but popular with those more interested in mountain scenery than body scenery, this park is quiet, with the Chelan Mountains behind and the jagged peaks of the Sawtooth Wilderness across the lake. The small beach is mostly for wading, though boaters fish in the lake. Open April through September only. There are picnic areas, restrooms, showers and moorage at the marina; a concession stand offers snacks, groceries and fishing supplies. ~ Located 20 miles up-lake from Chelan on Route 971; 509-687-3610, fax 509-687-3163.

▲ There are 61 tent sites, 19 RV hookups and a group camp for overnight use that can accommodate 88; $11 to $16 per night. Reservations, 800-452-5687.

LINCOLN ROCK STATE PARK 🚲 🏠 ⚓ 🛶 🏊 ⛴ ⛵
◟ Named for a rock outcropping that resembles Abraham Lincoln's profile, this is a heavily used state park in the Columbia River canyon a short distance north of Wenatchee. There is swimming, fishing for trout, perch and bass, and boating. Several species of wildlife reside in the park, including marmots, rabbits, deer, beaver, nighthawks and swallows. Facilities include picnic shelters, restrooms, showers, volleyball courts, a playfield and play equipment for children. ~ Located six miles north of East Wenatchee on Route 97/2; 509-884-8702, fax 509-886-1704.

▲ There are 27 tent sites and 67 RV hookup sites, 35 of which have full hookups; $11 to $16 per night. Reservations, 800-452-5687.

▼▼▼▼▼▼▼▼▼▼▼

Wenatchee Area

Famous for its apple orchards, the sunny Wenatchee Area is located in the heart of Washington. Popular with rafters and gold panners, this region is also home to one of the state's most picturesque gardens.

SIGHTS

You have a choice of two highways when leaving Chelan: You can continue along Route 97, which cuts through the Cascade foothills back to the Columbia River and south to Wenatchee, or cross the Columbia at Chelan Falls, hardly more than a junction, and follow the lesser-used Route 151 south through the orchard town of Orando to East Wenatchee. Stop at **Rocky Reach Dam** to visit the Fish Viewing Room where healthy numbers of migratory salmon and steelhead swim past the windows. The dam also has two museums, one showing the natural and human history of the Columbia River, complete with a handcarved American Indian canoe, parts of steamboats and orchard equipment. The Gallery of Electricity also has hands-on exhibits that let you create electricity. ~ Located 28 miles south of Chelan; 509-663-7522, fax 509-667-3449.

Wenatchee is the largest town in this region and directed more toward orchards than tourists, although you will certainly feel welcome. On the northern edge of town, overlooking the Columbia River, Wenatchee and Rocky Reach Dam, is **Ohme Gardens**. You will find nine acres of alpine gardens built by an orchardist on the steep, rocky outcroppings at the edge of his property overlooking the Columbia River. Admission. ~ 3327 Ohme Road, Wenatchee; 509-662-5785, fax 509-662-6805; www.ohmegardens.com.

Downtown, the **North Central Washington Museum** has several permanent exhibits including a 1919 Wurlitzer theater pipe organ and an apple-packing shed featuring an apple wiper, sizing machine and a 1924 orchard truck. In the gift shop area is an original WPA mural by Peggy Strong depicting the change of the postal service from its pioneer days to a modern, organized unit. Closed Sunday. Admission. ~ 127 South Mission Street, Wenatchee; 509-664-3340, fax 509-664-3356.

On the western edge of town is the **Washington Apple Commission Visitor Center**, which has an interpretive center offering apple tasting; samples are given of the different varieties of apples that are in season. The gift shop sells sweatshirts and other items with an apple theme. Open daily May through Christmas; closed weekends the rest of the year. ~ 2900 Euclid Avenue, Wenatchee; 509-663-9600, 509-662-3090 in winter, fax 509-662-5824; www.bestapples.com.

Ten miles west via Routes 2 and 97, **Cashmere**, so-named because it reminded a pioneer of Kashmir, India, has an Early American theme to its downtown buildings. The **Chelan County Historical Museum and Pioneer Village** has more than two dozen original buildings from Chelan and Douglas counties assembled to recreate a pioneer village, including a blacksmith shop, school, gold mine and hotel. Closed Monday and November through March. ~ 600 Cottage Avenue, Cashmere; 509-782-3230, fax 509-782-8905.

From Cashmere, Routes 2 and 97 follow the swift Wenatchee River into the Cascades. Shortly before reaching Leavenworth, Route 97 turns south toward the Route 90 Corridor towns of Cle Elum and Ellensburg by going over 4101-foot **Blewett Pass**. An alternative route, in the summer only, is to follow the **Old Blewett Pass Highway**, which has been preserved by the Wenatchee National Forest. The old highway is a series of switchbacks with sweeping views of the Cascades. No services are available until you reach Cle Elum and Ellensburg, other than a small grocery store at **Liberty**, a gold-mining town just off the highway that is making a comeback as people move into its modest cabins along the main street.

LODGING Most hotels in Wenatchee are along North Wenatchee Avenue. The largest hotel in this part of the state is the **WestCoast Wenatchee Center**, at nine stories one of the tallest buildings along the eastern edge of the Cascades. The 147 rooms are larger than at most other hotels in town and suites have double sofas and potted plants. A large lobby has a baby grand piano. There's a restaurant, an indoor-outdoor pool and a fitness center. ~ 201 North Wenatchee Avenue, Wenatchee; 509-662-1234, 800-426-0670, fax 509-662-0782; www.westcoast.com. DELUXE.

For a low-priced place, try the **Orchard Inn**. It has 103 rooms on three floors decorated with subtly flowered bedspreads, unobtrusive furniture and wallhangings. There is a heated pool and hot tub. ~ 1401 North Miller Street, Wenatchee; 509-662-3443, 800-368-4571, fax 509-662-3443. BUDGET.

If you want to be close to Routes 2 and 97, the best place is across the Columbia River in the **Rivers Inn**. With 55 units on two floors that surround the heated pool and hot tub, it is unpretentious and has basic, comfortable rooms with cable television. There's always coffee in the office (after 7 a.m. free rolls are available). ~ 580 Valley Mall Parkway, East Wenatchee; 509-884-1474, 800-922-3199, fax 509-884-9179. BUDGET TO MODERATE.

The **Village Inn Motel** is in the heart of town. The white-and-green motel has 21 units, six with refrigerators. A bit impersonal, but it's also clean, quiet and reasonably priced. ~ 229 Cottage Avenue, Cashmere; 509-782-3522, 800-793-3522, fax 509-782-2619. BUDGET TO MODERATE.

DINING

Want Italian? Try **Visconti's Italian Restaurant**. Both Southern and Northern Italian dishes are offered in a family-friendly atmosphere. Their wood-fired oven is used to "broil-roast" seafood and prime cuts of meat. ~ 1737 North Wenatchee Avenue, Wenatchee; 509-662-5013, fax 509-664-3853. MODERATE TO DELUXE.

A top-notch steakhouse is **The Windmill**. It's a down-to-earth place, with waitresses who have been there for years. A blackboard keeps a running total of the number of steaks sold there since 1982. Châteaubriand and lobster are now offered in addition to a wide selection of meat and seafood dishes. Fresh-baked pies round out the meals. Dinner only. Closed Sunday. ~ 1501 North Wenatchee

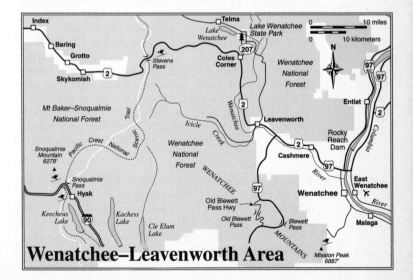

Wenatchee–Leavenworth Area

Avenue, Wenatchee; 509-665-9529, fax 509-662-5030. MODERATE
TO ULTRA-DELUXE.

As a reflection of Central Washington's growing Hispanic population, **Tequila's** is owned by former residents of Mexico. The
refried beans are homemade, and the salsa is as
tangy as you'd get in Guadalajara. ~ 800 North
Wenatchee Avenue, Wenatchee; 509-662-7239. BUD-
GET TO MODERATE.

Cashmere began life
in 1873 as the town
of "Mission," so
named for its log
Catholic church.

One of Wenatchee's apple-pioneer homes has become a popular restaurant. The owners of **John Horan's
Steak and Seafood House** have turned two upstairs bedrooms into a room for private parties and a cigar room.
The downstairs dining room has a fireplace, a welcoming
spot on chilly evenings. The menu boasts a large selection of seafood, steak, chicken, pasta and lamb dishes. Save room for the
homemade desserts. Closed Sunday. ~ 2 Horan Road, Wenatchee;
509-663-0018, fax 509-662-9543; e-mail johninga@johnhoran
house.com. MODERATE TO DELUXE.

SHOPPING   A wide range of Washington souvenirs and products, everything
from jam to table linens, can be found at **Pak It Rite**. ~ 126 North
Wenatchee Avenue, Wenatchee; 509-663-1072.

Victorian Village is a small mall constructed in the best of the
Victorian Carpenter Gothic style—round towers, falsefronts and
steeples. You will find a hair salon, clothing, antiques and, inter-
estingly for a Victorian theme, a Mexican restaurant. ~ 611 South
Mission Street, Wenatchee.

If you need a fix for an urban-size mall, the **Wenatchee Valley
Mall** has 39 stores and more under construction, making it the
largest shopping center you'll encounter in the shadow of the Cascades. ~ 511 Valley Mall Parkway, East Wenatchee; 509-884-6645.

Nearby Cashmere is the place to shop for a wide range of apple-
based food products and gifts. Especially tempting is **Liberty
Orchards**, which has been making fruit gelatin confections since
1920. Known for their Aplets and Cotlets, fruit-and-nut concoctions sprinkled with powdered sugar, Liberty Orchards also sells
a wide variety of apple-themed gifts. Tours of the candy-making
process are offered on weekdays. ~ 117 Mission Street, Cashmere;
509-782-2191.

NIGHTLIFE   Although Wenatchee is the largest town in the Cascades, the nightlife choice is slim. Aside from lounges in some of the chain motor
inns, **Mickey O'Reilly's Sports Bar**, with dart boards, pull-tab
gambling, a big-screen TV and seven other TVs scattered around the
bar, is about as good as it gets. ~ 560 Valley Mall Parkway, East
Wenatchee; 509-884-6299.

WENATCHEE NATIONAL FOREST 🚶 🚴 🐎 🎿 🏠 ⛵ 🐕   **PARKS**
⛷ 🚤 🛶 🛥 🏊 At 2.1 million acres, Wenatchee is one of the
largest national forests in the United States. It encompasses seven
wilderness areas, hundreds of lakes, downhill-ski areas and 2500
miles of trails for hiking, riding and biking (including the Pacific
Crest National Scenic Trail). Salmon, steelhead, searun cutthroat
trout, bull trout, bass, crappie, walleye and sturgeon are among
the fish found in streams and lakes. There are picnic areas and
restrooms. ~ The forest is crossed by Routes 12, 97/2 and 90;
509-662-4335, fax 509-664-2731.

▲ There are more than 120 campgrounds; RVs accommo-
dated in some campgrounds (no hookups); prices range from free
to $12. Most campgrounds do not take reservations; the five that
do can be reached at 800-280-2267.

Think Bavarian! If you like cuckoo clocks, fancy
woodwork, beer steins and alpenhorns, you'll love **Leavenworth Area**
making a stop in Leavenworth.

One of the major tourist spots in the Cascades, **Leavenworth** wel-   **SIGHTS**
comes visitors with oompah bands, specialty stores and impressive
alpine scenery. Almost everything here—architecture, hotels, restaurants, annual events—is centered around the Bavarian theme.
Mountains are on three sides, and a river rushes through town.
During most of the summer, free concerts and dancing exhibitions
are given in the City Park, and outdoor art exhibits are held on
weekends.

Just west of Leavenworth, Route 2 enters **Tumwater Canyon**,
which follows the Wenatchee River some 20 miles. It is marked
by sheer canyon walls, plunging river rapids and deciduous trees
along the riverbank that turn into brilliant colors in autumn.

Route 2 continues over **Stevens Pass**, a popular ski area and
where the **Pacific Crest National Scenic Trail** (see "Hiking" at the
end of this chapter) crosses the highway. Soon after crossing the
summit and passing Skykomish, the **Skykomish River** parallels the
highway. This is one of Western Washington's most popular whitewater rivers. Most trips originate in the small alpine village of
Index, a short distance off the highway. The sheer-faced, 5979-foot
Mt. Index looms behind the town. From there, the river rumbles
down past the small towns of Gold Bar and Sultan, then flattens
out onto the Puget Sound lowlands.

One of the most pleasant spots in Leavenworth is the **Hotel-Pen-**   **LODGING**
sion Anna. It has 15 rooms with furniture and decor imported from
Austria and has been decorated in a farmhouse theme. Heavy,
wooden bed frames and cupboards are used throughout, along

with feather beds and down comforters. Three suites come with fireplace and jacuzzi, and all rooms have private baths. Breakfast is included. ~ 926 Commercial Street, Leavenworth; 509-548-6273, 800-509-2662, fax 509-548-4656; www.pensionanna.com. MODERATE TO ULTRA-DELUXE.

A Bavarian wood carver was imported to fashion the rails and ceiling beams of the **Enzian Inn,** and the entire 104-room motel with its turret and chalet-styled roofs shows similar touches. The seven suites have king-size beds, spas and fireplaces. It has indoor and outdoor pools and hot tubs. During the winter, free cross-country ski equipment is available to guests. The complimentary buffet breakfast is served in the big solarium on the fourth floor. ~ 590 Route 2, Leavenworth; phone/fax 509-548-5269, 800-223-8511; www.enzianinn.com. MODERATE TO ULTRA-DELUXE.

For a change of pace, try renting one of the townhouses at the **Linderhof Motor Inn,** next door to the Enzian Inn. The ten townhouses are divided into one- and two-bedroom units that sleep six and eight respectively. They have cathedral ceilings with balcony bedrooms and full kitchens with all appliances. There are 22 additional units, some with fireplaces and spas, all with handcrafted furniture. There is an outdoor pool and hot tub. Continental breakfast is included. ~ 690 Route 2, Leavenworth; 509-548-5283, 800-828-5680, fax 509-548-6704. MODERATE.

More and more bed and breakfasts and inns are opening outside town. One is **Run of the River,** a mile east of Icicle River from Route 2. The building is made of logs and has cathedral ceilings with pine walls and handmade log furniture. The six rooms come with private baths and cable television. Three of the rooms have woodstoves and three have jacuzzis. Stay here, kick back and just contemplate the beautiful setting. There are complimentary mountain bikes for exploring the many surrounding trails and backroads and complimentary snowshoes in winter. Breakfasts are country-style. The inn accepts non-smokers and adults only. ~ 9308 East Leavenworth Road, Leavenworth; 509-548-7171, 800-288-6491, fax 509-548-7547; www.runoftheriver.com. MODERATE TO DELUXE.

Located in a wooded setting on the banks of the Wenatchee River, the **All Seasons River Inn** offers spacious rooms and suites, all with private decks overlooking the river and most with fireplaces and jacuzzis. The inn provides full breakfasts and bicycles for touring the nearby Icicle Loop. Nonsmoking; no children or pets. ~ 8751 Icicle Road, Leavenworth; 509-548-1425, 800-254-0555; www.allseasonsriverinn.com. MODERATE TO ULTRA-DELUXE.

Farther down the mountain you'll find the **Dutch Cup Motel,** which is popular with skiers. The two-story motel has 21 units with queen-size beds and cable television. ~ 918 Main Street, Sultan; 360-793-2215, 800-844-0488, fax 360-793-2216; e-mail dutch cupm@aol.com. MODERATE.

Café Mozart's wall sconces, gold chandeliers, honey-colored oak floors and candlelit tables create an intimate baroque-style atmosphere in each of the four dining rooms. The German-born chef prepares Bavarian favorites such as beef goulash soup and wild mushroom pork schnitzel. Seasonal fresh seafood entrées include sockeye salmon grilled in hazelnut butter and almond-crusted halibut with hollandaise sauce. If you have room for dessert or if you stop by between meals, treat yourself to Mozart's chocolate torte (seven layers of rich marzipan wine crème covered with dark chocolate). Weekend reservations recommended. ~ 829 Front Street, Leavenworth; 509-548-0600. MODERATE TO DELUXE.

Lorraine's Edel House offers an outdoor patio overlooking the Wenatchee River and an intimate dining room with candlelit tables, ceiling fans and Victorian furnishings. The menu offers an eclectic assortment of Northwest dishes, ranging from grilled wild king salmon to roast duck marinated in soy ginger and topped with an orange glaze. ~ 320 9th Street, Leavenworth; 509-548-4412, 800-487-3335. MODERATE TO DELUXE.

The Gingerbread Factory is a delight for children and parents alike, with decorated cookies and gingerbread houses. The café sells pastries, salads, espresso and all sorts of gifts related to gingerbread. ~ 828 Commercial Street, Leavenworth; 509-548-6592. BUDGET.

The first place to eat after coming down off Stevens Pass is the **Sky Chalet**. This large restaurant has booths with high backs and open tables, and serves country breakfasts all day. Lunch specials might be Swedish meatballs or chicken-fried steak. The dinner menu is unembellished—Swedish dishes, steaks, pork chops and chicken. ~ Route 2, Skykomish; 360-677-2223. BUDGET TO MODERATE.

In Index, the best place to eat is in the **Bush House Country Inn**. Here, in the century-old hotel dining room you will find a big

GET CRACKIN'

The only museum in the country devoted exclusively to nutcrackers, the **Leavenworth Nutcracker Museum** displays artifacts from as early as the 15th century up to modern times. The collection consists of more than 4000 nutcrackers from around the world, including Italy, Germany, Turkey, the U.S. and India. You'll see the popular soldier nutcracker, as well as nutcrackers in the shape of dragons, dogs and rams. Moses, Abraham Lincoln, Bugs Bunny, Thomas Edison and Shakespeare have all been immortalized as, you guessed it, nutcrackers in the museum's gift shop. Open daily 2 p.m. to 5 p.m. from May through October; open weekends only November through April. Admission. ~ 735 Front Street #2-B, Leavenworth; 509-548-4708; www.nussknackerhaus.com/museum.htm.

stone fireplace and gourmet country cuisine that uses very fresh meat, seafood, fish, fruits and vegetables. The Sunday breakfast is served until 3 p.m. and includes omelettes, homemade pastries and fresh fruit. ~ 300 5th Street, Index; 360-793-2312. MODERATE TO DELUXE.

The Dutch Cup Restaurant is one of the most popular restaurants on the Stevens Pass route. It opens at 6 a.m. to catch the ski crowd as they head up the highway and stays open until 11 p.m. to get them on the way home. The home-cooking menu includes country breakfasts, burgers, soups and sandwiches for lunch, and offers steaks, prime rib and chicken for dinner. ~ 927 Main Street, Sultan; 360-793-1864. BUDGET TO MODERATE.

SHOPPING   Leavenworth has the best selection of specialty shops in the Cascades; about 100 are crammed into a two-block area. A Different Drummer sells international greeting cards, other paper supplies and children's books. ~ 725 Front Street, Leavenworth; 509-548-5320. The Cuckoo Clock has a large collection of contemporary timepieces. It is a resonant place on the hour, quarter and half hour when the cuckoos perform a veritable symphony. ~ 725 Front Street, Leavenworth; 509-548-4857.

Train buffs will love the Train Store at Leavenworth for its railroad memorabilia, which includes pen-and-ink drawings, pins and artwork. ~ 636 Front Street, Leavenworth; 509-548-7246. Cabin Fever Rustics offers a quality assortment of antiques, collectibles, Pendleton blankets and Northwest gifts. ~ 923 Commercial Street, Leavenworth; 509-548-4238.

NIGHTLIFE   Leavenworth has little nighttime entertainment; its movie theater collapsed beneath a heavy snowfall several years ago and has not been replaced, and the only place that offers live music after dark is the Leavenworth Brewery. The brewery has live jazz and rhythm-and-blues on Saturday throughout the year. Cover. ~ 636 Front Street, Leavenworth; 509-548-4545.

Leavenworth's major sports bar is the Old Post Office Tavern, with TVs, pool tables and karaoke on Friday and Saturday nights. ~ 213 9th Street, Leavenworth; 509-548-6573.

PARKS   **LAKE WENATCHEE STATE PARK**   The lake is tucked away near Stevens Pass and is popular in summer for canoeing, kayaking, sailing, swimming and fishing (kokanee and whitefish) and in the winter for cross-country skiing. The secluded, wooded campsites are great. Picnic areas, restrooms, showers and evening interpretive programs are found here. ~ Located 18 miles north of Leavenworth and four miles off Route 2 on Route 207; 509-763-3101.

▲ There are 197 tent and RV sites (no hookups); $11 per night. Reservations, 800-452-5687.

Route 90 Corridor

This pristine area remains one of America's scenic icons. From snow-capped peaks to dramatic waterfalls, the corridor is one of the Northwest's hidden treasures. It extends from Snoqualmie across the Cascades to Ellensburg and the Kittitas Valley. Fasten your seat belts for a breathtaking ride past volcanic peaks, fir forests and rivers where you're likely to land tonight's dinner.

SIGHTS

The Cascades begin rising only a half-hour's drive east of Seattle. The town of **Snoqualmie** has an ornate, old railroad depot that is home to the **Snoqualmie Valley Railroad**, which makes a ten-mile trip through the Snoqualmie Valley on weekends (April or May through October) and runs a special Christmas train. ~ 38625 Southeast King Street, Snoqualmie; 425-746-4025; www. train museum.org.

Inside the depot, the **Northwest Railway Museum** displays old railroad equipment and sleeper and dining car paraphernalia. Admission. ~ 425-888-3030.

Nearby is **Snoqualmie Falls**, a thundering cataract with a small park, observation platform and trails leading to the river below the 268-foot falls.

The town of **North Bend** has adopted an alpine theme for its downtown buildings, but it hasn't caught on with the vigor of Winthrop and Leavenworth. Not to be confused with the coastal town of the same name, this hamlet sits snugly in the shadow of the looming Mt. Si.

The summit of **Snoqualmie Pass** has four major ski areas, for downhill and snowboarding, and one cross-country ski area with more than 35 miles of groomed trails. There's a Forest Service museum information center where you can pick up brochures and outdoor-recreation information.

> Twenty-seven dialects were commonly heard in Cle Elum during the town's early days as a mining center.

In **Cle Elum**, an American Indian name meaning "swift water," you will find the unusual **Cle Elum Historical Telephone Museum** which commemorates and explains (through exhibits of ethnic costumes, old switchboards and logging and mining items) why Cle Elum was the last U.S. town to switch over from a manual long-distance switchboard. Open Friday to Sunday during summer, or by appointment. ~ 221 East 1st Street, Cle Elum; 509-674-5080.

The **Carpenter Museum** is actually a 1914 house that belonged to the first successful banker in Cle Elum. It's one of the few historic houses in the state that still has original furnishings. Call for a private tour. ~ 221 East 1st Street, Cle Elum; 509-674-5702.

At the foot of 4th Street is the access point for the 25-mile-long **Iron Horse State Park**, a section of the former railroad right of way with the rails and ties removed and the roadbed smoothed over for walking, jogging, cross-country skiing and biking. It is part of the **John Wayne Pioneer Trail** that will eventually run the width of the state.

Three miles away from Cle Elum is the tiny town of **Roslyn**, used as the set for television's quirky *Northern Exposure*. It was formerly a coal-mining town with a large population of Italian, Croatian and Austrian immigrants who worked in the mines. There are separate cemeteries—23 in fact—for these nationalities.

As you drive through the Kittitas Valley to Ellensburg, notice that the prevailing wind off the Cascades gives trees a permanent lean toward the east. When you reach Ellensburg, you're out of the Cascades and entering the arid climate that characterizes most of the eastern side of Washington. **Ellensburg** is perhaps best known for its rodeo each Labor Day weekend, and in keeping with the Western legacy, the Western Art Association has its headquarters there and holds an annual show and sale each fall.

The **Clymer Museum Gallery** displays work by the famous Western artist, who lived in Ellensburg. ~ 416 North Pearl Street, Ellensburg; 509-962-6416; www.atellensburg.com/~clymer.

The **Kittitas County Historical Museum** displays American Indian artifacts and pioneer tools and has extensive rock and doll collections. Closed Sunday and Monday in winter. ~ 114 East 3rd Avenue, Ellensburg; 509-925-3778.

Three miles east of town is the **Olmstead Place State Park**, a working farm that uses pioneer equipment. The 217-acre farm and all its buildings were deeded to the state. Weekend tours are offered from Memorial Day to Labor Day. ~ 921 North Ferguson Road, Ellensburg; 509-925-1943.

LODGING

The **Salish Lodge at Snoqualmie Falls** perches on the cliff overlooking the spectacular falls, one of the more dramatic settings for a hotel and restaurant in the Northwest. The 91 rooms and suites are decorated in an upscale-country motif with down comforters, wicker furniture, woodburning fireplaces and jacuzzis. Only a few rooms have views of the falls, but the interiors are so well done that most visitors console themselves by watching the falls from the lounge or observation deck. There is also a full-service spa. ~ 6501 Railroad Avenue Southeast, Snoqualmie; 425-888-2556, 800-826-6124, fax 425-888-2420; www.coastalhotel. com. ULTRA-DELUXE.

A less pricey place to stay is the **Edgewick Inn**, three miles east of town. It is a straightforward motel with 42 clean and quiet units and two suites with jacuzzis. Three rooms are wheelchair accessible. ~ 14600 468th Avenue Southeast, North Bend; 425-888-9000, fax 425-888-9400. MODERATE.

About the only place to stay at Snoqualmie Summit is the **Best Western Summit Inn**. Outfitted for skiers, its 82 rooms come with king-size or two queen-size beds, and it has a complimentary ski-storage area and coin-operated laundry. Tired guests also enjoy the indoor sauna, jacuzzi and heated outdoor pool. The large lobby is stocked with comfortable leather sofas set around the native-stone fireplace. ~ P.O. Box 163, Snoqualmie Pass, WA 98068; 425-434-6300, 800-557-7829, fax 425-434-6396. MODERATE.

A former Milwaukee Railroad crew house and recognized in the National Historic Register, **Iron Horse Inn** has been converted into one of the state's best inns. The 12 rooms, half with shared baths, are named for former occupants. All are decorated in turn-of-the-20th-century antiques—with an emphasis, not surprisingly, on railroad trinkets and tools. There are two remodeled cabooses sporting queen-size beds, refrigerators and sundecks with hot tub. A deluxe honeymoon suite has a jacuzzi; an outdoor hot tub serves everyone else. The Iron Horse is adjacent to the Iron Horse State Park Trail, where cross-country skiing, bicycling, horseback riding and walking are popular. Full breakfast is included in the rate. ~ 526 Marie Avenue, South Cle Elum; 509-674-5939, 800-228-9246; www.ironhorseinn.uswest.dex.com. BUDGET TO DELUXE.

Although this is supposedly the state's oldest dude ranch, it is one of those places that keeps being "discovered." **Hidden Valley Guest Ranch** is eight miles from Cle Elum nestled at the edge of a broad valley and at the base of low mountains. In addition to the main building, where guests gather for trail rides, hikes and the community meals, the ranch has a total of 14 cabins and rooms that haven't had all the rustic removed, so don't expect sound- or cold-proofing. However, the fireplaces are great for

◄ HIDDEN

taking off the chill as are the heated pool and communal hot tub. All meals, and they are very large meals, are eaten in the buffet-style dining room. There are no telephones or TVs on this ranch; instead there is a sport court, horseback riding and 750 acres of nature to explore. Two-night minimum stay. In winter, only seven cabins (with studio kitchens) are available. ~ 3942 Hidden Valley Road, Cle Elum; 509-857-2322, 800-526-9269, fax 509-857-2130; www. ranchweb.com/hiddenvalley. DELUXE TO ULTRA-DELUXE.

For more impersonal lodgings, the **TimberLodge Inn**, on the western edge of town, has 35 bright, clean rooms and one deluxe suite with fridge and microwave, far enough off the street to deaden the noise of the busy main drag. Amenities include an exercise room and hot tub. There is a daily breakfast bar. ~ 301 West 1st Street, Cle Elum; 509-674-5966, fax 509-674-2737. BUDGET.

Twede's Café in North Bend served as the model for the diner in television's *Twin Peaks*.

Murphy's Country Bed and Breakfast, four miles west of Ellensburg, has two rooms in a ranch home built in 1915. It has a broad porch made of local stone with views across the valley. The large rooms have antique furnishings with private baths. A full country breakfast is served. ~ 2830 Thorp Highway South, two miles from Exit 106 off Route 90; 509-925-7986, fax 509-962-9498. MODERATE.

DINING

The **Salish Lodge at Snoqualmie Falls** offers spectacular views over the falls and canyon below, and the food is first rate. The menu leans toward what has become known as Northwest cuisine: lots of seafood, fresh fruits and vegetables, and game. The restaurant boasts the largest wine list in the state and a dessert list almost as long. ~ 6501 Railroad Avenue Southeast, Snoqualmie; 800-826-6124; www.coastalhotel.com. DELUXE TO ULTRA-DELUXE.

Twede's Café has faux gas lamps, wood paneling and neon across the ceiling. Stay only for a cup of "damn good coffee" and their infamous cherry pie. ~ 137 North Bend Way, North Bend; 425-831-5511. BUDGET

Cle Elum is better known for its inns and small hotels, but it has at least one good restaurant, **Mama Vallone's Steak House and Inn**. Tables are placed in most of the downstairs rooms, and you never have to wait for someone to replenish your water or bring more bread. A specialty is *bagna cauda*, a fondue-style mixture of olive oil, anchovy and garlic served with dipping strips of steak or seafood. ~ 302 West 1st Street, Cle Elum; 509-674-5174. MODERATE TO DELUXE.

Pub Minglewood's owner John Herbert, from the Isle of Jersey, has a menu of steaks, seafood, fish, chicken and light entrées for dinner. Dinner only. Closed Sunday. ~ 402 North Pearl Street, Ellensburg; 509-962-2260. BUDGET TO MODERATE.

A short walk away is **The Valley Café**. Food is American with a Northwest flair. Fish (frequently salmon) and chicken dominate the dinner menu. There is also lamb, steak and pasta on the menu. ~ 105 West 3rd Street, Ellensburg; 509-925-3050. BUDGET TO MODERATE.

SHOPPING

In North Bend, 31 miles east of Seattle, the **Factory Stores at North Bend** is a mall with 50 stores selling well-known brands—Nike, the Gap, Van Heusen, Big Dog, Bass, Hanes—at discount prices. ~ 425-888-4505.

Hedges Cellars is a Yakima Valley winery that has opened a full-fledged tasting room on the west side of the Cascades; some aging is done here. Hedges is known for its reds, especially cabernets and merlots. ~ 195 Northeast Gilman Boulevard, Issaquah; 425-391-6056.

Antique hunters will enjoy Ellensburg, which has at least half a dozen antique stores in a three-block area, including a mall. The **Showplace Antique Mall** is a restored art deco theater with up to 40 antique dealers displaying at a time. ~ 103 East 3rd Street, Ellensburg; 509-962-9331.

NIGHTLIFE

Cle Elum has almost nothing in nightlife other than taverns with jukeboxes, although occasionally **Iron Horse Inn** guests will bring their own instruments to the piano in the lobby area for a sing-along. ~ 526 Marie Street, Cle Elum; 509-674-5939.

In Ellensburg between the rodeos there is little entertainment, but **The Mint Bar and Grill** keeps 'em at the bar with beer and jukebox music. There's also a dancefloor and deejay on weekends. ~ 111 West 3rd Avenue, Ellensburg; 509-962-5448. **Pounders**, a bar and grill, occasionally has live or canned rock music on the weekend. Cover for live shows. ~ 315 North Main Street, Ellensburg; 509-962-4141.

PARKS

LAKE EASTON STATE PARK 🚶 🚲 🏕 🏊 🎣 🛶 🚤 ⛵ 🚣
On Route 90, near the summit at Snoqualmie Pass, this lakeside park with forested trails is used as a base for skiers and snowmobilers in winter, as a lunch stop for travelers in spring and fall, and for hiking, swimming and fishing in the summer. The lake is stocked with trout. Facilities include picnic areas, a swimming beach and restrooms. ~ Located on Route 90 a mile west of Easton; 509-656-2230.

▲ There are 90 tent sites near the Yakima River and 45 RV hookups near the lake, plus two primitive walk-in-only sites; $11 to $16 per night. Reservations, 800-452-5687 ($6 per reservation; $6 to cancel).

▼▼▼▼▼▼▼▼▼▼▼
Mt. Rainier Area

It is always a dramatic moment when Mt. Rainier suddenly appears ahead of you (in the Northwest it is often called just The Mountain). You could spend weeks in this area and only sample a small portion of its recreational possibilities. Whether you approach from the east or the west, the forest gets thicker and thicker and the roadside rivers get swifter and swifter. The national park is almost surrounded with national forest wilderness areas as buffer zones against clear-cut logging. Located southeast of Seattle, this peak is the site of the aptly named town of Paradise.

SIGHTS Coming from Route 5 down Route 7 toward Mt. Rainier, right before the town of Elbe is a turnoff that will take you north on Route 161 to **Northwest Trek Wildlife Park**. A free-roaming animal park owned by the Tacoma Metro Parks Department, it provides a rare opportunity to see native wildlife of the Pacific Northwest up close. The highlight is a 55-minute tram ride around a 435-acre expanse of forest and meadows inhabited by hundreds of large grazing animals, including bison, caribou, bighorn sheep, mountain goats, Roosevelt elk and a few elusive moose. Wild turkeys and migratory sandhill cranes and geese also live in the park. There is often a wait of an hour or more for the tram ride. In the meantime, you can walk around the more conventionally zoolike area near the tour station and see predators such as wolves, bears, cougars, owls and eagles as well as smaller animals like beavers, raccoons and badgers that would be hard to spot in a free-roaming setting. There's also a network of paved and unpaved nature trails that can take an hour or more to explore fully, plus a hands-on discovery center for kids. The gift shop features animal-motif gift items made by regional artisans, and the café has a full lunch menu as well as an espresso bar and an outdoor picnic area. If you're planning to visit Mount Rainier, Northwest Trek is right on the way. Admission. ~ 11610 Trek Drive East (off Route 161), Eatonville; 360-832-6122, fax 360-832-6118; www.nwtrek.org.

If you arrive via Route 706 you will have to go through Elbe on Route 7 which has the **Mt. Rainier Scenic Railroad**, a steam-powered train that makes a 14-mile trip through the forest and across high bridges to Mineral Lake. It runs daily in the summer, on Saturday and Sunday in September and on special holidays. A four-hour dinner train is offered Friday through Sunday in the summer and on Saturday the rest of the year. ~ P.O. Box 921, Elbe, WA 98330; 360-569-2588, 888-783-2611 (for dinner train only), 888-773-4637; www.mrsr.com.

Once inside the park you may be almost overwhelmed by the scenery. **Mt. Rainier** is so monstrous (14,411 feet) that it makes everything around it seem trivial. In fact, Mt. Rainier is the tallest mountain in the Northwest and has more glaciers—25—than any other mountain in the contiguous 48 states. **Mt. Rainier National Park** has numerous visitor centers and interpretive exhibits along winding roads. For park information, call the National Park Service at 360-569-2211 ext. 2357; www.nps.gov/mora.

In **Paradise**, head to the **Henry M. Jackson Visitor Center**, which has several exhibits and audiovisual shows. Paradise is one of the most beautiful places in the park, and the visitors center is one of the busiest. It has a snack bar and gift shop. Closed weekdays (except holidays) between November and April. ~ Paradise, WA; 360-569-2211 ext. 2328.

The **Longmire Museum** emphasizes the natural history of the park with rock, flora and fauna exhibits as well as with exhibits on the human history of the area. Its old historic buildings have stood since the 1880s when the Longmire family lived there. The museum also has an information center for hikers, and next door at the National Park Inn you can rent cross-country skis or snowshoes. ~ Longmire, WA; 360-569-2211 ext. 3314.

The **Ohanapecosh Visitor Center**, down in the southeast corner near a grove of giant, ancient cedar trees, has history and nature exhibits. Closed mid-October through May. ~ 360-569-2211 ext. 2352.

The **Sunrise Visitor Center** has geological displays and at 6400 feet is the closest you can drive to the peak. Numerous trails fan out from the center for day hikes, but be aware that even into July, there is often snow on the trails. ~ 360-663-2574.

Nearby, at the intersection of Routes 410 and 12 east of the mountain, you can watch elk and bighorn sheep being fed by game officials during the middle of winter at the **Oak Creek Wildlife Recreation Area**, which is accessible only from Route 12.

LODGING

Two inns are located inside Mt. Rainier National Park, and several other places to stay are around the park in Ashford, Packwood, Elbe, Crystal Mountain, Morton and the White Pass area.

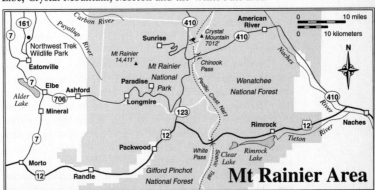

SCENIC DRIVE

The Mount Rainier Circle

Mount Rainier, the huge landmark mountain visible (on clear days) from every-where in the Puget Sound area, makes for a spectacularly scenic all-day trip from Seattle. Heading south from the city on Route 5, take Exit 149, drive two miles to Kent, and turn south on Route 167, another wide, fast, divided highway. Go seven miles to Puyallup, turn off on Route 161, and suddenly you're off the freeway and on your way through the forests and farmlands of Pierce County.

NORTHWEST TREK WILDLIFE PARK Located about 17 miles south of Puyallup is Northwest Trek Wildlife Park (page 292), Washington's premier animal park, where you can take an hour-long tram tour for an up-close look at large animals native to the Pacific Northwest roaming in a 435-acre natural habitat. There's usually a wait, so expect to spend two to three hours here.

PARADISE Ten miles south of Northwest Trek, Route 161 meets Route 7. Turn south (left) and go nine miles to Elbe, where Route 706, the well-marked road to **Mount Rainier National Park** (page 293), turns off to the east (left). Passing Alder Lake, it's about 15 miles to the park's Nisqually Entrance, where on sunny weekends you may have to wait in a long line to pay the $10-per-vehicle entrance fee. As you drive through lofty primeval forest at the base of the mountain, you'll see signs of a vast mudslide that occurred when the sleeping volcanic giant stirred and melted part of the glacier that caps its summit. About 15 miles into the

The most popular is **Paradise Inn**. Nineteen miles into the park, this nonsmoking inn has 117 rooms and a lobby that boasts exposed beams, peeled-log posts, wooden furniture, Indian-made rugs and two huge fireplaces. The views from outside are grand, but the rooms are ordinary. Closed October through April. ~ Paradise, WA 98398; 360-569-2275, fax 360-569-2770; www.nps. gov/mora. MODERATE.

The other in-park hotel is the **National Park Inn**, six miles from the Nisqually entrance. Built in 1916, the inn offers much of the rustic charm of the Paradise Inn, yet is much smaller with only 25 rooms, half with private baths. Some rooms have views of the mountain. In keeping with the rustic theme, there are no telephones or televisions. The lobby has an enormous stone fireplace. ~ Longmire, WA 98397; 360-569-2275, fax 360-569-2770; www. guestservices.com/rainier. MODERATE.

Equally popular with lovers of old inns is **Alexander's Country Inn**. This inn was built in 1912 as a small hotel designed to look park, a turnoff on the left takes you up to timberline at Paradise, where the busy visitors center has a cafeteria, trails that wend through alpine meadows, and exhibits about climbing the mountain.

SUNRISE   Beyond the Paradise turnoff, Route 706 is closed in the winter but stunning in the summer as it traverses Backbone Ridge, offering panoramic views of the jagged Catamount Range to the southeast. In about 15 miles you'll join Route 123 northbound. Another ten miles brings you to the summit of 4675-foot Cayuse Pass. Four miles farther on is the turnoff on the left that winds by switchbacks up the east slope of the mountain to **Sunrise Visitor Center**, a 16-mile climb to the highest point in the park that you can reach by car. Another network of alpine hiking trails starts here, and it's usually much less crowded than Paradise.

HOMEWARD   When you descend from Sunset, turn north (left) on Route 123 and you're on your way out of the park. The highway takes you 38 miles through **Mt. Baker–Snoqualmie National Forest** (page 270) to Enumclaw. Angle to the right on Route 164, drive 15 miles to Auburn, and hop onto divided four-lane Route 18 westbound. Three quick miles and you're back on Route 5, just 20 miles south of downtown Seattle. Allow one and a half hours for the return trip from Mount Rainier to Seattle.

like a manor with turret rooms and grand entrance hall. It retains the Old World look while adding modern conveniences such as a hot tub. Full-course country breakfast is included, as is wine in the evening. ~ 37515 Route 706 East, Ashford; 360-569-2300, 800-654-7615, fax 360-569-2323. MODERATE TO DELUXE.

In Packwood on the southern flank of the national park is the **Cowlitz River Lodge**. It is notable for clean, brightly decorated rooms and views of the mountains, although not "The Mountain." It is set back from the busy Route 12 far enough for the logging trucks to be a distant hum rather than an immediate roar. ~ 13069 Route 12, Packwood; 360-494-4444, fax 360-494-2075. MODERATE.

On the northeast boundary of the park is **Crystal Mountain Resort**, a year-round resort that is best known for its skiing. Visitors can choose from a number of places to stay, ranging from condominiums to inexpensive hotels, all of which are nonsmoking. Don't expect much charm because skiing, not hotel amenities, is the focus. Typical is **Silver Skis Chalet Condominiums**, which has a cluster of one- and two-bedroom units, some with fireplaces and views. All have kitchens and televisions and can sleep up to four people. They are decorated in the traditional rental-condo manner of plastic furniture and durable fabrics. ~ Resort headquarters, 33000 Crystal Mountain Boulevard, Crystal Mountain, WA 98597; 360-663-2558, 888-668-4368, fax 360-663-0145; www.crystalmtlodging-wa.com. MODERATE TO ULTRA-DELUXE.

A bit farther east toward Yakima is the White Pass ski area with **The Village Inn Condominiums**. The complex has 50 rental units designed for large groups, up to eight in many units, and they have a bit of variation in decor since all are privately owned. Some have fireplaces and sleeping lofts, while all have full kitchen facilities. ~ P.O. Box 3035, White Pass, WA 98937; 509-672-3131, fax 509-672-3141. MODERATE.

DINING

Good restaurants are hard to find around Mt. Rainier but there are a few worth mentioning.

Nearby is the more traditional **Alexander's Country Inn** serving breakfast, lunch and dinner. The dining room has windows looking out across the forest. Trout from the glacier-fed trout pond is a favorite, along with seafood, and all the breads and desserts are homemade. They also make box lunches. Open weekends only in the winter. ~ 37515 Route 706 East, Ashford; 360-569-2300. MODERATE TO DELUXE.

Mt. Rainier last erupted around 1845, and the mountain has been quiet since. However, steam vents on the summit are still active, and geologists warn another eruption is inevitable—someday.

Casual dining and great mountain views are staples of **Rainier Overland**, a cedar-sided restaurant in a forested setting. Good menu choices here are steaks, hamburgers, fresh grilled halibut and house-made soups and pies. The restaurant and saloon are open only in the summer. ~ 31811 Route 706, Ashford; 360-569-0851. BUDGET TO MODERATE.

Set on three wooded acres, which also include log cabins and an RV park, the **Gateway Inn** offers a wood-paneled coffee shop–style restaurant serving breakfast, lunch and dinner. The standard road fare of burgers, steaks and omelettes is enhanced by local trout and freshly baked breads and fruit pies. ~ 38820 Route 706, Ashford; 360-569-2506. BUDGET TO MODERATE.

One of the most popular restaurants between Mt. Rainier and Mt. St. Helens is **Peters Inn**, a large, old-fashioned place where they serve burgers, steaks, veal and some seafood and have a large salad bar. Pies and cinnamon rolls are made locally. ~ 13051 Route 12, Packwood; 360-494-4000. BUDGET TO MODERATE.

The **Whistlin' Jack Lodge** is a rustic lodge 20 miles east of Mt. Rainier National Park that offers a sophisticated level of dining unusual in these parts. Panfried rainbow trout boned table-side and a signature appetizer of crab-stuffed artichoke hearts served with garlic toast points are among the specialties. Prime rib, lobster and "bubbleberry" pie (a blend of apples, cherries, raspberries and huckleberries) round out the menu. Breakfasts are also exceptional, with items such as huckleberry coffee cake. The spacious dining area is set with white linen napery and features a huge fireplace built from local river rock. Picture windows overlook the Naches River. ~ 20800 Route 410, Naches; 509-658-2433, 800-827-2299. MODERATE TO ULTRA-DELUXE.

NORTHWEST TREK WILDLIFE PARK 🏃 Located 35 miles south of Tacoma this 600-acre nature preserve is operated by the Metropolitan Park District of Tacoma, which provides close but safe encounters with grizzly bears and other wildlife. Walking along the five miles of trails of Northwest Trek, visitors are also likely to see bobcats, martens, wolverines, eagles and owls. In the park's Bear Exhibit, the largest in North America, grizzlies and black bears live in outdoor enclosures designed to mimic their natural habitats. A tram tour takes visitors through 435 acres, where they will see bison, deer, elk, mountain goats, caribou, big horn sheep and waterfowl. There is also a Discovery Center where children can handle reptiles and observe bee and ant societies at work. Day-use fee, $8.25. ~ 11610 Trek Drive East, Eatonville; 360-832-6117, fax 360-832-6118; www.nwtrek.org.

PARKS

MT. RAINIER NATIONAL PARK 🏃 🚴 🐎 ⛷ 🏕 ⛵ One of the most heavily used national parks in Washington, Mt. Rainier is everybody's favorite because the mountain can be approached from so many directions and the area around it is glorious no matter the time of year. The mountain is open for climbing for individuals or groups under the leadership of Rainier Mountaineering Inc. (360-569-2227, mid-May through September; 253-627-6242, October to mid-May), or by direct registration with the climbing rangers, for experienced mountaineers. The park charges a climbing fee of $15 per person, per climb above 10,000 feet. Otherwise, you can hike the lower stretches of the mountain. The lower elevations are notable for the great views of vast meadows covered with wildflowers from July until August, and for dramatic fall colors in September and October. Numerous trails lead day hikers to viewpoints, and backpackers can register on a permit system for backcountry campsites. A backcountry fee may be charged for overnight trips during the summer months. The park is open year-round with special areas set aside for winter sports at Paradise. Fishing is permitted in designated waters without a state license. Check with a ranger for regulations. You'll find picnic areas, restrooms, four information centers, museums and self-guided nature trails. ~ Entrances to the park are located on Route 410 on the northeast, Route 706 on the southwest and Route 123 on the southeast; 360-569-2211.

▲ There are four car campgrounds, a few walk-in sites and overnight hike-in backcountry areas on a first-come, first-serve basis; RVs allowed (no hookups); $10 to $12 per night. Reservations for two campgrounds are at 800-365-2267 during the summer months, and include an additional $2 service charge.

▼▼▼▼▼▼▼▼▼▼▼▼▼▼▼
Mt. St. Helens Area

There are few certitudes in travel writing, but here's one: Don't miss Mt. St. Helens. At the southern end of the Washington Cascades an hour north of Portland, this peak might best be described as a cross between a geology lesson and a bombing range. East of this landmark is Gifford Pinchot National Forest and Mt. Adams Wilderness, the heart of a popular recreation area ideal for rafting and fishing.

On May 18, 1980, Mt. St. Helens, dormant for 123 years, blew some 1300 feet off its top and killed 57 persons, causing one of the largest natural disasters in recorded North American history.

Today, access to the volcano remains limited because the blast and resulting mudslides and floods erased the roads that formerly entered the area.

SIGHTS A major sightseeing destination, **Mt. St. Helens National Volcanic Monument Visitor Center** is on Route 504 at Silver Lake, five miles east of Route 5. The center is elaborate and includes a walk-in model of the inside of the volcano. A 22-minute film on the eruption plays almost continuously, and an equally dramatic nine-minute slide show runs every 30 minutes. ~ 3029 Spirit Lake Highway, Castle Rock; 360-274-2100, fax 360-274-2101. There is also the **Coldwater Ridge Visitor Center**, 38 miles farther east on Route 504. It is located eight miles from the mountain at milepost 43 and offers guided walks. Good for three days, the Monument Pass allows you to visit these two visitors centers, Johnston Ridge Observatory (360-274-2141) and any other fee sites on the monument. ~ 360-274-2131, fax 360-274-2151; www.fs.fed.us/gpnf.

Windy Ridge is the closest you can get to the volcano, and it is reached by driving south from Randle on a series of Forest Service roads. Hourly talks are given by rangers in the amphitheater there in summer. **Meta Lake Walk** is on the way to Windy Ridge, and rangers tell how wildlife survived the blast. A 30-minute talk is given in **Ape Cave** on the southern end of the monument. It includes a walk into the 1900-year-old lava tube that got its name from the first group of people who mapped and explored the cave, a boy scout group called St. Helens Apes.

East of Mt. St. Helens, continue south through **Gifford Pinchot National Forest** on paved national forest roads. First, buy a copy of the national forest map at the forest headquarters visitors centers, or from a ranger station. You can drive to the edge of **Indian Heaven Wilderness Area** and hike through peaceful meadows and acres of huckleberry bushes, or continue east to the edge of **Mt. Adams Wilderness** with views of that mountain reflected in lakes. Day and overnight permits are required to enter wilderness areas in the Gifford Pinchot National Forest. This whole area is known for wild huckleberries, and there are two seasons for them; in the lower elevations, they ripen in July and into August, then a week or two later the higher-elevation berries ripen. For more information, call the National Forest Headquarters. ~ 360-891-5001, fax 360-891-5245; www.fs.fed.us.

The roads will eventually take you to **Trout Lake**, a small town close to a wetland area of the same name near Mt. Adams. Here you'll find all services and a Forest Service Ranger Station. Just west of town is a vast lava flow called the **Big Lava Bed** and a lava tube called **Ice Cave**, which is chilly all through the summer. Both are reached on Forest Service roads.

From Trout Lake, drive east 16 miles to the small cowboy town of **Glenwood**. There's not much more than a country tavern and post office to the town, but in the Shade Tree Inn tavern you can get directions to some of the more unusual sights in the area,

◄ HIDDEN

Mt St Helens Area

such as a group of quartz crystals more than 200 feet in diameter and what is locally called "volcano pits," a series of small craters left behind by cinder cones.

From Glenwood, take the Glenwood-Goldendale Road to the junction with Route 142 and drive back southwest to Klickitat and the Columbia Gorge at Lyle. This takes you through the deep, winding Klickitat River Canyon with views of the river, a steelheaders' favorite. Mt. Adams often frames the scene.

LODGING

The **Seasons Motel**, about halfway between Mt. Rainier and Mt. St. Helens, has 50 rooms in a slate-blue, two-story, frame building at the intersection of Routes 12 and 7. All beds are queen-size, and the clean rooms have flowered drapes and bedspreads. ~ 200 Westlake Avenue, Morton; 360-496-6835, fax 360-496-5127; www.whitepasstravel.com. MODERATE.

HIDDEN ►

Located 17 miles west of Morton in the tiny town of Salkum, **The Shepherd's Inn** is about 45 minutes away from Mt. Rainier and one hour away from Mt. St. Helens. Guests can enjoy the region's natural beauty on any of the numerous walking trails that web through the 40 acres of wooded land on the property. The inn's five rooms offer country Victorian furnishings and brass beds. If you have the urge to tickle the ivories, you may do so on the grand piano. There's also a double jacuzzi. Full breakfast includes wild huckleberry crêpes. ~ 168 Autumn Heights Drive, Salkum; 360-985-2434, 800-985-2434; www.theshepherds inn.com. MODERATE.

The **Farm Bed and Breakfast** is situated on six acres in Trout Lake, close to Mt. Adams. Two rooms decorated in antiques with cozy quilts are available in this three-story 1890 farmhouse. Surrounding the B&B are perennial gardens, a barn, sheep and a vegetable garden. Hosts Rosie and Dean Hostetter serve a full farm breakfast complete with fresh raspberries and strawberries. ~

THE DAY THE MOUNTAIN BLEW

At 8:30 a.m. on May 18, 1980, the growing bulge that had been forming in the past weeks pushed a small section of rock down the slope of Mt. St. Helens, and suddenly the mountain exploded with the force of 21,000 atomic bombs the size of the one dropped on Hiroshima. It powdered the mountainside and blew it into the atmosphere at about 500 miles per hour. Simultaneously, practically the whole north flank lurched down the mountain at about 200 miles per hour. By evening, ash had covered a half-million square miles in three states and the silhouette of Mt. St. Helens was left standing with a huge bite taken out of its north slope—1300 feet shorter than its 9677-foot stature the day before.

490 Sunnyside Road, Trout Lake; 509-395-2488, fax 509-395-2127. MODERATE.

Also on the southwestern edge of Mt. Adams is the outdoor-oriented **Flying L Ranch**. Originally a working ranch, since 1960 the Flying L has been a guest ranch but now without horses. Hiking and photography are popular here, as is fishing in the nearby Klickitat River. Bikes are available free of charge to get around the mostly flat roads in the area. In the winter, cross-country skiing and snowshoeing access is nearby. The main lodge has five rooms, half with shared bath; a two-story guest house has five rooms with private baths, and three separate cabins sleep up to five. Full breakfast is provided and served in the cookhouse. The main lodge has a large common kitchen where guests can prepare their own lunches and dinners. Full breakfast is included in the rate. ~ 25 Flying L Lane, Glenwood; 509-364-3488, 888-682-3267, fax 509-364-3634; www.mt-adams.com. MODERATE TO DELUXE.

◀ HIDDEN

The **Wheel Café** has long been a local fixture in downtown Morton, with its all-pine paneling. Breakfast specialties include blueberry or strawberry pancakes, while dinner choices are a large salad bar, steaks, prime rib, burgers, fish and chips and house-made pies. There is also an adjoining bar area with dart boards, pool table and pull tabs. ~ 185 Main Street, Morton; 360-496-3240. BUDGET TO MODERATE.

DINING

Adventures Restaurant has a motif true to its name. A hang glider is suspended from the ceiling and the walls are adorned with photographs of skydiving, skiing and African safari scenes. Dining here is truly an adventure, with menu choices that include a salad of Caribbean jerk-spiced chicken with housemade poppyseed dressing. ~ 200 Westlake Avenue, Morton; 360-496-6660. BUDGET TO MODERATE.

MT. ST. HELENS NATIONAL VOLCANIC MONUMENT 🏃🚴

PARKS

🐎 🚣 🏕 🎣 ⛴ 🚤 🛥 🎣 The monument covers 110,000 acres and was created to preserve and interpret the area that was devastated by the eruption. Interpretive centers and overlooks show the destroyed Spirit Lake, vast mud flows and the forests that were flattened by the blast. Access to the east side of the monument is limited to a few Forest Service and county roads, most of which are closed in the winter. Guided tours are provided by several operators departing from Seattle, Olympia and Vancouver. Scenic flights in planes and helicopters operate out of area airports. Fishing is excellent for bass and trout in nearby Silver Lake and good for trout in lakes behind dams on the Lewis River, south of the monument. Facilities include interpretive centers, picnic areas, scenic overlooks and self-guided nature walks; viewpoints are on the east side close during the winter. ~ From the north, Forest Service roads branch off Route 12 at Randle. From the west, Route 504 from Route 5 leads five miles to the Mt. St. Helens National Volcanic Visitor Center on the shores of Silver Lake, and Route 503 leads up the Lewis River to the town of Cougar and the southern flank of the monument; 360-247-3900, fax 360-247-3965.

GIFFORD PINCHOT NATIONAL FOREST 🚶 🚴 🏇 🏕 🏊 ⛵ 🚣 🚤 🛶 This 1.37-million-acre forest covers most of the southern Cascades to the Columbia River, marked by the Mt. St. Helens Volcanic National Monument on the west and Mt. Adams on the east. Enclosing seven wilderness areas, the forest is well-accessed by a network of roads and trails used for a variety of recreational uses. Of particular interest are the **Big Lava Beds**, 14 miles west of Trout Lake, where unusual formations of basalt are found, and the **Ice Cave**, six miles southwest of Trout Lake, a lava tube where ice remains until late summer. Rivers and frequently stocked lakes offer excellent fishing. In late summer, huckleberry-picking is very popular. You'll find picnic areas and restrooms. ~ The easiest way to reach the forest is by Route 12 from the north. There is also access on smaller roads such as Route 14, State Route 503 off Route 5 at Woodland, and Route 504 off Route 5 at Castle Rock; 360-891-5000, fax 360-891-5245.

▲ There are more than 40 campgrounds; $6 to $22 per night. For reservations call 877-444-6777; www.fs.fed.us/gpnf.

▼▼▼▼▼▼▼▼▼▼▼▼▼▼
Outdoor Adventures

FISHING

Winter steelhead, Dolly Varden, rainbow trout, eastern brook trout, walleye, sturgeon, catfish, bass, perch and crappie all can be caught in the interior and along the flanks of the Cascade Range. Fishing is typically done from the banks or on private boats, but most resorts on lakes and rivers have boats and fishing tackle for rent.

The other Cascade rivers, such as the Methow, Wenatchee, Yakima, Snake and Klickitat, drain into the Columbia River. All have good trout, walleye and steelhead fishing. The Klickitat River has an excellent summer steelhead run as does the Columbia. As their numbers continue to dwindle, fewer and fewer salmon can be caught upstream from the Bonneville Lock and Dam, the first of 14 dams on the river.

You'll need a Washington State Fishing License to fish in most places, although not in all national parks. You can buy one at most bait shops.

NORTH CASCADES Several rivers in the area—Skykomish, Snohomish, Sauk and Skagit for example—provide year-round catches, notably steelhead and all species of salmon except sockeye (it's not permitted to take this fish from rivers). **Washington Fishing Adventures** specializes in fishing trips for small groups. Ken Elsea tries to help anglers both catch fish and sharpen their skills. His jet boat lets him take anglers onto sections of rivers inaccessible to boats with conventional motors. ~ Marysville; 360-653-5924.

Graybill's Guide Service offers full-day guided trips on Lake Chelan, seeking landlocked chinook and lake trout. Tackle and bait provided. ~ 509-682-4294; www.rgraybill.com.

RIVER RUNNING

"Mild to wild"—that's how one outfitter describes the range of whitewater-rafting experiences in the Cascades. From the easy Class I and II rapids on the Skagit, to the steady Class II and III staircase rapids on the Suiattle, to the Skykomish's Class IV and the Tieton's Class IV-plus rapids, whitewater-rafting trips are fun and popular throughout the Cascades. In the Wenatchee–Leavenworth area, the Wenatchee River, which has a relatively easy Class III rapid, makes a great trip for families with children. Depending on the river, outfitters generally operate April through October. From mid-December through January, the Skagit is the place for float trips to observe bald eagles, who migrate to the area to feed on salmon from the river. A caveat, though: One guide warns that classifications can be misleading, and inexperienced rafters may think they can handle rapids beyond their skill.

During salmon runs, American Indians still fish with their traditional dip nets from the Fisher Hill Bridge near Klickitat.

NORTH CASCADES Downstream River Runners rafts the Skykomish, Wenatchee, Tieton, Skagit, Sauk and Suiattle rivers in the North Cascades region, as well as several others elsewhere in the state. They do trips at all levels of difficulty (rivers range from Class I to Class V) Eagle-viewing trips are also offered. Downstream doesn't rent boats, but it offers many years of experience. ~ Monroe; 360-805-9899, 800-234-4644; www.riverpeople.com.

WENATCHEE AREA Besides whitewater trips, All Rivers Adventures offers eagle-viewing and scenic floats (accompanied by a naturalist) on rafts or inflatable kayaks on six rivers in Washington and one in Oregon. They can arrange rafting trips of all levels of experience, and for individuals using wheelchairs or with other special needs. ~ Cashmere; 509-782-2254, 800-743-5628; www.allrivers.com.

LEAVENWORTH AREA Alpine Adventures' Wild and Scenic River Tours concentrates its operation on rivers found within the Cascade Loop (the Route 2–Route 20 driving loop), including the Skykomish, Sauk, Nooksack, Wenatchee, Methow and Skagit. They also run trips on the Tieton River in September. Alpine's trips range from scenic floats to all classes of whitewater rafting, last from one hour to several days, and can accommodate from six to 200 people. ~ Leavenworth; 509-782-7042, 800-723-8386, and in Seattle, 206-323-1220. Experienced guides at Leavenworth Outfitters lead whitewater rafting trips on the Class III Wenatchee River. There's hardly an outdoor activity the company can't arrange an excursion or provide gear for: canoeing, kayaking, mountain biking, and cross-country skiing are among the activities they outfit. ~ 21312 Route 207, Leavenworth; 509-763-3733, 800-347-7934; www. thrillmakers.com. Located on the farthest reaches of Lake Chelan, accessible only by boat or floatplane, **Stehekin Valley Ranch** offers rafting on the Stehekin River (Class II to III). Children should be at least six. The trips are half-day and the rivers are tame. ~ P.O. Box 36, Stehekin, WA 98852; 509-682-4677, 800-536-0745. **Orion Expeditions** offers one- to seven-day raft trips on most of the Washington rivers ranging from Class I to IV. Lunch and lodging (camping) included. ~ 5111 Latona Avenue Northeast, Seattle; 206-547-6715, 800-553-7466; www.orionexp.com.

> If you're nervous about whitewater rafting, a scenic float is the way to go.

SKIING

In the winter, the Cascades turn into a wonderland for all types of skiing—cross-country, downhill and snowboarding. Several locations have night skiing. See the sidebar "Snow Bound" for more information. ~ Forest Service's Avalanche Center, 206-526-6677.

GOLF

It seems that nearly every community in the foothills has a golf course. And the courses are as varied as the individual communities that host them.

NORTH CASCADES In the foothills near Mt. Baker, the public **Baker's Edge Golf Course**, once pastureland, is a nice walking course without any water hazards. The nine-hole course, designed by Bill Eisenhower, is open year-round, weather permitting. ~ 8225 Kendall Road, Sumas; 360-599-2416.

METHOW VALLEY Along the eastern slopes of the North Cascades, in the Methow Valley, the public **Lake Chelan Golf Course** is fairly challenging, with small elevated greens and a tenth-hole canyon to hit over. This 18-hole course is open March through November, weather permitting, and has golf lessons, a driving range and full-service restaurant and bar. ~ 1501 Golf Course Drive, Chelan; 509-682-8026, 800-246-5361. The privately owned, public **Bear Creek Golf Course** has nine holes and two sets of tees. Designed by Herman Court, the course is scenic with valleys, hills and mountains. ~ 8-A Bear Creek Golf Course Road, Winthrop; 509-996-2284.

WENATCHEE AREA **Three Lakes Golf Course** is a pretty tough par-69, 18-hole public course, set on rolling terrain with a few water hazards. It includes a driving range, snack shop and restaurant. Weather permitting, it's open year-round. ~ 2695 Golf Drive, Malaga; 509-663-5448.

LEAVENWORTH AREA The Wenatchee River runs around the **Leavenworth Golf Club**, a semiprivate golf course that is closed to the public for a few hours each week. The spectacular mountain valley setting makes it worth the effort to get a tee time at this short, tight 18-hole course. The club, designed by members, is open April through October. ~ 9101 Icicle Road, Leavenworth; 509-548-7267. Tee off at the public 18-hole course at **Kahler Glen Golf Course and Condominiums,** designed by Randy Pelton. People ski on the course in winter. ~ 20890 Kahler Drive, Leavenworth; 509-763-2121.

ROUTE 90 CORRIDOR The 18-hole public **Mt. Si Golf Course** has breathtaking views of its namesake. ~ 9010 Boalch Avenue Southeast, Snoqualmie; 425-888-1541. **Tall Chief Public Golf Course** has a moderately challenging 18 holes at par 70. The front is open and forgiving while the back is hilly and challenging. ~ 1313 West Snoqualmie River Road South East, Fall City; 425-222-5911. Although it's relatively flat, **Cascade Golf Course,** with good drainage, is probably the best winter course in the area. The public nine-hole course, designed by LeRoy Jorgenson, has three sets of tees and easy access from Route 90. ~ 14303 436th Avenue Southeast, North Bend; 425-888-0227. **Sun Country Golf Course,** a public nine-hole course, is equipped with RV spots for golfers who want to stay. ~ 841 St. Andrews Drive, Cle Elum; 509-674-2226. The semiprivate **Ellensburg Golf Club,** designed by the Elks Club in the 1930s, has a nine-hole course available to the public. The Yakima River runs alongside the course. ~ 3231 Thorp Highway South, Ellensburg; 509-962-2984.

RIDING STABLES

Seen from atop a horse, the Cascades wilderness areas—deep mountain valleys, alpine meadows ablaze with wildflowers, heavily forested slopes and high peaks—take on new beauty. Winter weather limits horseback riding to the warmer months, from mid-April through October. Besides guided rides, some outfitters also schedule pack trips that last overnight or longer. Always call ahead to make arrangements.

NORTH CASCADES For a two-and-one-half-hour "nose-to-tail" guided ride—six riders maximum—through a pine forest to Coon Lake, which is in the North Cascades Wilderness Park, contact **Stehekin Valley Ranch** ~ Stehekin; 509-682-4677; www.courtney country.com.

METHOW VALLEY Guided rides at **Sun Mountain Lodge** are open to the public. The lodge's stable of 35 horses is one of the largest in the Cascades. The 90-minute ride is perfect for beginners; a four-hour trip through the aspen, pine and fir trees of the valley up to a lookout ridge is popular with more experienced riders. They can also arrange private rides based on experience. ~ Patterson Lake Road, Winthrop; 509-996-2211 ext. 735, 800-572-0493.

LEAVENWORTH AREA At **Eagle Creek Ranch,** a guided ride into Wenatchee National Forest follows a trail through alpine mead-

Text continued on page 308.

Snow
Bound

It's all downhill from here: Yes, friends, we are going to take you skiing. Whether you are into slopes or cross-country, the best ski areas in Washington are stretched along the Cascades from Mt. Baker to Mt. Rainier.

Beginning at the northernmost ski area and working south toward the Columbia River, **Mt. Baker** is 56 miles east of Bellingham and has an elevation range of 3500 to 5040 feet. Receiving the highest amount of average snowfall of any ski area in North America, Mt. Baker's ski park is all natural, including their half pipe. Eight lifts and two rope tows take you up to 38 trails. ~ Route 542; 360-734-6771, snowline 360-671-0211. The state's only helicopter skiing is **North Cascade Heli-Skiing**, which operates out of the Freestone Inn in Mazama. ~ 509-996-3272; 800-494-4354; www.mtbakerskiarea.com.

Some skiers prefer **Stevens Pass**, located on Route 2 about 65 miles east of Everett, because at times it has more powdery snow than spots at the summit of Snoqualmie Pass. ~ 360-973-2441; www.stevenspass. com. One of the area's smaller mountains is **Leavenworth Winter Sports Club**, a mile north of Leavenworth with a 400-foot vertical drop and a network of cross-country trails. ~ 509-548-5115.

Probably the best powder snow at a large ski area is at **Mission Ridge**, 13 miles southwest of Wenatchee. ~ On Mission Ridge Road, up Squilchuck Canyon; 509-663-6543, snowline 800-374-1693; www.missionridge.com. But the largest operation of all is **The Summit on Snoqualmie Pass**, 47 miles east of Seattle. Four major ski areas are to be found in a space of two miles: **Alpental, Summit East, Summit West** and **Summit Central**. The average summit elevation is 5400 feet and the average base is 3000 feet. The Summit at Snoqualmie offers the largest night-skiing operation in the country, as well as a tubing center, a lodge and a Nordic center where you can cross-country ski, telemark and snowshoe. ~ 425-434-7669, snow conditions 206-236-1600, road conditions 888-766-4636, information 206-236-7277.

Way up in the sky is **Crystal Mountain**. Forty miles east of Enumclaw just off Route 410 and in the shadow of Mt. Rainier, the summit has an elevation of 7000 feet. Crystal has 2300 acres including 1000 acres of backcountry terrain. The vertical drop is 3100 feet, and there are 50 trails, 13 percent of which are beginner, 57 percent of which are intermediate and 30 percent of which are advanced. ~ 360-663-2265; www.skicrystal.com. In the same general area, **White Pass** is 20 miles east of Packwood on Route 12 southeast of Mt. Rainier. A family-oriented ski area, this place is rarely crowded. A high-speed quad and rope tow serves 32 runs. Their 20-kilometer cross-country trail system is double tracked with a skating lane. ~ 509-453-8731; www.skiwhitepass.com.

Cross-country skiing is particularly popular on the eastern slopes of the mountains. Some of the best is in the Methow Valley, where 90 miles of trails are marked, the majority of which are groomed. The **Methow Valley Sport Trail Association** has a hotline for ski-touring information (800-682-5787) and a brochure showing the major trails. ~ P.O. Box 147, Winthrop, WA 98862; 509-996-3287.

Echo Valley offers downhill and cross-country skiing as well as rope tows, one lift, 14 miles of trails and a six-foot-wide skating lane for freestyle cross-country skating. A full-service rental shop stocks ski gear, and a school offers both downhill and cross-country lessons. In summer, there's a mountain-biking/hiking center. Echo Valley is ten miles northwest of Chelan on a dirt road off Route 150 and has elevations of 3000 to 3500 feet. ~ 509-687-3167. The Leavenworth area maintains several ski trails, including the **Icicle River Trail** (7.5 kilometers), kid-friendly **Ski Hill** (5 kilometers) and **Leavenworth Golf Course** (8 kilometers). You can actually ski from your hotel in downtown Leavenworth to the golf course trails (2 kilometers). ~ 509-548-7267; www.leavenworthgolf.com.

Leavenworth Outfitters, located a half mile from five snow parks in the Lake Wenatchee area, offers 35 kilometers of groomed trails. Cross-country ski lessons are available, and the store rents 120 pairs of cross-country skis, snowshoes and sleds. ~ 21312 Route 207, Leavenworth; 509-763-3733, 800-347-7934.

ows blooming with dozens of varieties of wildflowers before reaching a lookout peak for a spectacular view of the Cascades. The ranch also offers horse-drawn sleigh rides in the winter. ~ 7951 Eagle Creek Road, Leavenworth; 509-548-7798, 800-221-7433. **Icicle Outfitters and Guides** has hourly guided rides, day trips and summer pack trips that take two to ten people through timber past Nason Creek. You can rent mules, too. ~ P.O. Box 322, Leavenworth, WA 98826; 509-763-3647.

BIKING

For the most part, bicycling in the Cascades is not for the faint of heart or inexperienced. Besides that, unless you bring your own bike, it's hard to find bikes to rent. One exception is the Leavenworth area, where a relatively easy seven-mile loop will take you along the river and through town. You can pick up a free map at the **Leavenworth Chamber of Commerce**. ~ 894 Route 2, Leavenworth; 509-548-5807.

Several loop routes have been established along the eastern slopes of the Cascades. The **Leavenworth–Lake Wenatchee loop** is 50 miles long and goes from Leavenworth along Route 209 north to Route 207 at Lake Wenatchee State Park and south to Route 2 and back to Leavenworth.

The **Wenatchee–Chelan loop** is 90 miles along the Columbia River and Lake Entiat. It goes north on Route 2 from East Wenatchee, then north on Route 151 to Chelan Station, across the Columbia River, then south on Route 97 to Wenatchee again.

Bike Rentals **Leavenworth Outfitters** rents mountain bikes and offers guided tours. They can also arrange to shuttle you and your rental up into the Cascades for a 25-mile downhill cruise back into town. ~ 21312 Route 207, Leavenworth; 509-763-3733, 800-347-7934; www.thrillmakers.com.

HIKING

The Cascades are a backpacker's paradise laced with thousands of miles of maintained trails. All distances listed are one way unless otherwise noted.

NORTH CASCADES The **Pacific Crest National Scenic Trail** (480 miles) has its northern terminus just north of Washington at the Canadian border. It is a hard hike in many places but can be broken into easier chunks, such as from Stevens Pass to Snoqualmie Pass. Contact the **National Forest Service and National Park Service Outdoor Information Center** for further details. ~ REI building, 222 Yale Avenue North, Seattle; 206-470-4060.

The **Heliotrope Ridge Trail** (2.7 miles) leads to a precipice where you can look down on Coleman Glacier. This popular hike has three hazardous stream crossings and can be accessed from Road 39 at Heliotrope Ridge, just east of the town of Glacier. Purchase a one-day trail parking pass before parking at the trailhead. Contact the visitors center for more information (360-856-5700).

In Ross Lake Recreation Area, try the hike up Desolation Peak on the **East Bank Trail** (19.3 miles from the highway). The views of the surrounding mountains and Ross Lake are spectacular.

Perhaps the most historic route in the North Cascades is **Cascade Pass Trail** (3.5 miles), the American Indians' route across the mountains for centuries. It is also a route from Marblemount to Stehekin (9 miles), if you want to really make a trip of it.

Beat writer Jack Kerouac spent a summer at the lookout tower atop Desolation Peak.

All along **Route 20** are signs for trailheads—all are worth exploring. The signs show the destination and distance of each trail.

For a long trip—allow three or four days—**Image Lake** (16 miles) is considered one of the most beautiful in the Central Cascades. The lake mirrors Glacier Peak, the most remote and inaccessible of the Washington volcanoes.

METHOW VALLEY   **Goat Peak Trail** (2.5 miles) leads to a 7001-foot summit that has a staffed lookout tower. The fairly steep trail starts from a Forest Service road near Mazama; it is hikeable only from July through September. Contact the Methow Valley Visitors Center for information (509-996-4000).

LEAVENWORTH AREA   **Icicle Gorge Trail** (3.5 miles roundtrip) is an interpretive loop trail a short distance west of Leavenworth.

Enchantment Lakes (18 miles) is Washington's most beloved backpacking trip because the lakes are so otherworldly. They are approached from Icicle Creek near Leavenworth. The hike is a hard one, and permits must be obtained through the Leavenworth Ranger Station (509-548-6977).

ROUTE 90 CORRIDOR   **Iron Horse Trail State Park** (113 miles) is a former railroad right-of-way that is used by hikers, horse riders, cross-country skiers and bicyclists. No motorized vehicles are allowed on the trail, which goes from North Bend over Snoqualmie Pass to Vantage.

MT. RAINIER AREA   **Wonderland Trail** (93 miles) goes entirely around Mt. Rainier and can be made in stages ranging from the 6.5-mile section between Longmire and Paradise to the 39-mile section from Carbon River to Longmire.

Northern Loop Trail (34 miles roundtrip) runs through the wilderness with frequent views of the mountain between Carbon River and Sunrise.

MT. ST. HELENS AREA   **Klickitat Trail** (17 miles) takes you through a remote part of the Gifford Pinchot National Forest and is part of an old American Indian trail network. For more information contact Randle Ranger Station, one mile east of Randle on Route 12; 360-497-1100.

Willard Springs Trail (3 miles) winds through the **Conboy Lake National Wildlife Refuge** just south of Glenwood. It skirts the lake, which is dry in summer, and passes back through Ponderosa pines.

Indian Heaven (13 miles) is a beautiful section of the Pacific Crest National Scenic Trail that people return to again and again. It is near Trout Lake and goes past numerous lakes reflecting the surrounding mountains.

Transportation

CAR

Route 542 travels east from Bellingham through Glacier to dead-end at Mt. Baker Lodge. Route 20, also known as the North Cascades Highway, is one of the state's most popular highways and goes east from Route 5 at Burlington to the Methow Valley. Route 2, one of the last intercontinental, two-lane, blacktop highways, runs from Everett to Maine and is called the Stevens Pass Highway in Washington. From Seattle, Route 90 goes over Snoqualmie Pass to Cle Elum and Ellensburg.

AIR

Only one airport, Pangborn Memorial Airport in Wenatchee, serves this large area, and only one carrier, Horizon Airlines, offers scheduled service. The roadless Lake Chelan area is served by Chelan Airways, which makes scheduled and charter flights between Chelan and Stehekin.

FERRY

The Lady of the Lake provides daily transportation between Chelan, Manson, Fields Point, Prince Creek, Lucerne, Moore and Stehekin. Reduced service from November to mid-March. You can also catch the smaller Lady Express, which has fewer stops but faster service. The *Lady Express* also runs in the winter except on Tuesday, Thursday and Saturday. ~ 1418 West Woodin Avenue, Chelan; 509-682-4584.

BUS

Greyhound Bus Lines (800-231-2222) offers service to Leavenworth and Wenatchee and a stop in Cashmere. The Wenatchee station is at 300 South Columbia Street, 509-662-2183; while the Centralia/Chehalis Station is at 1232 Mellen Street, Centralia, 360-736-9811.

Link Transit serves Cashmere, Chelan, Dryden, East Wenatchee, Entiat, Leavenworth, Malaga, Manson, Monitor, Orondo, Peshastin, Rock Island, Waterville and Wenatchee. ~ 509-662-1155.

TRAIN

Amtrak travels from Seattle, Portland and Spokane to Wenatchee via the "Empire Builder." ~ 800-872-7245.

CAR RENTALS

At the Wenatchee airport are Budget Rent A Car (800-527-0700) and Hertz Rent A Car (800-654-3131. In Wenatchee are Hertz Rent A Car (800-654-3131) and U-Save Auto Rental (509-663-0587, 800-972-2298). Ellensburg has Budget Rent A Car (800-527-0700).

NINE

East of the Cascades

 If state boundaries were determined by similar geography, customs and attitude, Washington and Oregon as we know them would simply not exist. Instead, they'd be split into two more states using the crest of the Cascades as the dividing line or would run vertically from California on the south to Canada on the north with one state taking either side of the mountain range.

Well, who ever said life was perfect? So what we have is a state whose eastern and western halves bear almost no resemblance to each other. From the Cascades west, the land is damp, the forests thick and the climate temperate. The eastern side of the range is almost exactly the opposite: Very little rain falls and most crops are irrigated by water from the Columbia Basin Project created by Grand Coulee Dam, or by water from deep wells. Here, the winters are cold and the summers are hot.

If urban amenities such as hotels, finer restaurants, theater and shopping centers are what you're after, head to eastern Washington's larger cities—Spokane, Walla Walla, the Tri-Cities and Yakima. Elsewhere, you'll find RV parks and inexpensive but clean motels. On the lakes and streams are rustic resorts, some with log cabins.

Away from the cities, hunting and fishing abound. Many streams and lakes are stocked regularly with trout, and a few sturgeon are still caught in the Snake and Columbia rivers. Deer, elk and an occasional black bear are popular quarry, as are waterfowl, pheasant, grouse and quail. Don't be startled while driving along a mountain road during hunting season if you spot someone in camouflage clothing carrying a rifle emerging from the forest.

Some of the most interesting geology in North America is found in this part of Washington due to its tortured creation by volcanoes, lava flows through vast fissures and floods gigantic beyond imagining. Throughout this region you will find vivid reminders of this creation process, like the dramatic Coulee Country along the Columbia River and the beautiful Palouse Country with its steep, rolling hills. One stretch of landscape of unusual origin is the Channeled Scablands south and west of Spokane, which was created by floods from a lake formed at the end of the last ice age in the valley around Missoula, Montana.

The forests are mainly pine with little underbrush. Along some parts of the eastern slope of the Cascades, you will find larch, the only species of coniferous trees that are deciduous. They are brilliantly colored in the fall and stand out as vividly as sumac and maples in the dark-green forest.

East of the mountains is another treasure: peace and quiet. There are lonesome roads undulating off into the distance, small rivers stocked with trout, open pine forests, vast lakes made by man, and mornings so tranquil you can hear a door slam a mile away.

As is the case across much of America, the general rule here is that the smaller the town, the friendlier the people. Don't be surprised if folks stop to talk about anything or nothing in particular. Another plus is that you'll find nearly everything is less expensive than along the coast.

Traveling these remote areas you will have a continual sense of discovery as you visit places barely large enough to get themselves onto state maps. And you will find small towns that don't bother opening tourist bureaus but have a clean motel, a good café, friendly people to talk to and a small city park for your picnic.

A few remnants of the pioneer years still remain standing in eastern Washington. Here and there you'll see the remains of a cabin with perhaps the tall tripod of a windmill where a homesteader tried but failed to "prove up" the land given him by the Homestead Act. You'll also see remains of ghost towns (although some have been rediscovered and are peopled again). Most of these towns were built at or near mines and abandoned when the mines began coughing up only rocks and sand.

To help you explore this fascinating eastern strip of Washington, which extends from the Canadian border on the north to the Columbia Gorge that separates Washington from Oregon on the south, we've divided this chapter into the following sections:

The Okanogan Highlands, often called the Okanogan Country or simply the Okanogan, has boundaries that are fairly easy to determine: Route 97 to the west, the Canadian border to the north, the Columbia River on the east and the Colville Indian Reservation on the south.

Grand Coulee area includes all the Columbia River system from where it swings west at the southern end of the Colville Indian Reservation and follows past Grand Coulee Dam south to the Vantage–Wanapum Dam area, where the Columbia enters the Hanford Nuclear Reservation.

The Spokane area covers the only true metropolitan center east of the Cascades.

Southeastern Washington encompasses the famed Palouse Hills between Spokane and Pullman; the Snake River town of Clarkston; Walla Walla; the Tri-Cities of Pasco, Kennewick and Richland; and Yakima and the agricultural and wine-producing valley of the same name.

Okanogan Highlands

One of the pleasures of touring the Okanogan Country is simply driving down country roads to see where they lead. A number of ghost towns, some no more than a decaying log cabin today, dot the map.

Most visitors enter the Okanogan Country from Route 97, the north–south corridor that runs up the Columbia River Valley to Bridgeport, then follows the Okanogan River Valley north toward Canada. This is desertlike country with irrigated orchards on either side of the highway and open range climbing back up the mountains.

First, contact the **Omak Visitor Information Center** for brochures and maps. ~ 401 Omak Avenue, Omak; 509-826-1880, fax 509-826-6201; www.omakchronicle.com/omakchamber. The **Okanogan County Historical Museum**, also headquarters for the county historical society, has a collection of American

SIGHTS

Washington East of the Cascades

CANADA
UNITED STATES

Oroville

Wauconda

Tonasket

Republic

Kettle Falls

Colville

Omak

Okanogan

CASCADE RANGE

Lake Chelan

Pateros

Franklin Roosevelt Lake

Columbia

Grand Coulee

Coulee Dam

Spokane River

Chelan

Banks Lake

Spokane

Coulee City

Davenport

Wenatchee

Soap Lake

Quincy

Moses Lake

George

Ritzville

Potholes Reservoir

WASHINGTON

Pullman

Columbia

Yakima

Snake River

Toppenish

Richland Pasco

Dayton

Clarkston Lewiston

Kennewick

Walla Walla

N

OREGON

Goldendale

Columbia River

0   100 miles

0   100 kilometers

Pendleton

Indian artifacts, pioneer farm and ranch implements and historical photos. This is also a good place to start your travels because members of the volunteer staff have lived in the region for many years and know where everything is, including skeletons in the county's closets. Open Memorial Day to Labor Day and by appointment in the winter. Admission. ~ 1410 Second Street, Okanogan; 509-422-4272; e-mail ochm@mncdata.com.

HIDDEN ▶

Northwest of Omak is a region that was a silver mining area in the 1880s. Here, adventurers will find the remote town site for the short-lived **Ruby**. Named for either the type of silver prospectors hoped to find there or for a prospector's girlfriend or prostitute, the site has no structures left, only foundations and wagon roads. ~ Salmon Creek Road, 10 to 15 miles northwest of Omak.

West of Oroville, is **Nighthawk**, which was a ghost town until recently. The paved county road, which heads west from Route 97 near the Canadian border, curves along the Similkameen River Valley, then swings south into a valley between the mountains of the Pasayten Wilderness of the North Cascades National Park and a series of steep ridges to the east. This area is dotted with old mines, some still worked from time to time, but most of the land along the valley floor and stretching up the hillsides a few hundred feet has been turned into orchards or expanses of alfalfa with grazing cattle. Nighthawk now has two permanent residences, but mostly consists of a historic old store, post office, hotel and pink house from the few-year boom when prospectors found precious metals there in the 1890s. **Loomis**, the other mining town farther south on this loop drive, is no longer a ghost town. The highway passes Palmer Lake and Spectacle Lake, both of which have public beaches, before rejoining Route 97.

HIDDEN ▶

One of the most interesting drives is to **Molson**, a ghost town 15 miles east of Oroville off Route 97 near the Canadian border. Molson was founded when a nearby mine was attracting hundreds of prospectors and workers. Owing to a land-claim mix-up, a farmer took over the whole town, so a new one had to be built and it was named New Molson. The two towns, less than a mile apart, fought over everything except education for their children. They built a school halfway between the towns, and it became Center Molson. Today **Old Molson** is an outdoor museum with one historic building, two homesteads, sheds, early 1900s machinery, a steam engine and more. The **Center Molson school building** has three stories of artifacts and a tea room. Open in the summer. ~ Information, 509-485-3292 (ask for Mary Louis Lowe).

Route 20 is one of Washington's best highways for leisurely rural driving, especially as it traverses the Okanogan Country on its way to the Idaho border. It comes in from the Cascades to Omak-Okanogan, joins Route 97 north to Tonasket, swings east across the heart of the highlands through Wauconda and Republic, crosses the Columbia River at Kettle Falls and continues on to Tiger, where it follows the Pend Oreille River south to the Idaho border at Newport. There it disappears. The highway follows the path of least resistance beside streams and along valleys where ranches stretch off across rolling hills that disappear in pine forests. ~ Main Street, Okanogan.

Heading east from Tonasket, the first notable town you'll come to is **Republic**. Created by a gold rush in the late 1890s, Republic still hosts operative gold mines, such as Echo Bay mine a short distance outside town. The **Stonerose Interpretive Center** lets ◀ **HIDDEN** visitors dig for fossils on a hillside on the edge of Republic. The site is named for an extinct rose fossil found there. Closed November through April; closed Monday year-round and Sunday in summer. Admission to fossil test site only. ~ 509-775-2295; www. stonerosefossil.org.

Continue eastward and you'll reach a historical site called **St. Paul's Mission** where Route 395 crosses the Columbia River. It was built as a chapel for American Indians in 1845 and operated until the 1870s. A modest museum is also here. ~ Route 395, Kettle Falls.

In **Colville**, ten miles east of Kettle Falls, several buildings make up the **Keller Historical Park**. Sponsored by the Stevens County Historical Society, the complex has a museum, a fire lookout tower, Colville's first schoolhouse, a trapper's cabin, a blacksmith shop, mine, farmstead, cabin, machine shop, salt mill and the 1910 home of the pioneer Keller family complete with original furniture. Open summer to the public and by appointment the rest of the year. ~ 700 North Wynne Street, Colville; 509-684-5968.

Okanogan Highlands

LODGING   Surrounded by 178 acres of meadows, woods and orchards, **Amy's Manor** provides bed-and-breakfast lodging in a 1928 gray stucco home with green shutters. Three guest rooms upstairs provide river views and are adorned with queen-size beds. Small sitting areas are furnished with antiques from the home's original owner. Downstairs is a living area with a fireplace where breakfasts made with ingredients picked from the surrounding orchards and organic vegetable garden are served. ~ 435 Route 153, four and a half miles north of Pateros; 509-923-2334, 888-923-2334, fax 509-923-2691; www.amysmanor.com. MODERATE.

The most modern motel in Okanogan is the **Okanogan Cedars Inn**. It has 78 rooms (including two suites and four rooms with kitchenettes), an unpretentious dining room, lounge and heated swimming pool. ~ Appleway Street and Route 97, Okanogan; 509-422-6431, fax 509-422-4214. MODERATE.

A cheaper Okanogan motel is the **Ponderosa Motor Lodge** downtown, an older but clean one-story motel of basic design with a pool. ~ 1034 South 2nd Avenue, Okanogan; 509-422-0400, 800-732-6702, fax 509-422-4206; www.okanogan.net/ponderosa. BUDGET.

The **U and I Motel** has nine small "cabinettes" with rustic paneling; each unit has a microwave and refrigerator. They come with deck chairs, so you can sit and look across a lawn and flower garden to the Okanogan River. ~ 838 2nd Avenue, Okanogan; 509-422-2920. BUDGET.

One of the few bed and breakfasts in these parts is the **Hidden Hills Guest Ranch**, a Victorian-style inn surrounded by fields of wildflowers and pine trees. The ten guest rooms, most of which offer mountain views, have a turn-of-the-20th-century feel with flocked wallpaper, pedestal sinks, brass beds and gleaming woodwork. Full breakfast. ~ 104 Hidden Hills Lane, Tonasket; phone/fax 509-486-1895; www.hidden-hills.net. MODERATE.

Several small resorts are scattered along lakes in the area. Among them is the **Bonaparte Lake Resort**. This resort, 26 miles from both Republic and Tonasket, has ten airy and clean log cabins along the lake shore. Only one—called, of all things, the Penthouse—has a bathroom, bedding, towels and kitchen supplies. There are public showers and bathroom. ~ 695 Bonaparte Lake Road, Tonasket; 509-486-2828, fax 509-486-1987. BUDGET.

In Omak are several small, inexpensive motels including the **Omak Lodge**, which has rooms with jacuzzis. ~ 122 North Main Street, Omak; 509-826-0400, 888-700-6625, fax 509-826-5635. BUDGET. The **Leisure Village Motel** is also a clean, basic motel. ~ 630 Okoma Drive, Omak; 509-826-4442, 800-427-4495. BUDGET.

A mile east of Kettle Falls on Route 395 is **My Parent's Estate Bed and Breakfast**, one of the first bed and breakfasts in this part of the state. It formerly was a residential school in 1869, then a

CHAPTER FAVORITES

To feel like a millionaire while exploring eastern Washington's "Inland Empire," I indulge in the fabulous Sunday champagne buffet brunch at **Patsy Clark's**, a magnificent old mansion turned into a restaurant. *page 329*

A life-size diorama that fires my imagination is the **Yakama Nation Cultural Center**'s depiction of Yakama Indians catching salmon by hand at Celilo Falls. Imagining is all one can do since the falls vanished when The Dalles Dam was constructed and the Indians turned to growing asparagus and hops. *page 335*

Maybe you can't go home again, but I always return to **My Parents' Estate Bed & Breakfast** for a dose of rural living in Oregon's outback. The perfect starry nights and fresh pastoral mornings make me long for the country childhood I never had. *page 316*

Snow lovers swear that winter is the best season to visit **Mt. Spokane State Park** to sample its awesome ski trails. But I prefer the spring, when the mountain comes alive with birdsong and I can hike for miles through flower-covered fields. *page 331*

Catholic mission with a convent added later, then a boys' school. It offers three rooms with baths, queen-size beds and central air conditioning, plus a suite next to the gymnasium (separate from the main house) with a kitchenette, clawfoot tub and a view of Mingo Mountain. Each room is named for its period decor and furnishings: Queen Anne Lace, English Cottage and French Country. Included on the 47 acres are a gazebo, a gymnasium, a pond and a trail to the Colville River. ~ 719 Route 395, Kettle Falls; 509-738-6220. BUDGET TO MODERATE.

DINING

Basic, standard fare is pretty much the order of the day here. For starters, there is the **Cedars Inn Restaurant and Lounge**, which serves adequate, straightforward lunches and dinners and farmer-sized breakfasts. ~ Appleway Street and Route 97, Okanogan; 509-422-6431, fax 509-422-4214. BUDGET TO MODERATE.

For some local color and reasonable prices, try **Judy's Cafe**. This is a place where you can have an old-fashioned breakfast and lunch—complete with homemade soups and famous burgers—while listening to the auctioneer selling horses and cattle. Breakfast and lunch only. Closed Saturday through Tuesday. ~ Okanogan Livestock Market, Okanogan; 509-422-3660, fax 509-422-3717. BUDGET.

The choices are fewer in Omak, but one café and bakery that rates high is the antique-decorated **Breadline Café**, where lunch features big sandwiches on whole-grain breads and dinner includes shrimp Creole, jambalaya, mushroom marinara over pasta and pork loin medallion. Closed Sunday and Monday. ~ 102 South Ash Street, Omak; 509-826-5836. MODERATE.

Omak's **North Country Pub** serves nothing fancy—burgers, steaks, tacos and barbecue—but it's solid, filling food. The lunch specials are usually pretty good, and if you're there on a Thursday night, the steak special is a bargain. ~ 15 South Main, Omak; 509-826-4271. BUDGET.

One of the few deluxe dining choices in the region is provided by **Hidden Hills Resort**. This contemporary hotel has created a dining room built to resemble an 1890s mansion. The large room overlooks a mountain range and is handsomely decorated with cherry and maple furnishings, China cabinets and fringed lamps. The menu offers just one multicourse dinner selection that changes every night. Steaks and chicken breast are among the possibilities. ~ 104 Hidden Hills Lane, Tonasket; phone/fax 509-486-1895. DELUXE.

One of the more interesting places to stop for a snack or downhome American meal is **Wauconda**, the one-store town on Route 20 east of Tonasket. A breakfast and lunch counter to the left of the door is between the cash register and a smaller dining room with a few booths overlooking a valley and low mountains beyond. The food is uncomplicated and hearty, and the portions are generous, especially the Chinese food on Friday and Saturday. ~ 2360 Route 20, Wauconda; 509-486-4010. BUDGET TO MODERATE.

SHOPPING Omak's Main Street provides a few good browsing spots such as **Mustard Seed Gallery & Gifts**, which features artwork by local artists, plus crafts and collectibles. ~ 21 North Main Street, Omak; 509-826-2463. In the same block is **Lampe Jewelers**, known for custom-made gold and silver jewelry. ~ 26 North Main Street, Omak; 509-826-1280.

IT'S ALL RECENT HISTORY

Compared with the rest of the country, Washington's history is both recent and benign. The Northwest is so newly settled that East Coast visitors look askance when they find that the major cities weren't founded until the latter part of the 19th century. Very little recorded history goes back before 1800; the Lewis and Clark Expedition of 1804–1806 was the first overland crossing between the original 13 states and the Pacific Coast, and they were the first to describe the lower Snake River.

Western wear of all kinds plus handcrafted silver jewelry, Pendleton blankets and saddles are stock and trade at the **Detros Western Store**, a few miles north of Omak in Riverside. ~ 107 Main Street, Riverside; 509-826-2200.

You don't have many retail options in the small town of Oroville. However, **Prince's Center** may be all you need (or find). Half of Prince's is devoted to groceries; the other side carries general merchandise—everything from footwear and apparel to toys and garden tools. ~ 1000 23rd Avenue, Oroville; 509-476-3651.

Most nightlife in this cowboy and fruit-picking area is limited to taverns, a few of which have live bands on weekends and during the Omak Stampede, the rodeo held each August.

NIGHTLIFE

Big-screen TV, pool, darts, karaoke on weekends and beer on tap are provided by **Shorthorn Tavern** in downtown Omak. ~ 3 North Main Street, Omak; 509-826-0338.

CONCONULLY STATE PARK Strung along the edge of the town of the same name, this site is popular with boaters, swimmers, families and anglers seeking kokonee, large- and small-mouth bass, rainbow trout, German brown trout and Eastern brook trout. For hikers, there is a nature trail. Other facilities here include picnic areas, restrooms, a children's play area and a wading pool. ~ Located 15 to 20 miles northwest of Omak on Conconully-Okanogan Highway; 509-826-7408.

PARKS

▲ There are 71 standard sites, $10 per night; 10 utility sites with water only. Closed weekdays in winter except holidays or by appointment.

OSOYOOS LAKE STATE PARK This lakeshore park is one mile north of Oroville and stretches along the southern end of Osoyoos Lake. It has some of the few trees in the area for shade while picnicking and camping and is the most popular state park in the area. It is heavily used by Canadians and Americans alike since it is almost on the Canadian border. For nature lovers, the lake is a prime nesting area for Canadian geese; for anglers, this is a year-round spot for trout and spiny ray. Facilities are limited to picnic areas and restrooms. Closed weekdays (except holidays) in winter. ~ Located on the northern end of Oroville on Route 97; 509-476-3321.

▲ There are 87 developed sites; $11 per night. Reservations, 800-452-5687.

CURLEW LAKE STATE PARK This 128-acre setting is on the southeastern shore of a lake in a pine forest with several islands. Remnants of homesteaders' cabins can be seen near the park, and a large variety of animals, including chipmunks, squirrels and deer, lives in the area. Several species of birds also can be seen. The park is surrounded by Colville National Forest. Picnic area and restrooms are the facilities here. Closed October through April. ~ Located ten miles north of Republic on Route 21; 509-775-3592, fax 509-775-3592.

▲ There are 57 standard sites and 25 with RV hookups; $10 to $15 per night.

Grand Coulee Area

The centerpiece of the Grand Coulee Area, not surprisingly, is Grand Coulee Dam with its spectacular laser light shows during the summer months. The sheer mass of the dam is almost overwhelming and for decades was the largest concrete structure in the world.

Also of interest are the many lakes created by the dam that have become some of the Northwest's most popular recreation areas. The backwaters of the dam itself, named in honor of President Franklin D. Roosevelt, reach far north nearly to the Canadian border and east into the Spokane River system. A chain of lakes and some smaller dams were built to hold irrigation water for distribution south and east of the dam. These include Banks Lake and the Potholes Reservoir, known as the Winchester Wasteway. Don't be put off by the name—wasteway refers to the water that has been used for irrigation and has seeped along bedrock to emerge again ready for reuse. These lakes continue south to the Crab Creek Valley before re-entering the Columbia River below Vantage.

SIGHTS
Grand Coulee Dam was built in the 1930s and memorialized by the songs of Woody Guthrie. The area that became known as the Columbia Basin was so barren before the dam that locals liked to say you had to prime yourself to spit and that jackrabbits crossing the basin had to carry canteens. The dam was the largest concrete pour in the world for many decades after its completion at the beginning of World War II. It stands 550 feet above bedrock, as tall as a 46-story building, and at 5223 feet is nearly a mile long. While its 12 million cubic yards of concrete may be difficult to imagine, the Bureau of Reclamation points out that this is enough to build a standard six-foot-wide sidewalk around the world at the equator. ~ 509-633-9265, fax 509-633-9138.

In addition to powering the hydroelectric system with the 151-mile-long Lake Roosevelt, the dam serves the additional purpose of irrigating more than 500,000 acres. Water is pumped 280 feet up the canyon wall to fill Banks Lake's reservoir, from which the water is moved through canals and pipes to the area's farmland.

Visitors are welcome at the dam and can go on guided tours. One of the most popular events is the nightly **laser show**, a free, 40-minute demonstration that uses the spillway of the dam for its screen. It is shown nightly from Memorial Day through September. ~ 509-633-9265, fax 509-633-9138.

In Coulee Dam, the **Colville Tribal Museum and Gift Shop** displays authentic village and fishing scenes, coins and metals dating from the 1800s and many ancient artifacts. The gift shop sells local beadwork and other artwork by tribal members. Open May through September ~ 502 6th Street, Coulee Dam; 509-633-0751.

The best way to appreciate the stark beauty of the Grand Coulee Area is to drive south from the dam on Route 155 along **Banks Lake**. The artificial lake is used for all water sports, and its color and character change dramatically with the time of day and weather.

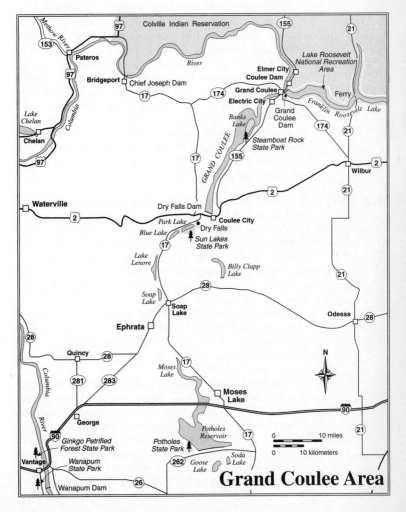

Grand Coulee Area

At Coulee City you come to the **Dry Falls Dam**, which holds Banks Lake water and sends it on south into a system of canals. Pinto Ridge Road heads due south from Coulee City and passes **Summer Lake**, a favorite picnic spot. The falls are created by the irrigation water from Banks Lake.

The main route out of Coulee City is across Dry Falls Dam, then south on Route 17 past Dry Falls and Sun Lakes State Park, along a series of smaller lakes in the coulees—Park Lake, Blue Lake, Lake Lenore (where you can see the form of a small rhinoceros that was trapped in a prehistoric lava flow) and finally to Soap Lake.

Soap Lake was so named because the water used to foam before the ground water rose. The water is rich in minerals—sodium, chloride, carbonate, sulfate, bicarbonate and plenty of others— and matches the contents of water in the Baden Baden Spa in Germany. It has attracted a number of motels that pump water for use in the rooms or into spas where people go to soak themselves seeking comfort for a variety of skin, muscle and bone afflictions.

South of Soap Lake the coulees flatten out, and the landscape away from the Columbia River becomes the gently rolling wheat-growing region. **Moses Lake** in the center of the Columbia Basin, is better known as a hub for farmers of the basin than as a tourist destination. The lake for which the town is named joins the Potholes Reservoir to the south.

LODGING If you want a room with a view, there are two good places near the dam. The **Columbia River Inn** is right across the street from Grand Coulee Dam. Most rooms have a view of the spillway, and nightly laser light shows are across the street in the summer. The motel has 35 rooms and an outdoor pool with a hot tub. Two rooms have jacuzzis, and you pay for it. ~ 10 Lincoln Street, Coulee Dam; 509-633-2100, 800-633-6421, fax 509-633-2633; www.columbiariverinn.com. MODERATE.

The other is **Coulee House Motel**, which is up a hill and provides a top-notch view. It has clean, unremarkable rooms and a swimming pool and hot tub. ~ 110 Roosevelt Way, Coulee Dam; 509-633-1101, 800-715-7767, fax 509-633-1416; www.coulee house.com. MODERATE.

Four Winds Guest House is a large, wood-frame Cape Cod–style bed and breakfast across the street from the former Chief Engineer's office for the Grand Coulee Dam construction project. It was built as a rooming house for engineers while the dam was being built in the 1930s. All guest rooms have furniture from that period, and all have washbasins. Two rooms have a shared bath and one room has a private bath; otherwise, the separate men's and women's dormitory-style bathrooms are at the end of the hall.

"World-famous" breakfast included. ~ 301 Lincoln Street, Coulee Dam; 509-633-3146, 800-786-3146, fax 509-633-2454; e-mail fourwind@televar.com. MODERATE.

Several budget-priced motels and resorts are located near Banks Lake and Lake Roosevelt. **Ala Cozy**, a mile and a half from the marina at the end of Banks Lake, offers ten motel-style units with private bathrooms and refrigerators. There's a pool on the premises. ~ 9988 Route 2 East, Coulee City; 509-632-5703, fax 509-632-5483. BUDGET.

In Soap Lake, **Notaras Lodge** is the best-known and most modern motel in town. The three-building complex plus restaurant has ten rooms, five of which have jacuzzis. The rooms boast unusual decor, with names like the "Old Mexico" room—with a red roof, stucco walls and wrought-iron balcony—and the "bunk house," complete with a wooden pack horse saddle and a 1900 cistern pump that turns the water on for the copper kettle sink. The accommodations are spacious and equipped with microwave ovens, refrigerators and breakfast nooks. Massages, whirlpool therapy and mineral baths in Soap Lake water are available. ~ 242 Main Street, Soap Lake; 509-246-0462, fax 509-246-1054. MODERATE.

Moses Lake is one of the most popular RV destinations in the central part of the state because several lakes are in the immediate vicinity, and hot, sunny weather is almost guaranteed. Several motels are also along the Route 90 corridor and the lake, including the **Best Western Hallmark Inn**, which has 161 units right on Moses Lake. In addition to boating and waterskiing, right off the dock, the motel has tennis courts, a heated pool and a sauna. ~ 3000 West Marina Drive, Moses Lake; 509-765-9211, 800-235-4255, fax 509-766-0493; www.hallmarkinns.com. MODERATE TO DELUXE.

The **Lakeshore Motel** is also on the lake, where a marina and waterskiing are available. The motel has 24 units, nine housekeeping cabins and a heated pool. ~ 3206 West Lakeshore Drive, Moses Lake; 509-765-9201, fax 509-765-1800. BUDGET.

COULEE CAN BE CONFUSING

This area is frequently baffling to visitors because of the similarity of place names. The towns of Coulee Dam and Grand Coulee are at the site of Grand Coulee Dam itself, while Coulee City is 30 miles away at the southern end of Banks Lake. In the same area are still two more small towns with names that often get confused: Elmer City and Electric City.

DINING   A well-known eatery in this region is the **Melody Restaurant &
Lounge.** With views of the Grand Coulee Dam and its summer laser
light show, the Melody offers standard American fare, seafood and
pasta. Breakfast, lunch and dinner. ~ 512 River Drive, Coulee
Dam; 509-633-1151, fax 509-633-2925. BUDGET TO MODERATE.

If you want Asian food, **Siam Palace** will have it. Thai, Chinese
and American dishes are served. Closed Sunday and Monday. ~
213 Main Street, Grand Coulee; 509-633-2921. BUDGET.

A light-filled, contemporary restaurant built of native stone,
Michael's at the Lake offers both indoor and outdoor dining. A
spacious deck overlooks Moses Lake. Prime rib, hamburgers, Oriental chicken salad and home-style desserts like apple crisp are especially popular here. ~ 910 West Broadway, Moses Lake; 509-
765-1611, fax 509-766-2804. MODERATE TO DELUXE.

SHOPPING   The **Colville Tribal Museum, Gallery and Gift Shop** sells local
beadwork and other items crafted by the tribal members. ~ 502
6th Street, Coulee Dam; 509-633-0751.

NIGHTLIFE   **Moses Lake** has a series of free concerts, all beginning at 8 p.m.,
on most Saturdays from July to September, in its 3000 capacity
outdoor amphitheater on the lakeshore. Nationally known musicians perform here. ~ Located 49 miles south of Coulee City;
509-765-7888, 800-992-6234.

PARKS   **LAKE ROOSEVELT NATIONAL RECREATION AREA** 🎣 🚴 🐎
🛶 ⛵ 🏊 🚣 🏄 🚤 ⚓ This area stretches 151 miles along the
entire length of Lake Roosevelt, including parts of the Spokane
and Kettle rivers. Owing to the arid climate, the lake has miles and
miles of sandy beaches and outcroppings of dramatic rocks. Only
when you get close to the Spokane River do trees begin appearing along the shoreline. It is a particular favorite for waterskiers.
Sailing and windsurfing are also popular activities. More than 30
species of fish are found here, including walleye, rainbow trout,

WHERE WATER WORKS

You may think of Washington as a rainy place, but without Grand Coulee
Dam and the string of smaller dams that came along later to turn the
Columbia and Snake rivers into a series of lakes, eastern Washington
would be barren. Instead, in this part of the state one of the most common scenes is an irrigation sprinkler going about its business of turning
the sand into a rich soil that grows wheat, wine grapes, fruit, soybeans,
barley, oats, rape, grass seed, corn, alfalfa, potatoes, peas and a host of
other crops.

sturgeon, yellow perch and kokanee, the land-locked salmon. There are only picnic areas. ~ The lake can be accessed from Grand Coulee and Davenport in the South and Kettle Falls to the north; 509-633-9441, 800-824-4916 for lake levels, fax 509-633-9332.

▲ There are 27 campgrounds with over 200 sites; $10 per night.

STEAMBOAT ROCK STATE PARK

This is one of Washington's most popular state parks and thus is one of the many parks where camping-space reservations are a necessity. The park is on the shores of Banks Lake at the foot of the butte by the same name. The ship-shaped butte rises 700 feet above the lake and has a good trail to the 640-acre flat top. Fishing for bass, walleye, trout, crappie, kokanee and perch is good year-round, and it's a popular place to ice fish. You'll find picnic tables, playground equipment, a bathhouse and a snack bar. ~ Located 13 miles south of Grand Coulee on Route 155; 509-633-1934, fax 509-633-1294.

▲ There are 92 primitive walk-in campsites, 26 standard sites, 12 boat-access sites and 100 sites with hookups. Fees are $5 to $16 per night plus a $6 reservation fee per site. Reservations must be obtained by contacting Reservations Northwest. ~ 800-452-5687.

SUN LAKES STATE PARK

This park is located on the floor of the coulee that was scoured out when the Columbia River's normal course was blocked by ice and debris at the end of the Ice Age. The river, three miles wide, flowed over nearby 400-foot-high Dry Falls, which was the original name of the state park but was changed because of the lakes and recreation. It is now home to boating, riding, jetskiing, hiking and golfing. Picnic areas and restrooms are here. Included in the park is Camp Delaney, an environmental learning center with a capacity of 84 people. ~ Located seven miles southwest of Coulee City on Route 17.

▲ There are 174 sites and 18 with RV hookups; $11 to $16 per night. Note: A private concessionaire (Sun Lakes Park Resort, 34228 Park Lake Road Northeast, Coulee City, WA 99115; 509-632-5291; www.sunlakesparkresort.com) operates a portion of the park and offers 50 cabins ($69 to $77 per night for three to four people), ten mobile homes ($108 per night for up to six people) and 112 full hookups ($22 to $24 per night). There's a general store, a snack bar, a heated swimming pool, boat rentals and marina, laundry and a nine-hole golf course.

POTHOLES STATE PARK

The potholes were created when water from the Columbia Basin Project seeped in to fill depressions around the coarse sand dunes in the area. Now the dunes stand above the water level and are used for campsites, bird blinds and picnic areas. The area supports a large population of waterfowl and other birds, including blue herons, white pelicans, sand-hill cranes, hawks and eagles. A lawn and shade trees, tables and stoves are beside the lake. Rainbow trout, bass, perch, crappie, bluegill and walleye are found in the park. There are restrooms and showers. ~ Located on Route 262, 17 miles southwest of Moses Lake; 509-346-2759, fax 360-664-8112.

▲ There are 126 sites: 66 for tents, 60 with RV hookups; $7 to $16 per night. For reservations, call 800-452-5687.

GINKGO PETRIFIED FOREST STATE PARK 🏃 More than 200 species of fossilized trees have been identified in this area of barren hillsides and lava flows, making it one of the largest fossil forests in the world. The park has an interpretive center overlooking the Columbia River with a wide selection of petrified wood and also has a one-mile interpretive hiking trail. No camping, fishing or swimming are permitted at Ginkgo, but you can head four and a half miles south on the Columbia River to **Wanapum State Park**. It also has hiking trails, swimming, canoeing and kayaking. You may fish for trout, salmon, walleye or steelhead and boat ramps are available. There are picnic areas and restrooms. ~ Located on the edge of Vantage, a tiny town on Route 90 where it crosses the Columbia River; 509-856-2700, fax 509-856-2294.

▲ Wanapum State Park has 50 sites with utilities; $15 per night. Call for reservations in the summer, 800-452-5687. Open weekends only in winter.

▼▼▼▼▼▼▼▼▼▼▼▼
Spokane

The northeastern corner of Washington is an area of pine forests, sparkling lakes, sprawling wheat farms and urban pleasures in a rural setting. Spokane is where the Midas-rich miners from Idaho came to live in the late 19th century, so the city has an abundance of historic homes, museums, bed and breakfasts and inns, and one of the most beautiful city park systems in the West.

SIGHTS

The best way to become acquainted with Spokane is to take the self-guided "City Drive Tour" outlined in a brochure from the city that is available in all hotels and at the **Spokane Convention and Visitors Bureau**. ~ 201 West Main Avenue; 509-747-3230, 888-776-5263; www.visitspokane.com.

Another useful brochure is the self-guided tour of historic architecture in downtown Spokane. The "City Drive Tour" takes you along Cliff Drive where many of the finest old homes stand and through **Manito Park**, one of the city's largest parks. Manito Park includes the Japanese Garden built by Spokane's sister city in Japan and the **Duncan Formal Gardens**, whose lush scenery looks like something out of a movie set in 18th-century Europe. ~ Grand Avenue between 17th and 25th avenues.

The tour continues past **Coeur d'Alene Park**, off 2nd Avenue, and the stately **Patsy Clark Mansion** at 2nd Avenue and Hemlock Street. It goes on to the **Northwest Museum of Arts & Culture** with its major collection of regional history and fine art. Closed Monday. Admission. The museum is closed for a major expansion; it will reopen in December 2001. ~ 2316 West 1st Avenue; 509-456-3931, fax 509-363-5303; www.northwestmuseum.org.

Next is **John A. Finch Arboretum**, which features an extensive collection of deciduous and evergreen trees from all over the world. From there the tour leads you back to the downtown area. ~ 3404 West Woodland Boulevard, off Sunset Boulevard; 509-625-6657, fax 509-363-5454.

The city is most proud of its **Riverfront Park** located in the heart of downtown and known for the natural beauty of its waterfall and island. A glorious addition to Spokane built for the 1974 World's Fair, the park has the restored 1909 Looff Carrousel, a gondola skyride over Spokane Falls, various other rides, food concessions and the 70mm IMAX Theater. It also has footpaths, natural amphitheaters, lawns and hills, and always the roar of the waterfall for a backdrop. Admission. ~ 507 North Howard Street; 509-625-6600, fax 509-625-6630; spokaneriverfrontpark.com.

Commemorating Spokane's most famous native son, Gonzaga University's **Bing Crosby Memorabilia Room** is home to the crooner's Oscar, gold records, photographs and other items. ~ 502 East Boone Avenue; 509-328-4220. More memorabilia is on dis-

Spokane

play at the **Gonzaga Alumni Association**, Crosby's boyhood home. ~ 508 East Sharp Street; 509-324-5999.

Another must see is the château-style **Spokane County Courthouse** across the river from downtown. Oddly enough, it was designed in the 1890s by a young man whose only formal training in architecture came from a correspondence course. It is a magnificent conglomeration of towers and turrets, sculpture, iron and brickwork in the French Renaissance manner. ~ Broadway just off Monroe Avenue; 509-456-5790. Occasionally, the director will take people on tours by appointment. Call 509-477-2255 and ask for Wes Whaley, fax 509-477-6447.

Spokane has several wineries with sales and tasting rooms. **Worden Winery** is one of the largest in the area with a capacity of 50,000 gallons. ~ 7217 West 45th Avenue; 509-455-7835.

Arbor Crest Wine Cellars is in a building designated as a National Historic Site on a bluff overlooking the Spokane River. ~ 4705 North Fruithill Road; 509-927-9894.

Latah Creek Wine Cellars has a Spanish-style building with a large courtyard and a tasting room decorated with oak. ~ 13030 East Indiana Avenue; 509-926-0164, fax 509-926-0710; www. latahcreek.com.

Knipprath Cellars is in the downtown area and offers a tasting room decorated with Victorian furnishings. ~ 5634 East Commerce Avenue; 509-534-5121; www.knipprath-cellars.com.

LODGING   Spokane has some pleasant hotels that don't carry big-city rates like those found in Seattle and Portland. You won't find deluxe or luxury accommodations here, but the down-home hospitality of the hotel staffs more than makes up for it.

Two of the largest offer perhaps the best rooms and service. The **Cavanaugh's Ridpath** is an old, yet renovated, establishment downtown divided into two buildings across the street from each other with a second-story skywalk connecting them. The second building has the larger rooms, which all look inside to the courtyard and large swimming pool. The lobby is small, but the staff is cheerful. There are two restaurants and a weight room. ~ 515 West Sprague Avenue; 509-838-2711, 800-426-0670, fax 509-747-6970; www.westcoasthotels.com. MODERATE.

The Doubletree Spokane Hotel was built for Spokane's 1974 World's Fair.

The **Doubletree Spokane Hotel** has the best location, right along the Spokane River and on Riverfront Park. The lobby is impressive, and most rooms have good views of the river, park and downtown. It also has a covered pool and two restaurants. ~ 322 North Spokane Falls Court; 509-455-9600, 800-222-8733, fax 509-455-6285; www.doubletreespokane.com, e-mail reservations@doubletreespokane.com. MODERATE.

The **Roadway Inn** is a favorite of many who visit Spokane frequently. Built on a hill west of town, it is roughly halfway between the airport and downtown, is quiet and affords good views of the city's growing skyline. ~ 4301 West Sunset Highway; 509-838-1471, 800-228-2000, fax 509-838-1705; www.roadway.com. BUDGET.

A newer downtown establishment is **Cavanaugh's Inn at the Park**. It has 402 rooms and is across North River Drive from the Riverfront Park. Unfortunately, it is just far enough away from the river to lose some of the waterfront charm. The inn is walking distance from downtown, and some of the rooms have private decks. ~ 303 West North River Drive; 509-326-8000, 800-325-4000, fax 509-325-7329; www.cavanaughs.com. DELUXE.

The **Fotheringham House** is Spokane's best bed and breakfast, and, for that matter, one of the best in the state. The fully restored Fotheringham House is in the Browne's Addition, Spokane's equivalent of San Francisco's Nob Hill, where many of the mining barons built their homes. There are four guest rooms with Victorian furnishings in keeping with the architecture. Full breakfast. ~ 2128 West 2nd Avenue; 509-838-1891, fax 509-838-1807; www.fotheringham.net. MODERATE.

DINING

Spokane's most popular Asian cuisine comes from the two **Mustard Seed Oriental Cafés**. The menu offers specialties from several provinces in China, as well as Japanese and American dishes. The downtown location is open and airy and the service brisk and friendly. ~ 245 West Spokane Falls Boulevard, 509-747-2689, fax 509-747-2454; and 9806 East Sprague Avenue, 509-924-3194, fax 509-924-7288. MODERATE.

The most striking restaurant in town is **Patsy Clark's**. It is in the mansion designed for a millionaire miner and has marble from Italy, wood carvings from England and an enormous stained-glass window from Tiffany's. Meals are served in several rooms. The restaurant maintains a high standard for steaks, seafood, duckling, lamb and veal. There is also a champagne buffet brunch on Sunday. ~ 2208 West 2nd Avenue; 509-838-8300, fax 509-838-0256. MODERATE TO DELUXE.

A favorite lunch and dinner spot is **The Onion**. Occupying a vintage downtown building, The Onion has a 1904 mahogany bar, 1890s prints and brass accents. A wide menu of appetizers and entrées includes onion rings, deep-fried mozzarella, burgers, caesar and taco salads, vegetable stir-fries and baby back ribs. ~ 302 West Riverside Street; 509-747-3852, fax 509-624-9965. BUDGET TO MODERATE.

SHOPPING

The Skywalk in the downtown core, a series of weatherproof bridges that connects 15 blocks on the second level, makes downtown shopping pleasant year-round. It leads to the major downtown department stores such as **Nordstrom** at Post Street and Main Avenue (509-455-6111) and **Bon Marche** at Wall

Street and Main Avenue (509-626-6000, fax 509-626-6007), several specialty shops, restaurants and art galleries.

With more and more Canadians driving just over a hundred miles to Spokane, where nearly all goods are less expensive, the city has had a surge of discount stores, from national chain stores to the West Coast warehouse stores. Shopping centers have sprung up on the north and northeast edges of town. Covered shopping areas include **Northtown Mall** at Division Street and Wellesley Avenue, **Franklin Park Mall** at Division Street and Rowan Avenue and **University City** at Sprague Avenue and University Street.

The **Flour Mill** is one of the more charming places to shop. It was built as a flour mill but was turned into a specialty shopping center in 1974 with more than 20 shops, including gift stores, cafés and restaurants. ~ 621 West Mallon Avenue; 509-325-2612.

NIGHTLIFE You'll find live jazz and dancing at **Ankeny's** on the top floor of Cavanaugh's Ridpath Hotel. ~ 515 West Sprague Avenue; 509-838-2711.

Fort Spokane Brewery serves pub food and brews their own beers daily. Live blues and alternative music are featured on weekends, and occasionally during the week. Cover on nights with live music. ~ 401 West Spokane Falls Boulevard; 509-838-3809.

> Idaho, Montana, Canada and much of Washington can be seen from the summit of Mt. Spokane.

One of the city's liveliest sports bars is **Finnerty's Red Lion**, which shows sports events on 15 screens. A bar menu features barbecue ribs. ~ 126 North Division Street; 509-624-1934.

The **Park Place Lounge** is a classic sports bar with a big-screen TV, three medium screens and a pool table. ~ Cavanaugh's Inn at the Park, 303 West North River Drive; 509-326-8000.

Dempsey's Brass Rail is a popular gay and lesbian nightspot with a dancefloor, piano bar and shows. Cover on Friday and Saturday. ~ West 909 1st Street; 509-747-5362.

The **Spokane Jazz Orchestra**, the oldest continually performing professional community jazz orchestra in the country, performs big band–style concerts as well as Latin, jazz, blues and more throughout the year at various venues around town. ~ P.O. Box 174, Spokane, WA 99210; 509-325-7328.

The **Spokane Symphony Orchestra** performs more than 40 orchestral concerts per year, including ten concert classic performances, six superpops shows and three pairs of chamber music concerts. ~ Spokane Opera House, 334 West Spokane Falls Boulevard; ticket office, 601 West Riverside Avenue; 509-624-1200.

The **Spokane Civic Theatre** presents musicals, comedies and dramas from late September through June. ~ 1020 North Howard Street; 509-325-1413.

RIVERSIDE STATE PARK 🚶🚴🏇🛶🛥️⛴️⛵ On the **PARKS**
edge of Spokane, this 7655-acre park includes nearly eight miles
of Spokane River shoreline (perfect for rainbow trout fishing), odd
basaltic formations in the river and Indian paintings on rocks. It
houses the Spokane House interpretive center, which tells the history of Spokane. Facilities include a 600-acre off-road vehicle park,
picnic areas with shelters, restrooms, hot showers and horse trails;
wheelchair accessible. ~ Located six miles northwest of Spokane at
the junction of Route 291, Rifle Club Road and Aubrey L. White
Parkway; 509-456-3964, fax 509-456-2902; www.riversidestate
park.org.

▲ There are 101 standard sites; $11 per night.

MT. SPOKANE STATE PARK 🚶🚴🏇🎿⛷️ This 5881-foot
mountain is used as much or more in the winter as it is in summer,
but warm-weather visitors find its views spectacular. It is especially
pretty during the spring when its slopes are blanketed with flowers and in the fall when the fields are brown and the leaves have
turned. For those into winter sports, there are skiing (downhill and
cross-country) and snowmobiling. During warm weather, the park
has some of the best mountain biking in Washington. There are picnic areas and restrooms. ~ Located at the end of Route 206, 30
miles northeast of Spokane; 509-238-4258, fax 509-238-4078.

▲ There are 8 primitive sites, $10 per night. For reservations,
call 800-452-5687.

TURNBULL NATIONAL WILDLIFE REFUGE 🚶🚴⛷️ One of
the most popular natural places for day trips in the Spokane area,
the refuge was established in 1937 primarily for waterfowl. It has
several lakes and wooded areas and a marked, self-guided auto-
tour route. You will also find hiking trails, cross-country skiing
areas and restrooms. Day-use fee March through October. ~ Located five miles south of Cheney on Plaza Highway; 509-235-4723,
fax 509-235-4703.

The drive from Spokane south into Or-   ▼▼▼▼▼▼▼▼▼▼▼▼▼▼
egon is one of unusual beauty, especially ## Southeastern Washington
early or late in the day, or in the spring
and fall. The entire region between the wooded hills around Spokane to the Blue Mountains is known as the Palouse Country. Here
the barren hills are low but steep, and wheat is grown on nearly
every acre. In fact, it is acknowledged as the best wheat-growing
land in the world.

Proceeding south from Spokane along Route 195, you'll find that   **SIGHTS**
the two best places to view the Palouse Hills are **Steptoe Butte State
Park** (see "Parks" below) and **Kamiak Butte County Park.** Kamiak Butte stands 3360 feet high and offers bird's-eye views of the

Palouse Hills. The park has picnic areas, a hiking trail and, unlike Steptoe Butte, a fringe of trees on its crest and over 100 kinds of vegetation, including the Douglas fir more common to the damp, coastal climate. Kamiak Butte is 18 miles east of Colfax and 15 miles north of Pullman just off Route 27.

The town of **Pullman** is almost entirely a product of Washington State University, although a few agricultural businesses operate on the edge of town. Continuing south from this campus town, Route 195 gains elevation through the small farming communities of Colton and Uniontown, then crosses over into the edge of Idaho just in time to disappear into Route 95 and then take a dizzying plunge down the steep Lewiston Hill, where you drop 2000 feet in a very short time over a twisting highway. The old highway with its hairpin turns is still passable and is exciting driving if your brakes and nerves are in good condition.

Clarkston, Washington, and Lewiston, Idaho, are separated by the Snake River, which flows almost due north through Hells Canyon before taking a sudden westward turn where Idaho's Clearwater River enters in Lewiston. Boat operators will take you up to the Snake River—you can't drive there. Most of the Snake River boat operators are headquartered in these two towns. For more information, contact the **Clarkston Chamber of Commerce**. ~ 502 Bridge Street, Clarkston; 509-758-7712, 800-933-2128, fax 509-751-8767.

The population has followed the Snake on its way west to join with the Columbia, but it is a tamed river now, a series of slackwater pools in deep canyons behind a series of dams: Lower Granite, Little Goose, Lower Monumental and Ice Harbor. The main highway doesn't follow the Snake River because of the deep canyon it carved, so from Clarkston you follow Route 12 west through the farming communities of Pomeroy and Dayton to Walla Walla, then on to the Tri-Cities area around Richland, where the Snake enters the Columbia River. Along the way is Dayton, an agricultural town with a large asparagus cannery. The town raised funds to preserve the beautiful **Dayton Depot**, a classic Victorian building that had an upper floor for the stationmaster's quarters. ~ 222 East Commercial Street, Dayton; 509-382-4825, fax 509-382-1969.

Walla Walla looks much like a New England town that was packed up and moved to the rolling hills of Eastern Washington, weeping willows, oak and maple trees included. Best known for its colleges, Whitman and Walla Walla College, the town with a double name has many ivy-covered buildings, quiet streets lined with old frame houses, enormous shade trees and, rather incongruously amid this Norman Rockwellian beauty, the state penitentiary.

You can learn about the heritage of southeast Washington at the **Fort Walla Walla Museum Complex**. A pioneer settlement composed of 16 early frontier buildings and replicas and five large ex-

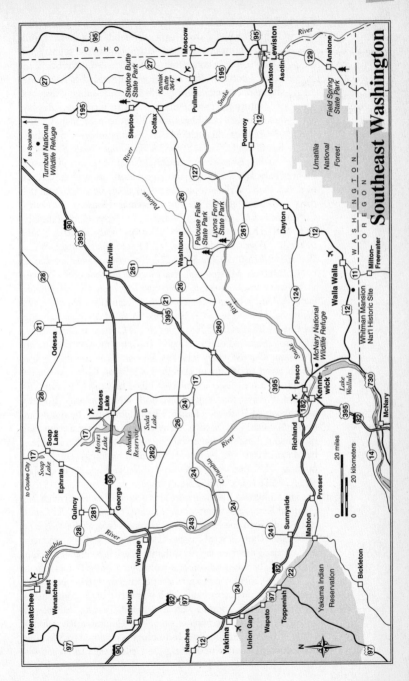

hibit buildings make this museum an excellent place to begin your visit to the Walla Walla area. A pioneer cabin built in 1877 and furnished with period artifacts, an old country rail depot, a completely outfitted one-room school and a doctor's office are among the highlights. Above the pioneer settlement, you'll find wide-ranging displays featuring family heirlooms, and an agricultural display featuring a combine with a 33 mule team hitch. Closed November through March. Admission. ~ 755 Myra Road, Walla Walla; 509-525-7703, fax 509-525-7798.

The cemetery at Fort Walla Walla contains victims from both sides of the first conflicts with the Indians.

You'll enjoy seeing the stately old trees centered around Pioneer Park and the Whitman College campus. With 360 acres of parks, Walla Walla is a pleasure to explore. Be sure to visit the town's splendid late-19th-century **Kirkman House**. ~ 29 North Colville Street, Walla Walla; 509-529-4373. To see more of the city by foot, stop by the **Chamber of Commerce** for the *Walking Guide to the Big Trees of Walla Walla*. ~ 29 East Sumach Street, Walla Walla; 509-525-0850, fax 509-522-2038; www.wwchamber.com.

At **Whitman Mission National Historic Site** one of the Northwest's worst tragedies occurred because of a basic misunderstanding of American Indian values by an American missionary, Marcus Whitman. He and his wife, Narcissa, founded a mission among the Cayuse Indians in 1836 to convert the Cayuse to Christianity. As traffic increased on the Oregon Trail, the mission became an important stop for weary travelers. Eleven years later the Cayuse felt betrayed by Whitman because his religion hadn't protected them from a measles epidemic that killed half the tribe. On November 29, 1847, the Cayuse killed both Whitmans and 11 others and ransomed 50 to the Hudson's Bay Company. The site is run by the National Park Service. There's a visitors center, a memorial monument, a millpond and walking paths to sites where various buildings once stood. None of the original buildings remain. Admission. ~ Located seven miles west of Walla Walla on Route 12; 509-529-2761, fax 509-522-6355.

The **Columbia River** runs free for about 60 miles through the Hanford Reservation, but when it swings through the Tri-Cities (Richland, Pasco and Kennewick) it becomes Lake Wallula, thanks to McNary Dam. Several city parks with picnic and boating facilities are along the river, such as **Columbia Park** in Kennewick. ~ Off Route 240, between Edison and Columbia Center Boulevard.

The Tri-Cities are best known for the nuclear-power plant and research center in nearby Hanford. It was here that the components for the first atomic bombs were assembled. Two nuclear-related visitors centers tell the nuclear story. The **Columbia River Exhibition of History, Science and Technology** is operated by Westinghouse for the Department of Energy and tells of the various sources of energy. The exhibits and historical displays focus on people's interaction with the environment, such as agricultural production, hydroelectric power, nuclear energy and environmental restoration. Admission. ~ 95 Lee Boulevard, Richland; 509-943-9000, fax 509-943-1770; www.crehst.org.

Another nuclear facility for visitors is the **Washington Public Power Supply System Plant 2 Visitor Center**, which offers information on the state's first commercial nuclear-power plant. Closed Monday through Wednesday. ~ Off Stevens Drive, 12 miles north of Richland; 509-372-5000, fax 509-372-5328.

From the Tri-Cities, the population follows the Yakima River, which flows into the Columbia at the Tri-Cities. The **Yakima Valley** is the state's richest in terms of agriculture: Yakima County ranks first nationally in the number of fruit trees, first in the production of apples, mint and hops and fifth in the value of all fruits grown. It is also the wine center of the state: Some 40 wineries have been built between Walla Walla and Yakima, and they have helped create a visitor industry that has encouraged the growth of country inns and bed and breakfasts. Brochures listing the wineries and locations are available in visitors centers and many convenience stores, and once you're off Route 82, signs mark routes to the wineries.

Fort Simcoe State Park is probably the best-preserved frontier army post in the West and was one of the few forts where no shots were fired in anger. It was used in the late 1850s during the conflict with the local American Indian people. There's a museum/ interpretive center (closed Monday and Tuesday). Five of the original buildings are still standing, including the commanding officer's home. ~ Located at the end of Fort Simcoe Road, about 35 miles south of Yakima; 509-874-2372, fax 509-874-2351.

Three important museums are in the Yakima Valley. One is the **Yakama Nation Cultural Center**. Here, the history of the tribe is told in dioramas and writings by and about the tribe preserved in a large library. The center also has a theater for films and concerts and a restaurant that serves traditional dishes. Admission. ~ Route 97, 100 Spilyay Loop, Toppenish; 509-865-2800, fax 509-865-6101; www.ohwy.com/wa/y/yakamncc.htm.

The **Central Washington Agricultural Museum** has a large collection of early farm machinery including a working windmill, a blacksmith shop, a furnished log cabin and a tool and artifact collection. ~ 4508 Main Street, Union Gap; 509-457-8735.

The **Yakima Valley Museum** has a comprehensive collection of horse-drawn vehicles, an extensive collection of furniture and other belongings of the late Supreme Court Justice William O. Douglas, a fine pioneer photo collection and special agricultural and American Indian exhibits. There is also an interactive chil-

Text continued on page 338.

Washington Wine

For a long time, Washington's liquor laws were so restrictive that it was illegal to bring wine into the state; you had to buy it from the state-run stores. The best Washington wine in those days was made by an Italian immigrant, Angelo Pelligrini, who taught Shakespeare at the University of Washington and made wine in his basement—illegally.

That has changed completely. Some 102 wineries are spread across the state, most in Eastern Washington, and many of those in the Puget Sound region own vineyards in Eastern Washington or buy their grapes there. The soil and climate are excellent for wine grapes, and the **Washington Wine Commission** likes to remind us that Eastern Washington is on the same latitude as some of France's great winegrowing regions. The wine commission publishes a free guide to wineries. ~ 500 Union Street, Suite 945, Seattle; 206-667-9463, fax 206-583-0573; www.washingtonwine.org.

Washington has four viticultural regions: Columbia Valley, which extends southward from the Okanogan Country into Oregon and east to Idaho; Yakima Valley, which runs from the foothills of the Cascades east to the Kiona Hills near Richland and is bisected by Interstate 82, making it the most convenient for visits; the Walla Walla Valley region, which straddles the Oregon–Washington border, taking in some vineyards in the Milton-Freewater area; and the Puget Sound region, which covers areas from Olympia in the south to Bellingham in the north, and includes various Puget Sound and San Juan Islands in between.

In keeping with the French adage that the best grape vines "like to be in sight of the water but don't want to get their feet wet," some of the best vineyards in Eastern Washington are on south-facing slopes above the Columbia, Yakima and Snake rivers, where they get as much as 16 hours of sunlight a day and fresh irrigation water on well-drained soil. As with all wine-producing areas, many wineries have been built in palatial settings.

One of the most dramatic is the **Columbia Crest Winery**. Built on a hillside overlooking the Columbia River, it produces more than a million gallons of wine annually and has a reflecting pool, fountain and courtyard, a luxurious lobby and tasting-and-sales room. ~ Route 221, Paterson; 509-875-2061, fax 509-875-2568; www.colombia-crest.com.

Running a close second is the eastern branch of **Stimson Lake, Ltd**. This is the state's oldest continuously operating winery and is the red-wine facility for the Château Ste. Michelle winery best known for its Woodinville palace. ~ 205 West 5th Street, Grandview; 425-415-3300; www.ste-michelle.com.

Located in an old converted gasoline station, **White Heron Cellars** emphasizes a natural winemaking process, leaving as much of the ecosystem undisturbed as possible. ~ 101 Washington Way North, George; 509-785-5521; www.vintners.net/wawine/white_heron.

A wine that keeps gaining new fans is the **Covey Run** label. The tasting room stands on a hill overlooking the winery's 100 acres of grapes. ~ 1500 Vintage Road, Zillah; 509-829-6235; www.coveyrun.com.

The Puryear family, Gail and Shirley, call **Bonair Winery** a "hobby that got out of hand." The winery not only offers a versatile range of wines, including fine chardonnays and cabernets, its gallery features exhibits of local artwork and photography. The setting, on a curve of land inside one of the valley's main irrigation canals, is inviting. ~ 500 South Bonair Road South, Zillah; 509-829-6027, fax 509-829-6410; www.bonairwine.com.

The quirky **L'Ecole No. 41** got its name from the retired schoolhouse near Walla Walla in which it was built. It is open daily with reduced winter hours. ~ 41 Lowden School Road, Lowden; 509-525-0940, fax 509-525-2775; www.lecole.com..

Joel and Pam Tefft focus on very limited bottlings of fine handcrafted wines at **Tefft Cellars** outside Sunnyside. Aside from cabernet sauvignon and lush, velvety merlot, the Teffts make unique, light, dry sparkling wines and ports, a rarity in Washington. ~ 1320 Independence Road, Outlook; 509-839-7651, 888-303-7651; www.tefftcellars.com.

Hunter Hill Vineyards is named for the well-known bird-hunting area around the nearby Potholes Reservoir. The tasting room is in the original farmhouse, which gives a feeling of a country home to visitors who come by to taste. ~ 2752 West McMannaman Road, Othello; 509-346-2736.

The most homey of the wineries is probably **Kiona Vineyards**. It is a family operation, with the tasting room, winery and the Kiona Vineyard at the home of John and Ann Williams. The winery was one of the originals to produce lemberger. ~ 44612 North Sunset Northeast, Benton City; 509-588-6716.

Sageland Vineyards is located in a French-country building set on a rolling hillside. The tasting room features a stone fireplace and cathedral ceilings. ~ 71 Gangl Road, Wapato; 509-877-2112, fax 509-877-3377.

Pontin del Roza came into being because the Pontin family's Italian heritage included a love of wine. They decided to add wine grapes to the crops they had been growing on their Prosser farm for two decades and produce both reds and whites. ~ 35502 North Hinzerling Road, Prosser; 509-786-4449.

Wine is only one of several agricultural products produced by Hogue Ranches. But the **Hogue Cellars** wines have been getting much more attention than their asparagus. ~ Wine Country Road, Prosser; 509-786-4557, fax 509-786-4580; www.hogue-cellars.com.

Cheers!

dren's museum and an operating ice cream soda fountain. Admission. ~ 2105 Tieton Drive, Yakima; 509-248-0747, fax 509-453-4890; www.yakimavalleymuseum.org.

HIDDEN ►

In Toppenish, the **American Hop Museum** chronicles a unique agricultural endeavor that has long been a Yakima Valley mainstay, now booming with the recent growth of the microbrewery industry. Antique harvesters, photographs and other artifacts depict the industry's beginnings in the second half of the 19th century. Open summers or by appointment. ~ 22 South B Street, Toppenish; 509-865-4677, fax 509-865-7649; www.americanhopmuseum.org.

Another museum that recalls the early days of the region is the **Sunnyside Historical Museum**. The elegant white building houses displays of American Indian artifacts and a pioneer kitchen and dining room. Across the street is the Ben Snipes Cabin, dating from 1859. Admission. Closed Monday through Thursday and January through April. ~ 704 South 4th Street, Sunnyside; 509-837-6010; e-mail saras1@beatonrea.com.

The main road leading from the Yakima Valley to the beautiful Columbia River Gorge (see Chapter Ten, "The Columbia River Gorge") is Route 97, which runs south from Toppenish, crosses Satus Pass (3107 feet) and reaches the Gorge just past Goldendale. An alternate route from the Yakima Valley down to the Columbia River is the **Mabton-Bickleton Road**, which heads south from the small town of Mabton through the even smaller Bickleton. An unincorporated town with a scattering of Victorian houses and falsefront store buildings, Bickleton's claim to fame is hundreds of houses for (are you ready for this?) bluebirds. Maintained by residents, the houses are on fence posts along the highway and country lanes and literally all over town. The one in front of the community church is a miniature copy of the church itself.

HIDDEN ►

The 1882 **Bluebird Inn Tavern** is one of the oldest buildings in the state. Inside is a pool table from 1903. ~ Bickleton; 509-896-2273.

Twelve miles outside Bickleton sits the funky **Whoop-N-Holler Museum**. The owners showcase a vast array of turn-of-the-20th-century pioneer memorabilia, much of which was handed down through their families. Highlights are the large classic auto collection and various horse-drawn vehicles, including an antique hearse on sled runners. Closed October through March except by appointment. Admission. ~ 1 Whitmore Road at East Road; 509-896-2344.

LODGING

It's difficult to find anything other than your basic, cookie-cutter motel in Southeastern Washington, although Yakima shows some imagination.

Pullman has about half a dozen motels, none particularly distinguished, and all budget or moderate in price. The best view is at the **Best Western Heritage Inn**. ~ 928 Olson Street at Davis

Way, Pullman; 509-332-0928, 800-528-1234, fax 509-334-5275; www.bestwestern.com. MODERATE. The **Quality Inn** is near both the campus and the airport. ~ 1050 Bishop Boulevard, Pullman; 509-332-0500, 800-669-3212, fax 509-334-4271. MODERATE.

The **Best Western** is a comfortable motel close to the town's center. With an indoor pool and a hot tub, plus free continental breakfast, it's above average for valley accommodations. Rooms are motel style, with queen-size beds, pastel decor and lots of formica and pressed wood. ~ 515 Elm Street South, Toppenish; 509-865-7444, 800-222-3161, fax 509-865-7719. MODERATE.

Dayton seems to be out in the middle of nowhere—gateway to the Blue Mountains and an agricultural center. The **Purple House B&B** is thus an unexpected pleasure. This elegant inn, on the National Register of Historic Places, is housed in an 1882 Queen Anne mansion that was built by a pioneer physician. Two upstairs bedrooms share a bath; the master suite downstairs has a private bath. All rooms are furnished in period antiques; there's a library and heated outdoor pool. A separate carriage house has full amenities and a private bath. The full breakfast is cooked to order. ~ 415 East Clay Street, Dayton; phone/fax 509-382-3159, 800-486-2574. MODERATE TO DELUXE.

Walla Walla has about ten motels, most of them in the budget to moderate range. The **Tapadera Budget Inn** offers a continental breakfast. ~ 211 North 2nd Street, Walla Walla; 509-529-2580, 800-722-8277, fax 509-522-1380. BUDGET.

The Tri-Cities area has several fair-size motels, many with meeting rooms since the Hanford Nuclear Center is nearby. One of the largest is the **Ramada Inn on Clover Island**, built on an island in the Columbia River. Half of the rooms have views of the river. The complex has a pool, hot tub, restaurant and lounge. ~ 435 Clover Island, Kennewick; 509-586-0541, 800-272-6232, fax 509-586-6956; www.ramadainn.com. MODERATE.

Peace and quiet are the overwhelming virtues of the **Apple Country B&B** outside Yakima. With two antique-furnished bedrooms in a 1911 house on a working farm, hard-working host-

A SCENIC DRIVE DOWN A CROOKED HIGHWAY

Only in the late 1980s was the highway completely paved between the Snake River Canyon and the Wallowas in Oregon. But now you can take one of the prettiest mountain drives in the Northwest by following Route 129 south from Clarkston in the southeastern corner of Washington through Anatone, then down into the Grande Ronde River valley over probably the most crooked highway in the Northwest. Be sure your brakes (and fortitude) are in good condition.

ess Shirley Robert wants her guests to feel as serene as the setting suggests. Sit outside your antique-furnished rooms overlooking the back yard and orchards beyond, sipping lemonade, and peace prevails. ~ 4561 Old Naches Highway, Naches; 509-965-0344, fax 509-965-1591. MODERATE.

Yakima does a lively convention business, and one of the best places to stay is next door to the convention center. **West Coast Yakima Center Hotel** has 153 large, comfortable rooms with colorful furnishings and spacious bathrooms, two heated pools, a dining room and a lounge. ~ 607 Yakima Avenue East, Yakima; 509-248-5900, 800-325-4000, fax 509-575-8975. MODERATE.

DINING

The **Hilltop Restaurant** shares the steep hill with the Best Western Heritage Inn, looking down on the city of Pullman. It caters to the local trade with thick steaks, Sunday brunches and afternoon dinners. ~ 920 Olson Street at Davis Way, Pullman; 509-334-2555, fax 509-332-3120. MODERATE.

If you're good at what you do, so goes the saying, the world will beat a path to your door. This could be the slogan for **Patit Creek Restaurant**. It has been in business since 1978 and has built a national reputation for excellent dishes in what is most accurately described as French country cuisine. Meat is the specialty—beef and lamb. Most of the food is grown locally, some by the staff, and since some of the luxurious plants inside and around the outside are herbs, they may one day season your food. Closed Sunday through Tuesday. ~ 725 East Dayton Avenue, Dayton; 509-382-2625. MODERATE TO DELUXE.

Washington is second in the country in wine production, behind California. The state's best-known varieties are chardonnays, cabernet sauvignons, merlots, rieslings and pinot noirs.

If you're feeling nostalgic for New York delis, **Merchant's Ltd.** will help. It has a wide choice of foods and a sidewalk café ideal for Walla Walla's mostly sunny weather. ~ 21 Main Street East, Walla Walla; 509-525-0900, fax 509-522-3065. BUDGET.

The **Cedars** is one of the Tri-Cities' most striking restaurants. It is cantilevered over the Columbia River with boat-docking facilities. The specialties are steaks, seafood and prime rib. Favorites include the bier garten steak and the daily fresh fish specials. ~ 509-582-2143, fax 509-582-6703. MODERATE TO DELUXE.

Emerald of Siam serves authentic Thai food in a former drugstore that has a combination of French, Thai and American decor and menu. A buffet lunch is served on weekdays, or you may order from the menu. Closed Sunday. ~ 1314 Jadwin Avenue, Richland; 509-946-9328, fax 509-946-8902. BUDGET.

Prosser is a farm town, pure and simple. But what better place for fine, gourmet country cuisine? At **The Blue Goose**, local wine and produce form the basis for a Tuscan/Northwest menu that ranges from veal marsala to chicken-fried steak (well, it is a country restaurant). The wine list features more than 50 local wines, some of them superb vintages, at prices you'll never see in any urban restaurant. ~ 306 7th Street, Prosser; 509-786-1774. BUDGET TO MODERATE.

Garza family members still return to their home village in northern Mexico every Christmas; a vivid mural painting of the village's square adorns the wall in the family's fine Toppenish restaurant, **Los Murales**. Among other things, the tamales are firm and flavorful, and the chile verde is made with tomatillos, not tomatoes. ~ 202 1st Avenue West, Toppenish; 509-865-7555. BUDGET TO MODERATE.

Located in Yakima's North Front Street Historical District, **Deli de Pasta** is a charming, small Italian restaurant located in a turn-of-the-20th-century storefront that was once the Commercial Saloon. House-made ravioli and other pastas are the specialty. Dinner only. Closed Sunday. ~ 7 Front Street North, Yakima; 509-453-0571. MODERATE.

Over the years, **Birchfield Manor** has won more magazine awards than any other Washington restaurant outside the Puget Sound region. The owners restored an old farmhouse and filled it with antiques, then opened the restaurant with a menu of seven entrées including fresh salmon in puff pastry, filet mignon, rack of lamb and chicken breast scallopine. Local fruit and vegetables are used, and the fixed menu includes an appetizer, a salad and a homemade chocolate treat. Closed Sunday through Wednesday. ~ 2018 Birchfield Road, Yakima; 509-452-1960, fax 509-452-2334; birchfieldmanor.com. DELUXE.

SHOPPING Yakima offers several intriguing shopping areas. One is the **North Front Street Historical District**, where the city's oldest buildings, some of them made of rough-hewn local rock, now house an assortment of boutiques, restaurants and brew pubs.

The **Paper Station** proffers books, cards and custom stationery. Half the store features toys. ~ 910 Summitview Street, Yakima; 509-575-1633.

Yesterday's Village is a collection of shops in the former Fruit Exchange Building. The remodeled building houses some 75 shops that sell antiques, glassware, collectibles, furniture and jewelry. ~ 15 West Yakima Avenue, Yakima; 509-457-4981.

Toppenish's antique district is dominated by two quite disparate stores. At **La Hacienda Gardens**, Italian espresso accompanies Southwest primitive furniture, Indian artifacts and Tibetan and Turkish jewelry. ~ 207 Toppenish Avenue, Toppenish; 509-865-1992.

Across the street, **Toppenish Antiques & Collectibles** is piled high with a mind-boggling array of stuff—some kitschy, some very fine—including an exceptional collection of Southwest Indian jewelry. ~ 212 Toppenish Avenue South, Toppenish; 509-865-4033.

NIGHTLIFE   Yakima has one of the widest selections of nightlife in southeastern Washington, ranging from cultural events to country-and-western taverns. **Grant's Brewery Pub** serves British pub food and frequently offers live music. Cover. ~ 32 North Front Street, Yakima; 509-575-2922. The **Golden Kayland Chinese Restaurant** has live music. ~ 40th Avenue and Summitview Street, Yakima; 509-966-7696.

In addition, Yakima has frequent concerts sponsored by the Ladies' Musical Club and the **Yakima Symphony Orchestra**. ~ 32 North 3rd Street #333, Yakima; 509-248-1414.

Square dancing is very popular in the Yakima Valley, and numerous clubs welcome travelers to their dances. For information, contact Daron Tandberg of the Square Dance Club of Yakima (509-576-4249). Dances are held Saturday nights at the Yakima Valley Square Dance Center. ~ 207 East Charron Road, Moxee.

PARKS   **STEPTOE BUTTE STATE PARK** 🏃 This park consists of the butte and a picnic area at the base but has no amenities at all. The reason for the park's existence is the butte itself, which rises to an elevation of 3612 feet out of the rolling Palouse Hills with panoramic views that are popular with photographers. The butte is actually the top of a granite mountain that stands above the lava flows that covered all the other peaks. The word "steptoe" has entered the international geological vocabulary to represent any similar remnant of an earlier geological feature standing out from the newer feature. There are seven picnic sites at the foot of the butte; no water. ~ Located roughly 50 miles south of Spokane just off Route 195; 509-549-3551, fax 509-549-3645.

FIELD SPRING STATE PARK 🏃 🚲 ⛷ This 800-acre park is in forested land on the eastern slope of the Blue Mountains. It is just below Puffer Butte, a 4450-foot mountain that overlooks the Grand Ronde River Canyon. For hikers, there are a one-mile trail to the summit of Puffer Butte and ten miles of hiking paths. Winter-sports enthusiasts will find cross-country skiing, snowshoeing and tubing. There are two lodges where groups or individuals can stay for just $7 per night. There are restrooms and showers. ~ Located four and a half miles south of Anatone on Route 129; 509-256-3332.

▲ There are 20 standard sites; $11 per night.

FORT WALLA WALLA PARK AND MUSEUM 🏃 🚲 This collection of pioneer buildings is located on a 208-acre former Army fort and cemetery containing victims from both sides of the first conflicts with the Indians. It also has 20 buildings, some authentic and others replicas, of pioneer homes, schools and public buildings. One of the largest collections of horse-drawn farm equipment in the Northwest is also owned by the museum (509-525-7703; admission). There are also nature and bicycle trails in the park. Other facilities include picnic areas, restrooms, play equipment and volleyball courts. Closed Monday. ~ Located on southwest side of Walla Walla on Dalles Military Road at Myra; 509-527-3770.

▲ There are 55 developed sites and 21 sites with hookups; $10 to $15 per night.

PALOUSE FALLS/LYONS FERRY STATE PARK This two-part, remote park is out in the rugged Channeled Scablands. The Lyons Ferry section consists of a pleasant, grassy area with boat ramps at the confluence of the Snake and Palouse rivers. About seven to eight miles up the Palouse River is the Palouse Falls section, with a dramatic picnic area and viewpoint overlooking the thundering Palouse Falls. There are picnic areas and restrooms; a wheelchair-accessible hiking trail there and at Lyons Ferry, as well as a boat launch ramp, concessionaire, hiking areas and a restaurant, are nearby. ~ Located 36 miles southeast of Washtucna on Route 261; 509-646-3252.

▲ Palouse Falls has ten primitive, walk-in sites ($8 per night) while Lyons Ferry has 50 standard sites ($11 per night). Both close in winter.

McNARY NATIONAL WILDLIFE REFUGE This is one of the major resting areas in the Pacific Flyway for migratory waterfowl, especially Canada geese, American widgeon, mallards, pintails and white pelicans. The population peaks in November, and the few summer migratory birds, such as the pelicans and long-billed curlews, arrive in the spring and summer. The refuge covers 3600 acres along the Snake River just before it enters the Columbia River at Pasco. Hunters look for waterfowl and upland birds, while anglers cast a rod for largemouth black bass, catfish and crappie. Self-guided wildlife trail through the marsh and crop-

THE OLDEST MAN IN WASHINGTON

The Tri-Cities area was the site of the 1996 discovery of the controversial Kennewick Man, one of the oldest human skeletons ever found in North America, radiocarbon-dated to about 6400 B.C. Because the skull was much different from those of modern American Indians, the find was first thought to suggest the presence of Caucasians in archaic America but is now believed to be "proto-Mongolian," with possible genetic links both to Russian Europeans and to native peoples' Asian ancestors. The Colville, Yakima, Umatilla and Nez Perce tribes each claim Kennewick Man as an ancestor, demanding reburial rights under the Native American Graves Protection Act. To resolve the dispute, the National Park Service is trying to test DNA samples from the ancient bones.

lands. ~ Located southeast of Pasco just off Route 395 on the Snake River; 509-547-4942, fax 509-544-9047.

Outdoor Adventures

Although eastern Washington is not, as one local guide puts it, "blue ribbon" fishing territory for most of the year, the region has its moments:

FISHING

come August, some big salmon show up in the Klickitat River; September starts the steelhead run in the Snake River; and trout in June and July make the Yakima River the most popular flyfishing stream in the Northwest. Some outfitters can also arrange hunting trips for game like elk, deer and bighorn sheep.

GRAND COULEE AREA   For information on fishing in Banks and Roosevelt lakes in the Grand Coulee area, contact **Coulee Playland**. ~ P.O. Box 457, Electric City, WA 99123; 509-633-2671.

SPOKANE AREA   G. L. Britton of **Double Spey Outfitters** has been flyfishing since he was a boy; he now guides visiting anglers for two-day walk-and-wade flyfishing trips for trout on the Spokane during August and September, and full-day steelhead trips on a driftboat on the Snake and Grande Rhonde rivers in October and November. The rest of the year, which is not necessarily peak fishing season in eastern Washington, Britton will take you out to one of the local lakes for a full day of fishing that's more "teach-you" than "trophy." Flies, rods and leaders are provided. ~ Nine Mile Falls; 509-466-4635; e-mail dean river@aol.com.

In winter, Banks Lake, near Grand Coulee, is a popular place to ice fish.

SOUTHEASTERN WASHINGTON   If you'd "rather be fishing," then call Dan Little at RBF **Excursions** to arrange a day of catch-and-release flyfishing for trout on the Yakima River. RBF also guides summer salmon and steelhead trips to the Klickitat River, about 65 miles away; for part of the year, Dan guides on Olympic Peninsula Rainforest rivers as well. ~ Yakima; 509-965-6308; www.rbfexcursions.com.

Fishing excursions on the Snake River between the Idaho/Washington border are offered by **Beamer's Hells Canyon Tours**. Spring and summer half-day to four-days trips on a fishing sled seek bass, trout and sturgeon; in fall, it's steelhead. Bait and tackle provided. ~ 1451 Bridge Street, Clarkston; 509-758-4800, 800-522-6966; www.hellscanyontours.com. **Snake River Adventures** also provides single or multiday guided trips for steelhead, sturgeon, bass and trout on the Snake, Salmon and Clearwater rivers. Bring your own bait and tackle. ~ 227 Snake River Avenue, Lewiston, ID; 208-746-6276, 800-262-8874; www.snakeriveradventures.com.

RIVER RUNNING

In September on the Tieton River, in southeastern Washington, water is released from the dam that controls the flow, creating Class III and some Class IV rapids and drawing ever-increasing crowds of rafters. It may not be a "hidden" spot, but it's still a thrill. Whitewater thrills come on the Snake River in Northeastern Oregon, where it cuts through walls of black basalt, forming Hells Canyon, the deepest gorge in the country. Spring is the best time to hit good whitewater, but be forewarned: classifications are arbitrary and the hard classes aren't necessarily the best. Watch water levels more closely than class.

SOUTHEASTERN WASHINGTON   **Chinook Expeditions** has been leading guided trips and eagle-watching tours since 1974. Rivers rafted include the Skagit, Snohomish, Skykomish, Toutle and Queets. Guide Shane Turnbull says all trips are very interpretive. Wetsuits, tents and gear can be rented. ~ P.O. Box 256, Index, WA 98256; 360-793-3451; www.chinookexpeditions.com. **Rivers, Inc.** offers full-day guided trips on paddle rafts down the Wenatchee, Methow, Suiattle and Tieton rivers in the summer. ~ P.O. Box 2092, Kirkland, WA 98083; 425-822-5296; www.rivers-inc. bizhosting.com. **Idaho Afloat** leads one-day rafting trips down Class II to Class IV rivers. ~ P.O. Box 542, Grangeville, ID; 208-746-6276.

Snake Dancer Excursions provides one-day jet boat tours down the Snake River and through Hells Canyon, with a stop at Kirkwood Ranch. Trips cover 85 sets of rapids that rate as high as Class IV. ~ P.O. Box 318, Clarkston, WA 99403; 509-758-8927, 800-234-1941; www.snakedancerexcursions.com.

Another popular location for rafting is the Snake River between the Washington and Idaho border. Contact **O.A.R.S. Dories** for guided tours on rafts, dories and inflatable kayaks on Class III and Class IV rivers. Trips on the Snake River last three days; Salmon River expeditions are 17 days. Classes are also available. ~ P.O. Box 67, 2687 South Route 49, Angels Camp, CA 95222; 209-736-4677, 800-346-6277; www.oars.com.

GOLF

Mountain valleys and high desert vistas give golfers satisfying course options, and greens fees that are lower than in urban areas sweeten the deal. Winter weather closes many courses for two to five months.

OKANOGAN HIGHLANDS   Hilly terrain makes a cart rental highly recommended at the nine-hole **Oroville Golf Club**. The scenic semiprivate course runs beside a river. ~ Nighthawk Road, two miles west of Oroville; 509-476-2390. Between Omak and Okanogan is the **Okanogan Valley Golf Club**. This public course is surrounded by hills on one side and orchards on the other. ~ Pogue Road off the Okanogan–Conconully Route; 509-826-9902.

GRAND COULEE AREA   **Banks Lake Golf and Country Club** offers nine holes for golf enthusiasts. The public course is next to Banks Lake, and offers a few canyons and wide fairways. ~ Route 155, two and a half miles south of Grand Coulee; 509-633-0163.

SPOKANE AREA If you've seen San Francisco's Lincoln Park Municipal Golf Course with its view across the city skyline, Spokane's **Indian Canyon Golf Course** will seem familiar. Set on a hillside that undulates downward toward Spokane, the public 18-hole course is well known throughout the region. ~ West 4304 West Drive; 509-747-5353.

SOUTHEASTERN WASHINGTON In Yakima the public, 18-hole **Suntides Golf Course** is fairly flat, so it's very walkable, making it popular with seniors and junior golfers. There's water on 13 of the holes. You'll find a restaurant and a championship 18-hole putting course on the premises. ~ 231 Pence Road, Yakima; 509-966-9065. The 17th hole at public **Apple Tree Golf Course** is called Apple Island, and is shaped like an apple and surrounded by water (this is apple country, after all). ~ 8804 Occidental Road, Yakima; 509-966-5877.

Sun Willows Golf Course is a public, 18-hole course that's very playable for all handicaps. It's fairly flat, but has several lakes. Carts are available for rent. ~ 2035 North 20th Avenue, Pasco; 509-545-3440. A canyon runs through **Canyon Lakes Golf Course**, which makes for plenty of interesting shots on this 18-hole public course. Rated one of the top ten courses in the Northwest, Canyon Lakes also has a champion putting course and full practice facilities. ~ 3700 West Canyon Lakes Drive, Kennewick; 509-582-3736.

SKIING

Ski areas in this part of the state, particularly the southeast part, are little farther away from the hustle and bustle of the larger, more popular spots elsewhere. The full-service resorts all offer equipment rentals for downhill skiing, cross-country skiing and snowboarding. In addition, lessons are available for all levels.

OKANOGAN HIGHLANDS Downhill and cross-country skiing are both popular in this region, particularly the latter because there is so much open country and powdery snow. Cross-country trails are maintained at most downhill areas, but any country road, most golf courses and parks may be used by skiers. **Loup Loup** has a 1240-foot vertical drop for downhill skiing and snowboarding. Its three lifts serve over a dozen runs. There is a small half-pipe for snowboarders, and 25 kilometers of groomed trails for cross-country skiers. Closed Monday, Tuesday and Thursday. Open from December to March. ~ Route 20, between Twisp and Okanogan; 509-826-2720.

Sitzmark has a base elevation of 3900 feet and a modest 650-foot drop. There are two chair lifts, a rope tow and runs for snowboarders. The majority of runs are intermediate (70 percent). Open mid-December to mid-March. ~ Located 20 miles northeast of Tonasket; 509-485-3323. **49° North** has five chairlifts on 1900

North America's Deepest Gorge

The Snake River's colorful Hells Canyon, deeper by 2000 feet than Arizona's Grand Canyon, is the center piece of a 652,488-acre parcel, much of it wilderness. The gorge defines the border between Idaho on one side and the Oregon–Washington boundary on the other, although the largest section of wilderness surrounding the gorge lies in Oregon. America's deepest gorge (with an average depth of 6000 feet), this 72-mile stretch of the Snake River (31.5 miles designated as wild; 36 miles designated as scenic and 4.2 miles unspecified) is accessible from Clarkston, Washington, and neighboring Lewistown, Idaho. It was saved from flooding after conservationists blocked a frightening proposal to dam this scenic region popular with anglers, rafters and jet boat operators. Visitors from all over the world make the pilgrimage to eastern Washington just to see **Hells Canyon National Recreation Area**, which encompasses three mountain ranges in Washington, Idaho and Oregon. ~ 88401 Route 82, Enterprise, OR; 541-426-4978.

The incredible scope of the gorge is apparent even to those who only see it from the surrounding hills. Visitors who continue farther into the canyon, either by water or by land, discover more than stark and spectacular scenery. Hells Canyon was well known to prehistoric American Indians and early white settlers alike, as evidenced by petroglyphs and 8000-year-old artifacts from Chief Joseph's Nez Perce, remnants of turn-of-the-century gold mines and homesteads.

On your trip you're likely to spot bighorn sheep, elk, deer and bald eagles, as well as American Indian petroglyphs and Nez Perce tribal landmarks. You'll also see old mining townsites and the site of one of the regions great tragedies, the Deep Creek Massacre of 1887, which took the lives of 32 Chinese gold miners.

Whitewater rafters, kayakers and drift boaters put in at the mouth of Hells Canyon Creek, just below Hells Canyon Dam, for trips downriver on the "national wild and scenic" portion of the Snake that extends north 79 miles to the mouth of the Grande Rhonde River in Heller Bar. In the fall, steelhead fishing trips are extremely popular on the Snake. The **Clarkston Chamber of Commerce** can provide the names of jet-boat and rafting operators. Overnight fishing trips can also be arranged with convenient stays at rustic Hells Canyon lodges. ~ 502 Bridge Street, Clarkston, WA; 509-758-7712. For private float boat reservations, call 509-758-1957. For private power boat reservations, call 509-758-0270.

feet as well as a snowboard park and 380 miles of groomed trails. They also offer free lessons for beginners. Open mid-November to mid-April. ~ Located ten miles east of Chewelah; 509-935-6649; www.ski49n.com.

SOUTHEASTERN WASHINGTON   Ski Bluewood, 22 miles southeast of Dayton at the end of a Forest Service road, has 1125 vertical feet of downhill skiing. There are two triple-chair lifts and one surface lift, as well as a snowboard terrain park. Open mid-November to mid-April. ~ 262 East Main Street; 509-382-2877.

BIKING

For the most part, automobile traffic is sparse in these regions, so bicyclists have little trouble finding long stretches of road that are practically deserted, and scenically beautiful. But they're also challenging and attract avid cross-country bicyclists, especially along Routes 3 and 86 in the Wallowa National Forest near Hells Canyon. Recreational bicyclists, however, have a couple of options. Along the bank of the Spokane River, the paved **Centennial Trail** extends from Riverside State Park to the Washington–Idaho state line (37 miles) and continues on to Coeur d'Alene, Idaho, 25 miles farther. The trail is a relatively flat, easy ride with a few hills in the park (and nobody says you have to go the full distance; you might just want to go as far as Plante's Ferry Park, where you'll find some interesting basalt rock formations in the water). Just west of Spokane is the forested Riverside State Park, which has several gravel trails for mountain biking. Mt. Spokane, which rises some 5800 feet, is another recommended destination.

In the Yakima area, besides an easy five-mile multi-use route along the **Yakima Greenway**, which meanders along the river, there are several possible routes through the local wine country. The **Yakima Valley Visitors and Convention Bureau** has information and maps. ~ 10 North 8th Street; 509-575-3010, 800-221-0751.

The **Snake River Bikeway** runs six miles between Clarkston and Asotin along both the Clearwater and Snake rivers. Access it from Beachview Park at the corner of Beachview and Chestnut in Clarkston. Also, a 24-mile tour from **Palouse** leads south on Route 27 to Clear Creek Road to Route 272 back to Palouse.

In some cities, you'll find some bicycle routes that double as hiking trails (see "Hiking," below).

Bike Rentals & Tours   There are three bike shops located along Spokane's main street. Rent or repair a mountain bike or buy equipment at **North Division Bicycle Shop**. ~ 10503 North Division Street, Spokane; 509-467-2453. **Spoke 'N Sport** rents and sells everything—tandems, mountain bikes, racks and trailers. A full-service bike shop, they also organize a variety of bike treks. ~ 212 North Division Street, Spokane; 509-838-8842.

In the Yakima area, contact the **Yakima Valley and Convention Bureau** for a map of bike routes through the local wine country. ~ 509-575-3010, 800-221-0751. Mountain-bike rentals, sales and repairs, as well as scheduled rides, are available through **Valley Cycling and Fitness**. ~ 1802 West Nob Hill Boulevard, Yakima; 509-453-6699. **Sagebrush Cycles** also has mountain and road bikes for rent. The shop also repairs and sells bikes and accessories, and offers 18- to 25-mile winery bike tours for eight to ten people as well as mountain bike day trips for the same number. ~ 5110 Tyson Boulevard, Yakima; 509-972-1330.

All distances listed for hiking trails are one way unless otherwise noted.

OKANOGAN HIGHLANDS Backpackers and day hikers alike enjoy this area because the weather is often clear and dry and the forest is more open than in the Cascades and Olympics. A number of established hiking trails are shown on Forest Service maps and in free brochures given out at the ranger station in Okanogan. ~ 1240 South Second Avenue; 509-826-3275.

A good walk for a family with small children is the one-mile trail leading from Bonaparte Campground just north of the one-store town of Wauconda to the viewpoint overlooking the lake. Another easy one is the **Big Tree Trail** (1 mile) loop from Lost Lake Campground, which is only a short distance north of Bonaparte. This one goes through a signed botanical area.

One of the most ambitious highlands trails is the southern segment of the **Kettle Crest Trail** (15 miles). The trek begins at the summit of Sherman Pass on Route 20 and winds southward past Sherman Peak and four other major mountains, the highest peak measuring 7135 feet. The trail is through mostly open terrain, and you'll have great views of the mountains and Columbia River Valley. ~ 509-775-3305.

GRAND COULEE AREA A system of paths and trails connects the four towns clustered around Grand Coulee Dam. The Bureau of Reclamation built a paved route about two miles long called the **Community Trail**, which connects Coulee Dam and Grand Coulee. An informal system of unpaved paths connects these two towns to Elmer City and Electric City.

The newest is the walking/biking trail called the **Down River Trail** (6.5 miles). It runs north along the Columbia River from Grand Coulee, beginning in the Coulee Dam Shopping Center. It is accessible for wheelchairs.

Bunchgrass Prairie Nature Trail (.5-mile roundtrip) begins in the Spring Canyon Campground, which is three miles up Lake Roosevelt by water and two miles from Grand Coulee. This loop trail starts in the campground, and self-guided booklets are at the trailhead. It goes through one of the few remaining bunchgrass environments here. ~ 509-633-9441.

SOUTHEASTERN WASHINGTON Cowiche Canyon (3 miles) starts five miles from Yakima. The trail is actually an old railroad bed that ran through the steep canyon. The canyon has unusual rock formations, and you can expect to see some wildlife.

Noel Pathway (4.6 miles) is a trail inside the city limits of Yakima that follows the Yakima River. The pathway is used by bicyclists, as well.

▼▼▼▼▼▼▼▼▼▼▼
Transportation

CAR

Eastern Washington is served by a network of roads that range from interstates to logging roads that have been paved by the Forest Service. **Route 97** serves as the north–south dividing line between the Cascade Mountains and the arid, rolling hills that undulate to the eastern boundaries of the states.

Route 90 runs through the center of the Washington, from Spokane southwest through Moses Lake, George and across the Columbia River at Vantage, where the highway turns almost due west for its final run to Puget Sound.

Route 5 bisects Portland, Oregon, and provides access from the north via Vancouver, Washington. This highway is also the main line from points south like the Willamette Valley and California.

Route 82 begins near Hermiston, Oregon, crosses the Columbia River to the Tri-Cities (Richland, Kennewick and Pasco) and runs on up the Yakima Valley to join Route 90 at Ellensburg. **Route 84** runs almost the entire length of the Columbia River Gorge in Oregon before swinging southeast at Hermiston and connecting Pendleton, La Grande and Baker City with Ontario on the Idaho border.

Other major highways are **Route 395**, starting south of Lakeview, Oregon, and continuing into Washington at the Tri-Cities to Ritzville. It joins with Route 90 at Ritzville only to emerge again at Spokane, where it continues north into British Columbia. Smaller but important highways include **Route 12** between Clarkston and Walla Walla, and **Route 195** running between Spokane and the Clarkston-Lewiston area.

Perhaps the most beautiful of all the highways in Washington is **Route 20**, which starts at Whidbey Island and continues to the North Cascades, through the Methow Valley, then straight through the Okanogan Highlands to Kettle Falls, where it merges with Route 395. It becomes Route 20 again at Colville, and continues southeast to Newport on the Idaho border.

AIR

Spokane International Airport is by far the busiest in Eastern Washington with seven airlines serving the area: Alaska Airlines, Delta Airlines, Horizon Air, Northwest Airlines, Southwest Airlines, United Airlines and United Express.

Other airports with scheduled service in Washington are **Moses Lake**, **Pullman**, **Wenatchee**, **Yakima**, the **Tri-Cities** and **Walla Walla**. All of these smaller cities are served by either Horizon Air or United Express, or both. In addition, Delta Airlines serves the Tri-Cities. Empire Airlines serves the Tri-Cities and Yakima.

Three bus lines operate in the region. From the Spokane terminal at 221 West 1st Avenue are **Greyhound Bus Lines** (509-624-5255, 800-231-2222) and **Northwestern Trailways** (509-838-4029). Greyhound also serves Yakima at the depot at 602 East Yakima Avenue.

Operating from Medical Lake (just southwest of Spokane) is **Alpha Omega Tours and Charters**. ~ 417 North Jefferson Street; 509-624-4116.

BUS

Washington is one of the few states to have two **Amtrak** routes. Both start in Spokane. The first route runs from Spokane due west with stops in Ephrata, Wenatchee, Everett and Edmonds before arriving in Seattle. The other route runs southwest from Spokane to the Columbia River Gorge with stops in Pasco, Bingen and Vancouver, and ultimately goes to Portland, Oregon. ~ 800-872-7245.

TRAIN

Car-rental agencies in Spokane include the following: **Rent-A-Wreck** (800-722-9732), **Budget Car and Truck Rental** (800-527-0700) and **Thrifty Car Rental** (800-367-2277).

Agencies in the Tri-Cities include **Avis Rent A Car** (800-331-1212), **Budget Rent A Car** (800-527-0700) and **Hertz Rent A Car** (800-654-3131). Walla Walla is served by **Budget Rent A Car** (800-527-0700).

CAR RENTALS

The Tri-Cities area (Pasco, Prosser and Richland) has **Ben Franklin Transit**. ~ 509-735-4131. **Valley Transit** serves Walla Walla and College Place. ~ 509-525-9140. Pullman has **Pullman Transit**. ~ 509-332-6535. Yakima has **Yakima Transit**. ~ 509-575-6175.

PUBLIC TRANSIT

Major taxi companies in the area are **Budget Taxi** (509-326-8294) and **Spokane Cab** (509-535-2535).

TAXIS

TEN

The Columbia River Gorge

The Columbia River cuts an 80-mile swath through the Cascade Mountains on its way to the Pacific, leaving in its wake a magnificent landscape of towering basalt cliffs, waterfalls and forested bluffs known as the Columbia River Gorge. Because it forms a natural border between Oregon and Washington, exploring the Gorge is a two-state proposition, with a lot to see and do on both sides of the river.

Since long before the two states existed, the Gorge has both fascinated and terrified travelers. For centuries this part of the river was a major trading ground for American Indians who came from as far away as Northern California and British Columbia to meet, talk and barter. Lewis and Clark marveled at the Gorge as they journeyed down the Columbia on the last stretch of their westward trek. Less captivated were the Oregon Trail immigrants of the 1840s who had to detour south around Mt. Hood or else mount their wagons on homemade rafts for a treacherous ride through the rocks and rapids west of The Dalles.

Today, visitors have it a lot easier. On the Oregon side, Route 84 parallels the Columbia River from Portland through such prime Gorge sightseeing areas as Cascade Locks and The Dalles. On the Washington side, Route 14 follows a mostly water-level route through the Gorge on the north bank, providing good views of the Oregon shore and such river traffic as tugboats pushing grain-laden barges downstream. Frequently sighted at the eastern edge of the Gorge, particularly near Hood River, are the bright sails of windsurfers attracted to some of the best conditions for their sport in North America. Although it's possible to tour the Gorge in a loop drive, taking Route 14 one way and Route 84 the other, we recommend crisscrossing it at various points in between. Declared a national scenic area by Congress in 1986, the Columbia Gorge, less than an hour east of Portland, has been a busy area for tourism development during the past several years. Although most hotels and restaurants are still concentrated on the Oregon side, it is the Washington side around Stevenson, with its interpretive center and deluxe resort, where the most recent activity has taken place. Fortunately, the Gorge is still largely unspoiled and provides much to keep waterfall lovers, windsurfers, kayakers, hikers and history buffs enthralled for days.

Although it's only half an hour from downtown Portland and the logical starting point for touring the Columbia Gorge region, many visitors to the region miss **Fort Vancouver**. What a pity. Located across the Columbia River from Portland, this national historic site is a cornerstone of Pacific Northwest history. Organized by the Hudson's Bay Company in 1825, the fort was a British fur-trading post and focal point for the commercial development of an area extending from British Columbia to Oregon and from Montana west to the Hawaiian Islands.

Ten structures have been reconstructed on their original fort locations. Collectively, they give a feel for life during the arrival of the first white settlers. One of the best ways to start your tour is at the visitors center with the introductory video. On your tour you'll see the re-created **Chief Factor's House**, once home to Dr. John McLoughlin, the British agent who befriended American settlers and is remembered as the "Father of Oregon." The phenomenal ability of the British to instantly gentrify the wilderness is reflected in the fine china, copper kettles and elegant furniture of this white clapboard home wrapped with a spacious veranda. You may be surprised to learn that the male officers dined without their wives.

The **Fur Warehouse** demonstrates how fur was collected and prepared for shipment to England. Also worth a visit are the **Blacksmith's Shop, Bakery, Kitchen, Wash Room, Stockade, Bastion** and a **Carpenter's Workshop**. At the **Indian Trade Shop and Dispensary**, you'll learn how American Indians bartered skillfully with the British. Because most of the items were imported, there was a two-year hiatus between ordering goods and receiving them. Fort Vancouver: Admission May 1 to September 30. ~ 1501 East Evergreen Boulevard, Vancouver, WA; 360-696-7655, fax 360-696-7657; www.nps.gov/fova/home.htm.

On nearby **Officer's Row**, you'll see 21 grand homes built for American Army leaders who served here during the latter half of the 19th and the early 20th centuries. These charming Victorians are the focus of a rehabilitation program combining interpretive and commercial use. Among the residences you can tour is the **Grant House**, which is the site of a folk art center featuring the work of local sculptors and quilters. Closed Sunday and Monday. ~ 360-694-5252, fax 360-737-9930. The **George C. Marshall House**, an imposing Queen Anne structure, also offers tours. Call for weekend hours. ~ 360-693-3103.

Next to Fort Vancouver is **Pearson Air Museum**. The field,   ◄ *HIDDEN* opened in 1905, is the oldest operating airfield in the United States. Exhibits feature a display on the world's first nonstop transpolar flight (Moscow to Vancouver) in 1937. The Soviet aviators were greeted by General George Marshall, who hosted them at his residence. The airpark exhibit features flyable vintage aircraft. Closed Monday. Admission. ~ 1115 East 5th Street, Vancouver, WA; 360-694-7026, fax 360-694-0824; www.pearsonairmuseum.org, e-mail pearson@pacifier.com.

Originally constructed as a Carnegie Library, **Clark County Historical Museum** has a better than good regional collection—from the American Indian artifacts and handicrafts to the historical doctor's office, general store and type shop. The doll collection includes everything from Eskimo creations to early Barbies. Not to be missed is the downstairs train room with a Pullman unit, railway telegram office, dining car china, a model train layout and photos of noteworthy local derailments. Closed Sunday and Monday. ~ 1511 Main Street, Vancouver, WA; phone/fax 360-695-4681; www.columbian.com/cchistorical/cchistorical.html.

To see more of Vancouver stop by the **Greater Vancouver Chamber of Commerce** and pick up the handy heritage tour brochure. ~ 404 East 15th Street, Suite 11, Vancouver, WA; 360-694-2588, fax 503-693-8279; www.vancouverusa.com, e-mail info@vancouverusa.com.

The taming of the Columbia River to provide low-cost power is one of the most controversial issues associated with the river. You'll get the pro side of the picture at **Bonneville Lock and Dam**, which is part of the **Bradford Island Visitors Center**. Extensive interpretive displays provide an overview of the dam's operation and history. ~ Route 84, Exit 40, four miles west of Cascade Locks, OR; 541-374-8820, fax 541-374-4516.

On the Washington side of the Gorge, you can also learn how the dam operates, see the fish ladders and visit the **Fort Cascades National Historic Site**. To get there, cross the Columbia River on the **Bridge of the Gods** (named for a natural bridge famous in Indian legend) and head west three miles on Route 14. The 59-acre historic site includes a one-and-a-half-mile trail featuring the sites of the old Portage Railroad, a onetime Chinook Indian village and an old military fort. ~ 541-427-4281, fax 541-374-4516.

Retrace your route across the Bridge of the Gods to the Oregon side and stop at the **Cascade Locks Museum** to see exhibits on American Indians, the first Columbia River locks, the portage road, logging and fishwheels. Water-powered, these rotating devices scooped so many salmon from the river that they were banned by the state in 1926. Closed October through April. ~ Marine Park, 1 Portage Road, Cascade Locks, OR; 541-374-8535.

The sternwheeler **Columbia Gorge** is docked in Cascade Locks from June through September. The multidecked old paddlewheel steamboat leads daytime and dinner cruises through the Gorge. ~ 541-374-8619, fax 541-374-8428.

Columbia River Gorge

PARKS
- **A** Ainsworth State Park
- **B** Goldendale Observatory State Park
- **C** Memaloose State Park
- **D** Northwestern Lake Park
- **E** Rooster Rock State Park
- **F** Viento State Park

Historic Columbia River Highway

This magnificent scenic route parallels Route 84, skirting the foot of sheer cliffs of the Columbia River Gorge with its wonderland of waterfalls, side canyons and verdant forest. The road was built by concrete tycoon Sam Hill, creator of the Maryhill Museum of Art, in 1916 as an attempt to convince Oregon legislatures to let him extend a highway up the length of the Columbia River. It was the first rural paved road in the Pacific Northwest.

VISTA HOUSE   Turn off Route 84 at Troutdale (Exit 17) to reach the Historic Columbia River Highway. At the mouth of the gorge, a road turns off to the right and winds up to Vista House in Crown Point State Park. This octagonal structure, perched 733 feet above the river, has an information desk, a gift shop, an espresso bar and an awesome view.

WATERFALLS   Among the major waterfalls that plunge into the gorge alongside the highway are **Latourelle Falls** (249 feet) in Guy W. Talbot State Park, **Sheppards Dell Falls** (two tiers, 50 and 60 feet) in Sheppards

On the Washington side of the bridge in Stevenson is the spacious **Columbia Gorge Interpretive Center**, where the focus is on the cultural and natural history of the Gorge. Located on a ten-acre site overlooking the river, the center includes a 37-foot-high replica of a 19th-century fishwheel, a restored Corless Steam Engine, a theater with a nine-projector slide show re-creating the cataclysmic formation of the Gorge and several exhibits drawn from the oral histories of local American Indians and pioneer settlers. The world's largest rosary collection is also housed here. Admission. ~ 990 Southwest Rock Creek Drive, Stevenson, WA; 509-427-8211, 800-991-2338, fax 509-427-7429.

Farther east on Route 14 is **Carson Hot Mineral Springs Resort**. On the Wind River, this resort is well-known by weary travelers for its mineral baths and massages, and can provide a restful stop for those who have been hiking all day on its beautiful hiking trails; there's also an 18-hole golf course. From here you can drive east along Route 14 to Route 141, which leads north along the White Salmon River Valley to Trout Lake, then return to Route 14 and the town of White Salmon. ~ 372 St. Martin's Spring Road, Carson, WA; 509-427-8292, 800-607-3678, fax 509-427-7242.

Just east of White Salmon in the small town of Bingen, Washington, is the **Gorge Heritage Museum**, where you can view his-

Dell State Park, **Bridal Veil Falls** (two tiers, 100 and 60 feet), and **Wah-keena Falls** (242 feet), where a mile-long trail leads to **Fairy Falls**, a magical 30-foot fan-shaped fall.

MULTNOMAH FALLS   The most popular tourist attraction in Oregon, this cascade plunges 620 feet, making it the second-tallest waterfall in the United States. Walk up the paved trail to the observation bridge between the upper and lower falls, where you'll get a misty view of the entire falls. In 1995, a 400-ton rock the size of a Greyhound bus fell from the top of the falls to the upper pool as a result of the ongoing erosion that originally formed the gorge. It caused about 20 minor injuries from flying debris, reminding us that the amazing geology here is still transforming on a grand scale.

STILL MORE FALLS   Two and a half miles beyond Multnomah Falls is **Horse-tail Falls** (176 feet). Nearby, a trail leads almost two miles through the lush greenery of Oneonta Gorge to **Triple Falls**, a 135-foot segmented fall. The historic highway rejoins the interstate at Ainsworth State Park—unbelievably a mere 18 miles from where it began.

toric photographs and American Indian artifacts, including tools, arrow points and beadwork. Closed Monday through Wednesday, and from Labor Day to Memorial Day. Admission. ~ 202 East Humboldt Street, Bingen, WA; 509-493-3228, fax 509-493-3149; e-mail mrno@gorge.net.

Your next stop should be on the Oregon side at **Hood River**, which has become a windsurfing capital thanks to the strong breezes here. Stop at the **Hood River County Visitors Center** for information on this scenic hub. ~ 405 Portway Avenue, Hood River, OR; 541-386-2000, 800-336-3530, fax 541-386-2057; www.hoodriver.org, e-mail hrccc@gorge.net.

The nearby **Hood River County Historical Museum** features exhibits on American Indian culture, the westward migration, pioneer farming, logging and the Columbia River. Also found here is a collection of period furniture and early-20th-century artifacts. Closed November through March. ~ Hood River, OR; phone/fax 541-386-6772.

One of the prettiest drives in Oregon is the 20-mile trip from Hood River to **Lost Lake** (elevation 3140 feet). At the lake you'll ◄ HIDDEN have a stunning angle on Mt. Hood—have your camera ready— and can rent a canoe or paddleboat (motorized boats are banned on the lake). In addition to fishing for rainbow trout, visitors like to walk the three-mile Lakeshore Trail that circles the lake. To reach the idyllic retreat, take Route 281 south to Dee and then follow the signs west to the lake. Do keep an eye out for logging trucks en route.

Although many visitors miss it, we strongly recommend a visit to **The Dalles**, on the Oregon side of the Gorge. The end of the Oregon Trail, where immigrants boarded vessels to float down the Columbia (the Barlow Trail later made it possible to complete the overland journey), this city has a superb old-town walking tour. Pick up a copy of the route map at **The Dalles Area Chamber of Commerce.** ~ 404 West 2nd Street, The Dalles, OR; 541-296-2231, fax 541-296-1688.

Highlights on this walk include the state's oldest bookstore, **Klindt's** (315 East 2nd Street), and the circa-1863 **Waldron Brothers Drugstore** nearby.

If you're traveling with children don't miss **WonderWorks A Children's Museum.** A storefront gem, this volunteer organization has hands-on exhibits for kids and a dress-up area. The young folk will love it. Closed Sunday. Admission. ~ 419 East 2nd Street, The Dalles, OR; 541-296-2444.

The **Fort Dalles Museum** is a favorite stop. Only one fort building, the Surgeon's Quarters, remains today. But the museum does preserve an excellent collection of pioneer artifacts, rifles, quilts and historic photographs. Open year-round, with reduced winter hours. Admission. ~ 15th and Garrison streets, The Dalles, OR; phone/fax 541-296-4547.

From here, take Route 30 east to Route 197 north. Cross the freeway to Bret Clodfelter Way and follow signs to **The Dalles Dam.** Perhaps the saddest part of this story focuses on the demise of the Gorge's best-known Indian fishing grounds. Wherever you go along this part of the Columbia River, in coffee shops and hotel lobbies, phone company offices and visitors centers, you're likely to see classic photographs of Indians dipping their nets into the river at heavenly Celilo Falls. To get the

THE LITTLE TRAIN THAT COULD

The scenic **Mt. Hood Railroad** excursion train links the Gorge with Mt. Hood along a route pioneered in 1906. The trip climbs up the Hood River Valley through steep canyons, orchards and forests. You'll enjoy panoramic views of the Cascades from the restored coaches on a 44-mile roundtrip journey. Special fall foliage trips are well worth your while as are murder-mystery and four-course dinner rides. The railroad runs April through October, with selected holiday trips between Thanksgiving and Christmas. ~ 110 Railroad Avenue, Hood River, OR; 541-386-3556, 800-872-4661; www.mthoodrr.com. e-mail mthoodrr@gorge.net.

full picture, leaf through the scrapbook of Celilo Falls fishing pictures at the Fort Dalles Museum.

If you continue on Route 84 east of The Dalles for 12 miles you'll come to a small **Celilo Falls Marker**, which indicates where these bounteous fishing waters prospered before being destroyed by the dam in the late 1950s.

A few miles farther east, on the Washington side, is one of the most isolated museums in America. **Maryhill Museum of Art**   ◄ HIDDEN
was designed in 1914 as the mansion residence of eccentric millionaire Sam Hill, and was supposed to oversee a Quaker agricultural town. But the plan for a new town flopped and the house on the hill eventually became a museum. This eclectic assemblage was dedicated in 1926 by Queen Marie of Rumania, which helps explain the presence of treasures from that nation's royal collection. Also here are Russian icons, a large collection of Rodin sculptures, Charles M. Russell's *Indian Buffalo Hunt*, French decorative arts, a good display of American Indian handicrafts and artifacts, and contemporary Pacific Northwest art, as well as one of the world's great chess collections. The museum now includes the world's only collection of post–World War II fashion mannequins. Views of the Columbia Gorge are spectacular, as are the sunsets. Closed mid-November to mid-March. Admission. ~ 35 Maryhill Museum Drive, Goldendale, WA; 509-773-3733, fax 509-773-6138; www.maryhillmuseum.org.

Although most are built with public funds, astronomical observatories are seldom accessible to the general public. One exception is the **Goldendale Observatory State Park Interpretive Center**. Just 11 miles north of the Maryhill Museum and Columbia River, this gem was created by four amateur astronomers and later taken over by the state. Afternoon instructional tours feature an opportunity to gaze at occasional sunspots and the bright planet Venus. Depending on night sky conditions, interpretive specialist Stephen R. Stout may allow visitors to view moon craters and the rings of Saturn and Jupiter through a 24-inch telescope. Be sure to call first for the observation schedule. ~ 1602 Observatory Drive, Goldendale, WA; 509-773-3141, fax 509-773-6929; www.perr.com/gosp.html, e-mail goldobs@gorge.net.

The **Cedarplace Inn Bed and Breakfast**, a white two-story home   **LODGING**
built in 1907, offers three large guest rooms and one suite, decorated in rose hues with antique furnishings including canopy or brass beds, clawfoot tubs, and soft featherbeds with down pillows and comforters. All these attributes may sound fairly typical of Victorian-style luxury B&Bs everywhere, but the location of this one, at the mouth of the Columbia River Gorge Scenic Area, makes it an extra special spot for a romantic getaway. ~ 2611 South Troutdale Road, Troutdale; 503-665-1189, 800-267-4744,

fax 503-665-6111; www.cedarplaceinn.com, e-mail cedarpl@aol. com. DELUXE.

Located just above the Columbia Gorge Interpretive Center in Stevenson, Washington, is the **Skamania Lodge**, a modern resort built in the tradition of the grand mountain lodges of the late 18th-century. Guests can congregate in the wood-paneled Gorge Room with its deep sofas and three-story river-rock fireplace. Public areas and the 195 guest rooms are handsomely decorated with mission-style furniture, Pendleton fabrics, petroglyph rubbings and American Indian–inspired rugs. The grounds include an 18-hole golf course, fitness center, whirlpools, swimming pool, and more. ~ 1131 Skamania Lodge Way, Stevenson, WA; 509-427-7700, 800-221-7117, fax 509-427-2547; www.skamania.com, e-mail lodge@gorge.net. DELUXE TO ULTRA-DELUXE.

Three miles east of Maryhill Museum of Art is Stonehenge, Sam Hill's memorial to local soldiers who died in World War I.

One of the frustrating facts of life on the road is the Sunday brunch. If you crave broccoli quiche, Italian sausages, artichoke frittatas, baklava, date tarts, fresh fruit and a dozen other treats, Monday to Saturday just won't do. Fortunately, the **Inn of the White Salmon** has solved this problem in an imaginative way. This lovely bed and breakfast offers brunch seven days a week. All you need do is check in to one of the inn's countrified rooms featuring brass beds and antiques, and this splendid feast is yours. Across the Columbia from Hood River, this inn also features a comfortable parlor. ~ 172 West Jewett Boulevard, White Salmon, WA; 509-493-2335, 800-972-5226; www.innofthewhitesalmon. com, e-mail innkeeper@gorge.net. MODERATE TO DELUXE.

HIDDEN ►

With rooms often in short supply during the summer windsurfing season, visitors who arrive in the Hood River area without reservations may want to call the **Hood River Bed and Breakfast Association** room-finder hotline for information on what is available at local inns. ~ 541-386-6767; www.moriah. com/hoodriverbba.

In Cascade Locks, 20 miles west of Hood River, **Bridge of the Gods Motel** provides affordable rustic rooms. All 15 units have queen-size beds; five of them offer kitchens. ~ 630 WaNaPa Street, Cascade Locks, OR; 541-374-8628, fax 541-374-2217; www. bridgeofthegodsmotel.com. BUDGET.

The **Columbia Gorge Hotel** is a 42-room landmark where strains of Bach waft through the halls, sculptured carpets highlight the public areas and the fireplace is always roaring. This Mediterranean-style hotel tucks guests into wicker, brass, canopy or hand-carved antique beds. The dining room, home of a popular five-course farm breakfast, offers splendid riverfront dining. Relax in the Valentino Lounge, take a walk through the manicured gardens or enjoy a mineral wrap at the in-house spa. ~

4000 Westcliff Drive, Hood River, OR; 541-386-5566, 800-345-1921, fax 541-387-5414; www.columbiagorgehotel.com, e-mail cghotel@gorge.net. ULTRA-DELUXE.

Beautifully located overlooking the Columbia, **Vagabond Lodge** offers spacious, carpeted rooms—some opening right onto the riverfront. All feature contemporary furniture, doubles or queens and a secluded garden setting. For the price, it's hard to beat this motel west of town. ~ 4070 Westcliff Drive, Hood River, OR; 541-386-2992, 877-386-2992, fax 541-386-3317; www.vagabondlodge.com, e-mail jcranmer@gorge.net. BUDGET TO MODERATE.

Three miles south of Hood River in the midst of apple and pear orchards is **The Beryl House**, a classic American woodframe farmhouse with a wraparound porch. The four guest rooms are simply decorated with reproduction antique furniture and have views of Mt. Hood, Mt. Adams and the surrounding orchards. Guests have access to a living room with a piano, TV, VCR and stereo system; breakfast includes fresh fruit from the Hood River Valley. ~ 4079 Barrett Drive, Hood River, OR; 541-386-5567, fax 541 387-8833; www.moriah.com/beryl, e-mail berylhouse@aol.com. MODERATE.

Located just five blocks from downtown Hood River is the 1908 Victorian **Inn at the Gorge Bed & Breakfast**. Three suites and one room have antique furnishings and private baths. Enjoy the surrounding gardens, nap in the hammock beneath the cedar tree or just laze the day away on the wraparound porch. Closed mid-October to mid-May. ~ 1113 Eugene Street, Hood River; phone/fax 541-386-4429; www.innatthegorge.com, e-mail inn@gorge.net. MODERATE.

The **Columbia Windrider Inn** is operated by an avid Columbia Gorge sailor and windsurfer who likes to play host to other sailboard afficionados. Situated on a quiet residential street, this historic 1921 home has maple wood floors and four large guest rooms, each with private bath, air conditioning and a queen- or king-size bed. Facilities include a swimming pool, a hot tub and a recreation room. ~ 200 West 4th Street, The Dalles; 541-296-2607; e-mail cwindrider@aol.com. BUDGET.

For contemporary motel accommodations try the **Quality Inn**. The fully carpeted rooms have oak tables and queen beds featuring spreads with floral designs. There's a pool on the premises, as well as Cousins, the only restaurant we know that has a John Deere tractor in the middle of the dining room. ~ 2114 West 6th Street, The Dalles, OR; 541-298-5161, 800-848-9378, fax 541-298-6411. MODERATE.

With a name like **Hidden House**, we couldn't resist. This structure and the adjacent residence (now a retail business) at 110 West 13th Street were built by Lowell M. Hidden and his son Foster.

DINING

◄ *HIDDEN*

Much of Vancouver was built with Hidden bricks from the family factory, still in operation today. Once the home of Clark College, this handsome red-brick Victorian offers dining upstairs and down. Antiques are an integral part of the decor, which includes three fireplaces, the original stained glass, ash and black-walnut woodwork and a covered veranda ideal for outside dining. The menu features steaks, seafood, chicken Kiev and veal dishes served with homemade poppy-seed bread. Northwest wines are featured. Dinner is served nightly except Monday. ~ 100 West 13th Street, Vancouver, WA; 360-696-2847. MODERATE TO DELUXE.

In business for over 70 years, **The Holland Restaurant** must be doing something right. Once a creamery, now a family-style restaurant with a contemporary look, this spacious establishment serves generous portions at low prices. American cuisine is the keynote here, with dishes ranging from prime rib to prawns. The on-premises bakery is known for its strudel, pumpkin muffins and danishes. Breakfast and lunch only. ~ Main and McLoughlin streets, Vancouver, WA; 360-694-7842, fax 360-750-8612. BUDGET.

In Stevenson, Washington, **Skamania Lodge** has a grand dining room with massive wooden ceiling beams and superb views of the Gorge. The specialties are Northwest-inspired dishes prepared in a wood-burning oven, including oak-crusted trout and roasted wild game, meats and seafood. ~ 1131 Skamania Lodge Way, Stevenson, WA; 509-427-7700, 800-227-7117, fax 509-427-2547; www.skamania.com, e-mail reservations@skamania.com. DELUXE.

The **Big River Grill** in downtown Stevenson is a convivial place with wooden booths and old photographs on the walls. Both locals and visitors come here to enjoy salmon chowder in bread bowls (Fridays only), pasta specials, salads topped with grilled meats and such vegetarian entrées as Mediterranean linguine and nutty garden burgers. ~ 192 Southwest 2nd Avenue, Stevenson, WA; 509-427-4888. MODERATE.

Almost smack dab on the railroad tracks in Stevenson is the **Crossing Café**, a tiny wood-framed cottage across from the *Columbia Gorge* paddlewheeler landing. Along with deli sandwiches and hearty soups, the Crossing has a changing menu of ethnic-inspired lunch items such as beef burritos and vegetable curries. Lunch only. Closed Christmas to mid-April. ~ 127 Russell Street, Stevenson, WA; 509-427-8097. BUDGET.

HIDDEN ▶

About 20 minutes north of the Gorge, and well worth the trip, is one of the Gorge's most intriguing restaurants, **The Logs**. You'll be impressed by the roasted chicken, hickory-smoked ribs, giant fries and huckleberry pie served in this log-cabin setting. The battered and deep-fried chicken gizzards and cheese sticks are a big hit with the regular clientele, which includes locals, rafters, skiers and devotees of the rich mud pie. In business for six decades, this is the place where city slickers will come face to face with their first jackalope, safely mounted on the wall. ~ Route 141, White Salmon, WA; 509-493-1402; e-mail logsres@gorge.net. BUDGET.

Tucked away in the woods on the Oregon side is **Stonehedge Inn**, an antique-filled home preparing Continental and Northwest dining at its finest. Set in a beautiful garden, this paneled restaurant has a tiny mahogany bar and a roaring fireplace. Among the dishes are scallop sauté, veal chanterelle, jumbo prawns and filet of salmon. Light entrées, such as a seafood platter, are also recommended. Call for summer hours. ~ 3405 Cascade Drive, Hood River, OR; 541-386-3940, fax 541-386-9391. MODERATE TO DELUXE.

◄ HIDDEN

It's hard to beat the breakfasts at **Bette's Place**, a small, mauve-toned café with floral curtains. Bette's bakes 13 kinds of muffins daily, including cinnamon and Oregon blackberry, and also serves eggs Benedict, omelettes, strawberry waffles and pancakes topped with fresh fruit. ~ 416 Oak Street, in the Oak Mall, Hood River, OR; 541-386-1880. BUDGET.

Pasquale's Ristorante has breezy indoor and sidewalk seating in the center of this resort town. The heart of the dining room is a handcrafted bar with an etched glass mirror. Entrées include filet of salmon, cappellini bolognese and rack of lamb. ~ In the Hood River Hotel, 102 Oak Street, Hood River, OR; 541-386-1900, fax 541-386-6090; www.hoodriverhotel.com, e-mail hrhotel@gorge.net. MODERATE TO DELUXE.

As its name suggests, **The Mesquitery Restaurant & Bar** is best known for its meat and seafood dishes cooked on a mesquite grill. Honey-glazed baby-back ribs and ahi tuna topped with rock shrimp are among the highlights, as are heaping main-dish cobb and caesar salads. The inside dining area is filled with high-backed booths and rich wood paneling, while outside is a two-level enclosed deck area with colorful planters. ~ 1219 12th Street, Hood River, OR; 541-386-2002, fax 541-387-4002. MODERATE.

An elegant dining room overlooking the Gorge, **Columbia River Court** is a romantic place to dine on roast pork tenderloin,

HOME ON THE HOOD

The chandeliered **Hood River Hotel** is a restored brick landmark with 41 rooms and suites. Brightly painted rooms are appointed with oak furniture, four-poster beds, casablanca fans, wing chairs and antiques. Some offer views of the Columbia River. Comfortable sitting areas, a lounge offering jazz music and a cheery café are all part of the charm. Kitchenette suites are available. ~ 102 Oak Avenue, Hood River, OR; 541-386-1900, 800-386-1859, fax 541-386-6090; www.hoodriverhotel.com, e-mail hrhotel@gorge.net. MODERATE TO DELUXE.

fresh Oregon salmon, rack of lamb or Dungeness crab with lobster sauce and risotto. Done in an Early American design with oak furniture and candlelit tables, this establishment is well known for its lavish farm breakfast. ~ 4000 Westcliff Drive, Hood River, OR; 541-386-5566, fax 541-387-5414; www.columbiagorgehotel.com, e-mail cghotel@gorge.net. DELUXE TO ULTRA-DELUXE.

Located in one of the most historic buildings in The Dalles, the **Baldwin Saloon** was built in 1876 and has an 18-foot-long mahogany back bar and turn-of-the-20th-century oil paintings on the brick walls. The restaurant is known for its seafood and oyster dishes (baked and on the half shell) and also serves thick sandwiches, burgers, soups and desserts. Breads are baked on the premises. Closed Sunday. ~ 1st and Court streets, The Dalles, OR; 541-296-5666. MODERATE.

For heaping platters of chicken, steak or shrimp fajitas, the place to go is **Casa El Mirador,** a cozy family-run restaurant with embroidered sombreros and decorative items from Mexico adorning the walls. Crabmeat burritos, chimichangas, tacos and other south-of-the-border staples also make good choices. ~ 302 West 2nd Street, The Dalles, OR; 541-298-7388. BUDGET TO MODERATE.

At **Bailey's Place,** locals swear by the prime rib, East Coast surf clams and Pacific salmon fresh from the nearby Columbia. Dinners, complete with fresh-baked bread, vegetables, salad and soup, include fettuccine with fresh scallops, chicken piccata, and sautéed scampi. The restaurant also boasts an impressive wine list, with over 500 wines to choose from. Dinner only. Closed Sunday and Monday. ~ 515 Liberty Street, The Dalles, OR; 541-296-6708, fax 541-298-8859. MODERATE.

Johnny's Café specializes in country home cooking that will stick to your ribs. For decades, locals have been coming here to feast on roasted chicken, chicken fried steak, fish-and-chips, homemade pies and puddings. ~ 408 East 2nd Street, The Dalles, OR; 541-296-4565. BUDGET TO MODERATE.

GORGING YOURSELF

After a visit to Multnomah Falls it makes sense to dine at **Multnomah Falls Lodge.** The smoked-salmon-and-cheese platter and generous salads are recommended. The European-style lodge building with a big stone fireplace, scenic paintings of the surroundings and lovely views will add to your enjoyment of the Gorge. ~ Off Route 84, Bridal Veil, WA; 503-695-2376, fax 503-695-2338; www.multnomahfalls.citysearch.com. DELUXE.

Fort Vancouver Gift Shop is the place to go for books, maps and
pamphlets on Pacific Northwest history. We recommend picking
up a copy of the *The Eagle in the Fort* by Dorothy Morris. ~
1501 East Evergreen Boulevard, Vancouver, WA; 360-696-7655,
fax 360-696-7657.

SHOPPING

Aviation buffs will want to stop by the gift shop at **Pearson
Air Museum**. The shop has an ace collection of memorabilia and
souvenirs for adults and juniors alike. ~ 1115 East 5th Street, Vancouver, WA; 360-694-7026, fax 360-694-0824.

Pendleton Woolen Mills and Outlet Store offers big savings on
irregulars. Tours of the mill, in operation since 1912, are available,
but call first for schedule information. ~ #2 17th Street, Washou-
gal, WA; 360-835-1118, fax 360-835-5451.

Also on the Washington side, Stevenson's small, walkable
downtown has a number of distinctive art galleries and gift shops.
Lewis and Clark Gallery sells American Indian arts and crafts. ~
240 Southwest 1st Street; 509-427-7754.

Carson, Washington, has a few sources for antique collectors,
including **Barely Antiques**. Closed Monday and Tuesday. ~ 1012
Wind River Highway, Carson, WA; 509-427-7727. You can also
find antiques, books and postcards at the **Wind River Trading Post**.
~ 981 Wind River Highway, Carson, WA; 509-427-4766.

A good place to find books on the region is **Waucoma Bookstore**, which is also well stocked with fiction, children's books,
cards, magazines, children's toys and handcrafted pottery. ~ 202
Oak Street, Hood River, OR; 541-386-5353.

Columbia Art Gallery represents over 150 artists, primarily
from the Columbia Gorge region. Featured are the works of photographers, printmakers, potters, glassblowers, jewelers, weavers,
sculptors and painters. ~ 207 2nd Street, Hood River, OR;
541-386-4512, fax 541-386-4841.

The Dalles is home to Oregon's oldest bookstore, **Klindts**,
which dates from 1870 and still has an old-time ambience with
high ceilings and glass-topped counters stocked with collectibles.
Books on the Pacific Northwest, both new and used, are a specialty,
as are rare and out-of-print books. ~ 319 East 2nd Street, The
Dalles, OR; 541-296-4342.

The Dalles Art Center, located in the historic Carnegie Library,
exhibits work by local and regional artists. Most of this fine art
is available for purchase. The gallery showcases paintings, pottery, jewelry, beadwork, glasswork, photography and baskets. ~
220 East 4th Street, The Dalles, OR; 541-296-4759.

A popular gay and lesbian nightspot in Vancouver, Washington,
is **North Bank Tavern**, which has a video area, dancefloor and
outdoor patio. Occasional cover. ~ 106 West 6th Street, Vancouver,
WA; 360-695-3862.

NIGHTLIFE

Text continued on page 368.

South of the Gorge

Since you've already dipped your toe into Oregon while visiting the Columbia River Gorge, you may now want to visit the place named the "Most Livable U.S. City" by the U.S. Conference of Mayors—Portland. Near the entrance to the Gorge, Portland boasts a rich cultural life and is blessed with some of the prettiest urban streets in the Northwest. A good place to orient yourself is the **Portland/Oregon Visitors Association**. Here you can pick up helpful maps and brochures. ~ Front and Salmon streets; 503-222-2223; www.pova.com, e-mail admin@pova.com

Walk west on Main Street to the **Portland Building**, a postmodern office landmark. This whimsical skyscraper represents the Northwest with an American Indian motif making extensive use of turquoise and earth tones. Above the entrance is **Portlandia**, the world's second-largest hammered-copper sculpture. ~ 1120 Southwest 5th Avenue; 503-823-4000, fax 503-823-6924.

On the Portland Building's second floor is the **Regions Arts and Culture Council**. You'll find *Portlandia* molds and renderings of the building, as well as pieces from the *Visual Chronicle of Portland*, a continually evolving series of works on paper meant to represent how the city views itself. ~ 1120 Southwest 5th Avenue; 503-823-5111, fax 503-823-5432.

Continue west on Madison Street to South Park and turn left to the **Oregon History Center**, a vast repository of Oregon history. This is the place to learn the story of the region's American Indians, the arrival of the Europeans and the westward migration. You'll find sea chests from early voyages and artifacts documenting the political and social evolution of the West. Closed Monday. Admission. ~ 1200 Southwest Park Avenue; 503-222-1741, fax 503-478-3021; www.ohs.org, e-mail orhist@ohs.org.

Adjacent to the Oregon History Center is the **First Congregational Church**, dating from 1895. This Venetian gothic–style basalt structure, modeled on Boston's Old South Church and crowned by a 175-foot tower. ~ 1126 Southwest Park Avenue; 503-228-7219, fax 503-228-6522.

Across the street is the **Portland Art Museum**, known for its collection of Asian and European art as well as 20th-century American sculpture. The collection of American Indian art and artifacts is one of the top collections of its kind in the U.S. The pre-Columbian pieces are notable, and the Cameroon collection is nationally known. Don't miss the skylit sculpture courtyard. Closed Monday. Admission. ~ 1219 Southwest Park Avenue; 503-226-2811; www.pam.org, e-mail info@pam.org.

Continue north to Yamhill Street and turn right. Walk two more blocks to **Pioneer Courthouse Square**, a popular Portland gathering point. A waterfall and 64,000 red bricks inscribed with the names of local residents who donated money for the square's construction are all here. Named for adjacent **Pioneer Courthouse**, the oldest public building in Oregon (completed in 1873), which you may want to explore, the square offers a variety of special events including concerts. ~ 701 Southwest 6th Avenue; 503-223-1613, fax 503-222-7425.

Continue walking east on Yamhill past the 19th-century Victorian Italianates and **Yamhill Marketplace**, site of many restaurants, coffee bars and a health club, will come into view. ~ 110 Southwest Yamhill Street; 503-227-3883.

Proceed onward to **Tom McCall Waterfront Park**, which is notable for being the green river frontage that 20 years ago replaced a busy, ugly stretch of freeway blocking the Willamette. ~ Front Avenue. Go south past **Mill Ends Park**; at just two feet wide, this is the smallest park in the world. ~ In the median at Southwest Front Avenue and Taylor Street.

Walk south past the Hawthorne Bridge on Harbor Way and you'll come to the sloped-roof buildings of **RiverPlace,** a popular shopping, hotel, restaurant and nightclub complex on the water. A promenade overlooks the Willamette River and the marina's plush yachts. To fully experience the waterfront, consider boarding an excursion boat departing from River-Place Marina. ~ 1510 Southwest Harbor Way behind the RiverPlace Hotel.

Then return north to the **Oregon Maritime Museum**. Here's your chance to learn Northwestern maritime history and see models of early ships, historical photographs and interpretive displays. You can also climb on board the fully restored *Portland*, a sternwheel steam tugboat. Closed Monday and Tuesday. Admission. ~ 113 Southwest Naito Parkway; 503-224-7724; www.teleport.com/~omcm/index.phtml.

The **Skidmore/Old Town** area illustrates Portland's commitment to adaptive reuse. This area between Front and 3rd streets both north and south of Burnside Street boomed in the later 19th century when the harbor was bustling. Eventually this became the rowdy part of town, and the buildings fell into disrepair. But interest has grown in the waterfront over the past 30 years, and historic commercial buildings and warehouses have been reborn as trendy shops, galleries, restaurants and nightclubs.

Next, head north through **Chinatown** on 4th Avenue. Not as large as it was a hundred years ago, it is still filled with Chinese restaurants and markets. The ornate entry gate at Burnside Street and 4th Avenue looks a bit out of place among the neighboring adult bookstores.

Finally, everyone should take time out to visit the **Church of Elvis**. Head down 6th Avenue to Burnside Street and take a right. Walk one block to Broadway and take a left; proceed one block to Ankeny Street, take a right and this 24-hour art gallery will be halfway down the block. The "church" fuses religion, rock and metaphysics in a multimedia window presentation. Open reliably on weekends, on weekdays by appointment. ~ 720 Southwest Ankeny Street; 503-226-3671; www.churchofelvis.com, e-mail church@churchofelvis.com.

For more information on Portland, consult *Hidden Oregon* (Ulysses Press, 2001).

The **Power Station** is a theater and pub located in the former Multnomah County poor farm. The theater presents movies and occasional special events in the farm's former boiler room. The pub serves a full menu in the converted laundry building. Also on the premises is the **Edgefield Brewery and Winery**. ~ 2126 Southwest Halsey Street, Troutdale, OR; 503-492-4686; www.mcmenamins. com, e-mail general@mcmenamins.com.

The **Skamania Lodge** has live acoustic music before a wood-burning fireplace on weekends in summer. ~ 1131 Skamania Lodge Way, Stevenson, WA; 509-427-2527, fax 509-427-2547.

Scootie's Bungalow Tavern has televised sports, two pool tables and dart boards. ~ Wind River Highway, Carson, WA; 509-427-4523.

Full Sail Brewing Company offers tastings of their very popular hand-crafted beers, as well as a pub-style menu and deck seating with fine views of the Columbia. ~ 506 Columbia Street, Hood River, OR; 541-386-2247, fax 541-386-7316.

PARKS

ROOSTER ROCK STATE PARK Offering more than three miles of sandy Columbia River frontage, this 872-acre park is near the Gorge's west end. The rock, named for a towering promontory, is adjacent to a camping site chosen by Lewis and Clark in 1805. Well-known for swimming and beginner windsurfing, Rooster Rock also has excellent hiking trails, a small lake, a disc golf course and a forested bluff. Anglers can fish for salmon. There are picnic tables and restrooms. Day-use fee, $3. ~ Located in Oregon 22 miles east of Portland on Route 84 at Exit 25; 503-695-2261, fax 503-695-2226.

VIENTO STATE PARK Originally a rest stop on the old Columbia River Highway, this 247-acre park includes a riverfront and Viento Creek forest section. Dramatic views of the Columbia River make this a popular camping and picnicking facility. It can get very windy, and be aware that trains

HAND-PICKED PRESENTS

Locally made jams, jellies, wine and other food products make terrific presents for the folks back home. **The Gift House** carries a variety of home-grown products, including wine and jams. ~ 204 Oak Street, Hood River, OR; 541-386-9234. Pick up a fine Oregon white or red at **The Wine Sellers**. ~ 514 State Street, Hood River, OR; 541-386-4647. **Rasmussen Farms** sells strawberries, Hood River apples, Comice pears and cherries. Apples and pears can be shipped as gift packs. ~ 3020 Thomsen Road off Route 35 south of Hood River, OR; 541-386-4622, 800-548-2243, fax 541-386-4702.

pass through the gorge at night. Facilities include picnic tables, showers and restrooms. Closed November through March. Day-use fee, $3. ~ On Route 84 Exit 56, eight miles west of Hood River in Oregon; 541-374-8811, fax 541-695-2226.

▲ There are 18 tent sites and 57 hookups; $14 to $16 per night.

AINSWORTH STATE PARK 🏃 Ranking high among the treasures of the Columbia River Scenic Highway is this 156-acre park. Near the bottom of St. Peter's Dome, the forested park has a gorgeous hiking trail that connects with a network extending throughout the region. A serene getaway, the only sound of civilization you're likely to hear is that of passing trains. There are picnic tables, showers and restrooms. Closed November through March. ~ Located on Route 30, the Columbia River Scenic Highway, 37 miles east of Portland on the Oregon side; 503-695-2301, fax 503-695-2226.

▲ All 45 sites have full hookups; $18 per night. There are also four walk-in sites; $12 per night.

MEMALOOSE STATE PARK The park is named for an offshore Columbia River island that was an American Indian burial ground. This 336-acre site spreads out along a two-mile stretch of riverfront and is forested with pine, oak and fir. Much of the park is steep and rocky. It can also be very windy. "Memaloose," in case you were wondering, is a Chinook word linked to the sacred burial ritual. There are horseshoes, a playground, interpretive programs in summer, showers and restrooms. Closed November through March. ~ Located off Route 84, 11 miles west of The Dalles in Oregon. Take the Memaloose Rest Stop exit, then make a right into the park. Westbound access only; 541-478-3008, fax 541-478-2369.

▲ There are 65 tent sites and 45 hookups; $15 to $19 per night. Contact Reservations Northwest for reservations; 800-452-5687.

Outdoor Adventures

FISHING

This is a prime fishing spot: Salmon, steelhead, walleye and sturgeon are all found in the Columbia River area. For guides or charters in the Portland area, contact **Page's Northwest Guide Service**. ~ 14321 Southeast Bush Street, Portland, OR; 503-760-3373. For trips specializing in sturgeon on the Columbia and Willamette rivers, try **Portland Fishing Adventures**. ~ P.O. Box 1131, Sandy, OR; 503-668-8541. In The Dalles, **Glenn Summers** offers fishing information. ~ P.O. Box 436, The Dalles, OR 97058; 541-296-5949. For both fishing and flyfishing information on steelhead, salmon and walleye in the Columbia and John Day rivers, contact **Fly by Nyte Guide Service**. ~ P.O. Box 24, Rufus, OR 97050; phone/fax 541-298-2770. Also offering guided fishing trips in the

Gorge area is **Northwest Guide Service**. ~ Woodard Creek Road, Skamania, WA; 509-427-4625; www.skamania.net/nwguide.

The art of flyfishing abounds on rivers in the Gorge region. **The Gorge Fly Shop** arranges flyfishing excursions to such popular destinations as Deschutes. All levels of lessons are available. ~ 201 Oak Street, Hood River, OR; 541-386-6977, 800-685-7309 ext. 1019; www.gorgeflyshop.com.

WIND-SURFING

One of the world's best windsurfing areas, the Columbia Gorge is a great place to learn this exciting sport. If you're experienced and want to rent equipment, contact **Hood River Windsurfing**. ~ 101 Oak Street, Hood River, OR; 541-386-5787; www.hood riverwindsurfing.com. The **Rhonda Smith Windsurfing Center** offers lessons and equipment, and has a beginner beach area in front of the Hood River Inn. ~ Port Marina Park, Hood River, OR; 541-386-9463, 800-241-2430; windsurf.gorge.net/rhondas. **Big Winds** offers rentals and instruction for children and adults, and a full-service retail shop. ~ 207 Front Street, Hood River, OR; 541-386-6086, 888-509-4210; www.bigwinds.com.

RIVER RUNNING

The White Salmon River north of the Columbia is a popular whitewater rafting spot.

There are some 30 Class II, III and IV rapids along the short course of the White Salmon River, a pool-and-drop mountain stream that is fed by rainfall and snowmelt from Mt. Adams, 30 miles distant. For a half-day guided whitewater adventure on the White Salmon, call **Phil's White Water Adventure**. ~ 38 Northwestern Lake, White Salmon, WA; 509-493-2641, 800-366-2004; business.gorge.net/philswwa. Also try **North Cascades River Expeditions**. ~ P.O. Box 116, Arlington, WA 98223; 360-435-9548, 800-634-8433; riverexpeditions.com.

River Drifters Whitewater Tours in Bend will outfit trips on the White Salmon, Deschutes and Owyhee rivers. Gorge trips may include lunch at a local winery. ~ P.O. Box 7962, Bend, OR 97708; 800-972-0430; www.riverdrifters.com.

Another often-rafted river in the Gorge is the Klickitat. **Renegade River Rafters** offers two- to three-day trips on the Deschutes

---

GIVE YOURSELF A BREAK

A little Washington gem on the White Salmon River north of the Columbia, **Northwestern Lake** is an ideal destination for a day trip where you can swim, fish, hike or just loaf. There are also summer cabins nearby for those who want to stay longer. ~ Head west from White Salmon on Route 14 to Route 141. Continue north five miles to the park.

and half-day trips on the Klickitat. ~ P.O. Box 263, Stevenson, WA 98648; 509-427-7238.

In Washington, there's also **All Rivers Adventures**, which offers day trips to the Klickitat as well as three-day trips elsewhere. ~ P.O. Box 12, Cashmere, WA 98815; 509-782-2254, 800-743-5628; www.allrivers.com.

SKIING

With Hood River and the Columbia River Gorge practically at the foot of snowcapped Mt. Hood, it's possible to ski in the morning (even in July) and windsurf in the afternoon. **Mt. Hood Meadows** spreads across 2150 acres and offers 87 trails, most of which are intermediate and expert level. In addition to alpine skiing, there are snowboarding parks with several half pipes and quarter pipes. Night skiing and 30 kilometers of cross-country trails are also available. ~ Take Route 84 Exit 64 in Hood River then follow Route 35 south to the Meadows entrance; 503-337-2222, 503-227-7669 (snowline); skihood.com.

Contact **Hood River Windsurfing** about ski rentals and repairs. ~ 101 Oak Avenue, Hood River, OR; 541-386-5787.

GOLF

It's only nine holes, but **Hood River Golf and Country Club** has full mountain views, pear orchards and a driving range. ~ 1850 Country Club Road, Hood River, OR; 541-386-3009. **Indian Creek Golf Course**, with its gentle rolling hills, is a dry, year-round 18-hole course. ~ 3605 Brookside Drive, Hood River, OR; 541-386-7770, 800-369-4137; www.indiancreekgc.com. In Stevenson, Washington, there's the 18-hole **Skamania Lodge Golf Course**, with views of the Columbia River and Bridge of the Gods. ~ 1131 Skamania Lodge Way; 509-427-2541, 800-293-0418. In Carson, Washington, the **Hot Springs Golf Course** has 18 holes and is great for beginners. ~ Hot Springs Avenue and St. Martins Road; 509-427-5150. Located on Route 14 in Washington between Beacon Rock and North Bonneville is **Beacon Rock Public Golf Course**. There's nine holes near the Columbia with sand traps and water hazards. ~ 509-427-5730.

RIDING STABLES

For equestrians, the Gorge area has limited options. **Mountain Shadow Ranch** provides guided trips on trails and also offers rides for young children. ~ 690 Herman Creek Road, Cascade Locks; 541-374-8592; business.gorge.net/mtshadow.

BIKING

The Columbia River Gorge along Route 84 is prime cycling territory, particularly along any portion of the 62-mile route from Portland to Hood River. The old Columbia River Highway, which parallels Route 84, is less trafficked, calmer, scenic and a wonderful way to experience the Gorge. The **Dalles Riverfront Trail**, a paved bike trail, extends from the west part of The Dalles to Dalles Dam.

During the summer, full- and half-day guided tours through the Hood River Valley and Columbia Gorge and on Mt. Hood provide a variety of riding options for all experience levels.

Bike Rentals   Discover Bicycles rents and sells mountain bikes, road bikes and tandems and can provide information about guided bike tours. ~ 205 Oak Street, Hood River, OR; 541-386-4820; www.discoverbicycles.com.

For mountain-bike rentals, sales and repair in The Dalles, try **Life Cycles.** ~ 418 East 2nd Street, The Dalles, OR; 541-296-9588.

HIKING   All distances listed for hiking trails are one way unless otherwise noted.

Latourell Falls Trail (2.2 miles), on the Columbia River Highway three miles east of Crown Point, is a moderately difficult walk leading along a streambed to the base of the upper falls. To extend this walk another mile, take a loop trail beginning at the top of lower Latourell Falls and returning to the highway at Talbot Park.

Near the Bridal Veil exit off Route 84 is **#415 Angels Rest Trail** (4.5 miles), an easy hike leading to an overlook. This route can be extended another 15 miles to Bonneville Dam by taking the **#400 Gorge Trail**, an amazing path that passes many of the Gorge's stunning cascades, including Multnomah Falls, Triple Falls and Horsetail Falls.

Eagle Creek Campground at Exit 41 on Route 84 is the jump-off point for the easy **#440 Eagle Creek Trail** to Punch Bowl Falls (2 miles) or Tunnel Falls (6 miles), the latter of which has a man-made tunnel passing behind the cascading water. You can continue to follow the wildflower-riddled path (part of the Pacific Crest Trail) through the Columbia Wilderness, up to Wahtum Lake (13 miles). Four campsites provide rest between Eagle Creek and the lake.

On the Washington side of the river west of Bonneville Dam is the one-mile trail leading to the top of **Beacon Rock,** an 800-foot monolith noted by Lewis and Clark. Ascended by a series of switchbacks guarded by railings, this trail offers numerous views of the Gorge.

East of Home Valley, Oregon, on Route 14 is the **Dog Mountain Trail** (6 miles), a difficult climb up 2900 feet for impressive views of Mt. Hood, Mt. St. Helens and Mt. Adams. During May and June, the surrounding hills are covered with wildflowers, making this an extraordinary time to hike the trail.

▼▼▼▼▼▼▼▼▼
Transportation

CAR

Route 84 runs the length of the Columbia River Gorge on the Oregon side and just east of the town of Troutdale is paralleled by the **Historic Columbia River Highway,** a windy road that offers awesome views of the Gorge. **Route**

14 travels along the river's Washington side. **Route 35** heads south from Hood River on the Oregon side toward Mt. Hood.

If you plan on flying to the Columbia River Gorge area, **Portland International Airport** is the closest airport. Air B.C., Alaska Airlines, America West Airlines, American Airlines, Delta Air Lines, Hawaiian Airlines, Horizon Air, Northwest Airlines, Southwest Airlines, Trans World Airlines and United Airlines all fly into Portland.

AIR

Greyhound Bus Lines (800-231-2222) offers service four times daily to Hood River. The Hood River terminal is at 600 East Marina Way, Hood River, OR. ~ 541-386-1212. They also service The Dalles at 201 Federal Street, OR. ~ 541-296-2421.

BUS

Amtrak provides daily service to Portland, Hood River and The Dalles in each direction. ~ 800-872-7245; www.amtrak.com.

TRAIN

Car rentals in Hood River are provided by **Knoll Motor Co.** ~ 1105 12th Street; 541-386-3011. In The Dalles, contact **Brace Brothers Rent A Car**. ~ 1119 West 2nd Street; 541-296-3761.

CAR RENTALS

Hood River is served by the **Columbia Area Transit**. Buses run to Parkdale, Odell and Cascade Locks. ~ 541-386-4202.

PUBLIC TRANSIT

In Hood River, call **Hood River Taxi and Transportation**. ~ 541-386-2255. In The Dalles, try **White Lion Cab**. ~ 541-296-6299.

TAXIS

Index

Lodging Index

LODGING SERVICES

HOSTELS

Dining Index

Travel With Someone You Trust®

Wherever you go, it's good to have a guide. Someone who knows the territory. Someone who can help you find those hidden spots and great deals. For generations of travelers, AAA has been that guide.

When you join AAA, you gain access to a world of information: AAA TourBooks, TripTiks, and maps help you find exciting things to do and wonderful places to stay. As a member of one of the world's largest consumer organizations, you receive the best deals from the world's best travel providers as well as valuable discounts from a wide range of Show Your Card & Save® partners. In addition, AAA financial and insurance services provide the freedom to help you pay for your travels and enjoy peace of mind on the ride.

As a AAA member, you join a community that numbers over 42 million members and that provides partnerships with the biggest names in travel. We invite you to explore the world. Let AAA be your guide. With over 4000 offices nationwide, you can find us in many local communities or on the Web at www.aaa.com.

Notes

Notes

HIDDEN GUIDES

Adventure travel or a relaxing vacation?—"Hidden" guidebooks are the only travel books in the business to provide detailed information on both. Aimed at environmentally aware travelers, our motto is "Adventure Travel Plus." These books combine details on unique hotels, restaurants and sightseeing with information on camping, sports and hiking for the outdoor enthusiast.

THE NEW KEY GUIDES

Based on the concept of ecotourism, The New Key Guides are dedicated to the preservation of Central America's rare and endangered species, architecture and archaeology. Filled with helpful tips, they give travelers everything they need to know about these exotic destinations.

Ulysses Press books are available at bookstores everywhere. If any of the following titles are unavailable at your local bookstore, ask the bookseller to order them.

You can also order books directly from Ulysses Press
P.O. Box 3440, Berkeley, CA 94703
800-377-2542 or 510-601-8301
fax: 510-601-8307
www.ulyssespress.com
e-mail: ulysses@ulyssespress.com